E415.2.P74 R45 2010

War with Mexico! :America's
 reporters cover the battlefront /

33663004733248

DATE DUE

War with Mexico!

War with Mexico!

America's Reporters Cover the Battlefront

Tom Reilly

Edited by Manley Witten

University Press of Kansas

© 2010 by the University Press of Kansas

Published by the University Press of Kansas (Lawrence, Kansas 66045), which was organized by the Kansas Board of Regents and is operated and funded by Emporia State University, Fort Hays State University, Kansas State University, Pittsburg State University, the University of Kansas, and Wichita State University

Library of Congress Cataloging-in-Publication Data

Reilly, Tom, 1935–2002.
  War with Mexico! : America's reporters cover the battlefront / Tom Reilly ; edited by Manley Witten.
      p.   cm.— (Modern war studies)
  Includes bibliographical references and index.
  ISBN 978-0-7006-1740-1 (cloth : alk. paper)
  1. Mexican War, 1846-1848—Journalists. 2. Mexican War, 1846-1848—Press coverage. 3. War correspondents—United States—History—19th century. 4. Journalism—United States—History—19th century. I. Witten, Manley. II. Title.
  E415.2.P74R45 2010
  973.6′2—dc22   2010026293

British Library Cataloguing-in-Publication Data is available.

Printed in the United States of America
10 9 8 7 6 5 4 3 2 1

The paper used in this publication is recycled and contains 30 percent postconsumer waste. It is acid free and meets the minimum requirements of the American National Standard for Permanence of Paper for Printed Library Materials Z39.48-1992.

To journalism students:
Know the past to examine the present and prepare for the future.

Contents

(A photo section follows page 127)

Preface

Journalism professor and historian Tom Reilly was a private person, and those of us who worked with him and whom he mentored knew little about his activities outside the classroom until after his death in 2002. What we did know is that he inspired, educated, and strove for excellence in journalism.

Born in 1935, Tom arrived in Southern California's San Fernando Valley with his father after his parents divorced in the 1940s. His mother was a civil service employee in New Jersey.

He enrolled in Valley College in the 1950s, but left school and joined the nearby *Van Nuys Daily News* from 1953–1958 and 1960–1961 as general assignment reporter, copy editor, sports editor, and assistant to the managing editor.

From 1958–1960, he was an information specialist in the U.S. Army. In 1961, he became public information officer for the Los Angeles City Schools, the nation's second largest district.

Reilly joined the Peace Corps in 1966 and spent two years in Bombay as consultant in mass communications to the Family Planning Department, where he worked on a pilot birth-control project, giving out transistor radios at train stations in exchange for vasectomies. In India, he witnessed problems that made concerns in the United States seem superficial.

He returned to the San Fernando Valley, completed his journalism degree in 1965 at San Fernando Valley State College (now California State University, Northridge), and began teaching journalism there in 1969. He obtained a master's degree in journalism with honors from the University of Oregon in 1970 and then moved from Northridge in 1971 to pursue his doctorate in mass communication from the University of Minnesota, which had become the center of communication research and journalism history. The latter had not yet been established as a field of study in its own right, and researchers without doctorates in history were frowned upon at the time.

Under the tutelage of press historian and professor Edwin Emery, director of the school's graduate studies, Reilly began work on his dissertation, "American Reporters in the Mexican War." Emery was best known for his book "The Press and America," first published in 1954 and regarded as the leading work in the mass media history field. Emery, who served as Reilly's dissertation adviser along with George S. Hage, professor of journalism and

American studies, became mentor for dozens of doctoral candidates and assisted them in finding media history teaching positions across the United States. Tom Reilly was one of those he mentored.

As Reilly conducted research for his dissertation—it was completed in 1975, but he continued his research for nearly thirty years until his death in 2002—he identified significant changes in journalism and news coverage that originated in the Mexican War:

- The war produced the first identifiable war correspondents and was the first time American reporters covered a foreign conflict.
- Coinciding with the advent of the "penny press" and popular journalism, it was the first war to be reported for mass circulation newspapers, and contributed to the rapid growth and expansion of the American press. The newspapers instinctively recognized the insatiable public demand for firsthand news of the war in Mexico and began printing eyewitness accounts of the battles that arrived far in advance of official government reports.
- News of the war gave rise to cooperative news gathering and transmission in the United States. Reports were shared among newspapers through a combination of telegraph, steamship, mail, and pony express. The Associated Press wire service began in 1848, the year the war ended.

Reilly delivered papers on his Mexican War research at meetings of the Association for Education in Journalism and Mass Communication and other academic groups, as well as authoring articles for academic journals. He continued to research the topic, with visits to the Library of Congress, National Archives, University of Texas at Arlington Libraries, U.S. Military Academy Archives at West Point, U.S. Army Military History Collection in Pennsylvania, New York State Archives, New York Public Library, Massachusetts Historical Society, University of Oklahoma, and Harvard University, among other research centers.

Reilly had returned to California State University, Northridge as a journalism professor in 1973 and served in a variety of capacities, including assistant editor of *Journalism Quarterly* from 1972–1973; founding editor of *Journalism History* in 1974; acting director of public affairs for the university from 1975–1977; journalism department chair from 1981–1985 and 1990–1998; and director of the university's Urban Archives Center from 1987–1990.

Reilly went on leave from 1985–1986 as a writing and editing adviser to the New China News Agency (Xinhua) in Beijing and spoke to journalism students at six universities and to staff members in Xinhua bureaus, becoming the first foreigner allowed to speak to the staff in Lhasa, Tibet.

For Reilly, scholarly research appeared more important than the end product, for there is no indication that he sought publication of his comprehensive research. When he became ill with prostate cancer for the second time in October 2001, however, he expressed interest in having his manuscript published.

Marcella Tyler, his friend and executor of his estate following his death on May 7, 2002, fulfilled his wish to establish a scholarship in his name for students at Cal State Northridge, make his archives available in the Oviatt Library Special Collections there, and encourage someone to get his manuscript published.

I began teaching part-time at Cal State Northridge in 1988, when Edwin Emery's son, Michael, who was coeditor of "The Press and America" with his father and was then Journalism Department chair, first hired me to teach graphics and editing. When Reilly returned to the chair position in 1990, he continued to hire me, and in 1997 I became full-time faculty adviser to the department's daily student newspaper.

In 2004, as I was completing my master's degree in mass communication at Cal State Northridge and was looking for a thesis project, I presented a number of ideas to my committee chair, Dr. Kent Kirkton, a colleague of Tom Reilly, who suggested that Reilly wanted his research on the Mexican War to be published. That was all the encouragement I needed. I had known Reilly for more than fifteen years, had been inspired by his love of journalism and teaching, and recognized an opportunity to fulfill his wish to have his research published.

Reilly's archives in the Special Collections at California State University, Northridge include sixteen boxes on the Mexican War—three on the biographies of newspaper correspondents, five on war news, and eight on general war research. In addition, there are the manuscript and notes he was continuing to revise when he died. Those have been edited and are presented here.

Throughout the process, I have attempted to do justice to the level of scholarship Reilly exemplified. As he indicates in the following Introduction, compiled from his research, there remain additional aspects of the reporting of the Mexican War to be studied. A note in his archives offers a glimpse of how important history research was to Reilly: "In preface, acknowledge debt to Cutler Andrews' books ('The North Reports the Civil War' and 'The South Reports the Civil War'). These represent a level of scholarship I strived for but could not reach. But it was fun trying."

That effort continues to inspire those who knew Tom Reilly to reach for excellence in the pursuit of journalism and journalism history.

Manley Witten
Northridge, California

Acknowledgments

The scholarship in these pages was provided by Tom Reilly. Two invaluable professors who guided and mentored the editor are Dr. Kent Kirkton and Dr. Jorge Garcia, both of whom have been enlightening, encouraging, and supportive with their seemingly infinite knowledge and wisdom. Others on whom the editor relied include Dr. Melissa Wall, Dr. Felix Gutierrez, Dr. Charles St. Cyr, Marcella Tyler, and Robert Marshall. Gratitude is extended to Dr. Richard Bruce Winders and Dr. Timothy D. Johnson for their careful review of the manuscript and constructive suggestions for improvements; to Michael Briggs, editor-in-chief of the University Press of Kansas, who allowed Tom Reilly's life work to be shared with others; and to Sanae, Aiko, and Mason, the editor's wife and children, for their love and support.

War with Mexico!

Introduction

The Southern mail comes in freighted with tidings of battle and carnage and I must hie along with it to New York.
—Horace Greeley, New York *Tribune*, May 27, 1846

The Mexican War (1846–1848) was one of the highlights of the American expansionist period. Fueled by a variety of motives, the United States and Mexico confronted each other at the Rio Grande in spring 1846. An American invasion of its weaker neighbor soon followed. A year and a half of sporadic fighting ended in September 1847, when American troops under General Winfield Scott captured Mexico City, effectively bringing most of the country under U.S. control. Peace negotiations followed over the next nine months, concluding at the end of May 1848, with the United States receiving the territory including California, Arizona, and New Mexico, plus the Texas boundary at the Rio Grande, as part of the settlement.

The Mexican War occurred at a time of great expansion in American journalism—especially for newspapers' newest form, the penny press. Starting with the New York *Sun* in 1833, the penny press had been spreading steadily through the 1830s and 1840s in the nation's fast-growing urban centers. The country's communication system also had been increasing throughout the 1830s and 1840s, with more miles of telegraph, railroad, canals, and roads being added every year. The improved communications, plus the energy of the penny-press editors, combined to make the Mexican War the first war to be reported extensively by American journalists.

Some journalism historians have observed that the mercantile and party press were still the dominant forms during the period prior to the Civil War, but the penny press, riding the wave of change caused in American society by the Industrial Revolution, was growing rapidly.[1] As a result, penny papers were sprouting in New York, Boston, Philadelphia, Baltimore, St. Louis, New Orleans, and numerous other urban centers. The penny papers were bringing about a shift in the content of news, also. Local news, sensational items dealing with crime and sex, and human interest stories all were becoming important elements of news selection.[2] The reading public, in turn, was responding to the new format, and circulation and profits of a number of key penny papers increased steadily.

Public reading rooms in Boston, for example, were jammed with news seekers, a reporter noted, adding, "If our troops do but make as vigorous a charge upon the enemy as newsboys do upon the public with their extras the victory will be ours without a doubt."[3]

Regarding the public's demand, a Charleston *Courier* correspondent noted, "Every rumor from the army is eagerly swallowed, and yet the cry is still like Oliver Twists for 'more' . . . the newspapers pour forth in a flood of extras, sometimes issuing two and three in a day."[4] During the opening days of the war in May 1846, the New York *Sun* stated, "Our extras over the past few days have averaged over 22,000 copies per day, making, with our regular daily edition, nearly 70,000 copies issued from our steam presses for several days in succession."[5]

Greeley's New York *Tribune* bragged it could get war extras on the streets in twenty minutes, and whether "favorable or unfavorable our readers may depend on receiving" the news first.[6] The New York *Herald* made similar promises, reporting its office "was thronged . . . with an excited and anxious multitude" waiting for extras. It crowed, "Look out Newsboys! Eyes right! Now for the halls of Montezumas."[7]

The papers rushed to keep up with demand for the news. The New Orleans *Delta* stated: "This is a busy . . . time for us editors and printers. We yesterday issued three editions of our paper, and the click-click of our Napier [press] never ceased."[8] A Charleston *Courier* correspondent noted, "'Any news from the army?' takes the place of 'How d'ye do?'—and any person going hurriedly into or from a newspaper office creates an instantaneous impression on the crowd, who always surround the bulletin board at the door, that an extra is about to be issued."[9] Newspaper offices frequently drew crowds, particularly when news was expected. An exasperated Boston *Post* editor wrote, "The dearest friend we have in the world we never desire to see more than five minutes at a time *in our office*. Business *is* business." The New Orleans *Picayune* agreed that "there is a sympathy of feeling on this subject."[10] The desire for war news was so great, some editors observed, that many papers did not reach their destinations, "disappearing" en route. The editors of the Clinton (La.) *Louisiana Floridian* said only one copy of the *Picayune* arrived by express in his part of the state after the battle of Monterrey in September 1846. "When the positive information was received," he wrote, "a salute was fired. This soon brought in the inhabitants from the country and our office was besieged from morn till night. . . . We distributed upwards of five hundred [extras] ."[11]

In addition to extra editions, the papers often ran extra copies with special items related to the war. After receiving a detailed list of the Americans killed and wounded at Monterrey, the *Picayune* announced in advance the list would appear, adding, "We shall print extras tomorrow for the use of gentlemen who may desire them to send off to friends or correspondents by mail."[12] When the New Orleans *Delta* ran a map and summary of the Monterrey battle, it reported the edition "sold out in less than an hour despite an extra large press run."[13]

An "extra edition" did not necessarily mean the republication of an entire newspaper. Many "extras" were only the size of a large galley (or tray) of newspaper type. A one-page extra published by the Washington *Union* in October 1847 containing news about the capture of Mexico City measured 18 inches in depth and two columns (about 5 inches) in width.[14] But, whatever their size, they were popular with the public. After one battle, a correspondent of the *Union* told of crowds in New York City mobbing newspaper bulletin boards, "extras flying noisily about by the thousands." The reporter wrote, "People were buying *Tribune* extras at two cents and reading them at the top of their voices."[15] In April 1847, after the news of the capture of Veracruz reached Philadelphia, the *North American* stated, "There never was an extra published in our city which was called for so long and eagerly."[16]

The widespread use of newsboys to distribute the penny papers brought an added dimension to the wartime press. When news of Zachary Taylor's victory at Buena Vista reached New York on April 1, 1847, an eyewitness reported: "Around the newspaper offices the excitement was intense; the people swarmed like bees, climbing up each other's backs to catch a glimpse of the notices on the bulletin boards; crowds of ragged news-boys fought their way into the different offices, and stood jammed up together, as tight as a compressed cotton bale. They were waiting for the extras . . . [which] are rapidly distributed, reeking wet."[17] When the newsboys hit the streets with the extras, the reporter wrote, they immediately broke into shouts: "Here's the extra 'Erald—got the great battle in Mexico! Here's the Sun—Got General Taylor Victorious! Here's the *seventh* edition of the Evening Express— Got Santa Anna cut to pieces!" There was little trouble selling the extras, according to the observer:

> The merchant rushes from his store and buys an extra . . . cartmen draw up to the sidewalk and stop with their loaded carts while they read. . . . The clerk, on his way to the bank, reads a full account. . . . The dandy on the hotel steps, the cabman on the stand, the butcher in his stall, the loafer on the dock, the lady in the parlor, the cook in the kitchen, the waiter in

the barroom, the clerk in the store, the actor at the rehearsal, the judge upon the bench, the lawyer in the court, the officer in attendance, even the prisoner at the bar, [read] of the victory and rejoice![18]

A Philadelphia *North American* correspondent was awakened in New York City by the cry, "War, War! Here's the extra Tribune with the war with Mexico!" He observed, "Our war news we get quickly," attributing the speed to the telegraph, fast composition, and "newsboy vagabonds, who scour the city in every direction." To him the youths were "war's [begrimed] and ragged messengers."[19]

At least fourteen correspondents were involved in some aspect of the war. Two in particular, George Wilkins Kendall and James L. Freaner, made major contributions. This study deals in depth with the methods the various American correspondents used, and the contribution they made to the general public's understanding of the war's events, progress, and outcome. Newspapers meant different things to different people, and the abundance of battle coverage provided the means for Americans to join the conversation about their country's expansion.

The coverage of the war resembled a jigsaw of a thousand pieces, and it was left to the reader to try to piece it together. Correspondents, editors, and readers included and excluded facts as they saw fit, representing nationalism, Republicanism, manifest destiny, racism, and political precepts. On the battlefield, the correspondents confessed to seeing only bits and pieces, yet they tried to reconstruct a whole. As Joseph Mathews has written, "Americans reported wars as they fought them: They ignored rules and precedents, introduced a spirit of competition unknown to the European press and welcomed rough writers as enthusiastically as rough riders. There were no legal restrictions on reporting the Mexican War."[20]

This study also discusses methods correspondents used to convey the news from the battlefields and army camps in Mexico to the newspaper readers in the American population centers. Through the use of pony express, boats, stagecoach, railroad, and telegraph the American correspondents constantly were able to reduce the period between the event's occurrence and its news report to the public.

Concurrently, the press improved the means of processing and publishing the news at home. High-speed presses, better typesetting procedures, and improved methods of distributing the news were developed during the war period. Although this study discusses these developments as they relate to reporting the war, it does not deal with them in depth.

The main thrust of the present study is how individual reporters carried out their assignments to witness the war's battles and major events firsthand

and then conveyed the accounts to readers at home. It also concentrates on events on the southern fronts. Reporting from the scene of military operations in the West was infrequent, and consequently that area is not included in this study. Nor does it include the development of the American press behind the army's lines in Mexico. This was a factor unique to the Mexican War. A large number of American printers volunteered to serve in the military during the opening stages of the war, and they later found opportunities to establish American-controlled newspapers in Mexican cities where the army maintained garrisons. Most of these publications were supported with military patronage, primarily for presenting propaganda about the Americans' motives in the war. But they also served the purpose of presenting news from America to the troops, and news about the troops to newspapers back home.

Included is the condition of American journalism in 1846, particularly the newspapers in New Orleans, which were crucial to the overall coverage of the war, and the major means of news communication during the period.

Another aspect of this study deals with the question of censorship and newspaper suppression by the military. For the number of problems faced by the army, and the amount of time it was forced to occupy large segments of territory in Mexico, the incidents of newspaper suppression were few and far between, but this issue, in general, is critical to the operation of a free press and, therefore, is explored in this study.

Relying heavily on extensive search of the key newspapers involved in reporting the Mexican War, this study also seeks to reconstruct the efforts, methods, lifestyles, achievements, and failures of the individual American correspondents and, to a lesser degree, the journalistic system in which they functioned. The combined efforts of the American reporters in Mexico and their enterprising editors at home made the Mexican War, in the words of historian Robert Selph Henry, "the first war in history to be adequately and comprehensively reported in the daily press."[21] In 1857 William Howard Russell of the London *Times* was to gain fame as "the world's first war correspondent" for his efforts in the Crimea, a decade after the extensive Mexican War reporting by the "special correspondents" of the American press. And it was not a case of one or two amateur American reporters in Mexico. Kendall of the New Orleans *Picayune* and Freaner of the New Orleans *Delta* were central figures in that effort, but so too, in their own ways, were Christopher M. Haile, Francis A. Lumsden, Daniel Scully, John E. Durivage, and Charles Callahan of the *Picayune;* George Tobin of the *Delta;* John Peoples of the *Delta* and the New Orleans *Crescent;* William C. Tobey of the Philadelphia *North American;* John Warland of the Boston *Atlas;* Jane McManus Storms of the New York *Sun;* Thomas Bangs Thorpe of the New Orleans

Commercial Times; and Josiah Gregg, whose work was published in the Louisville *Journal* and various other newspapers. The efforts and writing of these principal correspondents are singled out and presented in depth.

In addition to these reporters, there was a larger, but less important, body of writers, called in the language of the day "occasional correspondents." These were part-time writers, many of them former reporters or printers serving in the army, who were scattered across Mexico in the camps and towns occupied by the American army. A third category of correspondents was referred to as "letter writers." In the definition of the day these were often members of the army or navy who wrote letters to the country's political press, usually promoting or attempting to discredit the efforts of various leading military officers or units. These had political underpinnings to them. Added to this heavy volume of letters for the country's press was the extensive body of reporting provided in the colorful "occupation newspapers" that the Yankee printers established in the wake of the U.S. Army. Much of the content of these publications found its way to the papers at home, and the combined collection of letters, sketches, and eyewitness narratives made the Mexican War the most thoroughly and extensively reported war to that time.

The start of the Mexican War in 1846 was anticipated by most of the American press.[22] The Charleston *Courier* wrote on February 9: "There is a great lack of excitement, and a war with Mexico is what might be termed a 'real blessing to . . . correspondents and editors.' I wouldn't mind shedding my last drop of ink in the cause."

There had been steadily increasing coverage of the problems with Mexico since early 1845, when Congress and President John Tyler moved to annex Texas and President James K. Polk ordered General Zachary Taylor's small army to the Rio Grande to support the political action. The New Orleans newspapers, close to these events and with great enthusiasm for the American expansionist movement, had been providing continuing coverage of Taylor's army and events in Texas. Carried to the north by boat, horseback, train, and to a limited extent telegraph, the news from the Southwest made good copy for most of the country's newspapers.

The outbreak of the war coincided with a period of rapid growth for American newspapers and the continued emergence of the penny press as the dominant style of journalism. An 1846 prospectus for a new penny paper in New Orleans helped explain the changing newspaper climate: "The great object now is to obtain circulation and currency by publishing on terms so cheap that all may read. News is not exclusively for speculators and financiers. The whole community—the great masses of the people—claim these benefits, and this demand is silently working a radical change in the newspaper system."[23] The penny journals, the prospectus continued, were "more piquant and spirited, more elevated in their tone and temper, more free from partisan asperity and far better adapted to prevailing taste."[24]

Another penny paper, the New Orleans *Delta*, explained:

We [have]) witnessed the failure of too many newspaper enterprises established to carry out the purposes and objective of party cliques, sects or individuals. . . . [American] people are thoroughly investigative and deliberative. They will examine, discuss and decide for themselves; and to [do] this satisfactorily they will look on both sides of every question . . . and make their own inferences. . . . Therefore, one-sided or party journalism is becoming less successful in our country.[25]

A popular term for penny papers at the time was the "neutral press." But to be neutral did not mean to remain silent on the day's issues. The New Orleans *Picayune*, a popular and financially successful penny paper, explained: "All those matters which pertain to government or administration of public affairs are deemed political . . . we disclaim that sort of neutrality which acknowledges the exclusive right of the political or party press to monopolize all such topics."[26] The weakness of the party press, as the *Picayune* saw it, was that it was "absolute [in the] belief" that only "the peculiar creed it professes" could solve the country's problems. The independent press, according to the *Picayune*, judged each such issue in light of public good, regardless of politics: "With the clearest intentions a journalist may sometimes yield to the silent pressure of his personal political relations; but in so far as he does this his paper falls off from its high calling."[27]

But the neutral press had not quite won its place in the sun. A number of political papers questioned whether there was such a thing as neutrality in a publication. A prominent Whig paper, the Augusta (Ga.) *Chronicle and Sentinel*, stated: "The continued efforts to pass off the New York *Sun*, Baltimore *Sun* and Philadelphia *Ledger* as 'independent or neutral papers' . . . are certainly the grossest attempts at imposition on the public that can be imagined."[28] The infighting between the two journalism styles remained brisk throughout this period, and before the war was over, both forms made important contributions to reporting its many events.

When the Washington correspondent of the Philadelphia *North American* criticized "the neutral journals published in large cities" for being opinionated, the New York *Herald* retorted:

We think such censure is undeserved. Politicians and their organs, of the two great parties, ought to know that the independent press, which has been growing up for the last few years in New York, Philadelphia, Boston, and Baltimore, are the natural revolution of the age. . . . The time was when the political leaders could throw chain over the press, and make it speak as they spoke, and be silent when they wished it to be silent. That time is past. The independent press of our great cities hold now a stronger and more powerful position than the political leaders, or even their candidates for the Presidency themselves.[29]

Many Whig editors in the Northeast particularly felt boxed in by the events—their readers seeking all the news they could get of the war's events, but their political and ethical values telling them the war was unjust. "The papers from every section of the country contain little else than accounts from the seat of the army and speculations" about the war, the editor of the pro-Whig Claremont (N.H.) *National Eagle* observed. Democratic editors, he continued,

> are straining every nerve to make it popular . . . for the ostensible purpose of converting it into a hobby upon which to ride its immortal author [Polk] into a second term of the Presidency. The Whigs are denounced as enemies of the country—as traitors and tories—for presuming to express an opinion in relation to the cause of the war, and the motives of the men [who drew us into it].

The antiwar editor of the *Eagle* then judiciously added, "We have given all the news of the army up to the hour of going to press."[30]

Horace Greeley of the New York *Tribune* was one of the loudest and most consistent in opposition to the war. A correspondent in Taylor's camp wrote to him, "If you were to see the poor, ignorant and miserable people that inhabit this part of Mexico, I am sure your philanthropic feelings would get the better part of your political scruples and you would acknowledge that our people are really doing good in taking [this country]." Greeley rebutted, "So talked Cortez and Pizzaro."[31] On the eve of the conflict he warned his readers that the advance of the American army to the Rio Grande foreshadowed "the disgrace of a war with the nation whose territory has been despoiled by our selfishness and cupidity."[32] The *Tribune* consistently supported Taylor and the army,[33] but when Polk quickly pushed the war bill through Congress, Greeley predicted it would be a war "in which Heaven must take part against us."[34] He continued emotionally: "People of the United States! your rulers are precipitating you into a fathomless abyss of crime and calamity! Why sleep you thoughtless on its verge, as though this was not your business, or Murder could be hid from the sight of God by a few flimsy rags

Table 1.1 Mexican War Chronology

Date	Action
1845:	
March 4	James Polk begins presidency
July 25	Brigadier General Zachary Taylor lands force near Corpus Christi, Texas
1846:	
March 8	Taylor leaves for Rio Grande
May 8	Battle of Palo Alto begins the war with Mexico
May 9	Fighting resumes at Resaca de la Palma
September 20–24	Battle of Monterrey
1847:	
February 22–23	Battle of Buena Vista
March 9–28	Battle at Veracruz
April 17–18	Cerro Gordo
August 19–20	Contreras and Churubusco
September 8	Molina del Rey
September 13	Chapultepec
September 15	Scott takes Mexico City
1848:	
February 2	Peace treaty signed at Guadalupe Hidalgo
February 19	James L. Freaner of the New Orleans *Delta* hands treaty to Secretary of State James Buchanan
March 10	Senate ratifies treaty

SOURCE: Additional information from John S. D. Eisenhower, *So Far from God: The U.S. War with Mexico, 1846–1848* (New York: Random House, 1989).

called banners? Awake and arrest the work of butchery ere it shall be too late to preserve your souls from the guilt of wholesale slaughter! Hold meetings! Speak out! Act!"[35]

Throughout the war, however, Greeley demonstrated that whatever his personal convictions were about the morality of the conflict, they were not going to stand in the way of his journalistic sense. "Battle and carnage" sold newspapers, and political and penny-press editors alike took advantage of the opportunity for readers. The outpouring of coverage, and the unprecedented public demand for more, quickly gave shape to the press response to the events in distant Mexico.

The newspapers of the period worked hard to meet the demands placed on them for news of the events in Mexico. Spurred by the challenge to be "first with the latest intelligence," they continually sought ways to speed the news from the distant war zones and to print and present it to the public faster. It was a time of change within the press, the newer penny press attempting to replace the traditional mercantile and political press as the dominant form in American journalism. This competition continued throughout the period. It also was a time of inconsistency for the press—examples of good journalism mixed with bad, honest reporting mixed with exaggeration and occasional deceptions. The Mexican War, however, provided a timely and challenging opportunity for American newspapers, and they responded to it eagerly.

CHAPTER ONE

The War Press of New Orleans

"The Newsboy"
"The Delta, sir?" the newsboy cried—
The Pic and Delta here they go
The latest English news, beside
Another fight in Mexico!

....

Our boys have had another fight
With Santa Anna's mongrel crew—
The British money market's tight—
The royal household's in a stew—
And it is whispered that old Zack—
God bless him!—Has the inside track.
—New Orleans *Delta*, December 3, 1847[1]

This 1847 poem printed in the New Orleans *Delta* provides an example of the news mixture that the highly competitive New Orleans papers used to good advantage throughout the Mexican War. During the war, New Orleans was the fourth largest city in the United States, and its strategic location at the mouth of the Mississippi River made it one of the nation's busiest seaports. The city's commercial activities were so diversified that twenty-six governments had consuls stationed there during the war.[2]

Moses Yale Beach, editor of the New York *Sun*, visiting New Orleans during the war, described it as "second but to one city in the Union." He added, "New Orleans looks just like what it is, a foreign born city, naturalized and nourished under the kind American wing." A correspondent of the Louisville *Daily Journal* who visited the city during the war said he was "bewildered by the dazzling whirl of busy pleasures and noisy delights of this cursed, dear city, whose brilliant dissipations, fascinating excitements and eminent advantages as a commercial mart make it . . . the favorite resort alike of the trifler, the worldling and speculating adventurer." The writer added soberly, "Its floating population . . . is composed of the odds and ends of every State and all nations, without any tie save concentrated selfishness to bind them to the city of the temporary adoption." Another New York writer who visited during the war observed, "Work, work, work, is the unceasing cry. . . . New Orleans is decidedly entitled to be called the Calcutta of America." In considering the impact of the war on the bustling seaport city, one historian has noted: "Nowhere in America was the Mexican War more popular, and nowhere was the direct profit from that adventure in imperialism greater."[3]

Among those profiting from the war were the city's leading newspapers. Because of the proximity to Texas and Mexico, and the country's continuing expansionist activities, the city's papers had long given special coverage to Mexican and Texan affairs. With the outbreak of fighting in May 1846, the city became the funnel through which soldiers and equipment moved en route to the battle areas, and news about the armies and fighting moved from the battlefields to the nation's press. As a result, the city's papers aggressively expanded their war coverage.[4]

The New Orleans press, dating from 1803, was among the most colorful in the nation. Frederic Hudson, former New York *Herald* managing editor turned journalism historian, observed in 1872: "New Orleans . . . has always been an important place for journalism. . . . Most of the news from Mexico came through that port." Another New York journalist noted that in contrast to most of the country's newspapers, New Orleans papers "possessed very distinctive and celebrated characteristics." The Mobile *Alabama Planter* claimed the New Orleans daily press could be compared favorably to any in the country and was "unrivaled as to beauty, ability and cheapness." The *Planter* said its readers "have at home in the south better and cheaper newspapers for the masses than at the north."[5]

At various times during the war the city had at least thirty papers, publishing in four languages—French, Spanish, German, and English. Many were small political papers that "had a personal touch which was savored by a small group of adherents." The political newspapers, and the French papers in particular, were highly volatile and usually had two qualifications for a successful editor—he had to be "an excellent writer and a first rate marksman." The French-language papers added greatly to the flavor of New Orleans journalism. "French newspapers sprang up like mushrooms and died like flies," yet the 1840s still were considered the golden age of French journalism in Louisiana. Their content reflected a journalism more of ideas than news.[6]

The main effort of reporting the war firsthand and transmitting the news throughout the country fell to the English-language press. At various times during the war, twelve daily papers published in the city: the *Picayune, Delta, Tropic, Crescent, National, Courier, Bee, Bulletin, Jeffersonian, Commercial Times, Republican,* and *Evening Mercury.* A historian of New Orleans life during the 1840s has explained how it was possible to have so many daily newspapers:

> The founding of a new paper in the middle [1840s] did not require great financial investment. Only the larger journals had rotary, power driven presses. For the smaller ones, the type was set by hand from two or more compartmented cases. Once set, the type was locked into frames. From these the sheets could be printed by a hand-operated press. Such equipment could easily be bought at second hand from defunct sheets, or more often, from established papers wishing to improve their appearance with fresh, new type.[7]

In addition to being able to establish their publications on a shoestring, the New Orleans papers frequently exhibited energy and zest. An English writer who visited during the war wrote that the city's editors were politically opinionated but did not "let politics cause any disturbance of good feelings towards each other." He identified the *Picayune*, *Bulletin*, *Commercial Times*, and *Delta* as "neutral papers," the *Tropic* and *Bee* as "the leading Whig journals in the state," and the *Jeffersonian* and *Courier* "the two leading democratic [*sic*] papers." The *Picayune*, the writer observed, "is one of the most noted papers in the Union, a witty, lively, gossiping sheet . . . enjoying a circulation and advertising patronage which renders it one of the most profitable of the American newspapers." The author's only complaint was that the *Picayune* "dislikes the English government, and is always suspicious that it is intriguing to the injury of the United States."[8] When a new daily, the *National*, opened in June 1847, the Charleston *Courier* noted New Orleans had "one Democratic daily, two Whig and four neutral—all fighting." The Philadelphia *North American*, a vigorous daily in its own right, observed: "The press of the Crescent City . . . occupies as elevated a position as that of any other city and is distinguished for its energy and ability." The people of New Orleans had good newspapers, according to the Savannah *Georgian*, "because they know how to patronize them." Another Savannah paper, the *Republican*, commented, "We have been constant and critical readers of almost every paper published in New Orleans and we question whether there is another editorial corps in the country which combines greater caution and regard for truth with equal promptness and despatch [*sic*]."[9]

Cosmopolitan, bustling New Orleans was ripe for the aggressive penny-press style of journalism. A press historian for this period explained:

> The newspaper scoop was not born in New Orleans, but it grew tall in stature along the levee, in the counting houses and . . . . where the exchange later was located. Newspapers put extra editions on the street with

surprising speed, despite their handicap of setting type by hand. In some instances important news was sent out as a brief bulletin in an extra, to be followed by two or three editions as fast as printers could set up additional details.[10]

Many of these details came from the numerous ships that arrived daily from Mexico, Cuba, Europe, Latin America, the Eastern Seaboard cities, and up and down the Mississippi River. Everyone was seen as someone to "pump for news," in the language of the day: boat captains, military officers, government officials, merchants, civilian passengers—even rival journalists. A New York *Herald* correspondent writing from New Orleans described one such arrival: "[The ship] came crawling along and the newspaper people soon boarded and buttonholed every man or boy who would be likely to know anything at all of the passing events."[11]

Among the New Orleans papers during the war, the *Picayune* was the most important. The *Picayune,* although it did not cost a penny, was the first penny paper in the city. The *"Pic"* cost a *picayune,* worth a little more than 6 cents. When the *Picayune* was started January 25, 1837, by George Wilkins Kendall and Francis A. Lumsden, there were five other daily newspapers in the city, but all cost 10 cents. The lively, humorous paper quickly caught on and, during the war, built its regular daily and weekly circulation to 5,500. The weekly edition was particularly influential throughout the Southwest (not unlike the New York *Tribune* in the Northeast). The paper became an advocate for expansionism, Texas annexation, and settlement of the territorial problems with Mexico and Great Britain, by war if necessary.[12]

The *Picayune* had started running expresses from the Northeast as early as 1838 in order to speed the delivery of news. During the war it joined with the Baltimore *Sun* and other northeastern papers to establish an express that repeatedly beat the U.S. mail by 24 to 72 hours. Until the telegraph extended south to Richmond in 1847, the newspaper express went by train between Baltimore and Washington, then by boat, train, stage, and horseback to Mobile. At that point it went on a boat to New Orleans. To speed the process, the *Picayune* put printers on the steamers that carried the mail from Mobile. When the vessels docked, the news was in type, ready to be run off as soon as the small connecting rail line between the docks and New Orleans (four and a half miles) could deliver the forms to the press. Such enterprise moved the *Picayune* into the leadership of the New Orleans press. It thrived on competition, continually promising readers it would serve them better. "Let us be judged by our acts," it stated.[13]

The value of the *Picayune*'s efforts was not lost on the better known editors of the American press. Horace Greeley of the New York *Tribune* believed the *Picayune* was one of the best newspapers in the country, despite its "habit of interlarding its news with its opinions so that it is often difficult to separate the two." The New York *Sun* described the *Picayune* as "one of the ablest and best, as well as profitable newspapers in the country" and praised its Mexico coverage as "valuable and able." The Charleston *Courier* believed the *Picayune* to be "[better] informed on all matters connected with" Mexico than any other paper in the country. On another occasion, after war news had arrived, the *Courier* praised "our enterprising friends of the *Picayune* . . . who are ever on the alert to obtain and forward early intelligence."[14]

Kendall and Lumsden were northern men—they had worked on a number of eastern papers as printers and reporters—and had good knowledge of the new machinery and news content that were transforming the country's press. Kendall met Lumsden while they were working at the Washington *National Intelligencer*, where Lumsden was a reporter-printer for nine years. When they founded the *Picayune*, Kendall was 27 and Lumsden 37. Kendall later wrote, "All the money I had when I started the *Picayune* was $75 (and Lumsden was about that much in debt). Such was our capital." Their relationship was a success from the start and they remained close friends until Lumsden's death in 1860.[15] Since Kendall spent most of the war in the field, organizing the paper's network of correspondents and express riders and sending back detailed letters about the war's major battles, the *Picayune* editorial staff in New Orleans also played a crucial part in the paper's coverage. Lumsden headed this staff for part of the war, and during periods he was away, co-owners A. C. Bullitt, A. M. Holbrook, and coeditor George Porter coordinated editorial activities.[16]

The *Picayune* took a hard line against Mexico throughout the war. Before fighting even started, it editorialized: "[Should Mexico] attempt again to invade Texas, she must be met promptly and efficiently, and the lesson inculcated must be one that will be remembered throughout all time. . . . [T]he city of Mexico is but four hundred miles distant . . . and in a few short weeks the capital of the Montezumas may witness the approach of that Anglo-Saxon race whose destiny it is to subjugate and occupy the entire continent of North America." The *Picayune* also frequently warned against European designs on Mexico, campaigned for higher pay and recognition for soldiers, demanded California as the price for the war, and generally praised the performance of the American troops. The most important contribution of the *Picayune*, however, was not its editorial positions but the scope and depth of its reporting about the war's main events. By combining Kendall's first-hand accounts with those of other correspondents, the paper provided the country with the most comprehensive and informed picture of the two-year struggle.[17]

The New Orleans *Daily Delta* was the *Picayune*'s principal competitor throughout the war. It opened October 12, 1845, organized by a group of former *Picayune* employees—Denis Corcoran, M. G. Davis, A. H. Hayes, and J. E. McClure. Corcoran was a popular and gifted court reporter and sketch writer. He transferred his ability to his own paper, and it soon took on the appearance and style of the *Picayune*.[18]

An editorial in the first issue declared the *Delta* to be "strictly neutral." Events of the war and the predilections of the editors, however, made the paper pro-Democrat, and as the war continued the *Delta* became increasingly involved in war-related political battles with its local rivals. The *Delta* finally admitted it was not going to be "a neutral press," as the party press classified independent papers. "To hold and express no opinion upon questions of national concern is to be faithless to the trusts of Republicanism and the obligation of patriotism," a *Delta* editorial argued. Regarding its Mexican War coverage, the paper explained: "Our main object is to make the *Delta* a faithful history of the times, so that it may be filed and placed in libraries for future reference. Especially in regard to that most interesting event on this continent, the Mexican War, we seek to present full and authentic details so that our successive volumes may present the best history extant of the war." Although it admitted the cost of the war coverage was quite "heavy," the *Delta* stated, "We trust the public will see an earnest of our desire to continue to deserve the very handsome support which we have received from a liberal and appreciating public."[19]

The paper's business picked up so sharply after the start of the war that it bought a new Hoe double-cylinder press. "Increasing advertising patronage" was cited by the paper when it added a seventh column to its pages in January 1847. The new Hoe press started operating in January 1848. It was capable of 6,000 impressions per hour, and the paper proudly announced "it is the size and capacity used by the London *Times*." The *Delta* claimed its daily circulation was "near 4,000" and its weekly circulation "near 6,000." The *Delta* also showed a high degree of competitiveness in attempting to be first with the news. On at least one occasion during the war, an extra edition of the paper was printed in Veracruz and distributed in New Orleans after it arrived by boat. The paper noted the edition was prepared by "our agent in Vera Cruz in view of the importance of the news." The *Delta* served as a clearinghouse for the government's official military dispatches, which were being forwarded by the paper's principal correspondent in Mexico as part of the express package carrying his own reports. The paper later explained it had received many of General Winfield Scott's war messages and official battle reports and forwarded them to Washington. "Nearly all of the official dispatches from the army to the government have been brought by our couriers and passed through our office at our own expense," the paper claimed.[20]

The *Delta's* policy toward Mexico was blatantly hostile. At the beginning of 1846, the paper stated, "A few bombs tossed into Vera Cruz would be a most convincing argument of the folly of [Mexico's] course." When the news of the first skirmishing at the border reached New Orleans, the paper editorialized: "The soil of the United States [has] been invaded, some of its citizens have been killed, more have been captured. It is a disgrace. It must be wiped out. . . . We must avenge our slaughtered, we must rescue the prisoners, we must vindicate our honor." Several weeks later, the paper was happy to note that most of the country's editors, except "the fanatical few," agreed that it "should be a big and brief war . . . as a demonstration to other and more arrogant nations of the immensity of our power and the magnitude of our resources." The *Delta* was particularly vehement regarding European interest in Mexico. "Self-preservation demands from us prompt and efficient resistance" to all European interests "in this continent," the paper wrote. Among other positions the *Delta* took were "applying the Monroe Doctrine to keep Europeans out of the American continent"; using a draft to raise an army to fight the war; higher pay and land bounties for soldiers; officer commissions for noncommissioned officers who distinguished themselves on the battlefield; urging the states of northern Mexico to "voluntarily annex themselves" to the United States, which it said would "meet with a very general approval in this section of the country"; and urging better treatment of the volunteers by the regular U.S. Army.[21] As the American advantage grew stronger, the *Delta's* militant position regarding Mexico became bolder. "Slaves in the American South" were infinitely better off than the "poor and laboring classes of Mexico," the *Delta* insisted. The paper finally moved to a policy of demanding that all of Mexico be occupied and annexed.[22]

In competition with the *Picayune*, the *Delta* sent several war correspondents into the field. The most important were John H. Peoples and James L. Freaner. Although Kendall had the more established reputation, Freaner benefited greatly from the Polk administration's support for the pro-Democrat *Delta*, as well as from officers and civilians with the army who supported the administration.[23]

In March 1848, another New Orleans penny paper—the *Crescent*—came into existence and competed successfully against the *Picayune* and the *Delta* during the closing months of the war. The *Crescent* was started by a spin-off from the original *Picayune* group that had started the *Delta*. Hayes and Mc-Clure, who had joined the founders of the *Delta* in October 1845, left that publication and started the *Crescent*. The *Crescent's* objective was to take the middle of the road between the pro-Whig *Picayune* and the pro-Democrat *Delta*. "There is room for us all, without in the least stepping on each others [*sic*] toes," the new paper argued. "The *Crescent* will take no side in the party contests of the day, either directly or indirectly. But upon important questions, involving the welfare or the honor of the country, it will freely and fully express the opinions of its conductors, regardless of what [others] may think or do." The *Crescent* also faithfully carried out the *Picayune* formula—it resembled its rival and carried a similar mixture of hard news, commercial and shipping information, and numerous tidbits of humor and gossip. Its war position was similar to that of the *Delta* and *Picayune*—hawkish.[24]

The new paper took immediate steps to add reporting from Mexico equal to the *Picayune* and *Delta*. It hired John Peoples, the former *Delta* correspondent who had earned a national reputation writing under the pseudonym "Chaparral." He had reported the war for more than a year for the *Delta* and had been instrumental in setting up several American newspapers in Mexico. The *Crescent* obtained the services of Peoples, it explained, because he "is unsurpassed in enterprise, energy and correct views of Mexican affairs." Among the editing talent at the new paper were Walt Whitman, formerly of the prowar Brooklyn *Eagle,* and William Walker, soon to gain filibuster fame. Despite its late entry, the paper rivaled its older competitors in delivering army news during the war's closing months.[25]

Another key New Orleans paper was the *Commercial Times.* It was started November 1, 1845, as a daily paper "devoted to commerce, agriculture, literature and the arts . . . the causes of the mercantile and agricultural classes" of New Orleans. Its first editor was Thomas Bangs Thorpe, a noted painter and writer in the Old Southwest School of humor. The *Commercial Times* format placed heavy emphasis on commercial and shipping news, commercial directories, financial reports, import and export statistics, and advertisements related to shipping. It provided considerable coverage of events throughout the war and was particularly effective in news about the Gulf fleet. The paper also was interested in developing express routes and the telegraph to the North, primarily for their commercial value rather than coverage of the war.[26]

Thorpe left the *Commercial Times* in April 1846 to join another New Orleans daily, the *Tropic.* Robert Sawyer and Charles E. Hall were partners in the *Tropic.* Although it had a strong Whig tone, the paper also supported the nativist American movement in Louisiana. Not as financially strong or colorful as the *Picayune* and *Delta,* the *Tropic* had a good reputation with other New Orleans editors and the Eastern press. Thorpe helped the paper soon after the start of the war by going to General Taylor's camp on the Rio Grande and writing extensive anecdotes about him and the opening battles. The *Tropic* stopped and restarted publication a number of times during the war. "The *Tropic* has large influence," the *Delta* observed, "because Sawyer never allows it to descend to 'scurrility.'" After one failure, the paper was sold at a sheriff's auction and underwent a reorganization. It resumed in June 1847 as the New Orleans *National*. Thorpe was back as editor, and its flavor was "Whig, all Whig," the *Delta* observed. The new *National* clearly identified its purpose. At the top of its page-two editorial column was the boldface line: "For President of the U.S. Zachary Taylor."[27]

In October 1846, William C. Jones, owner of the New Orleans *Bulletin*, sold that paper to another veteran New Orleans editor, William L. Hodge, in order to establish a new afternoon paper in association with another experienced New Orleans editor, C. R. Cessions. The *Evening Mercury* made its debut on November 9, 1846. The *Picayune* said the *Evening Mercury* was publishing in the afternoon "because the field is more open." Another benefit, the *Picayune* noted, was the late arrival of the Eastern mail "that makes an abstract of the news desireable on the same day instead of the following one." As an afternoon daily, the *Evening Mercury* had another advantage over its morning rivals—if important news arrived from the war zones during the day, it did not have to worry about assembling its staff in order to put out an extra edition. The paper also became proficient at running expresses to New Orleans from the point where boats entered the Mississippi, about 60 miles south of the city. By running the short expresses, and having its staff already on hand, the paper was able to be first on the streets with the news after several of the war's major battles. "It's frequently the first to publish news of interest," the rival *Crescent* noted, attributing it to the *Mercury*'s editorial ability.[28]

The *Bee-L'Abeille*, the city's best known English-French daily, also provided some firsthand coverage of the war. The paper had been founded in 1827, and during the war years it was owned by G. F. Weiss. Dr. Samuel Harby was the principal editor of the pro-Whig paper, which ran two pages in English and two in French. Although the paper's news space was quite small, it generally followed the *Picayune*'s formula in mixing police court reporting and small humorous briefs with European, Mexican, and commercial news.[29]

The English-language newspapers of New Orleans received their strongest local competition in their war coverage from a controversial, outspoken contemporary that printed in Spanish—*La Patria*. The publication emphasized commercial news about Cuba, Mexico, and Central and South America. Editors and co-owners of *La Patria* were E. J. Gomez and Victoriano Aleman (and later I. A. Irisarri). "It is conducted by a society of able and intelligent writers," the *Delta* noted. The *Bee* agreed, stating the editors were "well informed on Mexican affairs and we place much reliance on their statements." The paper specialized in rapid translation from Mexican newspapers.

Another advantage *La Patria* had over its contemporaries was an effective chain of correspondents, particularly in Havana and Mexico, where most American newspapers could not establish contacts. *La Patria* also interviewed Spanish-speaking merchants and diplomats passing through New Orleans and printed biographical sketches about leading Mexican military and political leaders, who generally were unknown to the American public. The publication did not limit its interests to New Orleans, but instead it sought subscribers from throughout the Gulf region and from the 30,000 Spanish nationals it estimated lived in the United States at the time.[30]

As the war continued, *La Patria* increasingly became the target of attacks by American newspapers. These usually were caused by *La Patria*'s frequent pro-Mexican and pro-Cuban editorials and its occasional erroneous reporting, which trapped many American newspapers into the same mistake because of the wide practice of reprinting *La Patria*'s foreign correspondence. *La Patria* had a running feud through most of the war with the influential *Picayune*, often presenting the Mexican view of the war. In May 1847, the two papers got into a dispute over the condition of American prisoners in Mexico. It started when the New Orleans *Commercial Times* published a letter to Mexican president Antonio López de Santa Anna from five imprisoned American officers in Mexico City, asking for improvements in their prison's condition. When a *Picayune* editorial supported this demand, *La Patria* stated the *Picayune* should not comment on it because it did not "possess the facts." The *Picayune* replied sarcastically, "*La Patria* will next deny outright that these American captives have been imprisoned at all." Such arguments were to "the advantage of the enemy," the *Picayune* contended.[31]

La Patria's editors seldom sidestepped such attacks, but after continuous mistakes and disputes, the paper started to fade as a source for the American press. Editors grew irritated with what they considered carelessness on the part of *La Patria*. After one erroneous report, the New Orleans *Evening Mercury* explained, "We give it place in our columns simply because there is no other Mexican news to give." The Petersburg *Republican* of Virginia said of a *La Patria* item: "We give it for the purpose of letting our readers know all that is to be known and suppose it will be taken for what it is worth." *La Patria*, the Charleston *Courier* observed, "seems to have a way of getting the latest Mexican news, tho,' as in the case of the other [New Orleans] journals, a very large portion of it turns out to be incorrect."[32]

The concern for accuracy was a continuing theme in the nation's press. The New York *Commercial Advertiser*, for example, claimed Zachary Taylor "has relied too much upon the disparaging braggadocia [*sic*] of the New Orleans papers" regarding the ability of the Mexicans. "But he has found out his mistake, and so have the New Orleans papers, as we may judge from the wild and excited clamor with which they are now shouting for thousands of reinforcements . . . [for] the beleaguered general." The *Tropic* responded that the New Orleans press was "dignified and consistent . . . and without regard to party strife or political distinctions" in its calls for volunteers. Writing about wartime conditions in Tampico, a *Picayune* correspondent complained to the editors, "You and your fraternity throughout the United States are continually finding some piece of bombast in the Mexican papers, or some speculations or rumors . . . rather wide of the mark, which afford you all, apparently, infinite amusement at their expense." But, the writer continued, "I doubt if anything ever appeared in the Mexican press so highly absurd and without so little foundation as the thousand and one rumors [about Tampico] one finds in every paper from the United States." After the battle of Buena Vista, the newspaper *American Pioneer* at Monterrey printed a series of corrections for stories that had appeared in the New Orleans press. Such errors were important, the *Pioneer* observed, because "it is to the New Orleans papers that the whole country looks for early and correct information, and their statements are generally copied and believed, no matter how erroneous."[33]

In New York, the center for the nation's press, Horace Greeley of the *Tribune* praised the work of individual New Orleans papers yet protested their overall tone, wrathfully calling them "the War Press of New Orleans." In contrast, the editor of the New York *Courier and Enquirer* provided a broader view:

> We cannot forebear to express our high admiration of the spirit and enterprise which the New Orleans press has exhibited in obtaining news since the commencement of the Mexican war. All the papers have done themselves credit, but we . . . specially commend the *Picayune* and *Delta* for the remarkable efforts they have put forth. . . . The London Times has never evinced more zeal or enterprise than have been shown by these journals.[34]

Regardless of the concerns about quality, it was to the pages of the New Orleans press that editors everywhere turned for the news of the war. Led by the *Picayune* and the *Delta*, the New Orleans newspapers provided the tone, direction, and content for the reporting of the conflict—and in the journalism style of the day, most of the nation's press followed their lead.

CHAPTER TWO

The Corps of *Scribendi*

I shall, as I am on the spot, by every opportunity,
send you the earliest intelligence.
—*Delta*, May 17, 1846[1]

In March 1846 Zachary Taylor's army broke camp for the march south. As he packed his gear, Lieutenant William S. Henry wrote to the *Spirit of the Times* in New York, "The general will pick his route and then, to the tune of 'The girls I left behind me' (who will be rather hard to discover, unless they are some of our veteran camp women, whose name is legion) we will bid farewell to Corpus Christi. . . . Hold your horses till I get to the [Rio Grande] and we'll see if I can pick up anything for you."[2] The invasion army, which seldom exceeded 10,000 men, formed one of the most interesting stories of the war. It invariably fought larger forces holding better ground, and it invariably showed courage and initiative. In proportion to its numbers, one military historian described it as "about the 'fightingest' crowd we have ever assembled, and its excessive pugnacity, when not united into common action against the enemy, vented itself in internecine quarrels." When not fighting with the Mexicans, army soldiers engaged in squabbles that took the form of disputes between the president and his two top generals, Taylor and Winfield Scott; disputes among many of the leading officers; northerners against southerners; Democrats against Whigs; regulars against volunteers; and volunteers with volunteers.[3]

Newspapers started reporting problems with the volunteers even before they reached the war zones. "The public journals from the vicinity or routes taken by the volunteers," *Niles' National Register* reported, "bring to us, we are sorry to say, inumerable [*sic*] proofs of the lack of discipline and the prevalence not only of insubordination, but also of disgraceful rowdyism, amongst the volunteers."[4] Horace Greeley of the New York *Tribune* protested: "The idea of sending our Philadelphia rioters, Missouri riflemen and Arkansas dragoons to Mexico as missionaries of Christianity and civilization is a little too preposterous for words, even for an age of cant and hollow profession."[5] A New Orleans *Commercial Times* correspondent with Scott's army observed:

"It is the volunteers of the Cities, the Empire Clubmen of New York, the Killers of Philadelphia, the Gamblers and Loafers of Baltimore and New Orleans that have given the Volunteers the bad character under which they now labor."[6]

Taylor's march to the Rio Grande angered the Mexicans, who considered the annexation of Texas and the arrival of the American troops as acts of war. On April 25, 1846, 1,500 Mexican troops crossed the river and captured a small detachment of Americans. Writing under his own name, Lieutenant Henry (soon to be captain) notified the *Picayune* on April 26 from Taylor's camp that the capture of Captain Seth B. Thornton's party (and deaths of two other officers) "are rather melancholy commencements of the war. I say *war*, for there is no doubt of its existence." Taylor's official report of the attack reached President James K. Polk in Washington on Saturday, May 9, 1846. The following Monday the president sent a declaration of war message to Congress, which immediately approved it. At the Rio Grande, the larger Mexican army attempted to win a quick victory. It crossed the river in force, hoping to encircle Taylor's army of about 4,000. But on May 8, at Palo Alto in southern Texas, and the following day at nearby Resaca de la Palma, the Mexicans were badly defeated and retreated back across the river. Taylor followed slowly, handicapped by a shortage of boats, wagons, mules, and other supplies.[7]

Civilian correspondents were not assigned to the army when it fought the opening battles, but there was no shortage of correspondence about the fighting. "The victory for us has been a very great one," Lieutenant Ulysses S. Grant wrote home. "No doubt you will see accounts enough of it in the papers."[8] Henry quickly wrote accounts to the *Spirit of the Times*, somewhat sobered by American deaths: "My details will be melancoly [*sic*] and sad, and in your true heart, I know there will be a responsive throb for the true hearts who have left us."[9]

From these initial observations of the soldiers on the battlefield grew the reporting of the war. As the conflict continued, writers fell into several broad categories: letter writers, occasional correspondents and, finally, special correspondents. In the definition of the day, a letter writer most often was a member of the army who wrote letters to newspapers to promote or detract from the accomplishments of various officers or military units.[10]

Letters from participants and eyewitness observers started to reach the papers, particularly in New Orleans, in such large numbers that the *Picayune* eventually was moved to comment, "The fact is you might just as well stop the rations of the regulars as bridle the tongue or *pen* of the volunteers."[11] And a *National Intelligencer* correspondent observed, "The complaints, sufferings and achievements of [the] army . . . have been given to the public by almost as many pens as there are bayonets among its numbers."[12] "The number of letters written from Mexico for publication is almost incredible," the Philadelphia *North American* observed at the height of the war.[13] The venerable *Niles' National Register,* which reprinted more army correspondence than any other publication, described the problem: "As faithful chroniclers of passing events, it has been a task of no little difficulty to cull from the mass of writers; . . . to give a full, and yet an impartial view of the operations . . . our difficulty is culling [out] things which ought never to have been said, and [which] censure where strict justice would have perhaps awarded praise."

The *Register* concluded, "Much too free use has been made of the pen."[14]

The New Orleans *Tropic* joined in censuring volunteers' letters to newspapers, pointing out, "Such letters printed anonymously, and many miles [from the camp], relieve their authors from the fear of detection, or from the responsibility of their authorship." Letter writing allowed unhappy privates to "vent malice" toward their officers, the paper contended, and officers to "curry favor . . . by bestowing undue praise" on superiors. The *Tropic* fretted, "The public has no means of judging of the truth or falsehood of these statements and erroneous opinions are necessarily formed."[15] The New York *Spirit of the Times* complained about "the thousand and one letters from volunteer privates and others, which are to be seen in the . . . papers far and wide, written from no-body knows where to no-body knows who [and] are not [infrequently] downright [inventions]."[16] Many such letters had bits of news and thus appealed to editors who already were working in a system that published considerable material from unclear sources. Editors had to read through considerable personal opinion and political bias in search for news. In too many cases, the pressure to be first with the details pushed newspapers to print rumors and faulty, unverified, biased accounts. On occasion, deliberate distortions made it into print. It was a practice that left readers the final responsibility of sorting out the news from the nonsense.

In one example of an unsolicited letter, an army officer based at Buena Vista wrote to the editors of the *National Intelligencer* with some area news in spring 1848. Signing it "Yours, X," he added this postscript:

Messers. Gales & Seaton—
Respected Sirs: The times of information which I have and may send you, from time to time, relative to the troops, movements, etc., on this line are, where they do not fall directly under my own observation, derived from various officers in the Regiment upon whose authority reliance may be placed. . . . I am attentive . . . to glean what I can in the hopes that

it will prove of such local interest as will justify its publication, at least as far as you think proper.[17]

Many officers were appalled at the flood of letters. Lieutenant George Meade, with Taylor's army, wrote to his wife, "I cannot express to you how thankful I am you refused [an editor's] request to publish my letter. . . . Many letters have been published which their authors would have given a great deal to have *revised* before meeting the eyes of their fellow officers." Newspaper notoriety "is the curse of our country," Meade told his wife, and he expressed fear it would seriously injure "our little army."[18] Captain E. Kirby Smith, who wrote copious letters to his wife about the unit's movements and personnel, cautioned her, "*Not a word I write must get into the papers.*"[19] A member of the army who wrote to the Little Rock *Arkansas State Banner* pleaded: "I beg that I may be [not] classed among the 'scribblers from the Army,' who write *only* to trumpet forth their own fame and that of their corps—doing justice to none, injustice to many and blinding the people as to the operations of the army."[20] Editors usually tried to salvage most of these letters for publication, the Pensacola *Gazette* noting on one such occasion, "Omitting the speculations and opinions of the writer, we make the following matter-of-fact extracts."[21] Other editors would trim out the attacks on officers if they felt they were not warranted by the official battle reports.[22]

The practice of criticizing superiors in print could backfire, as in the case of Lieutenant Lauriston Robbins of the Illinois Volunteers. He wrote in a letter of apology: "I was never so mortified in my life, as to see in the 'Alton Banner' a letter of mine . . . with my name appended there to in glaring capitals. As to the *publication* of the letter itself, I requested [a friend], if he thought it worthy, to hand it to the Editor of that paper, not doubting but that even that Editor had common sense enough to withhold my name from his dingy sheet."[23] Many officers were at a loss as to how to prevent the letters, despite an order in paragraph 650 of the Army Regulations of 1825 that prohibited officers, upon pain of dismissal, from writing to the press. The order, which had first appeared in the General Regulations of the Army in 1825 but had been excluded when the regulations were reprinted in 1841, was revived during the Mexican War (see Chapter 20 of this volume).

Colonel W. B. Campbell of a volunteer regiment observed: "The officers are always subject to a public opinion in camp which has an influence on them in spite of all the regulations of the army. The soldiers are writing home constantly and can annoy them very much." This hampered discipline, the colonel explained, because "after the short term of service the officer goes back to a society composed in part of his soldiers."[24]

The need to sort out the honest reporting from self-serving letters was never fully resolved. As the war progressed it became a contentious problem for the press and contrasted the values of the agenda-driven political press and the emerging penny press, which favored a more independent, balanced view. For many editors the story was too important to leave in the hands of inexperienced correspondents. The Boston *Daily Mail* complained about the "looseness and uncertainty" of the news from the army: "Even good news, to produce the best and most soul-stirring effect, should wear at least the appearance of authenticity; it should be clear in its statements and exact in its details." The paper pinpointed the issue: "The hap-hazard conjectures of excited men—the guesswork of those who have pointed guns at the enemy . . . are never to be depended on."[25]

The term *occasional correspondent* also was widely used, overlapping at times with the term *special correspondent*. The reporting of the occasional correspondents was more consistent than that of the letter writers. Many of the occasional correspondents were former members of the press, often printers or editors from small papers who had volunteered and joined the army. Stationed at scattered camps and towns over the vast area of Mexico occupied by the American army, they helped pass time by sending mostly unsolicited letters with news and speculations about the war. Using colorful pseudonyms such as "Antelope," "Hombre," "Cactus," "Truth," "Lancer," "Our Private," "Corporal," "Pony," "Rinconda," "Chihuahua," "Indicator," "Amigo," "American Reporter," "Peppercorn," "The Major," "Marinus," "Americano," and "White Hat," their letters formed a large portion of the war's firsthand reporting.

The art of letter writing to newspapers was a well-established practice in American journalism in 1846. Many of the country's leading newspapers regularly received such letters from Washington, D.C., and major commercial cities.[26] Authors were paid a few dollars an article or, more commonly, a penny per line, resulting in many long, wordy, highly detailed reports. Most of these accounts were written in a rambling antebellum style that preceded development of the telegraph. They were similar to casual letters one might write to a friend or relative, with news interspersed with opinion and often buried among a variety of unrelated events and activities.

The practice was not without its detractors. The New Orleans *Delta* promised it would not copy items from "those unreliable, gossiping eavesdroppers the Washington letter writers . . . not one word said by those truthless scribblers can be relied on—not a word."[27] A surprising amount of accurate information was supplied by the Washington letter writers, however. At various times they correctly predicted the government's war strategy, appointments and movements of major officers, U.S. military plans to invade northern and central Mexico—even the contents of the secret peace treaty to end the war.

In 1847, after the Charleston *Courier*'s Washington correspondent predicted (correctly) an attack at Tampico, the New Orleans *Delta* commented: "There is not a government in the world that takes less pains to conceal its plans and purposes of war than our own . . . by some clairvoyant principle possessed by Washington letter-writers [plans are announced] almost as soon as known. . . . They do not always tell the truth, yet, in most cases certain members of the corps are generally right as to facts."[28] This often was the case for the army letter writers as well. Many letters contained rumors, as well as incomplete or incorrect information, but, as the newspapers discovered, even negative reports had value. An editorial in the Baltimore *Sun* defended the use of the letters with this argument: "At the present time, when the greatest interest prevails with regard to [our military] . . . an intelligent correspondent at any place accessible for information is a valuable adjunct to the press."[29] The Washington *Union* explained: "In the absence of the official dispatches we continue to lay before our readers the private letters from the troops which are pouring into newspaper offices." The *Union* added: "We only regret that the correspondents from the camps, or their publishers in the cities, do not sometimes keep back reflections which are calculated to wound the feelings of some, and produce a feud with others. There are laurels enough for all to share."[30] The corps of *scribendi* had arrived.[31]

In one letter to the *Union*, a writer stated he was "sorry to find a new branch added to the army—soldiers who cater for the press."[32] The Washington correspondent of the Charleston *Courier* observed: "There are some corps in the army which appear to be favored by the exertions of trumpeters in their own ranks connected with editors at home."[33] The uneven quality of the letters caused the same writer to complain, "The corps of correspondents attached to the army does not seem to be very well organized." The writer suggested a unique plan for organizing the reporting: "The demands of public [curiosity] would justify the issue of a daily bulletin, under the direction of a judicious editor, at headquarters, which would contain a full account of every proceeding, as furnished by a very full corps of reporters. The press might be worked while the artillery were playing or the cavalry charging, and as soon as the action were over, a full report of it . . . [might] already be in print, and ready for the expresses."[34]

There was another issue with letter writing: the problem of the "planted" letter, a document that originated in the United States and was meant to harm or promote the political ambitions of prominent officers. An editorial in the Philadelphia *North American* noted many of the letters from Mexico "are marked by a high order of talent, and many others, as might be expected, are wholly unsuited for the public eye."[35] The paper asked, "But of the vast number of letters which are published purporting to have been written in Mexico, and indulging in (unwarranted) remarks upon officers there or on parties at home, how many are genuine?" Most letters from the army that included political attacks were "*spurious*," the paper charged, adding: "We suspect that the domestic manufacture of Mexican letters is becoming an extensive branch of industry." The press itself held the responsibility for ending the practice, the *North American* contended: "No respectable journal will give currency to a calumny upon anonymous authority. . . . It is a base mode of attack, cowardly and contemptible."[36]

As the war continued, letters attacking various officers grew, leaving the nonpolitical press in a quandary as how to handle the contents. When a letter criticizing General Stephen W. Kearny appeared in the press, the New Orleans *Picayune* explained, "We are compelled to give it as part of the history of the times. . . . But . . . we wish the letter had not been written."[37] On another occasion, after it ran a letter from Zachary Taylor to a friend in New Orleans telling details of the battle of Buena Vista, the *Picayune* stated, "The letter was not intended for the press; but we make no apology for publishing such portions of it as are of public concern."[38] Stating the complaints of many, a letter to the Washington *Union* from an unnamed army officer said: "I agree, as do most of the officers of the army, with you, at disgust at that wretched . . . legion of correspondents to the numerous papers in the different parts of the states. . . . Many of [the letters] are exaggerated or highly colored, if not altogether fabulous, and the writers and scenes fictitious and imaginery. Half of the stories told . . . are purely imagination." The writer concluded: "This world is sadly given to humbug and lying! But what can you expect when there is any number of penny-a-liners belonging to different papers out here, in quest of matter and news."[39]

The work of the occasional correspondents fell into a different category than that of the letter writers. For the most part more reliable, the occasional correspondents grew from a special phenomenon of the Mexican War—a large number of American printers, journalists, and editors volunteered to serve in the army. So many joined that at one point the New Orleans *Picayune* reported, "it is computed that over 500 printers have enlisted for the Mexican war."[40] The Philadelphia *Public Ledger* noted, "There is no profession or trade which, in proportion to its numbers, has sent so many men to war as the [press]."[41] Soon after the opening battles, a correspondent of the *Picayune* wrote, "There are too many [writers] in the field. General [Persifor] Smith's command might in truth be called the 'press gang,' for the greater part are . . . printers. They won't fight any the worse for that, however."[42]

A popular anecdote regarding the printers in the army was related in the St. Louis *Reveille*. General Scott, according to the tale, needed some military orders printed at a local newspaper but was told "due to a shortage of hands it couldn't be done." The next morning at parade Scott is supposed to have ordered all printers to take three steps forward, only to find several hundred men obeying the command.[43]

New Orleans papers were hurt by the loss of editorial staff. The *Delta* lost its assistant editor and a reporter. So shorthanded was the paper that its editor wrote, "We are in a predicament—in a plight—in a quandary—in a fix."[44] The New Orleans *Commercial Bulletin* reported seven of its printers had enlisted, and the New Orleans *National* had four of its five-man staff serve in the war.[45] The *National* observed: "As a body [printers] are talented but not tenacious, courageous but not cautious, wise without, of course, being wild, and being very erratic in their dispositions, are always of necessity poor." When some of the printers refused their volunteer bonuses, the *Louisiana Courier* urged them to take it, cautioning, "The time may come when it will serve a good turn."[46] The shorthanded New Orleans *Tropic* boasted, "In every important crisis in the history of our country the Printers have shown themselves conspicious [*sic*] by their patriotism."[47] Picking up this theme, the Baton Rouge *Gazette* claimed, "Printers have at all times shown a great share of patriotism." The paper claimed the same circumstance had occurred in the War of 1812, the Florida War, and during "the Texas difficulties."[48] The New Orleans *Bee* gushed, "[a] printer who lives by his daily toil, in surrendering everything to fly to the scene of danger, offers a glorious illustration of a Republican Government and proves him worthy of the noble institutions under which he lives."[49]

It became evident that life in the field could be a challenge for the civilian printers, more accustomed to the comforts of city life. In northern Mexico the correspondents had to cross several hundred miles of semiarid desert to reach Monterrey. It required long, slow, tiring travel on poor roads between small dusty towns. Good water, food, carrying equipment, horses and mules, and forage for their animals were scarce and often expensive. Rain, hot days followed by cold nights, dysentery, fever, an often hostile population, and acclimation to different customs and culture added to their problems. Boredom was the primary tropical disease for many.

Some of the volunteer correspondents wrote under difficult conditions. One for the New Orleans *Delta* apologized for having to write his letters with pencil: "You will find [it] difficult to read."[50] Another *Delta* correspondent reported: "I write in camp on a chair, or bed, on anything or with anything I can find. . . . I'm [rushed] so if you condense or shape it so as to make it publishable, it will do me great pleasure."[51] A volunteer who wrote regularly to the Baltimore *Sun* said, "There are no stationery stores in this part of the world . . . so I have paid our sutler a *dime* a sheet for this."[52] A *Delta* correspondent, who used the pen name "Hombre" and wrote from an army post on the Rio Grande throughout the war, noted on one occasion: "Some of the good folks, after reading Hombre's last letter, grumbled that it was not 'spicy and rich!' Now I would like to know how the deuce one is to get up anything spicy and rich without the necessary *material*."[53]

Lack of news was the primary weakness of the "occasional correspondent" system. After the frontline units moved to other areas, the writers from the camps and occupied towns often relied on rumors and exaggerated anecdotes to fill their letters. A correspondent of the *Picayune*, after reading an exaggerated item about a captain of the Texas Rangers, observed: "I greatly fear our Mexican friends will not believe us at all after a while, even if we should overrun all Mexico. . . . These ridiculous puffs do no good and make honest men doubt even the truth when it is told."[54]

A correspondent for the *Delta* wrote: "Every vague rumor [is] made the subject of a long letter to one of your public journals. Could these letter writers look beyond their own personal gratifications, or . . . their private interests, it would seem that humanity would dictate to them at least to [withhold] their information until the truth is ascertained."[55] During a visit to the army camps near Matamoros, the *Picayune*'s Christopher Haile observed, "Rumor is always busy enough, spreading ridiculous tales from one encampment to another, and the wags and 'green'uns,' and literary aspirants, have no doubt kept the newspapers abundantly supplied with this species of 'important news.'"[56]

After looking at the initial avalanche of letters and stories from the army camps, *Niles' National Register,* the Baltimore weekly magazine that reprinted news from many of the nation's newspapers, commented in a tone of exasperation, "We have found it no trifle of a task to sift the . . . facts from such a heterogeneous mass of exaggeration and preposterous stories as filled the daily newspapers and 'EXTRAS.'" Many of the stories and resulting extra editions, the *Register* continued, were "made up for speculation and utterly regardless of anything but to make a market of public credulity." The public should protest "such impositions," the *Register* said, and the practice would stop.[57]

After excerpting a variety of letters from New Orleans newspapers, the Cincinnati *Enquirer* warned its readers:

In the present excited state of the public mind, news from the border, coming as it often does through uncertain, and poorly informed channels, must be received with much doubt, especially in the matter of details. We do not, of course, vouch for the accuracy of the accounts we publish from the border; we give them as we receive them, leaving the intelligent reader to judge for himself how much to believe, and how much to disbelieve.[58]

The *Enquirer* continued to use such letters, it explained to readers, because "some of the descriptions sent back by the volunteers are very amusing, and often rich."[59]

Many of the war's early correspondents had short careers, as the reality of army life became clear. "Tom," who had a prolific but brief time in the field for the New Orleans *Delta*, blamed the officers' treatment of the volunteers. Many in the military, he explained, "have yet to learn that volunteers are neither asses nor fools, but as they have been known and respected at home as gentlemen, they intend to be regarded as such here." The excessive heat, poor conditions, and "green hands at a new business necessarily give trouble," he admitted, but he also stated it did not justify cursing and kicking them. "Tom" was Thomas Stringer, a former *Delta* reporter, serving as a captain in a regiment of the Louisiana Volunteers. He started publishing army material in the *Delta* on May 20, 1846. In one of his first letters to the paper, he reported en route "sea-sickness, as usual, assailed every landsman, your humble servant coming in for a full share." Stringer's military activities took most of his time, apparently, as his letters appeared infrequently.[60]

Another of the early correspondents to reach the camps was John C. Larue, who wrote to the *Delta* under "Our Private." He sent letters to the *Delta* throughout the first summer, mostly observations about camp life. However, he had no hesitation in leaving the army to return to New Orleans when the Louisiana Volunteers were mustered out. "It was much too boring to wait for the next battle," he explained. Larue tried war correspondence, but his feelings often came through in his letters.

At one point in midsummer 1846, when there was no activity in the army camps, he sent the *Delta* a long speculative article on what the army's next move might be. He concluded:

> But you who are always news-mad may turn up your noses and ask, what has this to do with the matter? What do we care for all these speculations? Why write this trash? What's the news? Good sirs, I write these things because I have nothing else to write about . . . for news there is none. . . . Therefore, take such as you get, and either publish or burn, as you may see fit.[61]

In another letter, it was clear Larue was quickly tiring of the war: "Drink the brackish water . . . and warm mud of the Rio Grande for a month and then you must feel eternal [gratitude] to the man who will furnish you with good brandy, pure water, fresh mint and sparking ice."[62]

Similar sentiments were expressed by other printers, one writing to the editor of the Evansville (Indiana) *Journal:* "To tell the truth, *sogerin'* ain't what it was cracked up to be no how. I had rather be sticking type in your office than eating beef and mouldy bread and drinking brackish water on the Rio Grande."[63] Some resented losing their civilian independence. John B. Borden, junior editor of the Little Rock *Arkansas State Gazette,* wrote of his experience in the Arkansas volunteers: "This serving one's country as a soldier in actual harness is no frolic I tell you [because] one submits to be restrained of his liberty."[64] Many had no news. William Osman of the Ottawa (Ill.) *Free Trader* noted, "This lying in camp waiting for supplies and further orders . . . where there is no enemy to harass us, is poorly calculated to furnish material for newspaper paragraphs."[65] A correspondent of the New Orleans *Bee* started one letter, "Gentlemen—There is little to communicate since my last," and another, "I have written you so many letters without sending you any information that I am now almost ashamed to address you."[66] Similarly, a Veracruz correspondent admitted to his editors at the New Orleans *Commercial Times,* "I must write though I have little to say indeed."[67]

The New Orleans *Crescent* said, "Having engaged gentlemen of character, in whom we have confidence . . . we shall not crib and trammel them, nor cut out every line that does not coincide with our own mind."[68] When the Savannah (Ga.) *Republican* was critical of some of its letters from the army camps, the New Orleans *Delta* explained: "We do not adopt or endorse everything that is said by our correspondents. Newspaper letter-writers, like other men, will indulge in the expression of their opinions."[69] When another New Orleans paper complained about the contents of a letter from one of its correspondents, the *Picayune* defended the writer, stating, "We are so loath to interfer [*sic*] with the independence of the writers for this journal that it is not one time in a thousand that we in any way abridge their contributions." The paper added, "We have allowed him to speak his mind even though often against our own opinions . . . and convictions."[70] The *Picayune* had no qualms about running the correspondents' letters at length, explaining, "We presume the reader will prefer to study the operations in letters written on the spot, rather than in such abstract as we might make." This system generally was followed, but later in the war the papers occasionally found it expedient to abstract letters in order to meet deadlines; accounts usually arrived in large batches, sometimes filling five and six columns of space.[71]

The work of the letter writers and occasional correspondents was a factor in the public perception of the conflict throughout the two-year period. The letter writers, many with political motives, continued to support or attack various leading officers, using the political press as their primary channel for publication. A number of these letters, though, because they contained some genuine news or provided some previously unreported background on the war's events, found their way into the nonpolitical press. On several occasions the president, the War Department, and the commanding generals attempted to halt the practice, but the letters continued to appear right to the end of the war.

With so many printers in the army camps, the next step in the reporting of the war seemed logical. With little fighting and little to do, many printers decided to try to start camp newspapers. Before the war ended, the enterprising Americans had established no fewer than twenty-five such papers at fourteen locations (thirteen in Mexico and one in southern Texas). Their existence quickly proved a boon to the rest of the nation's press, providing a steady, fresh, and fairly timely supply of news about the army and events at the front line and in the camps. But under the difficult field conditions, the quality and content of most were uneven and incomplete.

Before the war ended, many more of these publications appeared. A number of attempts were made by Americans to analyze their appearance. The Polk administration's paper, the Washington *Union,* wrote, "The press is a necessary accompaniment of our armies. Wherever our armies have penetrated, and the press can find an abiding place in a convenient locality, a printing press makes its appearance. It has become the herald of information and the pioneer of civilization."[72] The New Orleans *Delta* said the American papers in Mexico gave the army an advantage over all others in history "by enabling them to be their own trumpeters." As official military reports often did not do the soldiers justice, it was fortunate, the *Delta* said, that "they carry about with them their Homers, Xenophones and Thucydides in the shape of some printers and editors, who, as soon as the fighting subsides, throw aside their muskets, and hunt up a few reams of paper."

The *Delta* observed, "The printing press is following the Yankees" because "it is the oxygen that secures to them their social and political respirations."[73] The New York *Sun* said such papers were the "mental fruits" of the American occupation,[74] and to the New York *Herald* it was an "omen full of meaning."[75]

As the war continued, the American newspapers in Mexican territory continued to expand. Responding to the need for news at home and news in the camps, they found small markets for their publications wherever the American forces penetrated into Mexico. They also proved of use to the U.S. military governments, printing orders and regulations pertaining to both the troops and the civilian population. Recognizing this latter function, many of the papers took pains to publish portions of their contents in Spanish as well as English. Several, through the hard effort of their practical printer-owners, obtained permanency. But most, like the American occupation forces, were transient, and as the war wound down and the troops withdrew, the war papers' role ended.

CHAPTER THREE

"Mr. Kendall of the *Picayune*"

The most influential, productive, and enterprising journalist during the war was George Wilkins Kendall of the New Orleans *Picayune*. He has been called the first American war correspondent, and though he was among the first, it is difficult to say if he was *the* first (as can be seen in the following discussion). Kendall's articles, however, were the most widely reprinted and quoted around the country, and by the end of the war he was recognized as its leading correspondent.[1]

Although Kendall was coeditor of the *Picayune*, he had little taste for desk work and was a reporter in the field for much of his career. Prior to the Mexican War, Kendall, an avid outdoorsman, went hunting and exploring across the vast Texas expanses at every opportunity. In the process he became an outspoken booster of the region's future. One biographer has written that he became one of that state's "greatest publicists. His enthusiasm for Texas was unbounded—exaggerated, a non-Texan might sometimes think." On one occasion the Boston *Post* published a letter Kendall had written to a New England friend about the future of Texas, and the *Picayune* editor received 300 letters from interested parties. "Croakers" was the term Kendall reserved for those who belittled the future of the state.[2] In later years he acknowledged, "If any man worked hard for the annexation of Texas . . . it was your humble servant."[3]

For Kendall, the war with Mexico began before 1846. In 1841 he was invited to accompany an expedition to Santa Fe organized by the president of Texas, Mirabeau Buonaparte Lamar. Kendall seized the opportunity "to find new subjects upon which to write" and agreed to go, "subject to no control, civil or military." Three days before the expedition was scheduled to begin, Kendall shattered his ankle and injured his back when he fell off a cliff above the Colorado River while heading for a swim at night. Unaware of this incident as a possible omen, Kendall rode in a wagon to begin an expedition that was doomed from the start. Poorly organized, delayed a month until the cattle and drinking water had dissipated in the summer heat, with little idea of the route it would travel, the expedition encountered one hardship after another. Finally, the Santa Fe Expedition was deemed to be a group of

invaders by Mexican governor Manuel Armijo, and its members were captured by Mexican troops.[4]

Kendall was captured along with more than 200 Texans on the expedition
and was imprisoned in Mexico for six months. The mistreatment, suffering, and humiliation he and other prisoners underwent "blazed into a burning hatred of Mexico and all things Mexican," his biographer noted.[5] When
Kendall returned to New Orleans he wrote about his adventures and imprisonment in a 900-page book, *Narrative of the Texan Santa Fe Expedition*. Of
the man in charge of the prisoners, Kendall wrote: "Never shall I forget this
Don Jesus. He had a coarse, dark, hang-dog face, a black but vicious eye, a
head which I am phrenologist enough to know was destitute of the organs
of benevolence and the better attributes of our nature as outer darkness is
of light, and if he had a heart at all, it legitimately belonged to a hyena or a
prairie wolf."[6] The book became a best-seller for its time, with 40,000 copies being purchased over the next eight years. He became an influential and
well-known national figure as a result, but the experience left Kendall critical of the Mexican character, influencing his reporting of the war. Kendall
explained that he wrote the book because he wanted "to tell his story in a
plain, unvarnished way—in the homely, every-day language which is at once
understood by all."[7] Most of his war correspondence also was characterized
by the "plain, unvarnished" style he sought. Unlike some regional journalists
of the time, Kendall was not a pro-South extremist. He considered himself
as mildly Whig but generally tried to keep politics out of his wartime writing. At the same time, he clearly supported slavery as an institution, hated
abolitionists, had strong, negative views about Mexicans, and was concerned
blacks were getting "saucy and impudent."[8]

He was widely known for his sense of humor and storytelling. One contemporary called him "genial, witty, gentlemanly." Frederic Hudson, the
New York *Herald*'s longtime managing editor, said Kendall "never lost a
joke, or a bit of wit, or scrap of humor, or a ray of sunshine." As a result,
Hudson said, Kendall "became a Treasury of Wit." What allowed Kendall
to give the *Picayune* "great character," the New York editor wrote, was his
reporting of the Santa Fe Expedition and the Mexican War. His descriptive
letters "were among the first of the kind in this country," Hudson said. He
called Kendall's work "excellent and very graphic," a form of reporting that
only a few newspapers "indulged in" at the time. Newspaper contemporaries
considered him a "keen observer," with "quick perception of character." A
military friend who spent long months in the field with Kendall said he was
known for his "bluntness and frankness."[9]

From a young age Kendall worked hard and traveled widely. During this
time he became self-sufficient, experienced, and eventually prosperous. He

was energetic, outgoing, organized, even-tempered, and reliable. He valued common sense, simplicity, tolerance, persistence, and, importantly, action in place of words. He disliked politicians and politics, diplomats and diplomacy. By his own description he was "blessed, or cursed, as the case may be, with strongly-developed organs of self-will, obstinacy, and 'go-a-headity.'"[10]

Historian Milo Milton Quaife called Kendall "the world's first great war correspondent" and observed that the Mexican War presented him "a unique journalistic opportunity . . . and he was not the man to permit it to pass unimproved."[11] Other historians have agreed, but there are challengers, and the question remains unsettled: Was Kendall the first war correspondent? The answer seems to be a matter of definition. English historians, for example, claim the distinction for William Howard Russell of *The Times* of London, who covered the Crimean War in 1854. By one definition Russell is said to be first because his work was "the beginning of an organized effort to report a war to the civilian population at home using the services of a civilian reporter."[12]

Regarding Kendall and other Americans in the Mexican War, some writers have argued they were only "gifted amateurs" who were soldiers first, journalists second. Yet Kendall, Christopher Haile, James Freaner, John Peoples, Thomas B. Thorpe, John Durivage, Jane McManus Storms, and other Americans spent various periods of the war working exclusively in the role of civilian journalist. Thus, Kendall, and the others, have a fair claim to be included among the first war correspondents, a position, not surprisingly, taken by a number of American journalism historians. As a closing thought about who was first, Kendall wrote a letter to the *Picayune* from Paris, arguing in 1854 that British and French military authorities should allow civilian journalists such as Russell to cover the Crimean War. Kendall wrote, "It will be utterly impossible for [them] to head off or drive back correspondents from their lines." A better plan, he suggested, would be to select writers "of honesty and character" and "give them all facilities" for reporting "to the craving multitudes at home." This would prevent unreliable reports and misrepresentations. Kendall believed "the position of an honest and faithful" army correspondent "is not particularly pleasant at the best of times." No promotion or pension awaited them, regardless of the battlefield dangers they faced. Without the correspondents, he argued, the public would get only "the dry and imperfect details in official reports."[13]

Despite his knowledge and experience, Kendall apparently did not expect the war to start when it did. Nonetheless, in early April 1846, with Taylor on the Rio Grande, Kendall traveled closer to the scene in northern Texas to report on a council the U.S. government was holding with Indian tribes to seek a treaty. As his biographer notes, Kendall never had seen the Comanches in camp and did not want to miss the sight. Although this moved him a bit closer to Taylor's forces, he was out of touch with the events on the Rio Grande because of the council's isolated location. A special courier caught up with him on May 21, thirteen days after the first battle occurred. Kendall immediately started for Taylor's camp. It required a 400-mile trip across the barren, roadless state to reach the American forces. Kendall's description of the journey in letters to the *Picayune* provides some insight about the man and the conditions in Texas. It rained for the first ten days of the seventeen-day trip, forcing him to dismount frequently to cross swollen streams and rivers. One day, after riding 30 miles in pouring rain, he wrote, "We reached our lodging house, soaked through and through, and although we were obliged to sleep on the floor, in a small room with 15 persons of all nations and all languages, contrived to get through the night comfortably enough." On another day he wrote, "One does not feel after riding thirty or thirty-five miles, altogether so much like writing as he might."

Nearing the end of the journey, Kendall joined a large group of Texas volunteers headed south for the army camps. Kendall reported it was necessary for the group to travel at night, "owing to the heat of the noon-day and the swarms of prairie flies that annoy our horses." For food, the volunteers killed wild bulls, which Kendall noted were "tough as wagon tire . . . and required a bark mill to grind and digest it."[14]

Kendall's trip ended June 6, when he reached Fort Polk at Point Isabel on the southern Texas coast. Christopher Haile, the *Picayune* correspondent who had preceded Kendall to the Rio Grande, noted he looked "rather thin from hard riding, but in other respects in good order and well conditioned." Another *Picayune* correspondent wrote, "Our friend is just in from the region where the summer uniform is a 'piece of rope around the waist.'"[15] Kendall also met "Indicator," a naval officer who corresponded regularly through the war for the New Orleans *Tropic*, and, later, the New Orleans *Commercial Times*. "Indicator" found Kendall camped with Colonel David E. Twiggs's division, "perfectly at home, but I'm sorry to say, quite unwell; not sufficiently so to prevent his writing, for I observed a good deal of his manuscript ready for the press." While talking, "Indicator" and Kendall were surprised when a "large number of Indians inundated the tent." They were members of the Tonkwa tribe who had come "to settle terms with the victorious party," the *Tropic* correspondent explained.

A New York *Tribune* correspondent also reported meeting the *Picayune* editor at Matamoros: "I met [him] at Col. Twigg's tent, which he makes his home while in the neighborhood. He tells me he shall leave here on an expedition in the interior. . . . He is a strange genius indeed." Kendall apparently was satisfied with the extensive coverage Haile and other *Picayune* correspondents were providing from the camps. Although he continued to send letters almost daily to the paper, the editor concentrated on extending the *Picayune*'s network of correspondents. Like Haile, Kendall heard a number of anecdotes about the opening battles, but oddly he avoided reporting them, observing, "A man does not like to carry about a note book and pencil to clap down every story he listens to."[16]

Kendall's early letters were dominated by Taylor, Indians, Mexicans, war speculation, and particularly Texas Rangers. He agreed with Haile's position that Taylor needed boats and other transportation in order to advance to Monterrey. "Gen. Taylor is now worse cramped and hampered for want of transportation than ever," Kendall wrote on June 23. A week later he expanded: "Volunteers are still arriving by regiments and still Gen. Taylor is without transportation or any means of moving them. Where are the steamers ordered to be purchased long since for the use of the army?" He reflected: "I cannot conceive a situation more mortifying to the feelings of the commander-in-chief than the one he is now placed in. With men enough to march on any quarter he has not the means to move them an inch." Widely reprinted, such comments would soon burn the ears of the War Department and the Polk administration.[17]

Kendall found Matamoros "completely overrun with a little bit of everything." This included regular and volunteer soldiers, "speculators, settlers, camp followers, Texas rangers, loafers, gamblers, and what not of the Anglo-Saxon stock, besides a goodly portion of the Mexican population." A few days later he wrote, "Matamoros is to be decidedly an American city. . . . The Americans have got in here, now, have opened stores, coffee-houses, restaurants, billiard-rooms, hotels . . . have introduced ice and mint-juleps—a long step towards civilization—and their *back tracks* will never be discovered." It was all for the best, according to Kendall, because, "The Mexicans would never had made anything out of the country . . . more than a living."[18]

Kendall and John Peoples both reported the growing hostility between Mexican civilians and Texas Rangers. There were frequent ambushes of individuals on both sides, particularly at night. In mid-July 1846, Kendall reported: "Several Mexicans were killed in rows last night—some say five or six—by drunken brawlers who hang about the camp of the Texans. . . . The misfortune is, that a large portion of Texans are obliged to suffer for the faults of a few."[19] Kendall, a friend of many of the Texans, generally tried to minimize the issue.

The same month, Peoples wrote to the New Orleans *Bee* that three or four Mexicans were found shot almost daily, adding, "Those of our men who become engaged in these broils are *bad men*—who join with some [Texas] rangers of similar character." A few weeks later, Peoples reported that three or four more Mexicans "were found by the road side, their faces turned up to heaven, a bullet in either their heads or their breasts." Most of this was "attributed to the Rangers, and such things are generally allowed to pass off," he observed. Peoples noted the almost 1,000 American civilians working in and around Matamoros wore their sidearms because of the hostility. "I have little confidence in Mexicans," Peoples wrote. "They have too much Indian in them to forget the deadly enmity . . . and whenever their brain becomes befuddled with liquor their real sentiments find vent."[20]

Long after the war, George Kendall expressed reservations about using volunteers. "Our volunteer system will not do for a long contest," he wrote on the eve of the Civil War. Short enlistments, he believed, "in seven cases out of ten make a shirk of him—learn him to neglect instead of perform his duties." Volunteers' difficulties included "muddy coffee, soggy bread, half cooked or entirely burnt bean soup and constant camp-fire quarrels and bickerings" about camp chores. Kendall also noted, "It is too much the custom of volunteers in choosing their officers, thinking thus to make their terms of service easier, to select men *who can be commanded,* and not those who will have the will and capacity *to command.*" If volunteers were "under the command of experienced and energetic captains or first lieutenants of the old line," Kendall said, they behaved and performed well.[21]

At Matamoros, Kendall joined the Texas Ranger company of Captain Benjamin McCulloch, which was to scout the road to Monterrey for Taylor. It was a "Texas spy company," in Kendall's words, and he described himself as a "high private" in the unit. McCulloch's company of seventy men departed Matamoros on July 7 and headed for Reynosa on the road to Monterrey. In a letter from Reynosa, Kendall said scouting with McCulloch's Rangers "may be exciting enough but it is far from being agreeable." The Rio Grande had overflowed its banks, he wrote, causing the troops to "wade, dig and flounder through water, mud and mire until the patience of the men and strength of the poor horses was entirely exhausted." There was a hot sun overhead and not a breath of air stirring, he wrote: "Not a sign of a tent do we take along, while shade and shelter are matters not pertaining to the country. You can form some idea of campaigning among the 'greasers' and then weep."[22]

Kendall praised the Rangers throughout the war. Against Indians and Mexicans, he contended, "a single company of the old Texans is worth any three companies of the line . . . or any thirty for that matter." The reasons were tactics and mobility. He explained: "Fast horses and good riding, Colt's revolvers and close shooting no matter how insignificant the force, will always strike terror [on] the great western plains which an army with banners displayed could not produce." It was at the battle of Monterrey that the Rangers and the regular army came to appreciate each other, Kendall wrote. Earlier, the Rangers had been looked upon by the regulars as a set of "wild, harum-scarum, impracticable scouts, who might fight or might run as the notion took them. They had no discipline, no apparent tactics or method." The regular army did not expect help from them when it came to the "brunt of the battle." The Rangers' success at Monterrey, however, showed the regulars their apparently undisciplined allies "had a method which told upon the enemy if it said but little for science." And the Rangers, who had scoffed that the army's "tictacs" would not work in chaparral or house-to-house fighting, "found themselves closely backed up by men, who combined steadiness of movement with indomitable courage" and the Texans "frankly confessed they had been mistaken."[23]

Kendall also reported that Indians were "committing depredations and murdering the inhabitants with impunity" on the Mexican side of the Rio Grande. Although they outnumbered the Indians ten to one, Kendall wrote, the Mexicans would not fight the Indians: "It is because they are too lazy in the first place, and too timid in the second." Horse theft was considered the worst of crimes. Kendall reported one incident in which a Mexican who stole horses from the Texas Rangers received 100 lashes: "It is almost certain further punishment followed. No doubt the unfortunate man was shot by men who lost their horses." At the same time, Kendall urged action be taken against bands of Mexicans who were raiding American supply trains. "[Our] conciliatory system has been lost upon them, and some other should be tried," he wrote. "We are treating thousands of individuals here with consideration and respect who would turn around and cut our throats the first opportunity that occurred, and *con mucho gusto,* to use one of their favorite expressions."[24]

After Kendall departed with McCulloch's company, Haile remained behind to provide the *Picayune's* regular correspondence from the army. Noting the heavy summer rains, Haile commented that wherever Kendall was "he has enjoyed the luxury of a *shower*-bath every day since they have been out." Regarding the rain, Kendall later wrote that it showered every day for fourteen days. On the fifteenth day, the scouts reached Reynosa. Kendall related that they were "as hard a looking set of customers as the rear guard of Peter the Hermit's crusading host. I had not taken off my boots, jacket nor cravat for a fortnight, had not been under shelter and my only regret was that I could not have my daguerreotype taken just as I was." Commenting on Kendall's adventures, Haile wrote, "With his usual luck he will see the elephant again. He has become so familiar with the animal, though, that the critter no longer looks formidable to him."[25]

As the war continued, Kendall made a number of such trips into the

Table 3.2 Correspondents List

Newspaper	Correspondents
Boston *Atlas*	John Warland
Louisville *Journal*	Josiah Gregg (work also published in other newspapers)
New Orleans *Picayune*	George Wilkins Kendall
	Christopher M. Haile
	Francis A. Lumsden
	Daniel Scully
	John E. Durivage
	Charles Callahan
New Orleans *Commercial Times*	Samuel Chester Reid Jr.
	Thomas Bangs Thorpe
New Orleans *Delta*	James L. Freaner
	George Tobin
	John Peoples (also of the New Orleans *Crescent*)
(New York) *Spirit of the Times*	William S. Henry
New York *Sun*	Jane McManus Storms
	Moses Yale Beach
Philadelphia *North American*	William C. Tobey

field, sending back to the *Picayune* a steady stream of correspondence signed "G. W. K." He took care at each camp to set up a reliable express system to relay the *Picayune*'s letters. The newspaper maintained an interesting relationship with him while he was in the field. It frequently called attention to and supported his opinions regarding the war and various Mexican and American participants. Kendall's views were widely quoted in the American press; phrases such as "Mr. Kendall's letters from the Army," "Mr. Kendall says," "Mr. Kendall believes," "Mr. Kendall's Accounts" and "Mr. Kendall thinks" appeared frequently in letters, editorials, telegraph summaries, and the small headlines of the day.[26] The *Picayune* also was proud of Kendall's effort to obtain and forward his reports, noting, "We hope our readers will recognize in Mr. Kendall's enterprise his characteristic energy and liberality—a determination to do everything in his power to promote the character and interest of this paper."

At the same time, the *Picayune* staff at home, primarily co-owners A. M. Holbrook and A. C. Bullitt, retained the right to disagree with Kendall. "We by no means always agree with him," the paper explained after printing his analysis of the American master war plan in May 1847. But, it acknowledged, "He has facilities for forming an opinion . . . which [we do not]."[27]

It was these "facilities"—being with the army and its leadership and sharing its wartime experiences—that gave weight and authenticity to Kendall's

Table 3.3 Newspaper Correspondents Who Witnessed or Wrote about Battles

Battle	Correspondents
Palo Alto, May 8, 1846	William S. Henry, *Spirit of the Times*
	Thomas Bangs Thorpe, New Orleans *Tropic*
Resaca de la Palma, May 9, 1846	William S. Henry, *Spirit of the Times*
	Thomas Bangs Thorpe, *Tropic*
Monterrey, September 20–24, 1846	Samuel Chester Reid Jr., New Orleans *Commercial Times*
	George Wilkins Kendall and Christopher M. Haile, New Orleans *Picayune* (double coverage of General Worth's division)
	William S. Henry, *Spirit of the Times*
	James Freaner, New Orleans *Delta*
Buena Vista, February 22–23, 1847	George Tobin, *Delta*
	Josiah Gregg, Louisville *Journal*
	William Osman, Ottawa (Ill.) *Free Trader*
	Rufus R. K. Arthur, Vicksburg (Miss.) *Whig*
	Albert T. Pike, Little Rock *Arkansas Advocate*
Veracruz, March 9–28, 1847	George Wilkins Kendall, Christopher M. Haile, and Francis A. Lumsden, *Picayune*
	James Freaner, John Peoples, *Delta*
	William C. Tobey, Philadelphia *North American*
	Jane McManus Storms, New York *Sun*
	"Truth," *Spirit of the Times*
Cerro Gordo, May 17–18, 1847	George Wilkins Kendall, *Picayune*
	John Peoples, *Delta* and New Orleans *Bee*
	William C. Tobey, *North American*
	George M. C. Davis, Alton (Ill.) *Telegraph*
Contreras and Churubusco, August 19–20, 1847	George Wilkins Kendall, *Picayune*
	James Freaner, *Delta*
	John Peoples, *Delta*
Molino del Rey, September 8, 1847	George Wilkins Kendall, *Picayune*
	James Freaner, *Delta*
	Henry, New York *Courier and Enquirer*
Chapultepec/Mexico City, September 12–14, 1847	George Wilkins Kendall, *Picayune*
	James Freaner, *Delta*
	John Peoples, *Delta*
	William C. Tobey, *North American*
	John Warland, Boston *Atlas*
	James R. Barnard, Tampico *Sentinel*

correspondence. His drive to be at the center of the war's action, and to be first to report it, provided the *Picayune* a successful competitive edge it seldom relinquished. In this process, most American newspapers used Kendall's letters first, and the reading public's first impressions about the war often were Kendall's impressions.

CHAPTER FOUR

Pardon Jones Goes to War

After defeating the Mexicans in the battles of May 8–9, 1846, at Palo Alto and Resaca de la Palma, General Zachary Taylor crossed the Rio Grande and peacefully occupied the key town of Matamoros near the mouth of the river. It soon was apparent that he would not be able to advance rapidly into Mexico. He had insufficient supplies, ammunition, and wagons for his forces. The rainy season began, and Taylor was forced to spend the summer on the Rio Grande waiting for additional equipment and men before he could advance. Several other small towns along the river—Reynosa, Camargo, and Mier—were occupied by the Americans, but it was September before fighting resumed.[1]

The summer lull was not readily apparent to the press in the States. The demand for war news was so great that the New Orleans *Picayune* decided to send a full-time correspondent to the army's camp to supplement the coverage supplied by the "occasional correspondents." Before long, a group of "special correspondents"—the country's first war correspondents—were writing to the newspapers on a regular basis.

The earliest full-time civilian writer on the scene was the *Picayune*'s Christopher Mason Haile (his signed correspondence carried only the capital letter *H*). Haile has remained generally unrecognized, but his reporting and writing were among the most extensive of the war. Born in Warren, Rhode Island, he was one of the state's appointees to the U.S. Military Academy at West Point in 1836 (he left in 1837 but is listed in the Class of 1840). An obituary in the *Picayune* at the time of his death in 1849 stated he graduated from West Point "with distinction," but academy records show he resigned after the first year because of ill health. While at the school, however, he performed well enough to score in the upper one-third of his class in grades and conduct. Haile's brief experience benefited him during the war: twenty-nine graduates of the Class of 1840 saw service in Mexico, and Haile had contact with many of them. He also had an understanding of military history, ordnance, and tactics, reflected in his *Picayune* reports.[2]

After leaving West Point, Haile traveled briefly to Texas, then moved to Louisiana. On March 19, 1839, he married 16-year-old Mary Clarisse Hébert, the sister of his West Point classmate Paul Hébert. The couple settled at

Plaquemine, Louisiana, upriver from New Orleans. Haile edited the Plaquemine *Planter's Gazette*, farmed, ran a general store, and served as an officer
in the local militia company. The *Picayune* observed Haile made his paper
"the vehicle of a never ending flow of genuine wit and humor." Haile started
corresponding for the *Picayune* in 1840, writing a series of letters during the
years before the war that utilized the Old Southwest style of humor to depict
life in rural Louisiana. This writing style combined tall tales, thick regional
dialect, and ironic humor. Although Haile also provided occasional straight
news coverage, the humor letters, signed "Curnel Pardon Jones," established
a local literary reputation for Haile long before the war.[3]

In mid-May 1846, the *Picayune* decided to hire the 29-year-old Haile and
send him to the Rio Grande. The awkward wording of the paper's announcement that Haile "was actually" going to be with the army led the rival *Delta*
to observe in a teasing tone, "Mr. Haile, . . . a first-rate fellow by the way,
has 'actually' left for Matamoros. . . . Now with George Wilkins Kendall
to do the fighting, and (Haile) to do the writing, the Mexicans must be, as a
matter of course, expunged—wiped clean out of the journals of creation—
surrounded by black lines, which will be a barrier to after ages knowing aught
of their history."[4] Haile left New Orleans on May 18 and reached Fort Polk
at Point Isabel, Texas, on May 25. His first report to the *Picayune* appeared
May 30. In it he correctly predicted: "The fighting having ceased for some
weeks to come, at least . . . I am inclined to think there will be no more of it
on the Rio Grande. Our army must seek the enemy in their own country if
they desire to meet them in any considerable bodies."[5]

Haile immediately began to collect firsthand accounts about the battles of
May 8–9. Officers who had participated in the fighting opened their private
journals to him, and he started inserting accounts of individuals and units
into his letters. "I do not believe that serious inaccuracies exist in any of
these narratives," he assured the editors. These interviews led him to a position he stated frequently:

> The officers who have undergone so many dangers and privations dur-
> ing this war are becoming disgusted and discouraged with the thousand
> ridiculous and injurious reports that have emanated from irresponsible
> sources. These scribblers frequently praise, censure, or omit to mention
> the deeds of members of the army, without the slightest regard to truth.
> . . . Our officers and men have acted nobly in this war—their country is
> justly proud of their achievements, and the press should be ready on all
> occasions to defend them against any imputations that could arise from
> the idle tattle of busy-bodies.

The former West Point cadet did not limit his support to the army's upper ranks. He was among the first correspondents to criticize the poor pay for privates and other noncommissioned ranks. Haile also urged better equipment and transport be provided for the army; more activity for the volunteer units to "quiet the restless spirits among them"; taking the captured Mexican brass and copper shells and using them for medals for "men of all grades" in the battles of May 8–9; and promotion of younger officers to fill numerous vacancies in the higher ranks. In the past, he noted, it took an army officer a lifetime to reach higher ranks, and as a result "the majority of the field officers at the breaking out of the Mexican war were in the decline of life." He urged an honorable retirement "for those who have grown gray and infirm in the service" and the promotion of "younger officers who have distinguished themselves" to fill the openings. The volunteer units were in great confusion, he noted. "The sutlers," Haile wrote, "put the screws to the poor soldiers here at a cruel rate in the way of charges."[6]

Haile was appalled at conditions in the Rio Grande campsites. Volunteers already were starting to "suffer severely" from the effects of sun and bad water, Haile observed, many "very much weakened and emaciated by dysentary." Haile quickly put his finger on a problem that caused trouble for the army throughout the war. "Nothing disheartens the volunteers so much as inactivity," he wrote, a theme sounded for the army's problems many times by many writers.

Sand fleas, flies, mosquitoes, spiders, scorpions, heat, and blowing sand added to the troops' mounting unhappiness. Shortages of transportation and supplies, particularly good tents, compounded the situation, as did the changeable weather. Days often were hot and still, but rainy spells turned many of the camps into pools of mud, and sudden storms frequently flattened the flimsy tents. Haile told of one wild night he spent chasing "a certain dilapidated straw hat" he liked across the sand dunes after a sudden gale "stripped my tent as if it had been a sheet of tissue paper." Haile also had some fun walking around for several days in a Mexican army brown linen summer coat that had been found on the battlefield. "It came into my possession as a reward, no doubt, for what I might have done had I been in the battles," he wrote. After heavy rains left stagnant puddles in many of the camps, Haile told of an encounter with "musquitoes—none of your common sized Louisiana musquitoes, but the genuine Mexican gallinippers." He wrote: "They came in clouds, fairly encrusting our horses and filling our eyes, noses, and mouths, and *biting*—it makes me shudder even now to think of it." Even mosquito nets failed to help, Haile reported, because there was no way to spread them without getting insects inside the net. "We were at last obliged to lie down and satisfy the appetite of those we had taken to bed with us," he explained, adding: "Our eyes and noses were badly swollen when we rose."[7]

Kendall reached Point Isabel on June 4, 1846, and Haile temporarily joined forces with the *Picayune* editor. They visited nearby camps, then traveled to Matamoros. Haile also visited army hospitals and toured the two battlefields. The hospitals he found in generally good condition, except for "millions of house flies." He found the battlefields still covered with bodies of Mexican troops and horses. "The buzzards and wild dogs were fattening upon the carrion," he wrote in the graphic style that characterized much of the Mexican War reporting. Haile, with his military knowledge, was impressed with the use of the American artillery and gave a detailed description of its effectiveness upon the Mexican troops: "Some had been nearly severed in two by cannon balls. Others had lost part of the head, both legs, a shoulder or the whole stomach. Of many of them nothing but the bones, encased in uniform, was left; whilst others had been transformed into mummies and retained the expression of countenance which their death agonies had stamped upon them." Haile was surprised at Matamoros's "pleasant appearance." People were starting to return to the streets, he noted, "and good-looking female faces are seen looking forth from the windows." Commenting on the rising attacks against volunteers, Haile observed, "The inhabitants that remain . . . are mostly of the lowest class, and they appear sullen and inclined to seek revenge . . . they hate us cordially."[8]

Haile responded emotionally regarding violence directed at American volunteers. After an officer from Ohio was murdered, Haile reported, "His heart was cut out and hung upon a shrub to show us, I suppose, how deeply seated was their hatred towards us." The correspondent wished he commanded 200 mounted men "with unlimited power over the country." He continued, "My first act would be to shoot every man in Mier; then go and burn every rancho on the route [to Monterrey] for ten miles right and left, and shoot every man at Cerralvo—and then continue to shoot them in that region as fast as they made their appearance."[9]

Haile was one of the few major American correspondents who also took head-on the conduct of the volunteers. In the second month of the war, Haile predicted the volunteers "will give a good deal of trouble to the army before the campaign is over." Haile related an incident of a Mexican being shot by a Texas Ranger, who accused the victim of "adding to the distress of the Mier prisoners some years ago" (referring to an incident in 1842). Haile observed, "The assassin will find that he cannot with impunity act as an avenger of blood in a city that old Zachary has taken under his special protection." He added, "There is a spirit beginning to manifest itself among a certain class of the Texas volunteers, who have been pulled up occasionally for their irregularities . . . which looks decidedly seditious." "The restless spirits" among the volunteers would give little trouble, Haile believed, if they were kept active. "But the same patience and regularity can scarcely be expected from them as is exacted from the regulars." All volunteers were called Texans by the Mexicans, Haile noted, "and the word Texan is a fearful one to them." The Texas volunteers were amusing themselves at Camargo by shooting cattle, horses, and mules owned by Mexicans, Haile later wrote. "This is disgraceful, but it is hard to remedy."[10]

Some correspondents, volunteers themselves, were consistent defenders of the volunteers. William Tobey of the Philadelphia *North American* was concerned about the war's effect on volunteers. "The harsh treatment and privations the men are subjected to soon make one callous to all but his own feelings and interests." He continued, "I daily witness painful spectacles of human [degradation] and selfishness that before seemed impossible to our nature. Men we have known at home as generous . . . become, here, the most narrowminded, sordid, hoggish . . . creatures imaginable; yet, *vice versa,* some who were accounted of no great moment at home, turn up bright sides and astonish us as much by their liberality as do others by their cupidity."[11]

Tobey and John Durivage of the *Picayune* occasionally commented on the problem, but not with Haile's sustained tone of moral indignation. Influential writers such as Kendall, James Freaner, Francis Lumsden, Peoples, George Henry Tobin of the *Delta*, and John Warland of the Boston *Atlas* generally ignored the issue or mentioned it only in passing.

The volunteers' behavior had been "too long neglected" by the press, Haile believed, admitting it gave him "great pain" to report it. The volunteers, he wrote, were guilty of numerous "outrages against Mexican citizens," including robbing, "assaulting the women," breaking into houses, and similar violent acts. Haile advised, "Let a few of the fiends who commit [outrages] be strung up upon the nearest trees, and some of the officers who wink at such conduct be . . . exposed and dismissed from the service and our national honor will not often be tarnished by such gross and horrible violations."[12]

Haile was particularly critical of volunteers stationed in small towns along Taylor's supply route to Monterrey: "The women have been repeatedly violated—[almost] an every day affair, houses broken open, and insults of every type have been offered to those *whom we are bound by honor to protect.*" He wrote the criticism with the approval of many army officers, he explained. "I am determined, hereafter, to notice every serious offense [of this kind]. The American army shall not be disgraced without the [light] falling on the guilty parties, if I can be instrumental in exposing them. It would be criminal of me to overlook these outrages and, for the sake of our national honor, as well as for that of the U.S. Army, I shall not do so."[13]

Haile also made a firsthand inspection of another American import to the Rio Grande: the Mississippi River steamboat. "The idea of a steamer ascending such a stream as the Rio Grande at night, at the rate of eight miles an hour, and with no soul on board who had ever navigated the river before is wonderful, and has created a sensation here," he wrote from Matamoros. The boats soon became the backbone of the army's supply route in the Rio Grande Valley. On a later trip Haile was surprised to discover the boat's captain was the former editor of the Vicksburg (Miss.) *Sentinel.* "You find ex-editors and printers in departments of the service here, from officers of rank down to the 'bone and sinew' who carry the musket," Haile wrote, "and I have not yet had the misfortune to meet a *black sheep* among them." The correspondents made liberal use of the boats for travel and forwarding their letters.[14]

A number of Haile's letters during the summer interlude dealt with camp life. Describing the numerous military bands on the scene, Haile commented, "The music is soul-stirring enough to open the eyes of the veriest sluggard in camp. . . . No fond mother ever used more ingenious or honied language to win her darling from its bed in good humor than these musicians do." The arriving volunteers, he reported, were mostly bewildered: "Volunteers are constantly arriving fresh from home and 'full of glory,' though a little subdued by sea-sickness. . . . Water is found to be brackish. . . . The poor fellows are exposed to the burning sun, surrounded by white, hot sand and choked with thirst."

In another letter he gave this description of the scene:

The beach at the landing is strewn with barrels, boxes, baggage, hay, horses, wagons, drums, muskets and a thousand other articles, and a thousand or two of men—soldiers arrived, soldiers discharged, boatmen, sailors, fishermen, Mexicans, dogs, oyster shanties, coffee tents, sick men, Dutch, Irish, English, Italian, Spanish, Yankees, Virginians, Buckeyes, Pukes, suckers, Creoles of Louisiana, Mississippians, Chinese, Indians, Carolinians, negroes, and representatives of all of the nations of the earth.[15]

Haile spent considerable time traveling from camp to camp, visiting with regulars and volunteers, and interviewing officers. Character studies started to fill his letters, providing the *Picayune* (and other newspapers that copied his letters) with detailed accounts of army men who were becoming popular heroes. This description of army Captain Charles A. May, one of the early popular figures of the war, is typical of Haile's observations:

He is a soldier, heart, hand and soul. In height he is about six feet four inches, rather slim, but bountifully supplied with bone and sinew, with a beard hanging down upon his breast, and his hair resting upon his shoulders—his figure as straight as an arrow, a clear blue eye, handsome teeth, and in the very prime of manhood, say 28 to 30 years of age; his appearance is as *distingue* as the most romantic could desire for one whose courage and activity has won for him so high a name. . . . In his manners he is frank and pleasing, but there is energy in all that he says or does.[16]

An important news source for Haile was General Zachary Taylor. Like most of the writers with the army, Haile had a high opinion of the commander. "The old gentleman goes poking about just like other folks," Haile wrote admiringly, after observing Taylor riding around camp one morning looking for newspapers. In August at Camargo, as the army was preparing for its assault on Monterrey, Haile watched Taylor reviewing his troops and wrote:

He was on his war-horse, which he rode with more grace than usual, and his coat and forage cap were in apple-pie order; in short, a stranger would not have been surprised, as some are, when told that they saw before them the hero of the glorious 8th and 9th. The more I see of General Taylor the more I am impressed with the conviction that he is a man of extraordinary ability, and the very man to occupy the place that he does.

On another occasion Haile related one of many Taylor anecdotes about volunteer troops taking "a peep at the old lion." "The General's tent is just like those around him, only perhaps, a *little more so,*" Haile explained. For this reason, and the fact Taylor used little military formality, the volunteers often had trouble identifying him. Haile wrote:

[The volunteers] saw an honest looking elderly man seated in a tent eight or ten feet off and neither knowing or caring who he was, they chatted awhile rather loudly, canvassing the merits and demerits of "Old Zach," some saying he was "a d—ned tough old cock;" others that he was "pretty d—ned tight on the Americans sometimes." Finally they struck up *Old Dan Tucker* in real Kentucky style, beating time on the benches, not uproariously, but heartily.

At first Taylor paid no attention to their comments, Haile wrote, but finally sent an aide to quiet them. As the aide approached, the volunteers spoke out:

"See here . . . I'll bet that yonder is old Zach!" "Oh, h-ll no!" exclaimed another positively, "*that* old General Taylor!" and he laughed the other into silence. But the first speaker thought he would make *sure,* and so he stepped up to [the officer] and asked, "Is that the old fellow, yonder?" pointing towards the General. "What old fellow do you mean?" . . . "Why the old general—*that* ain't him, is it?" "That is General Taylor, yes sir." . . . "The h-ll it is," exclaimed the fellow, stalking off after old Rough and Ready—"come on boys! that's him, by Jupiter, I *told* you so!"—and the company started off in pursuit of their game.

Similar anecdotes, sprinkled through many of the correspondents' letters, added to the popular Taylor image of an accessible, unpretentious leader willing to meet volunteer and professional troops alike. It supported the notion of all Americans being equal, from professional generals to volunteer privates. Taylor often was portrayed in the anecdotes as a great but ordinary man, one who shook the hands of even privates—the common man—and asked them to sit and talk with him. This image, constantly nurtured in media coverage of the war, was to aid Taylor immeasurably when he ran for president in 1848.[17]

These items also demonstrate Haile's ability to tell a story. His use of dialogue, particularly vernacular, gave life, color, and humor to many of the incidents he related. As a writer he exhibited two personalities: one, a formal, patriotic side that praised the army and the country unquestioningly and insisted others should do so, too; the other, that of a lighthearted humorist who used wit, dialogue, and exaggerated characters to poke fun at the serious, sometimes pretentious side of army life. Nowhere is Haile's humor more evident than in his "Curnel Pardon Jones" letters. Haile had developed his Pardon Jones character as early as 1840 and constantly refined it in the years prior to the war. His letters commented on society, customs, and life on Louisiana's plantations, changing social conditions in America, and, as the war drew closer, the dispute with Mexico. Pardon Jones was the commander of a fictional New England volunteer militia unit, "The Dead Cow Brook Artillery." The letters about Pardon Jones's adventures used a mixture of misspelling, slang, vernacular dialogue, and colorful characterization to convey humor. The letters had wide appeal, the *Picayune* often reported. As early as 1842 the paper had gushed, "We are sure Pardon is the most popular man of his generation."[18]

Twelve Pardon Jones "war letters" appeared sporadically in the *Picayune* over a period of fourteen months, from September 10, 1845, to November 11, 1846. The letters started commenting about the possibility of war when Taylor first went to Corpus Christi. When the American army advanced to the Rio Grande, the fictional "curnel" soon followed. After Haile's visits to the camps along the border, his Pardon Jones character commented humorously about many facets of army life. The letters ended abruptly in November

1846, with Pardon Jones explaining his "exploits" in the battle of Monterrey to President James K. Polk. The unique Pardon Jones letters remain the most creative part of Haile's work during the war. Like much humor, its effectiveness has faded with time, but it still retains qualities of originality, wit, liveliness, and clues to the American character of the 1840s.[19]

The first Pardon Jones letter from the army camps appeared in the *Picayune,* July 16, 1846. Typical of the other Pardon Jones letters, it started:

LETTER FROM PARDON JONES

Mattymorus
Junne the 20 tooth, 1846
My Dear Pic: The war is goin' on glorusly. I'n Capting Potter has just goot farely intu the sperrit on't, and you won't see no more on us till you hear that diffikilties is eended.

. . . .

My regisment is camped in a house, in this town. Ginrel Taylor hasn't made no 'jection tu our stayin' in the army, and he's right, for if he gets intu a snap with the Mexicans he'll know where tu look for a reed tu lean on. 'Fore we come intu town tu camp, we had our tents pitched over 'tother side, and had a good deal of trouble tu keep the privates in order. We've got only three privates left in the regiment, and they give us more trouble then all the officers put together, besides bein' a bad example for the officers. If ever I go tu the wars agin with my regiment, I shan't take no private along.[20]

In his final camp letter, following the battle at Monterrey, the "curnel" reports to General Taylor the "extraornary conduct of my ridgement, and as I'm the curnel, of coarse, the fust honners comes to me." He closes by assuring Taylor, "You've dun your duty, Ginral, and I shall speak to Mr. Polk." As promised, he follows with a "report" to the president:

To Jamie K. Polk, our President tu Washington:
My Deer Frend—As a good many reports is going home about capterin this devoted city, I take my pen in hand tu do myself justice, and to inform you that I took it myself! It ain't necessary for me to prove this, for fax is stubborn things. I have been very hansumly supported in this glorious acheevement by Ginral Taylor and his army, speshly by the 2d Division, the officers is all officers of great Ginral Worth, or of great worth ginrally, which is the same thing backwards. I feel very greatfull for this

assistance, and hope none of these gullant men will be overlooked when you come to reward me. I don't want to cast nobody in the shade, but want to have the sun of your good graces shine putty bright and warm on my patriotic fame.[21]

Pardon Jones emerges from Haile's letters as a second-generation character in the Old Southwest school. Historian Walter Blair has noted southern characters of the period often were fun but not necessarily smart or insightful in most matters. Pardon Jones fits this evaluation. He shows occasional wit and brightness and serves as a tool to help understand a segment of American society. But the literary quality is limited. Although the use of a wholly fictional character to relate aspects of life in the army was unique, Haile's more important contribution, of much greater volume, was that of straight reporting. Serious, intelligent, and hardworking, as a war correspondent his talent soon became apparent to the press and public alike, and he was widely reprinted throughout the first year of the war.[22]

CHAPTER FIVE

Meeting the Demand

*No war has ever been fought, of which there were so many
historians as there is likely to be of this, our little war with Mexico.
. . . The avidity of all classes for news from the army, places in
constant requisition some thousands of printing presses, & mails,
expresses, steamboats, locomotives, magnetic telegraphs, are flying
in all directions. In order to keep the supply, fairly up to the mark,
some thousands of ready writers are required. The army and its
retinue promptly meet the demand.*
—*Niles' National Register,* November 21, 1846

As Haile and Kendall arrived on the scene, they were joined by scores of
other writers—volunteer soldiers, army officers, merchants, printers, country editors, and a variety of journalists—many attracted by the momentary
excitement, opportunity, and patriotism of the war's opening months. The
army's retinue swelled quickly, as did the temporary correspondents who
dashed off letters to newspapers and magazines. A large number of the earliest writers made interesting but mostly brief contributions to the overall
reporting of the war; others, through the quality of their work, or their publications, had more impact.

One of the war's most important and prolific military writers was William
Seton "Guy" Henry, a personable young officer (as mentioned earlier, lieutenant then captain) attached to the 3rd Infantry Division. Even before the
war, Henry was a popular contributor to the *Spirit of the Times,* a weekly
New York sports and entertainment magazine. He signed his work with the
nom de plume G** de L**, which gave him anonymity during the war to
write critically from the field (see more on Henry in Chapters 6 and 11).
Under the patronage of Secretary of State Martin Van Buren, Henry entered West Point in 1831, one month after turning 15. A family friend, Van
Buren wrote to War Secretary John H. Eaton: "I do not know the lad, but
the stock is enough for me." Although unusually young, Henry completed
the rigorous West Point course ranked thirty-eighth in the 1835 class of fifty-

Table 5.1 Newspapers and the War

Supported	Opposed*	Neutral
Albany *Argus*	Albany *Evening Journal*	New Orleans *Bulletin*
Baltimore *Sun*	Alton (Ill.) *Telegraph*	New Orleans
Boston *Atlas*	Augusta (Ga.) *Chronicle and*	*Commercial Times*
Boston *Post*	*Sentinel*	
Brooklyn *Eagle*	Chicago *Democrat*	
Charleston *Courier*	Claremont (N.H.)	
Charleston *Gazette*	*National Eagle*	
Nashville *Union*	*La Patria* (Spanish-language)	
New Orleans *Crescent*	Louisville *Daily Journal*	
New Orleans *Delta*	*National Intelligencer*	
New Orleans *Picayune*	New Orleans *Bee*	
New York *Courier and*	New Orleans *Tropic*	
Enquirer	(pro-Whig)	
New York *Herald*	New York *Journal of*	
New York *Post*	*Commerce*†	
(mildly supported)	New York *Tribune*	
New York *Sun*	Pittsburgh *Gazette*	
Philadelphia *North American*	St. Louis *Republican*	
Philadelphia *Pennsylvanian*		
Philadelphia *Public Ledger*		
St. Louis *Union*		
Washington *Union*		

*Whig newspapers opposed the war.
†David Hale opposed the war, while his partner, Gerard Hallock, supported it.

six members. He joined the 3rd Infantry as a brevet second lieutenant and served in Louisiana, Arkansas, Kansas, and the Seminole War in Florida before joining Taylor's army in Texas in 1845. He advanced to captain after the May 8–9 battles and was appointed brevet major for "gallant and meritorious conduct" in the battle at Monterrey in September 1846.[1]

Henry started corresponding to the *Spirit* from Texas months before the fighting began. Regarding his letters, Henry explained to the *Spirit*'s editors, "I had intended to give you a journal of each day's march but it would clean *break my back* to attempt to write it in this camp, separated from chair and table." Nevertheless, most of his accounts were in the form of a daily diary: "I give you these reports simply to show you the pulse of the army from day to day, so that you and your readers may go along with us and understand our feelings." In a modern context his writing might be described as a "G.I. Joe" style, a participant's account of the good and the bad in the camps and battlefields. Publications, on occasion, communicated with their correspondents by inserting comments into the writer's published article.

In one article to the *Spirit* in which Henry wrote that his description of the battles of May 8–9 "would fill pages were I to go on," the editor inserted, "You *must*, though, at your leisure." Henry wrote one of the first detailed reports when Matamoros was occupied by the Americans. After visiting the city prison, cathedral, and Mexican hospitals, he assured his editor "there is no such thing as refusing us anything—'might gives right.'" The hospitals were "filled with wounded and dying" Mexican soldiers, he reported. Most who were hit at Palo Alto had bullet wounds, he observed, whereas "the amputated limbs told of the cannon's fearful execution" at Resaca de la Palma. "I left the hospital shocked with the horrors of war," he wrote to the *Spirit*. A happier moment came later: "This afternoon Gen. Taylor very properly divided his captured cigars among his command; such a happy set of smoking dogs, you never saw, and all at the expense of the *enemy!*" Henry also worried about the large number of volunteer units arriving at the Rio Grande. "I fear, for their gratification, the fighting is all over. If all tales be true, there will be enough here to overrun the whole country." Henry admitted he did not know Taylor's plans but predicted "he will take all the towns upon the river, if he does not advance into the interior."[2]

Henry also fretted about the timeliness of his items, fearing some were so old that they might "rank among 'Boston News' to you. At the risk of this, I will cull from out of my note-book, some few events that may have escaped the press, and trust to your generosity to bury them if they are deemed stale and unprofitable." To the contrary, the *Spirit* noted, Henry's reports were being reprinted and praised by half the country's papers. Some of the army officer correspondents were killed or wounded in the war's opening battles. After receiving a letter from Henry, the *Spirit of the Times* confessed, "We open his letters . . . with fear and trembling. Two of our correspondents and one of our intimate friends have fallen [in battle]."[3]

For an army officer, Henry was quite outspoken as a correspondent. He strongly praised and urged the government to enlarge and improve the artillery units. "I hope that the press throughout the country will take this matter in hand," he wrote. He claimed much of the army's equipment was poor—swords too long and too light; transport lacking and hampering Taylor's advance; canvas tents "miserable," with many troops having no tents at all. He urged the government to establish a retirement home for old soldiers and to advance younger ones into higher ranks, and he praised the leadership provided by West Point graduates. Shortly before the war started he suggested the government buy California for $20 million: "I'm a volunteer for the Californias. If there is a truly delightful country, that must be it." After the capture of Monterrey he recommended the government appoint civilian governors and courts of justice in captured territories, observing, "[Now] there is no way to bring a criminal to justice." And he had words of praise for generals Worth and Taylor, at the time perceived as Whigs, opinions apparently not fully appreciated by the Polk administration.[4]

James L. Freaner of the New Orleans *Delta* began writing letters in May 1846, but his most important work as a war correspondent came a year later in summer 1847, when General Winfield Scott marched from Veracruz to Mexico City. Freaner (pronounced FRAY-ner), who was born and raised in Hagerstown, Maryland, worked on the Hagerstown *Mail* before making his way as a printer to New Orleans. He was working as assistant editor at the *Delta* when the first call for volunteers came, joined the Louisiana Volunteer Regiment, was in the first batch of volunteers to arrive at Point Isabel, and started writing letters immediately.[5]

Freaner had some trouble selecting a pseudonym he liked. He briefly used "Corporal" and "J. L. F." on his letters but settled on "Mustang" in June 1846. The *Delta* later claimed Freaner was nicknamed "Mustang" after killing a Mexican lancer at Monterrey and capturing his horse. But it is clear from Freaner's correspondence that he was using "Mustang" for months before the battle. He used that name for the remainder of the war, and before it ended "Mustang" and Freaner were as well known to the nation's press and public as any of the war's correspondents.[6]

Unfortunately for Freaner and the other New Orleans journalists who had joined the first rush of army volunteers, their service came to an abrupt end. It became clear it would take all summer to build up Taylor's army to the point it could march farther into Mexico. In the meantime, the ninety-day enlistment of the Louisiana Volunteers ran out. By early June, Freaner reported, "We are now lying here in the most perfect state of 'masterly in-activity' that can possibly be imagined." The camp was full of rumors that Taylor was going to march to Monterrey, he noted, but "we all know very well that Gen. Taylor . . . will 'have to wait for the wagon.' At present we have not got sufficient ammunition, provisions, or the means of transport for one-half the army."[7] Seeking action, Freaner left the Louisiana unit and joined a Texas Rangers company headed by Jack Hays. It put him closer to the heart of the army, but the unreliable mail system undercut his reporting efforts. He went on to serve an important role in the war by delivering the peace treaty to Secretary of State James Buchanan (see Chapters 13 and 22 for more on Freaner).

Another Louisiana volunteer who wrote from the camps throughout the war was George Henry Tobin, a New Orleans reporter and soldier of fortune. Tobin was working for the *Delta* when the fighting broke out, and his letters, some serious but most filled with humorous sketches about army life, appeared in that paper throughout the two years. The *Delta* frequently referred to him as "our favorite correspondent" and as "that prince of epistolizers."[8]

Tobin was born in Wicklow, Ireland, and attended Trinity College in Dublin before traveling to the United States. He had a good understanding of classical literature, occasionally quoting it in his articles. Referring to his Irish background, the *Delta* said teasingly he had been "raised on goat's milk . . . and this may account in some measure for his eccentricities." Another contemporary described him as "a good fund of amusement, fun and frolic. . . . His eccentricities and oddities were without end, and, when directed to a particular point, they furnished him with arguments which were certainly unanswerable."[9] Tobin had seen prior military service in Florida and in the Texas Navy and was among the first New Orleans newspapermen to volunteer when the fighting broke out, serving briefly as a captain. His first letter from the army appeared in the *Delta* June 16, 1846, but he wrote only occasionally during the first summer of the war.[10]

After the Louisiana Volunteers were discharged in August, Tobin returned to New Orleans and began the humorous army sketches that were to earn him a national reputation. He started writing under the title "Notes from my Knapsack." This was later shortened by the *Delta* to read "From Tobin's Knapsack" or, occasionally, "From Capt. Tobin" or "Capt. Tobin's Last." The first "Knapsack" article appeared in the *Delta* on September 23, 1846, and the *Spirit of the Times* reported that it "set the whole country in a roar."[11] Like many of his subsequent articles, it dealt with differences the regulars and volunteers had toward army life and regulations. Most of the humor was based on puns ("The men called the *three* of us the Siamese Twins") or play on words ("My company *conglomerated* and *promiscuously* just mixed up."). Regarding Tobin's humor, the *Delta* explained: "There is a good deal of George's humor which we would like to soften and modify, but it is a difficult and dangerous task, and we must give him with all his faults, praying that our readers will bear in mind he is a wild, rollicking dragoon, who, in his multifarious duties hasn't time to polish and refine [his] style." The Philadelphia *North American,* praising Tobin's "humorous letters," added: "He is a soldier, every inch of him. . . . There is no whipping such a man as George H. Tobin." The Baltimore *Sun* called his Knapsack items "rich and rare," and on the whole "if not sublime, belong at least to the beautiful." The St. Louis *Reveille* believed his work to be the "most original" being sent by the writers in Mexico.[12]

Another active correspondent during the war's opening months was Thomas Bangs Thorpe, New Orleans newspaper editor and nationally established writer and artist. Thorpe was "well known to the 'press gang' on both sides of the Atlantic," William Trotter Porter, editor of the lively *Spirit of the Times,* observed. Thorpe often was referred to as "Tom Owen, the Bee Hunter," after the title of one of his popular short stories. Thorpe was born and raised in the Northeast and attended Wesleyan College in Connecticut before moving to Louisiana in the late 1830s and starting his popular sketches about outdoor life in the Old Southwest, primarily Louisiana and Arkansas. Thorpe, who was 31 when the war broke out, is described as having been "a short, thick-set young man, with a big nose and saturnine face." He had been active in Louisiana politics and journalism for several years before the war.[13]

In April 1846, on the eve of the war, Thorpe became editor of the pro-Whig New Orleans *Tropic.* He left that paper in September and moved to Baton Rouge, where he started the *Louisiana Conservator.* The paper was not successful, and in June 1847 Thorpe returned to New Orleans to become editor of another new daily, the pro-Whig *National.*[14]

It was while serving as editor of the *Tropic* in late spring and summer 1846 that Thorpe played his most active role in covering the war. From the start, Thorpe's biographer noted, the young Whig editor "shared the common attitude that the war was a stirring and adventurous affair." In mid-May, after the opening battles, Thorpe was selected by a group of Louisiana politicians to travel to Zachary Taylor's camp and honor the general. As Thorpe set off to "furnish the latest war news for the *Tropic,*" the paper wrote, "well, *we*—that is, the remaining *editors*—are disposed to go too!" Thorpe arrived at Matamoros in the last week of May and was happy to report he was received "with distinguished kindness by the officers of the army wherever I have met them."[15]

Thorpe repaid some of the kindness in his letters back to the *Tropic.* They contained glowing descriptions of a number of the high-ranking officers, such as this one of Colonel (later General) David E. Twiggs: "The brave Colonel is before me; he is grey-haired, remarkably stout, and a perfect military looking man. His face is almost covered with tremendous whiskers, joined together with a mustache that looks exceedingly fierce and very like old Blucher." Thorpe's power of description carried over to other people, as well, such as a group of Mexicans who were being questioned by Twiggs in his tent:

They are dressed in large palmetto hats covered with glazed cloth, and ornamented by bands of the most tremendous size, and silver "fixins" on the side that resemble the knob of an old-fashioned bureau. Their waists are encircled with gay belts, and their pantaloons tanned deer skins, and open on the side seam from the hip down, exposing their white linen drawers; they are very Mexican and very picturesque.

Thorpe's articles often referred to Mexicans in terms of cowardice, brutality, and inferiority. In recounting anecdotes from the battles of May 8–9 in which dead Americans were reportedly mutilated and robbed, Thorpe said, "For the cause of humanity we relate that the gallant [American officer] was dead when these indignities were offered to his remains." He concluded that the Mexican army officers "deserve the execration of every civilised nation and the contempt of every Christian people." Reinforcing one of the key ideas of Manifest Destiny—that the American system was best—Thorpe wrote, "It is time these Mexicans were better informed in the most simple precepts of civilization."[16]

Thorpe also walked about Matamoros and provided descriptions of its buildings and cathedral. He reported, "Men sit sullenly about in their fantastic dresses, half of them looking as if they (had been) stolen out of a stock company of a theatre. . . . There is a flaunting, stilletto-you-in-the-dark look about the whole of them." The appearance of an American newspaper in Matamoros "showed that the white man was coming," Thorpe explained, adding, "A new order of things had commenced and sudden and singular improvements for the better were bound to follow in Matamoros." In one of his most descriptive sketches, Thorpe visited makeshift hospitals in Matamoros for the Mexican troops wounded in the opening battles. He was appalled at the conditions and suffering he saw: "The [veil] is torn away in these receptacles of suffering humanity, and it was a matter of serious speculation whether the horrors of war were not eclipsed by the horrors of the social condition."[17]

Although he did not witness any fighting and was with the army for less than six weeks, Thorpe was involved in the war's coverage off and on for approximately 18 months, partly as a New Orleans editor and as the author of two books of anecdotes about the army. He also was active in promoting the growing hero image of Taylor, which eventually helped boost the relatively obscure frontier general to national prominence. Thorpe was among the first writers to suggest publicly that Taylor might become president. In the *Tropic* of June 25, 1846, after another New Orleans paper had criticized Taylor's generalship, Thorpe countered: "Any attempt to persecute Genl. Taylor or lessen his high standing before the people of the United States, *will most certainly make him president of the United States.* Let 'Old Rough and Ready' alone, he is a hero, and he cannot be slandered out of his position by all the presses in the world."[18] As a Louisiana Whig, Thorpe had good access to Taylor and his staff. During the short time he spent in the army camps, Thorpe collected a number of interviews and anecdotes regarding Taylor, the army, and the May 8–9 opening battles. Many of these found their way into the pages of the *Tropic*, and from there to the newspapers along the Eastern Seaboard and in the Midwest.[19]

Additionally, Thorpe started work on his first book soon after his return from the camps. He wrote enthusiastically to his publisher that he had material for "one of the most readable books of the season, containing more stirring incidents, serious and comic, together with the many particulars than is often in a volume." He expanded, "I would say that I have the only *descriptions of the battles* and subsequent scenes ever published. . . . I gathered *my materials from the actors in the scene* and [went to] a great deal of difficulty to obtain what I have." By September 1846, *Our Army on the Rio Grande* was on sale in New Orleans. Thorpe's publishers, Carey and Hart of Philadelphia, printed his second book, *Our Army at Monterey*, the following year. The books, according to one analysis, showed "signs of haste in composition both in language and structure, but the narrative moves easily and is lively and colorful." In the second book, dealing with Taylor's subsequent victory at Monterrey, Thorpe did not go to the Mexican city but relied instead on interviews with returning participants, plus his previous material.[20]

Taylor's supporters apparently liked Thorpe's work well enough to have him compile a third book, *The Taylor Anecdote Book*. This publication, filled with biographical and anecdotal material about Taylor, was published in summer 1848 as part of the Taylor presidential campaign. Thorpe also contributed to Taylor's campaign by delivering stump speeches and corresponding to newspapers about the general's activities. Altogether, Thorpe's war coverage, while helping Taylor's candidacy, was too brief to have lasting importance. "He had done his work as a journalist," a biographer noted, "seeking to capitalize on the excitement over the war."[21] Overall, his version of events was often romantic, shallow, and stereotyped.

Also caught up in New Orleans's war fever was Kendall's *Picayune* partner Francis A. Lumsden, who went to the war zone in summer 1846. He had started organizing the Orleans Regiment, but when a Georgia volunteer company called the Gaines Rangers arrived in the city, it elected him captain. The *Picayune* coeditor quit recruiting and agreed to accompany the Gaines Rangers to Taylor's army. Lumsden reached Galveston on June 21, 1846, and immediately started writing letters to the *Picayune*, signing them "F.A.L." He celebrated the Fourth of July at the tiny town of Egypt, Texas, where he wrote, "There is no good water to be had, the temperature is 98 degrees in the shade and no one in the place has ever seen ice." He observed the holiday "with a small party of Gaines' Rangers, by quaffing them down in *old rye* for want of something more agreeable and listening to our thumping of tin cups on the counter."[22]

Lumsden spent some of his time visiting the battlefields at Palo Alto and Resaca de la Palma. He observed, "There is something that is beautiful in these [fields] . . . the soft and waving grass of the one and the deep chaparral of the other. Yet there, where all was still and silent and beautiful, man had met his fellow man in deadly strife, sabre had clashed against sabre, and the earth had drunk the life of valorous men." The Gaines Rangers disbanded, and Lumsden followed Kendall's example and made arrangements to join one of the Texas Rangers scout companies (headed by Colonel Jack Hays). On one of the unit's early missions to the town of San Fernando in northern Mexico in August 1846, Lumsden wrote to the *Picayune,* "Here your humble servant and his messmates are comfortably stored away, each of us with a separate bed, servants to attend us, and 'living in clover,' as if there were no war."[23] Lumsden did not enjoy the long trips into the field, however, and returned to New Orleans in early September, a decision that cost him an opportunity to participate in the coverage of the major battle at Monterrey.[24]

Another early writer on the scene was Samuel Chester Reid Jr., who corresponded to the New Orleans *Commercial Times.* Following the footsteps of his sea-captain father, Reid had served as a merchantman as a teenager and later as a deputy U.S. marshal. A New Orleans attorney when the war started, he joined the rush of Louisiana volunteers headed for Taylor's camp. He reached south Texas in early June but soon became dissatisfied and resigned, fearing his unit would be confined to rear garrison duty. He went to Matamoros and joined Captain Ben McCulloch's Texas Rangers company, which Taylor assigned to advanced scouting duties. A habitual diarist, Reid described the unit's early war experiences in what he called "a simple journal of events." He later interspersed his own collection of anecdotes with published articles by Kendall, Haile, and Lumsden of the *Picayune* and authored *The Scouting Expeditions of McCulloch's Texas Rangers.* The highly popular book went through four printings and helped add to the growing national image of McCulloch and the Texas Rangers.[25]

Reid's letters, usually signed "Adios, R.," often commented on Mexican customs and culture. When the Mexican army was not around, he observed, the general population was friendly toward the Americans. But when the Mexican army approached, the people grew "more surly and hostile . . . and all their smiles and apparent friendship had been only bought with gold." Reid expressed dissatisfaction, as did most of the correspondents, with the army's policy of paying Mexican civilians for supplies: "For the most ordinary things of no value, but still requisite, they exported the most outrageous prices." As the Rangers moved farther into Mexico, Reid claimed, "we bettered the condition of the people in every way . . . not only by filling their pockets, but by introducing civilized arts and customs among them, and luxuries which they never knew before." Such sentiment characterized

Reid's writing, but he made a telling observation about the stream of war-related letters the Americans were sending to their newspapers. If reporting mistakes occurred, he explained, "it must be recollected that men do not see, think, speak, or act alike, and therefore diversity . . . of opinion will exist, but even different constructions will be given [and] some events may be unknown, while others are overlooked."[26] Before the war ran its two-year course, there would be many occasions when the highly independent correspondents did not see, think, speak, or act alike.

CHAPTER SIX

Battle of Monterrey

My Dear Brother
Yesterday we read accounts of the Battle of Monterey. You may
easily imagine the feeling of intense anxiety with which the news
was read & listened to by all parties. I came to the list of killed &
wounded, here my eyes failed me, my voice grew tremulous. But
heaven be praised you were not in the list.
—Joseph E. Davis to his brother,
Jefferson Davis, October 7, 1846[1]

Monterrey was the first major battle that the American correspondents witnessed. It also was the first major battle of the war that American troops fought on what was indisputably foreign soil, and when the news of the victory arrived it exploded with the force of a bombshell. "The [American] victory at Monterrey is one of those brilliant achievements which will be cited in history as proof of the superior courage and ability of the Anglo Saxon race," the Philadelphia *North American* proclaimed, as it reported the enthusiasm sweeping over the city. "Had such a victory been achieved by British arms," the *North American* continued, "it would have figured in the London *Times* as a deed of the most heroic character." With a mixture of pride, patriotism, and news sense, the country's papers spared little effort in publishing the details of what was, at least to the prevailing American point of view, "a deed of the most heroic character."[2]

In reality, the victory was costly, marked by a number of military mistakes. But it was a victory. A combination of luck and fighting skill on the part of Zachary Taylor's small, spirited army allowed it to overcome a larger Mexican force during a four-day struggle, September 20–24, 1846. Lacking adequate transportation, Taylor's 6,000-man army had slowly, almost painfully, moved forward from Matamoros during August and September. Taylor made no pretense of hiding his destination. Heavy press coverage of the general's plans finally led the New York *Tribune* to observe, "The proposed movement of General Taylor on Monterey is well known in all parts of Mexico."[3]

Taylor had not expected a major battle at Monterrey, but when he reached the city on September 19 he found it fortified and a Mexican force of more than 10,000 waiting for him. The next day he split his forces: General William Jenkins Worth took the 2nd Division (2,200 men) to the western side of the city for the main attack, while the 1st Division (Lieutenant Colonel John Garland substituting for the ill General David E. Twiggs) and General William O. Butler's 3rd Division of volunteers were to make a diversionary attack on the eastern side. Communication was poor, and the east flank attacked before Worth was in position on the west. During the next two days the east flank suffered heavy losses and made little headway, while Worth was advancing successfully house to house on the lightly defended western side. Surrounded, the Mexican forces surrendered on the night of September 23. Taylor, aware of his heavy losses, agreed to a controversial armistice that allowed the defenders seven days to evacuate, and both sides promised not to fight for at least eight weeks.[4]

In spite of his mistakes at Monterrey, Taylor emerged as a national hero, pushed along on a wave of newspaper coverage before and after the battle. In early September it seemed to the American press and public that Taylor's army had disappeared. "Where is General Taylor?" an editorial in the St. Louis *Reveille* asked. Was it true, the paper wondered, that he was advancing undermanned and ill-equipped against a fortified city as the New Orleans papers suggested? The *Delta* wrote, "Great anxiety is now felt and expectation is on the tip-toe to hear from the . . . army." The administration paper, the Washington *Union*, observed: "We are looking for news from the army with much more anxiety than they are looking for news from Washington." The *Picayune* commented, "Where the suspense is so prolonged human curiosity will be at work and in divining what *may* have happened, it is not strange that conjectures have taken the form of positive rumors, and that reports have been circulated that can be traced to no authentic source." Such statements of anxiety became a pattern before each major battle of the war. As a result, the suspense that newspapers helped create heightened the public relief and jubilation at the news of each victory.[5]

Samuel Chester Reid Jr. of the New Orleans *Commercial Times*, George Kendall and Christopher Haile of the *Picayune*, Captain William Henry of the *Spirit of the Times*, and James Freaner of the *Delta* all were at Monterrey. Haile, in particular, mailed stories back at every step of the advance, but the slow, irregular deliveries hindered their publication. During the months Taylor was preparing to move his troops to Monterrey, Kendall had organized a system to relay the *Picayune*'s reports to New Orleans. This foresight provided the key for the paper's success in being first to report the battle's results. In addition to his journalistic sense, Kendall had sound knowledge of express deliveries and horses. In Mexico, he once wrote, "Every man had to have a horse under him on which 'you could run for your life' and save it." With care and forethought, he applied this attitude to establishing his express system.[6]

Throughout summer 1846, Kendall's letters were widely reprinted, appearing regularly in papers in Charleston, St. Louis, Chicago, Washington, Cincinnati, Baltimore, Philadelphia, Pittsburgh, New York, and Boston—even in Mexico City. The *Picayune* commented that their appearance in Mexican newspapers "was a little unexpected by us" and added "they do *not* fail to mention that he once visited their country under different auspices." When the army started its slow advance to Monterrey, Kendall again joined the Texas Ranger scouts. Notifying the *Picayune*, another correspondent observed that Kendall "can't sleep if anyone gets ahead of him, so he had to go along."[7]

The army's main staging depot for the march to Monterrey was Camargo, a small Rio Grande town. Kendall described it as "that hottest of all holes." Henry wrote to the *Spirit of the Times*, "I'm sick of Camargo and its precincts." Leaving the town for the march to Monterrey, Henry told the *Spirit*, "It was *withering* hot when we started. . . . Even my dog Sancho walked quietly by my side, instead of ranging for birds." Haile reported, "Had we been in the focus of a sunglass, ten miles in diameter, it would not have been much worse." On a hot day in August 1846, with the sun "darting down rays which were like arrows of fire . . . with not a tree to protect or a breath of air to relieve," Haile daydreamed of cooler times in New Orleans. He recalled sitting "in an easy arm-chair, with my foot thrown lazily upon another, a white linen coat on—shirt-collar open—a delicious Havana between the lips, and—oh—that *large,* sweating tumbler of iced mint julep sitting on the table."[8]

Haile arrived at Camargo on August 10 and immediately sought out Taylor to ask his plans. "Everything betokens an early movement of the troops on Monterey," Haile reported. "It has always been my opinion," he wrote confidently, "that the Mexicans would give Gen. Taylor another chance to whip them, and on a large scale, at or near Monterey, and I find that most of the officers here agree." Taylor had placed Camargo under martial law, and Haile asked for and received a written permit from the general that allowed him to remain with the army. In two weeks' time, Haile observed, the camp that had stretched "12 tents wide and one mile long" had grown to 3 miles. "It is no child's play, this campaigning in Mexico," the *Picayune* reporter wrote, as the heat and illness took a mounting toll on the volunteers.[9]

As the time drew near to leave for Monterrey, Haile notified the *Picayune* he was going to travel with the command of Worth. He was sure Worth, who had missed the opening battles of May 8–9, was "determined to do something brilliant at all hazards." Haile also noted he personally "was determined to see it out," although the march to "the interior of the enemy's country, almost unknown to us, causes everyone to reflect deeply." Assuring the *Picayune* "the best *horse* for a long journey in this [hot] country is a *mule*," Haile purchased one for the trip to Monterrey. "He is a sleek, grave looking old fellow, perfectly docile, and has a lively, easy gait," Haile explained. In his characteristic light manner, Haile concluded, "I shall mount my faithful mule and make a forced march, in time to enter Monterey with the first and engage a choice room at one of their crack hotels."[10]

Reaching Cerralvo on September 8, Haile caught up with Kendall: "I hunted him down as soon as I arrived . . . but could not succeed in ascertaining his exact whereabouts until I happened to espy *Spriggs*, his favorite charger, standing near the door of a dwelling. I have never seen Spriggs and his doating master very far apart in Mexico, and knew very well that my search was at an end." Haile found Kendall in "robust" health. "He seems to be in his element while dashing around the country with the spy company," Haile wrote. Henry also met Kendall, telling the *Spirit*, "When I saw him he was the busiest man, loading as fine a shooting iron, as I have seen in some time." On September 12, Kendall departed with the Texas Rangers as they were sent forward to Monterrey on a scouting mission.[11]

Haile soon was on the road to Monterrey, riding with the 7th Infantry. The mood of the army was confident and lighthearted, he judged, noting that "the officers are busy today writing 'one more letter home'" and some were working on "last wills and testaments." Whenever an army express rider started for the States, Haile would take the opportunity to send a letter to the *Picayune,* often tearing pages out of his notebook to include. He also would make notes on the contents of his letters in case they were lost and he had to send them again. Although Haile made better time than most of the marching soldiers, the trip between Camargo and Monterrey took him fifteen days. Riding and camping in Mexico could be exhausting, Haile explained:

> The dew had been so heavy during the night that, as we slept without tents, we found ourselves damp to the skin when reveille beat (at 4:30 A.M.). On rising from my blanket to stretch my limbs, my head came up in one of the eternal thorn bushes, leaving several points in the skin. . . . To dress, gather your *plunder,* saddle your *Caballo,* pack a cross, cunning mule, and all this in the dark, is a job that requires much practice to render it pleasing.[12]

James Freaner of the *Delta* also was en route to Monterrey, but he would not be as successful as the other correspondents. When the original Louisiana

Volunteers were mustered out in August 1846, Freaner stayed at Matamoros and joined the Texas Rangers unit of Colonel Jack Hays. Whereas the *Delta* had been in a quandary when Freaner and other staff members left New Orleans with the volunteers in May, it was now praising "Mustang" for his "indefatigable efforts" to obtain army news.[13] Freaner also was encountering the hardships Kendall, Haile, and Henry faced. When Hays's company was sent on a scouting mission to protect the southern flank of Taylor's army as it advanced toward Monterrey, Freaner wrote, "We are now in the very heart of the enemy's country." The scouts had only dried beef to eat for the final four days of a fourteen-day ride, he noted. Hays's company continued to scout in the forward areas until Taylor reached Monterrey. At that point the general assigned it to Worth's division as it began the flanking movement to the city's western side.[14]

"Well, the ball has opened!" Haile reported at midnight on September 18. For the first time he was able to use the dateline "Camp before Monterey." Haile's unit had planned to camp about 4 miles from the Mexican city when the troops heard a "brisk cannonading in that direction." Rushing to the scene, he learned the Mexicans had fired at Taylor and his staff when the general first arrived at the city. "The first ball came within about ten yards of the General," Haile recorded. The reporter quickly entered the camp and began observing the tense atmosphere around him. "How do the troops act on the eve of an expected battle?" he asked.

> Only that they are a little more precise in the performance of their duties—a little more careful in arranging their arms and knapsacks to be in readiness for an instant's notice—and a little more careful to procure rest while they may—I see no change in their demeanor. The only conversation is, *how* they might go to work to take the city. . . . It is the settled belief that the Mexicans will fight, and it is also believed that many lives will be sacrificed on both sides.

The next day, September 19, was one of "excitement and interest to our isolated little army," Haile reported. Most of the day was spent scouting the Mexican defenses. He decided to stay with the 7th Infantry, especially because it was moving with Worth's 2nd Division. Haile was impressed with Worth. "A handsomer officer than he appeared, I never saw," Haile wrote. "His handsome face was lighted up with a proud, but affable smile, as he motioned gracefully to his officers . . . the directions they were to take with their commands," Haile noted, using the gregarious antebellum writing style of the day. The mood of the troops, the reporter predicted, "renders this body of men invincible." As the troops lay around him sleeping by their rifles, Haile added, "No one expects an easy victory . . . all have made up their minds to see much bloodshed." On September 20, Worth's troops broke camp to begin their encircling movement. McCulloch's company was part of the division's reconnoitering party, and Kendall moving with it. Haile, meanwhile, stayed with the 7th Infantry, farther back in the division's ranks. In the confusion of the camp, the two correspondents did not coordinate their plans. "Kendall and I both came out with this division, neither knowing that the other was coming with it, until it was too late to return," Haile wrote after the battle was over.[15]

The double coverage of Worth's division, although accidental, led to overemphasis of its role, whereas the 1st and 3rd divisions on the eastern side of the city received heavier casualties but much less coverage. Like all reporters, Haile and Kendall saw the story from their particular vantage points. Although Worth's division played a major role, the fighting at the eastern end of the city was fierce and costly. Three out of four American casualties were suffered in that area, and the troops did not perform as well.[16]

Haile kept extensive notes of what he witnessed with Worth's troops, and when he finally was able to sit down four days later to begin his letters to the *Picayune,* he emphasized those incidents. The first published reports, primarily Haile's, concentrated on Worth and the Louisiana Volunteer Company, a strong local angle for the New Orleans press. Rushed to send his reports with the first express riders to leave, Haile had time only for a short summary of events on the other front.[17]

Haile and Kendall realized the imbalance and later spent a number of days collecting interviews about the fighting at the eastern end of the city. But the follow-up report did not reach New Orleans until two and a half weeks later, long after it was established in the public mind that Worth's division had carried the day. Taylor's role did not suffer in the unbalanced coverage, as he was the victorious army's acknowledged commander; in fact, Taylor may have benefited from it. Some historians have noted Taylor mishandled the troops on the eastern front, causing higher casualties. Most of the initial news coverage did not report the problems on that front.[18]

On the morning of September 21, Haile, advancing with the 7th Infantry, watched as a charge of Mexican cavalry opened the battle. The attack was quickly broken, Haile recorded. The Americans started advancing cautiously again, Worth ordering four companies, including the 7th Infantry, to halt along a fence. The unit remained there for more than two hours, Haile reported, while a Mexican cannon continued to fire at it. "The balls fell directly in their midst all this time without wounding a man!" Haile noted, somewhat astonished, because he felt "the Mexicans manage their artillery in battery as well as the Americans do." Worth next ordered his troops to take Independence Hill, which was providing the Mexicans with a commanding position. To Haile, the enemy's position appeared to be "in the clouds," so steep was the hill. The troops, including the 7th Infantry and the Louisiana Volunteers, charged up the hill in a "shower of grape and round shot," shouting and firing as they ran.[19]

The next morning, the correspondent watched as the troops charged and captured the Bishop's Palace. One of the soldiers Haile spotted in the charge was Sebastian D. Allis, a former *Picayune* office boy. A number of officers considered Allis a hero in the affair, Haile said. "He would rise and open up—up—like a jack-knife, until he obtained his full altitude, and would then level his piece, take good aim, fire, and *fold up* again behind a rock or bush," Haile explained.[20]

During the battle, Haile joined Worth's small staff as a volunteer aide. It gave him a better view of events and reinforced the positive feelings he held for the general. When the battle was over, Haile wrote: "The achievement is a glorious one—sufficiently to satisfy the ambition of any man on earth. I was expecting to see Gen. Worth rushing his men into unnecessary danger in order to win for them and himself great military fame, but his conduct has been very different from this. His great study has been in gaining these commanding points with the least possible sacrifice of life." The battle continued for forty-eight hours, during which the troops, and Haile and Kendall, had only raw corn to eat.[21]

Kendall, meanwhile, was with the Texas Rangers, Worth's forward scouts. At one point during the first day of fighting, the *Picayune* editor volunteered to find and warn the general when it appeared a large body of Mexican cavalry was about to charge the Texans. The attack failed to develop, however, and after spending the day with McCulloch's Texans, often under fire, Kendall slept with them that night in some nearby huts. The next morning, September 22, McCulloch's unit did sustain a charge from the Mexican lancers, and Kendall and the rest of the troops had to fight back while still in the saddle, "pouring in a perfect storm of lead from . . . rifles, double-barreled guns and pistols." The lancers' attack was broken, yet many still charged forward on foot, and a hand-to-hand struggle followed. Walking around the area afterward, Kendall counted 150 Mexican casualties. That afternoon, Worth decided to attack Federation Hill, a Mexican strongpoint protecting the western approach. Kendall again was in the thick of the fighting with the Texas company as it charged up the hill with other American units and dislodged the defenders at the top. Haile also observed this attack.[22]

In the afternoon, Kendall watched as the Americans turned captured Mexican cannons on the Bishop's Palace. On the final day of heavy fighting,

September 23, Kendall served as a messenger for Worth as his troops advanced from house to house through the streets of Monterrey. Because they were narrow, the streets were easily defended by well-placed guns. This forced the Americans to move forward through the houses by knocking holes in wall after wall. On several occasions Kendall dashed down the narrow, dangerous streets with orders for the forwardmost troops. By the end of the day, the advance had hemmed in the Mexican troops and thousands of civilians, and the defenders brought out a white flag. Both armies halted, exhausted.[23]

Kendall was exhausted as well. Having participated so much in the fighting, he was in no condition to write long newspaper reports. On the night of September 29, he sent an explanation to the *Picayune:* "I should have written to you before this late hour, but I knew all the while that our regular correspondent [Haile] was keeping you well acquainted with the stirring events of this past week, and little time had I, even could I have put my hands upon writing materials." Instead, Kendall concentrated on getting the express rider ready to carry Haile's detailed letters back to the paper.[24]

Haile had time on September 24, the day after the fighting ended, to start his battle story. He datelined it "Bishop's Palace, Monterey," explaining: "Even now, though I write in a palace, I am obliged to hold the sheet of paper in one hand on my knee, for want of a desk. But I have no time for extra remarks—a chance offers to send you the news, and I must hurry to give you a glance at what has been done here, before the express goes off." The courier took eight days to cover the distance to New Orleans, keeping pace with the official government messengers. News of the battle reached the New Orleans papers on the night of October 3, and while they all rushed out extras using scanty details from ship officers, the *Picayune* soon was on the streets with Haile's complete story, eight letters filling six columns. The street in front of the paper was jammed with people seeking copies, the *Picayune* "despairing" it could not satisfy the demand even though its press was "throwing off between five and six thousand sheets an hour."[25]

Express riders left for the North as soon as copies of the *Picayune* extra were available. When the news arrived, the Charleston *Courier* observed, "It is spreading rapidly throughout the country . . . as the newspapers, in a daily increasing circle, [are] teeming with it." It reached Charleston October 10; Washington the night of October 11; Baltimore, Philadelphia, and New York on October 12; Boston on October 13; St. Louis on October 15; and Cincinnati on October 16.[26]

With the first dispatches under way to the *Picayune,* Haile continued his follow-up stories. He started to compile a highly detailed unit-by-unit casualty report of all the Americans killed and wounded, including a description of the wounds. It was an ambitious project. Two weeks later he wrote, "Even now all of the names have not been gathered, the Kentucky regiment not having sent in any and some other corps having failed to report the names for several days of the fight." Haile persisted, however. "My object in collecting these names will be appreciated by the friends of the brave men who have fallen, as well as those who will be relieved from anxiety from reading over the lists," he explained. The report appeared in the *Picayune* on November 4 and filled four columns of agate type. Haile's list was accurate to within ten of the official army report. It had to be tedious to compile; the American casualties were high in comparison to the size of the force, and some historians have complained Taylor did not report all of the casualties.[27]

Haile's innovation of compiling the detailed casualty list touched off praise and controversy. The St. Louis *Reveille* called his list "the most elaborate and complete document of the kind that we have ever seen." The Baltimore *Sun* had strong praise for the report. "The press has by its enterprise, easily beaten the government casualty reports," the *Sun* stated, adding: "The public demand upon the celerity of the modern press is too exacting to admit of the delay necessary for that accuracy required in the official details of the battle."[28]

The New Orleans reporters compiled the lists after all of the war's major battles. Their accuracy got to the point that a year later, in November 1847, when the government issued an official list of the killed and wounded at Mexico City, the Charleston *Courier* commented, "It appears less accurate than that of the New Orleans correspondents . . . we therefore deem it unnecessary to publish it." At one point the War Department complained about the newspapers compiling the lists, claiming it was making the job more difficult. This was greeted with strong rebuke from the press. A number of newspapers had argued from the start that the government should make the casualty lists available to the press immediately. The *National Intelligencer* urged "on the score of humanity" that the lists of "privates as well as officers" be made known. The Philadelphia *North American* made an even stronger argument: "Wars are always popular at a distance. The bulletin that announces the destruction of a thousand fellow beings is received with . . . pride, pomp and circumstance of glorious war." In the public's celebrations of victories in Mexico, the newspaper said, "The main features of the terrible truth are suppressed. . . . We should like to have a list of all [casualties] with the details and names. Let our people realize the price paid for conquered provinces and military glories."[29]

In addition to the casualty report, Haile compiled a detailed report of the captured Mexican arms and rode over the battleground at the eastern end of the city with army officers who had fought in that area to reconstruct the portion of the story he and Kendall had not seen. He wrote: "I only regret that it is impossible, in one article, to furnish the public with [all] those details. . . . This can only be done in the form of *sketches*, and in that manner I propose to present to your readers the particulars . . . as fast as you will find room to publish them." The detailed summary that followed, filling almost two columns of type, ran in the *Picayune* November 4, a month after the first Haile and Kendall stories, which had emphasized the events at the western end of the city. Haile concluded: "I fear that you will find my communication too long, but you will readily see that I could not have given it a much more condensed form. I have done my best, under the circumstances, and shall always hold myself in readiness to make corrections when any errors in this paper shall be pointed out to me."[30] After the fighting ended, Kendall explained, "Operating at different places at the same time, it is impossible to get hold of everything [about the army] in a day." It was at this point that the *Picayune* editor began assembling a thorough "history" of the struggle, including details on Taylor's eastern line. The history, filling more than three pages of the *Picayune*, appeared in an extra edition on November 19, six weeks after the first news had arrived. To that point, the majority of the *Picayune*'s reports (and, therefore, much of the nation's coverage) had been written by Haile.[31] In addition to the fuller reports from Kendall and Haile, the *Picayune* also had access to letters written by Allis, the paper's former office boy who was serving in the Louisiana Volunteer Company. He wrote a vivid, first-person account of the Louisiana Volunteers in the battle, including the charge up Independence Hill "through a shower of musket balls." Allis also saw Haile during the fight. "He was riding about quite indifferent to the balls which fell around him," Allis reported, observing, "Although he did not run into danger, he did not appear to try to avoid it when it visited him."[32]

Where Haile and Kendall succeeded at Monterrey, Freaner failed. Although it waited hopefully, the *Delta* did not receive a letter from him regarding the battle until early November. When his correspondence finally came through, the *Delta* reported he had written letters twice a week since the city fell, but "we have not received one of them." The paper claimed there was a "system of espionage at the camp" that intercepted letters that did not contain "a certain admixture of *soft soap* for certain parties." The paper was forced to get its first reports of the battle from returning army officers and ship captains. The earliest published letter from "Mustang" at Monterrey was dated October 13. By that time he had switched to discussing the resumption of normal camp life.[33]

The lost letters prevent establishing Freaner's exact role in the battle, but the *Delta* later reported he had participated in the fighting as a member of Colonel Jack Hays's Texas Ranger Company. This put him on the same front with Haile and Kendall. A year later the *Delta* stated: "At the battle of Monterey, where, it's said, he killed in a single combat an officer of the Lancers and captured his Mexican horse, [Freaner] gained the familiar cognomen of 'Mustang' over which signature he has since been a regular correspondent of the *Delta*." Although the paper might have been right about the incident, it was wrong about the origin of the pseudonym: Freaner started signing his letters to the *Delta* with "Mustang" on June 3, 1846.[34]

Another graphic account of the battle was sent by Captain Henry to the *Spirit of the Times*. As an officer in the 3rd Infantry, he was on the eastern flank with Taylor's forces. Although his two articles were thorough and covered both wings of the assault, they appeared in the *Spirit* after the *Picayune*'s accounts had swept the country. Ordered forward toward the city on the morning of September 21, Henry noted, "Little did we know what was in store for us." Frequently lost, all the units were under heavy fire: "From all its embrazures, from every house, from every yard, showers of balls were hailed upon us. Being in utter ignorance of our locality, we had to stand and take it. . . . There was no resisting the deadly concealed fire; on every side we were cut down." The units rallied, and then fought an extended house-to-house battle: "The moment we left [cover] we were exposed to a galling fire of musketry, escopets, and artillery," he wrote. "Crossing one street we were exposed in full [to a hidden battery] and the men were knocked over right and left as they crossed." Still, the troops advanced, and Henry exalted: "Here it was that the undaunted courage and bravery of the American soldier presented itself." Finally, "The night set in cold, and to complete our misery, it rained all night." On September 22, progress was still slow on the eastern flank, but the troops pushed forward when they realized the considerable progress on Worth's front. Ever the military critic, Henry observed the army's light guns at work: "They did very little good, as the weight of metal was entirely too light. I look upon the exposure of the field artillery in the streets as perfectly useless—a sacrifice of life without a corresponding return." When one 3rd Infantry officer near him was shot in the leg, Henry saw him clap his hand over the wound and exclaim: "Boys, I've *got my ticket*, I'm off for camp."[35]

Henry also fretted about Taylor: "[He was] on foot, walking about perfectly regardless of danger. He passed over this cross street, in which there was such a terrible fire, in a walk, and by all chances should have been shot." On September 23 the tide turned, and as Worth advanced from the west and cut off the retreat road to Saltillo, the Mexicans pulled back. Henry praised their performance: "Thus far they have fought most bravely, and with an endurance and tenacity I had no idea they possessed." He also admitted he was "tired of this spilling of blood." Henry's first report to the *Spirit* detailed his own experiences on the eastern front with Taylor. He followed it three weeks later with a summary of the battle on Worth's front.[36]

So many officers were killed and wounded at Monterrey that the *Spirit of the Times* could not disguise its relief when it heard from Henry after the battle: "Thank God he is safe! . . . We are not at liberty to name him but sooner or later—perhaps in his very next letter—his identity will be disclosed." The paper went on to explain that Henry had written the Monterrey reports "on a valise placed across his knees." Over the next few weeks, Henry provided voluminous accounts of the fighting and a detailed list of the killed and wounded—but his identity remained unreported.[37]

Several key stories followed on the heels of the battle. Although Taylor's generous truce proved controversial at home, all the correspondents at the scene accepted the decision. American casualties were about 500, Haile reported, adding: "A considerable number of the wounded will die, so that the number who have lost their lives will be about 300." He continued, "The large fort at the north end of town is a very strong work and would have cost a heavy sacrifice of life to have taken it. . . . It would have cost many a valuable life to have taken the city at the point of a bayonet." "A great many are discontented at the terms," Kendall reported, "and think that [the Mexicans] will certainly fight again after being let off so easily." Kendall said if the American attack and bombardment on "this Gibraltar of a town" had continued even three more hours, "the loss would have been fearful" and "a terrible carnage [might] have ensued." Taylor realized this, Kendall wrote. "To carry out the known conciliatory policy of our Government . . . appears to have been his aim—to spare life and property, in accordance with his instructions, his object—and this should relieve him from all censure in the matter." But Kendall was exasperated: "I believe the whole policy of our Government is, and has been wrong for years." A magnanimous policy would not work with Mexicans, he argued, because "they neither feel nor appreciate it."[38]

Henry wrote to the *Spirit* that the armistice was a "humane decision" and that "the terms are excellent, and the country should be satisfied with them." Samuel Chester Reid Jr. wrote to the New Orleans *Commercial Times:* "At first a burst of indignation and angry discontent" was expressed. But slowly the troops' anger subsided: "It was a terrible moment—but their cooler judgment told them it was for the best, and gradually they became more reconciled."[39]

In another story, Haile said he was impressed by the strength of some of the defeated Mexican units as they marched out of the city after the surrender. "Most of the soldiers looked sullen, and their eyes gleamed with hatred and a desire for revenge," he wrote while watching the colorful units and their camp followers file past. The Americans particularly were watching for the U.S. Army deserters who had formed an artillery unit in the Mexican army, the San Patricio Battalion, under their leader, John Riley. Henry, who earlier had written about problems of desertion and officers' slaves running away, reported: "Several of our deserters were recognized in the ranks of the enemy [and] some of our men hissed one of them. He was marching by the side of a tall Mexican, who looked down upon him and laughed . . . as much as to say: 'You have to stand it, old fellow!' How degraded the poor wretch must have felt!" Kendall was not impressed with the American deserters or the Mexican forces as they departed. "A worthless scoundrel . . . [Riley] received a passing salute from his old comrades . . . which he will not forget in a twelve month," Kendall observed. "Other deserters were in the ranks of the enemy—runaway negroes as well—but not one of them was as well known as the traitor Riley, not one of them received such a blighting shower of contempt, such a withering tornado of scorn."[40]

By the middle of October, life had returned to normal at Monterrey. "Everything is as dull here as possible," Haile wrote. He was upset that the Mexicans had captured two American mail shipments and that he had not heard from his family for more than six weeks. It would not have happened, Haile charged, "if the economical quartermaster at Camargo had not hired a Mexican to run the gauntlet for *fifteen dollars*." Haile admitted, "No American citizen could be hired to take the mail through alone for $100." Additionally, Taylor was not discussing his plans. "The Washington letter writers probably know more about it than a majority of the officers under Gen. Taylor at the moment," Haile wrote after interviewing the general. "Is the war ended?" he asked. "Knowing nothing of what is passing at home we can only judge by what we see and hear around us."[41]

Freaner's life in camp also became routine. "We are now with hardly news enough to afford usual conversation—even 'camp rumors' are scarce," Freaner wrote. Although he had little to report, he remained at Monterrey until late November before returning to New Orleans.[42]

In addition to having no news, Haile came down with "double dysentery." "The health of the army is bad," he wrote, noting "a very heavy proportion" of it was on the sick list. "As for the curiosities—the scenery—the habits of this singular people, and many rich scenes I have come across here, my notes will enable me to pen descriptions of them for your readers when in health and at leisure," he assured the *Picayune*. Taylor assured him no fighting was imminent, and Haile decided to return home. As he departed, Haile analyzed the military situation: "It is useless to conciliate. . . . We must whip them into a family union before we can negotiate with them. They must be compelled to become either Mexicans or Americans, and those who choose to preserve their nationality must . . . organize a government that shall be responsible."[43]

Haile closed his Monterrey correspondence with a short treatise on army affairs. He again complained about the shortage of field-grade officers; noted "the army is woefully deficient in medical officers"; urged Congress to elevate Worth to major general; and suggested that a number of unit commanders who fought well at Monterrey be given permanent promotions to match their temporary assignments. "These are matters of vital importance to our Army," Haile wrote, expressing confidence Congress would do justice "to all concerned." Haile left Monterrey October 24, anxious to make the trip to New Orleans as fast as possible. At Reynosa, on November 1, he saw his original battle report to the *Picayune* for the first time: "It was copied into the N.Y. *Herald,* but as there was only one copy of it in the place, and as we had not time to read it and could not *borrow* it, I am yet unable to learn what you and the people generally at home think about it." Haile's long tour, which had started in mid-May, ended the night of November 13 at Hewlett's Hotel in New Orleans, as he jauntily signed the register: "C. M. Haile, Monterey."[44]

Haile's extensive reporting was widely praised, and the other New Orleans dailies paid him the compliment of reprinting his work. The *Picayune* was delighted. "We cannot withhold the expression of our admiration of the letters of Mr. Haile. They possess the best qualities of such a correspondence—unpretending simplicity of detail and studious accuracy. He is ever most solicitous to correct the slightest error. . . . His state of narration rises with his subject as will allow all who read the letters." The Charleston *Courier* commented admiringly: "To the *Picayune* is due the credit of getting the news through. . . . Their correspondent [Haile] writes graphically and spares no trouble in collecting his materials." "We have read [Haile's letters] with such interest," the Baltimore *Sun* explained, "that notwithstanding our crowded columns we cannot refrain from laying them before our readers." In New York, the *Tribune* commented, "The details of the struggle at Monterey will be read with a profound though painful interest."[45] Haile's letters were used in full by the Washington *Union,* but not without a degree of restraint. Under a one-column headline reading simply, "Very Interesting News from Gen. Taylor's Camp," Haile's letters filled six columns on the paper's second page. The *Union* primly cautioned, "Of course we cannot vouch for the entire accuracy of these statements." The next day, however, the *Union* published Taylor's first official battle reports and pointed out "they confirm last night's . . . accounts," referring to Haile's extensive letters.[46]

The reporting at Monterrey also provided the first clear indication of a major problem the correspondents faced. John Peoples of the *Delta* later charged that the *Picayune*'s accidental "double coverage" of Worth's division caused a "great" public misconception. He wrote: "From the tone of the newspapers throughout the United States, a person unacquainted with the important events of [Twiggs's division] would look upon it as being of minor consideration. This is the greatest error that ever was committed, and owes its origin altogether to accident." Peoples did not criticize the reporting of Kendall and Haile; he felt they "fulfilled their task very well." The problem, he said, was that no one from the daily press accompanied the troops at the eastern end of the city to provide the same record the *Picayune* reporters had of Worth's troops at the western end. Further, Peoples noted, when the *Picayune*'s "voluminous and interesting" reports were copied by newspapers around the country, some distortion was inserted into the original copy by local editors. "Generals Taylor, Twiggs, Butler, Quitman, etc. were forgotten and paragraphs crept into the original account derogatory to the character and standing of those gentlemen as officers and soldiers." In the absence of all official accounts, Peoples said, the American public accepted the newspaper accounts that "Worth was the hero" and that "he did *all the work*."[47]

The criticism was not so much about what the correspondents did as about what they could not do—they could not see all of the battlefield at one time. Each saw only a slice, and many of their reports left a distortion of the whole. Kendall later explained, "No man knows so little of a battle, as he who is actively engaged in it." The "bewildering terms of the fight" hindered comprehension, he believed. After the war, having had time to reflect on his experience, Kendall wrote that one of the great problems of battle reporting was the complexity, stress, and confusion of the action. Each observer or participant could honestly hold different views of what had actually transpired, he noted.[48] William Henry predicted, "Many accounts [of Monterrey] will be contradictory—hardly any two will see through [the same] medium. *Gen. Taylor's official report must and will be the standard.*" As for himself, Henry explained, "In all that I have written I have striven to record all that occurred in the simplest language, exaggerating nothing." Samuel Reid Jr., the occasional correspondent for the New Orleans *Commercial Times*, explained: "In describing the operations on the eastern side of Monterrey, we cannot be expected to give our readers as particular an account of the details of the fight as those given on the western side, where we were an eyewitness."[49] Reid, like all the other correspondents, rode over the eastern battlefield after the fighting to reconstruct the events. Clearly Taylor, Worth, Ben McCulloch, and the Texas Rangers had benefited from the coverage. Regarding McCulloch, his biographer observed:

The legend of Ben McCulloch was now firmly fixed. [Kendall's] lavish coverage of his role in the Monterrey campaign . . . syndicated throughout the world, established McCulloch's reputation as a *beau sabreuer*. In 1847 [Reid], in his vastly popular account of his adventures with the spy company, intended to "give the reader the continuation of the exploits of this daring partisan." [It] was reprinted four times before the Civil War and further buttressed McCulloch's romantic image.[50]

The lesson to be learned, as some realized about Worth's good fortune, was that first impressions count. It was an issue that would come back to plague the press as the war's major events unfolded.

CHAPTER SEVEN

The "Americanization" of Tampico

By the start of 1847 it became evident the war was going to continue longer than many Americans had assumed. "The first and grand mistake [in our war effort]," the St. Louis *Reveille* noted, "arose from the very natural contempt we felt for the enemy, and in this mistake the whole country shared." In New York, members of the 1st New York Volunteer Regiment publicly burned an effigy of *Tribune* editor Horace Greeley to protest his critical remarks about their behavior. The influential Albany *Argus* scolded Greeley for his "anti-Americanism," adding that the volunteers' behavior "is to be regretted and censured." The prowar paper cautioned such "acts of violence, however harmless in themselves," might help "the friends and apologists of Mexico." In Washington, the Polk administration reluctantly selected General Winfield Scott to head a new, major invasion inland from Veracruz on the Gulf of Mexico to Mexico City. Troops to bolster Scott's invasion army were taken from Zachary Taylor, who was ordered to hold his position at Monterrey in northern Mexico. It was an ambitious plan, involving the first American amphibious landing, and it took extensive military preparation. As a result, events centered at the Gulf of Mexico port city of Tampico, and in northern Mexico during winter 1846–1847, while the military carried out the buildup.[1]

It was during this period that another important correspondent, John H. Peoples, emerged. Peoples, formerly a printer and ship news reporter at the New Orleans *Bee,* was active as a journalist the entire two-year period of war, establishing a number of American papers in the occupied territory and sending a stream of correspondence from Mexico. Peoples used the pseudonym "The Corporal" in his early letters to the *Bee,* and "Chaparral" in later articles for the *Delta* and the New Orleans *Crescent.* His heaviest volume of letter writing was for the *Delta* from November 1846 to April 1847. He stopped his letters to the *Delta* and *Bee* after the battle at Cerro Gordo in April 1847, when he became involved in publishing newspapers for the army camps. His letters resumed in March 1848, when the *Crescent* began publication. During the war, he gained national recognition with his "Chaparral" letters, which were widely reprinted.[2]

One of the first national publications to recognize Peoples's ability was *Niles' National Register,* the Baltimore newsmagazine that reprinted many wartime letters. Calling his early reports from Matamoros "exceedingly lively and well written," the *Register* said his work was "keeping the public well posted up as to the affairs on the Rio Grande." The New Orleans *Crescent* later called Peoples "the person, who without any other motive than a desire of spreading truth before the public, has been so indefatigable in furnishing his contemporaries in the United States everything of interest and importance." The *Delta, Bee,* and *Picayune* agreed he was one of the most "indefatigable" of the correspondents—a term of high praise at the time. Peoples, the *Picayune* observed, persisted in his labor throughout the war only for "peace and the improvement of his country."[3]

Peoples joined the Louisiana Volunteers in the first exuberant days of the war. His newspaper letters, together with his penchant for establishing "army papers," made him one of the war's most influential journalists. Young, outspoken, adventurous, and a firm believer in the concept of American destiny, Peoples followed the army from Matamoros to Monterrey, Tampico, Veracruz, and on to Jalapa, Puebla, and finally Mexico City, constantly reporting about and praising its activities. He placed high value in what he called "sure enough" men, and he fretted that the "greater part" of the American population was "much fitter to sell thread and needles" than to face the challenges of the prairie and the West.[4]

Peoples joined Isaac Fleeson at the Matamoros *American Flag* as a coeditor in summer 1846. This experience prepared him for establishing subsequent camp papers at Tampico, Veracruz, Jalapa, Puebla, and Mexico City. Peoples missed the battle at Monterrey, but the lure of renewed fighting caused him to end his relationship with Fleeson in November 1846. As he departed for the front, Peoples wrote to his editors at the *Delta:* "With permission, [I] shall remain with the army until they get up a fandango in the Capital, should they do so. I left the army before with the conviction the fighting was over, but I shall now stick to it as long as there's a 'shot in the locker.'"[5]

Reaching Monterrey in late November 1846, Peoples found the army in disarray. The Kentucky Volunteers and Mexicans "are having a war" over the death of some Kentucky troops, he wrote, and he estimated "50 Mexicans have been found dead in the last five days." Taylor, angry that Scott had superseded him and was taking his best troops, ordered a series of marches and countermarches. Peoples said it was "general knowledge" in the camp that the Americans would soon march to Victoria, 200 miles southeast. He named the American units and the route to be followed. "From this you may infer that headquarters will be at or near Tampico." Taylor and his troops departed for Victoria on December 14, Peoples joining them, marching with a volunteer unit. After traveling 65 miles, Taylor received an emergency message requesting him to return the army to Monterrey immediately; an attack by Santa Anna was feared. Confusion followed as the return march started at 4 A.M., Peoples related, with almost everyone "ignorant" of what was occurring. The army, its supplies, and its animals soon stretched 25 miles on foot, and an exhausted Peoples arrived back at his former Monterrey boarding-house. The alarm proved false, and within three days the troops again were on the road to Victoria. The pace was grueling. The volunteers had to walk 25–30 miles a day over rough, rock-covered, rutted roads strewn with dead mules and horses. Peoples complained mildly about the early morning starts: "As early as it was, the 'greasers' were about the camp with their little articles of merchandise and followed the army for miles, until all they had were disposed of. These people make money out of us every way. . . . When they are not engaged in disposing of their wares, they will ferry sick soldiers over the rivers, by placing them on their own horses, and then jumping up behind them . . . [some] are making [to them] a fortune by the business, charging for each person thus ferried a picayune [6 1/4 cents]." Peoples spent Christmas Eve 1846 listening to the soldiers exchange stories about holidays at home. Later, the men grew silent and "everyone was left to his own reflection," the reporter observed. "I can't say that mine were of a very serious nature," he confessed, "those large bowls of egg-nog that annually sit upon the counter at Hewlett's [in New Orleans] were continually flitting before my eyes." On Christmas Day, the army covered 25 miles. "The march was too heavy for men under any circumstances," Peoples felt, and the "company called the 'laggers' had swelled to a regiment." It was particularly dangerous for troops to fall behind. Several were killed daily by the Mexican guerrillas who followed on the fringe. The twelve-day march ended at Victoria on the morning of January 4, 1847. "Now that we are all here, what is to be done?" wondered Peoples, as he described the bemusement of the officers and men camped around him.[6]

Peoples was the only correspondent with Taylor's 3,500-man army at the time, and his *Delta* accounts of the march and encampment received extensive use in the States. Although Victoria was in a remote interior region, Peoples's letters reached New Orleans in about three weeks, because he was allowed to send them with the army's special express service operated by the quartermaster's unit. This avoided the regular mail service, which operated by way of Monterrey and took six to eight weeks to reach New Orleans. Life in the temporary camp was quiet, except for numerous rumors. One day, Peoples was visiting with the Illinois Volunteers when General Taylor arrived. The correspondent wrote,

The way the boys crowded around him threatened immediate suffocation. By way of salutation I verily believe the old General pulled at his cap five thousand times. . . . The General was mounted on a large and gentle mule, whilst his orderly rode a splendid dragoon horse and was himself dressed in a clean and handsome uniform, whilst the General had on the same old black frock coat and a big Mexican straw hat. . . . The orderly got about six salutes to the General's one, the 'Suckers' taking him for the General.

Taylor took time to shake the hand of every volunteer. "By the time the two regiments finished squeezing [Taylor's hand]," wrote Peoples, "there could have been little feeling left in it." Finally, the general rode off on the mule, "many wondering if that was the animal on which he had charged the Mexicans."[7]

Peoples also started to piece together the army's plans through conversations with officers. By January 11, 1847, he was able to make a highly accurate forecast: "I trust I am not wrong in telling Vera Cruz to tremble," he wrote. "We can all be in Tampico by [January 25] . . . [and the army] can be moved to Vera Cruz by land or water before the first day of March; giving us six to eight weeks to take the place—for take it we will, if we attack it—and then fall back, out of the range of the [yellow fever] epidemic." Peoples's prediction appeared in the *Delta* on February 4, a month before the American assault began at Veracruz. The question of whether it was ethical for reporters to use such advance information does not appear to have been an issue during the Mexican War, as it was later during the American Civil War. There is evidence the Mexicans closely monitored the New Orleans papers for military information, but at Veracruz they did not capitalize on it.[8]

After ten days at Victoria, Taylor returned to Monterrey with a reduced force, his units transferred to Scott continuing on to Tampico. The army's march from Victoria to Tampico began on January 15 and proved a repeat of the previous disorganized, difficult march. The column stretched out for more than 7 miles, with Peoples noting that "the road was so rugged that it was impossible to keep up." In most towns through which it passed, the army "bought every pig, chicken and egg in the place," Peoples wrote. He favored a policy of the military living off the land, and he often wrote about the army's problems obtaining food. He noted, "So hostile are the people around Tampico at this time that they will not bring in their cattle, or sell them to our butchers for beef." Peoples attributed this to pressure from the Mexican government. "There is one thing certain," Peoples reported, "that if they will not bring in their cattle and receive pay, the army will go after it, and take it for nothing." On January 23, weary from eight days on the road, Peoples awoke at 3 A.M. and, leaving the troops behind, rode the final five hours to Tampico, observing happily, "Although it is January, everything looks as green as May."[9]

At Tampico, Peoples found a busy port city, crowded by the rapid buildup of U.S. troops and supplies. He joined the other correspondents in praising the "Americanization of Tampico," writing, "To those who have been a long time about Monterey, and in the interior, . . . Tampico has a very pleasing appearance—rendered so by the numerous articles of [merchandise] on sale here from home. It is a perfect Orleans." Other arriving journalists sounded a similar theme. "Truth," the pseudonym of a correspondent of the New York *Spirit of the Times,* commented, "You would hardly think you are in a Mexican town, the streets are filled with bustling Americans." George Kendall also was impressed: "Everything in and about this place would go to prove the go-aheadity of the Anglo-Saxon race, and that every thing is fast Americanizing. Here we have an American newspaper, the American theatre, the United States Hotel, the Union Restaurant and an American Court of Justice."[10]

When settled at Tampico, Peoples continued his letters to the *Delta.* "The sale of spiritous liquors has been stopped . . . and it cannot be procured publicly, but from the number of drunken men about, and the frequent rows that occur, it must be as plenty as water . . . somewhere," he observed. A few days later he had the answer. "There is not a [Mexican] house or shanty . . . that does not exhibit something in the eating or drinking line for sale. . . . And a sober man can always go into a back place and obtain *aquadiente, muscal* and American whiskey." The result, Peoples observed, was a guardhouse filled with "rowdies and *voluntarios.*" Much more enjoyable were fandangos. Peoples found them "more chaste and agreeable" than those at Monterrey, particularly because an armed soldier stood in every corner to assure order. In addition to the drunkenness and misbehavior by the volunteers, Peoples was concerned about the rate at which they were being murdered. He observed, "There was a time in Matamoros that the dead bodies of our countrymen found in the streets ceased to attract attention, so numerous were the assassinations, and the chances are much in favor of the same thing here. The Mexicans, independent of their natural hatred at this time, will kill an American for the smallest sum of money, or his clothing, and many a volunteer will fall to their knives." U.S. Army regulars did not have as severe a problem, Peoples reported, because they were confined to camp at night. Volunteers did not face such restrictions, and their officers seldom attempted to curtail their activities.[11]

Peoples also reported dissatisfaction among officers at Tampico about having to find out the army's movements by reading the New Orleans papers.

However, he surmised Scott would be issuing all his orders through proper channels, and "they shall be news when issued." He refrained from guessing Scott's assault plans, stating he was satisfied "to hold my peace . . . until I positively *know* something." Because the army might move at any moment, Peoples decided to send letters to the *Delta* by every departing ship, even "if it is to say there is no news." As a result, he supplied the *Delta* with a prolific series of letters on the army's Tampico activities. His work was not without hindrance, though. The *Delta* complained it was being punished by post office department workers for editorials critical of postal service. Peoples agreed this was the case and switched to addressing his letters to the proprietors' full name—Davis, Corcoran & Co.—rather than to the *Delta* by name. To get news, Peoples spent most of his days alternating between the army camps, which were several miles from town, and the city's commercial exchange. The exchange, he wrote, was "where newsmongers 'most do congregate.'" The exchange was the center for ship news, traveling foreigners (who often came from Mexico City or Veracruz), commercial mail, and Mexican newspapers from the interior.[12]

During his travels with the army, Peoples worked hard at building his sources with officers, particularly the veteran general David Twiggs. Peoples felt Twiggs had not received proper credit for his contribution at Monterrey because the *Picayune*'s Kendall and Haile "by accident" had accompanied Worth's division. When the news reached Tampico in mid-February that Twiggs had been promoted to major general, Peoples wrote, "The advancement of the brave old general fills me with joy." Peoples took the occasion to provide a detailed account of Twiggs's involvement at Monterrey, concluding, "I never should have alluded to this subject had not the promotion . . . called for it, for I had hoped that some more able pen than I can wield would have referred to it." Peoples received so much praise for his correspondence that the *Delta* was startled when he was criticized by the *American Pioneer*, an American newspaper published at Monterrey. The *Delta* wrote that Peoples "is a gentleman incapable of slandering intentionally any person, or of falsifying any fact."[13]

While at Tampico, Peoples also took time to go from the pen to the printer's case. With so many American troops stationed at the Mexican port city, it became possible for the American newsmen to establish a newspaper. On February 6, 1847, the Tampico *Sentinel* made its debut. Two New Orleans printers, James R. Barnard and William Jewell, published the paper, with assistance from Peoples. Francis Lumsden of the *Picayune* participated for a short period as editor. Lumsden described it as a "neat little paper." Regarding the publishers, he said, "They are worthy, respectable and enterprising practical printers. . . . This is another improvement—an American newspaper in Tampico!" Barnard, Jewell, and Peoples operated the paper until March, when they sold it and followed the army to Veracruz.[14]

Lumsden, Kendall's partner, had missed the battle at Monterrey and was determined to witness the assault at Veracruz. Lumsden traveled to Tampico aboard the steamer *Cincinnati* with Brigadier General James Shields and his staff and arrived in time to enjoy eggnogs on Christmas Day 1846. "[Tampico] is being *Americanized* very rapidly," he informed the *Picayune*. Lumsden praised the American "improvements": "There is no fighting, dissipation, rowdyism or disturbance of any kind, and it is not probable that the people of Tampico—the former inhabitants—ever saw so still and peaceable a place before." He took up the task of defending the conduct of the American volunteers, contradicting Peoples and the *Picayune*'s Christopher Haile, who were more critical in their observations. "It falls to my lot to speak in the fullest terms of praise of the volunteers . . . at this post," Lumsden wrote. "I have never seen a more orderly set of men encamped anywhere."[15]

The army and the press watched closely as Scott directed the invasion buildup. There is no evidence Scott discussed his plans with the correspondents, as Taylor did. Describing Scott's activities on one occasion, Lumsden observed, "It is not given to common people to know what is going on as regards the immediate future operations of our army; so I cannot, even if I would, enlighten you on that score." In mid-February Lumsden made arrangements to accompany Shields on the Veracruz assault. Confident it would be an easy victory, he asked his readers, "Who doubts the issue?" Lumsden's writing was the most jingoistic of the American reporters. He frequently overstated the strength and performance of the American forces, and his main purpose in moving with the army was to participate in the fighting as a volunteer aide rather than report about it. However, with his outlet on the pages of the influential *Picayune*, his work was widely reprinted. As a result, the impact of his observations and reporting, although biased, still carried some weight.[16]

Also arriving in Tampico was Christopher Haile, who rejoined the *Picayune* staff in late December 1846 for another tour as special correspondent with the army. The *Picayune* boasted proudly, "Hereafter we will be kept always posted upon war news by a gentleman whose experience in military affairs is scarcely inferior to his accomplishments as a correspondent." Although Haile's previous army reporting had been voluminous, the *Picayune* added, "we never had occasion to correct any revelation of his." Haile originally planned to rejoin Worth's division near Monterrey. At Camargo, fearing he might not reach Worth's division in time for a battle, Haile made arrangements to travel to Monterrey immediately with a small courier detachment.

Although under threat of guerrilla attack, the couriers and an escort of seventy dragoons covered the 300 miles to Monterrey in fourteen days, arriving January 8. The trip was hectic and difficult, but Haile was "exhilarated to be back in the wilds of Mexico." "Isn't this better than sitting on a high stool in a counting room?" he asked in a letter to the *Picayune*. Expanding on his feelings of why he wanted to be a war correspondent, he wrote:

> Is not this glorious appetite, this free air, this wild scenery, the novelties we are constantly meeting with—is not an idea of all of this enough to make you feel dumpish as you sit poring over the 'last mail,' and reading and making deductions from the 'rumors from Washington' . . . ? If not, so much the better for you, but I try to lash myself into the belief that you are all miserable there at home, and that *we* are the only happy fellows who belong to the States.

On January 5, 1847, Haile wrote from camp, "We never know what the morrow will bring forth. We travel all day along this dusty, rough, tedious road, our noses and lips cooked by the sun, and lie down at night, wrapped in our blankets. . . . We dream about ice creams, dogs' noses, and other cooling notions. We awake—chilled to the very bones."[17]

At Monterrey, Haile was surprised to learn Worth's command was preparing to travel the Rio Grande, en route to join Scott's army for the assault on Veracruz. Haile decided to stay with Worth and made immediate plans to retrace his steps. "Wherever Worth goes I shall follow him," Haile wrote, "for I know if anything is to be done he will have a hand in it." Regarding the pending invasion, Haile wrote, "We are now coming into a field that is new, and I will promise you that I shall write often and shall probably frighten you with the length of my epistles."[18]

Events, meanwhile, were moving to a conclusion at Tampico. Kendall arrived on March 3, close behind Haile. James Freaner of the *Delta* also was on hand. It was clear to the correspondents that the weather and the army were starting to move rapidly. By the middle of February it was getting warmer, and another problem was developing. "With all its pleasure, Tampico has one drawback upon a stranger's comfort," a correspondent of the *Delta* wrote. "Musquitos [sic]. Well may it be said, 'there's no rest for the wicked'; and the pious suffer some, for the hot sun in the day time and the clouds of poisonous insects at night." On this theme, John Peoples noted the weather in Tampico was getting "hot and oppressive" and predicted "the generals will lose no time in mounting the Vera Cruz attack since vomito [yellow fever]—feared more by American soldiers than anything else—is due in 4 to 6 weeks."[19]

CHAPTER EIGHT

Buena Vista—"Carpe Diem"

*Since the fight is over and the enemy has vomosed [sic], every
body is telling anecdotes, some of which are decidedly good.*
—Letter from army volunteer "MOSE"
in Ottawa (Ill.) *Free Trader,* April 23, 1847

Buena Vista, one of the bloodiest and most desperate battles of the war, received poor eyewitness press coverage. Winfield Scott was moving men,
supplies, and ships south along the Mexican coast, and it seemed logical Veracruz would be the next major engagement. Kendall departed from New
Orleans in late February to join Scott, the *Picayune* announcing he "was
headed for Brazos, Tampico and the seat of war." Haile and Lumsden of the
Picayune already were en route to Tampico, as were Freaner and Peoples of
the *Delta.* By this time the scope and length of the war had become clearer to
the New Orleans press, and the *Delta* and the *Picayune* took steps to expand
coverage. A correspondent wrote to the St. Louis *Reveille:* "Both [papers]
have a powerful corps of reporters with the army." Each had "five people in
the field with the title 'special correspondent,'" the writer said, concluding,
"we may rely on them for correct news."[1]

One key player in the drama was not headed for Veracruz. Santa Anna,
recently returned from exile in Cuba and again named president of Mexico,
was headed north toward Monterrey in an attempt to take advantage of the
divided American forces. The Mexicans had intercepted secret American
messages and were aware that Scott was taking troops from Taylor's army
for a flanking attack at Veracruz. Moving rapidly, Santa Anna marched north
from Mexico City, hoping to defeat Taylor, or at least cause him to retreat
from Monterrey, before Scott could become established at Veracruz.[2]

Taylor, meanwhile, had overextended his position beyond Saltillo, 65
miles south of Monterrey. He was poorly prepared for the sudden arrival of
Santa Anna's forces on February 19, 1847, but withdrew quickly to a prese-
lected defensive site at Buena Vista, 7 miles south of Saltillo. Santa Anna had
the numerical advantage, about 21,000 troops to Taylor's estimated 6,000,
most of whom were volunteers. But in a two-day battle February 22–23,

1847, Taylor's smaller force held its ground and forced the Mexican army to withdraw. Casualties were heavy on both sides and the outcome in doubt to the end. It was the last major battle fought in the north and, as with the previous battles, the news was received at home as a great victory, further reinforcing Zachary Taylor's war-hero image and boosting him toward the presidency in 1848.[3]

By early 1847 the New Orleans press started printing rumors that Santa Anna was headed north. But all reports were unsubstantiated, and Scott continued to shift experienced troops away from Taylor for the long-planned assault at Veracruz. The Santa Anna rumors continued, however, and soon became a flood in American newspapers. There were "Mexican rumors" and "American rumors," depending on the source. A writer for the Charleston *Courier,* after reading the latest papers from Mexico, Texas, and Havana, observed: "It is enough to bewilder any brain of common capacity to go through the tangled maze of rumors and come to any 'fixed facts' or definite conclusions as to what are truths, and what not."[4]

Amid garbled reports that Taylor was retreating and possibly defeated, the St. Louis *Reveille* stated it "would support General Taylor come what will," adding, "the suspense and anxiety [are] painful." The Baltimore *Sun* attempted to bolster public opinion by stating it had confidence in Taylor's "skill, prudence and valor." As the rumors of a defeat continued, however, it admitted, they "oblige us to admit there is serious cause to apprehend disaster." The New York *Tribune* warned, "The next news may be of the darkest character."[5]

The New Orleans papers were trying hard to sift out the truth. The *Picayune* noted the continuing reports "leave little doubt Santa Anna . . . made an important move . . . but the direction is a mystery. . . . A very pretty state of things for newsmongers this." Kendall arrived at Tampico on March 4 and found the city rife with rumors regarding Taylor's situation. He attempted to get the facts and ended up reporting there had not been a battle. "Mr. K announces that General Taylor has fallen back, and without an action, in so confident a manner that we place very great reliance upon his news," the *Picayune* stated on March 19, not knowing that the battle already had been fought and won.[6]

Amid all the garbled accounts, the *Delta* observed that the most definite statement it had seen about Santa Anna was in a letter from Mexico, printed in the Spanish-language *La Patria* of New Orleans. It had been mailed from Tampico on February 9 and claimed Santa Anna was advancing toward Saltillo with "16,000 good troops." Another report believed authentic was in the semiofficial Mexico City *El Republicano.* It said Santa Anna was en route to Monterrey with 21,000 troops, and it gave a unit-by-unit breakdown of his forces. Taylor was reported at Saltillo with 6,000 men and sixteen guns. The details led the *Picayune* to comment: "This shows again the accuracy of the information possessed by the Mexicans of our movements."[7]

George Tobin of the *Delta,* author of the popular "Captain Tobin's Knapsack" articles, was the most experienced correspondent at Buena Vista. Tobin, who had been discharged with the Louisiana Volunteers the previous summer, rejoined in January 1847 as a sergeant in Major Ben McCulloch's Texas Mounted Volunteers. Tobin wrote to his *Delta* editor, *"My Dear Fellow*—I'm off to the wars again. What were men invented for, except for war, wine and making love to the ladies, (God bless 'em . . .)." He had been on scouting missions in the Monterrey-Saltillo area with the unit for a month prior to the battle, sending occasional reports to the *Delta.*[8]

Tobin had a firsthand view of the two-day struggle. After Santa Anna's troops moved into position on February 22, skirmishing began. Tobin wrote, "We were idle spectators, sitting on the ground with our bridles in our hands. It was a pretty sight; but both parties fired at 'a foolish distance.'" The situation grew critical the next morning, as Santa Anna's infantry advanced. "The Mexicans fought well," Tobin wrote. But each time the larger Mexican forces pushed back the Americans, Taylor's artillery batteries would arrive and check the advance. "We were sure to see the artillery galloping through the ravines and checking them instantly," Tobin reported. "They appeared to me to be gifted with ubiquity—they were here, there and everywhere at the same time." At first, Mexican forces withstood the cannon fire: "Whenever a roundshot got amongst them, the lane was immediately filled up; and when the grape plunged in, that gap was instantly closed." As the day wore on, however, the artillery took its toll, moving Tobin to note, "The Mexicans suffered horribly . . . dreadfully."

The *Delta* correspondent spent a busy afternoon. McCulloch, riding next to Tobin, had his horse shot out from under him. "It was my first time under fire," Tobin confessed. "I had a couple of shots, and hit—nothing." At one point he observed two American dragoons dismount their horses and start a fistfight with each other. At another he watched as two Americans cornered a Mexican lancer: "He made a gallant charge, but they both shot him at once, and his arms and blankets became prizes to the victors." Tobin was upset as hundreds of the Americans ran "from the battlefield never to return," but he cheered to see "some of the retreating Indians mixed up with the Mississippians fighting like devils." Soon after, an American major "captured a pair of colors, but they belonged, I am sorry to say, to one of our own regiments, which was afflicted with a sudden panic."

There was brutality everywhere: "They killed all our men who were taken prisoners, and were too badly wounded to march away. . . . They stripped them naked too." He estimated Santa Anna's force at 21,000, "besides some thousands of banditti and women, brought on to plunder the dead and murder the wounded." He marveled at the courage of the Mexican lancers, adding, "but many of them bit the dust." In the midst of the carnage, a heavy hailstorm hit the battlefield, Tobin reported, and later some snow. "All that while you are luxuriating on juleps," he tweaked the *Delta* editors.[9]

Tobin's account of the battle was delayed when McCulloch's mounted unit was assigned by Taylor to pursue the retreating Mexican army. On March 4, Tobin wrote to the editors: "I'm broken down and in low spirits: two nights riding after the retreating remains of the conquered enemy and the third in copying the names of the killed, wounded and missing, which copy I transmit to you, as I suppose their relatives and friends, as well as those of the survivors, must be anxious to be relieved from suspense."[10]

The Louisville *Daily Journal*, Ottawa (Ill.) *Free Trader*, Vicksburg (Miss.) *Whig*, and Little Rock *Arkansas State Gazette* also received eyewitness accounts from experienced correspondents. The Louisville *Journal*'s graphic report came from Josiah Gregg, a noted author, trader, explorer, doctor, and occasional newspaper correspondent.[11] He was author of an influential book about the western plains and Santa Fe Trail, *Commerce of the Prairies*. Gregg had joined General John E. Wool's command in 1846 as a member of the Arkansas Volunteer Regiment. Because of his knowledge of the region, he had expected to be utilized extensively by Wool as a scout and adviser, but he was not. Gregg grew impatient with the army's slow progress and had personality problems with Wool, who suspected (correctly) that Gregg was writing critical letters about him to newspapers. Gregg had a difficult personality and was highly critical toward much that he observed, including the army, the Mexicans, and their culture. "He was that anomaly in society," one biographer has noted, "the one who appears to betray his kind by standing apart and observing them; and for him they inevitably hold a sort of uneasy derision." For Gregg, the campaign had become a series of "irritations, inefficiencies and humiliations," for which he blamed Wool.[12]

By the time of the battle, Gregg's role with the army was unclear, and he no longer considered himself officially attached to it. "I'm on my own hook," he wrote to his brother. One biographer observed "unofficially he was a war correspondent." Another said Gregg was "tempted many times to give up his association with the army and set out as a free-lance reporter of the campaign."[13]

But Gregg seemed reluctant to associate with the press. He corresponded regularly with John Bigelow, a coeditor of the New York *Post*, and made the clear admonition, "I wish it understood that *I do not write for the press.*"[14] In his letters to editor George Prentice of the Louisville *Journal,* Gregg added apologies for their "familiar, hasty and careless" tone. Prentice explained to readers: "It is but justice to Mr. Gregg to say that his letters come to us in the form of private communications and that they are necessarily written in great haste and under many disadvantages." Rebuffed in a last-minute attempt to serve General Taylor as a "volunteer aide or any other creditable capacity," Gregg decided to witness the battle from "high and commanding points. . . . Nevertheless, I was frequently in about as much danger from both musket and cannon shot, as if I had been actually engaged in battle."[15]

Whatever his journalistic status, Gregg's eyewitness account of Buena Vista is among the best. On February 21, with fighting imminent, Gregg joined the Arkansas Cavalry at an advanced position in the small town of Agua Nueva, where the unit was guarding supplies. Late that night, Santa Anna's cavalry reached the area, causing panic and a rapid evacuation by the American units. Gregg was appalled as the fleeing Americans burned supplies and nearby ranches. "This last was not only useless, but I think improper and even detrimental," as it allowed the Mexicans to see the American positions and "exasperated the *rancheros,*" who would seek revenge, Gregg wrote.

He arrived at the battlefield early February 23 just as the first massive Mexican attack began. "The force of the enemy was overwhelming—3 or 4 to one," he wrote. "The fire was incessant . . . a most terrible roar. I did not expect raw volunteers to stand so severe a fire, and less did I expect the Mexicans to endure it." As the Mexicans continued to advance, Gregg feared the battle was going to be lost: "Prospects were now gloomy." He moved to a high point toward the rear of the battle area and witnessed an attack by American cavalry that dispersed Mexican rancheros who were threatening the Americans' rear. Gregg wrote cryptically, "Some . . . endeavored . . . to give much credit to the *charge* of Col. May's command in this case. For my own part, I saw nothing praiseworthy in the affair, and, if justice should be meted out with impartiality, I fear the reverse would be the result."[16]

Gregg attempted to ride to areas where the fighting was most intense. After Mexican cavalry successfully charged into some Arkansas and Kentucky troops, Gregg rode to the site and found his friend, Colonel Archibald Yell of the Arkansas regiment, dead from a lance wound. Shortly afterward, Gregg, about 200 yards behind the center of the American line, found himself under intense fire. He wrote: "A more incessant fire of volley after volley, of musketry, accompanied by the rapid fire of artillery, too high, almost universally, I was perhaps in more danger than if I had been in the line. . . . Such a whizzing of balls on either side—before—behind—above—could only be compared to a hail-stone in a hurricane. . . . I heard one strike upon the blanket of my saddle but it was too far spent to penetrate."

The Americans rallied, he wrote, held their lines, and gradually the fighting fell off as the Mexicans pulled back amid "great slaughter." Gregg was confident "the Mexicans were whipped" and rode around to tell others. When night fell he returned to Saltillo and then awoke to the news the Mexicans had indeed retreated. He returned to tour the battlefield, writing, "and dreadful was the view. Large numbers of our own dead yet lay upon the field! But still greater quantities of Mexicans were scattered there." He came to a spot where seven Mexicans "had been mowed down by a single cannonball." In other areas he saw three, four, or five killed by one shell. The effectiveness of the American artillery, he concluded, had made the difference.[17]

In his letter to the Louisville *Journal*, Gregg claimed, "Such a battle, and such a victory . . . is hardly on record in modern history." The reason, he explained, was because Taylor's "4,000 'raw volunteers'" had defeated 20,000 of Mexico's "best troops." He continued, "Veterans could have done no better than a large portion of [the volunteers] did. The Mexicans too fought with much more resolution and obstinacy than I had anticipated." Gregg continued to collect details for his report in the week following the battle, and he transmitted it on March 1 using regular mails. It took five weeks to reach Louisville, where it was published in heavily edited form on April 7.[18]

Another experienced journalist, William Osman, editor of the Ottawa (Ill.) *Free Trader* and a member of the Illinois Volunteers, sent a detailed eyewitness account to his paper. Mindful of his history, Osman opened: "We have met the enemy, and although they may not be ours, the day and the victory at least are ours." He continued, "The whole of [Santa Anna's] army of 15 to 20,000 men . . . have been beaten, whipped out terribly, by a mere handful of Volunteers." Osman gave a fairly accurate account of the two-day struggle, describing all the major incidents, including a controversial retreat by the 2nd Indiana Regiment. During the fight, Osman watched a costly charge by Illinois colonel John Hardin's troops, first with fascination, then with horror as it faltered and fell back: "No other forces were sent to their aid, and indeed it would have been folly to do so . . . our boys were cut down by the dozens. Not a man got out of the ravine but made a hundred hair breadth escapes. But many a noble fellow fell, and not one dropped but was pierced with a dozen lances. No quarters were given to such as wished to surrender, and not a wounded man was found in the ravine." Osman witnessed the death of Hardin, as well as Colonel Henry Clay Jr., son of the Kentucky senator Henry Clay. Clay Jr. had been wounded in the ankle and was being helped from the field, "but the lancers came upon them so fast that he told [the men] to drop him and save themselves which they did and poor Col. Clay was immediately pierced in a hundred places and stripped of every thread of clothing he had about him." Hardin "was struck down by 2 or 3 lancers, and the scoundrels that did it never left him until they had pierced him in a dozen places." The U.S. artillery finally broke the lancers' attack, Osman wrote. "Thus ended the most unfortunate charge—the heaviest—indeed the only reverse of the day." The attack had been Hardin's own request, Osman reported, "and whether wise or not, it cost him his life, and that of many gallant spirits besides." At that moment, Osman believed, "the Mexicans had us completely whipped, if they had only known it."[19]

The report to the Vicksburg (Miss.) *Whig* came from a Mississippi volunteer, Rufus R. K. Arthur, brother of the paper's editor. Arthur reflected the perilous position of Taylor's smaller army on the eve of the battle when he wrote, "This little army may *possibly* be whipped, but there will not be many left if it should." The Mississippi regiment played a crucial role in the battle, and the *Picayune* called Arthur's account "one of the most vivid" written.[20]

The main action for Arthur's unit came on the second day. As it arrived on the field, Arthur wrote, "The first sight that met our view, was the 2nd Indiana Regiment, and Cavalry, fleeing from the enemy—closely pursued—the hills and vales covered with them; a portion of them met and passed through our ranks." At this point, Taylor ordered the Mississippians to check the Mexican advance. Arthur estimated they were facing 8,000 foot soldiers and cavalry: "There was no time for hesitation or doubt . . . or the day was irretrievably gone." Using superior rifles and with close, effective artillery support, the regiment broke the Mexican attack. "They were now for a short time too far for our rifles, but we looked on while our skilled artillerists thinned their ranks," Arthur wrote. Santa Anna mounted another frontal attack, and the regiment was repositioned to face it. "Col. [Jefferson] Davis cautioned the regiment to stand steady and firm, until they were within 50 or 60 yards," Arthur noted. "It would have done the heart of a Quaker good, to hear the clear rifle, the hoarse musket, the 'deep mouth cannon,' and witness the gaudily dressed scoundrels drop from their mustangs—the front ranks fell as if stricken by a thunderbolt."

Arthur expressed anger and outrage that many American wounded were murdered and that the dead were robbed, stripped, and some mutilated. "The comrades of the fallen men wreaked terrible vengeance upon the inhuman monsters," he wrote. Arthur's account emphasized the role of Davis and his regiment but summarized fairly accurately other battle highlights. He explained, "I have taken the first leisure moment to [write], and have been much hurried; it is therefore imperfect, but I have endeavored to be strictly correct and impartial."[21]

Albert T. Pike, an officer in the Arkansas volunteer cavalry, was another experienced correspondent at Buena Vista. Poet, author, political journalist, and former editor-owner of the Little Rock *Arkansas Advocate,* Pike was practicing law and serving as captain of the volunteer Little Rock Guards when the war broke out. A Whig, he opposed the war but remained with his decidedly prowar unit when it was assigned to join General Wool's command. The commander of the Arkansas Volunteer Regiment was Governor Archibald Yell, who had defeated Pike in an election for the post; they remained political enemies, and Pike criticized Yell's leadership in newspaper articles he wrote prior to Buena Vista. Like many volunteer units, the Arkansas regiment was racked by strong partisan politics and disputes. Yell, a friend of President Polk's and a popular politician without military experience, did not control his men, and the unit compiled one of the army's worst records for ineffectiveness and insubordination.[22]

Shortly before the battle, Pike's company was reassigned to a regular army dragoon unit under Lieutenant Colonel Charles May. The unit was held in reserve guarding supply wagons during the battle, except for one brief charge in support of retreating volunteers. Pike wrote about Buena Vista in prose and poetry, and his work was widely reprinted. He reported to the Little Rock *Arkansas State Gazette* that the two armies spent most of February 22 maneuvering into position. That night "the troops rested on their arms," he wrote, "the Mexicans starving and ours [eating] hard bread and raw bacon." The next morning Pike was surprised at the effectiveness of the initial Mexican charge: "Confident of an easy victory, they fought well." The ferocity of the attack, Pike wrote, caused a number of the Arkansas and 2nd Indiana volunteers to flee. He watched as Yell attempted to move the Arkansas regiment a short distance out of the reach of Mexican cannon fire, only to see the volunteers panic and run. "Totally undisciplined, the men understood the word *retreat* to be an order to make, each man, the best of his way to the rear and turned and ran off in great confusion." General Taylor rode up, "conspicuous on a white horse," and attempted to close the gap with reserves. Pike's company found itself tangled up with the retreating 2nd Indiana Regiment. "The aspect of things was now most alarming," he wrote. "Our men were mixed up with the Indiana fugitives who filled the ravine . . . and were flying from the field, throwing away their arms, and some even crying like children for terror." Pike's men held their ground, and a few moments later he observed General Wool berating the fleeing volunteers and striking an Indiana officer with his sword in an attempt to get him to stop running.

Looking at the confusion, Pike expressed his fears: "Affairs looked really desperate. . . . I thought everything was lost." Shortly afterward he saw Yell killed. "The want of discipline in the Regiment cost him his life," Pike wrote, as he described the charge of the Mexican lancers into the disorganized

Arkansas Volunteers. American troops and teamsters nearby stopped the Mexican charge "with a warm fire of musketry, which killed many of them and some of our own men." It was at this point that May ordered his dragoons to charge the Mexican lancers. "I had a momentary glimpse of the enemy," Pike later wrote, but the surprised lancers turned and retreated before the units met. Meanwhile, on the main battlefield, Pike reported, the American artillery was deciding the outcome.

Pike's after-battle analysis to the *Arkansas State Gazette* provided an example of the political bias that characterized many of the Buena Vista letters. He claimed, "No man living could have won the battle but Gen. Taylor. . . . While he sat there unconcernedly on his white horse, a target for the balls and yet unhurt, every man felt [confident]." Pike was not as kind to President Polk: "What punishment from an indignant people does not this administration deserve, which either from spite, malice, fear of a successful General's popularity and without any necessity, leaves 5000 men hundreds of miles in an enemy's country to be sacrificed! It is frightful to think of!"[23]

Another experienced correspondent serving at Buena Vista was Lieutenant Lew Wallace of the 1st Indiana Volunteers. (Wallace in the Civil War was a Union Army major general and author of the novel *Ben Hur*.) Wallace worked briefly before the war as a state legislative reporter for the pro-Whig Indianapolis *Daily Journal*. In a letter to the paper prior to Buena Vista, he observed, "The wonders of war are gradually revealing themselves to my sight. There is nothing else on earth in which splendor is mingled to a greater degree with misery. It is strange, also, how soon it blunts the finer feelings of our nature, and absolutely murders all sympathy or pity." At Buena Vista, Wallace saw this firsthand. During the battle his unit was positioned "at the fringe" and played only a minor role. Afterward he rode across the battlefield, describing it as "the most horrible . . . I ever saw. The dead lay . . . body on body, a blending and interlacing of parts of men as defiant of the imagination as of the pen."[24]

But a greater impression was made on Wallace by Zachary Taylor's stern criticism of the 2nd Indiana Regiment's controversial performance. A long-running controversy occurred after the 2nd Indiana troops apparently were ordered to retreat by their commander during a Mexican attack and ran in panic. Taylor's official report confirmed they fled, but it was not published until after nationwide newspaper accounts had condemned all the Indiana troops. The commander thus essentially reinforced rather than created the public's perception of what had occurred. Many Indiana Volunteers, politicians, and newspapers objected to being branded "cowards" in the press, and a long public dispute followed.[25]

The eyewitness letters of Pike, Tobin, Gregg, Arthur, and Osman all reported the 2nd Indiana Regiment (and the Arkansas Volunteers, as well) ran from the field. In the absence of their regular correspondents, the New Orleans papers used numerous accounts from participants. Many of the articles were romantically written and filled with unsubstantiated facts and opinions. One problem was that most participants had seen only a part of the whole, and so they emphasized their own experiences, observations, and biases. Politics and mistakes also inevitably crept into this process, and some newspapers found themselves in heated crossfires between writers and readers. The New Orleans *Tropic*, for example, used a long letter signed "Buena Vista" written by army Lieutenant C. P. Kingsbury that included several sentences criticizing the Indiana Volunteers. It was widely reprinted. The paper steadfastly refused to identify the author, but a year later Kingsbury wrote a weak apology to an Indiana newspaper admitting that his "Buena Vista" letter was hastily written "the day after the battle and with the views and impressions which, you will remember, were at the time prevalent, to a very general extent, in the army . . . under circumstances it was almost impossible not to have fallen into some errors." So many accounts were garbled that even the proadministration Washington *Union* lamented, "It is a matter of much regret that one of the able correspondents of the *Picayune* had not remained with General Taylor's division . . . to have furnished a graphic account of the battle."[26]

Such controversy was not the only issue that occupied the writers. Also important were depictions of Zachary Taylor as a war hero, as well as the role of the volunteer soldier. Rufus Arthur reported that Taylor "could not be induced to protect himself, he was a constant mark for the guns of the enemy." He continued, "He rode his white horse, and from the prominent manner in which he exposed himself, he was a constant target. . . . His clothes were several times cut by bullets but his person was untouched." George Tobin wrote, "If they killed 'Old Rough and Ready' . . . they'd have made little out of his toggery, his coat had two or three bullet holes in it . . . but it's a lucky color, salt and pepper, with capacious pockets." Prior to the start of the battle, Santa Anna reportedly gave Taylor an opportunity to surrender his outnumbered army. "Let him come and take us," Taylor replied, according to Tobin. "Short and pithy. . . . You may think this is a joke," Tobin reported, "but it is a true one." William Osman wrote that Taylor "was hardly out of reach of [the Mexican] batteries, and rode 'that same old bay horse' that moves about as Taylor hunches him with his knees, and never was known to move faster than a dog trot. Decidedly, the general was in a bad fix for a run." Osman reported Taylor had been fired upon seven times by Mexican cannons manned by American deserters in the San Patricio Battalion by "Captain Riley . . . a rare villain, and our boys will venture far to get his head."[27]

Post–Buena Vista newspaper coverage also produced one of the war's most famous phrases: "A little more grape, Captain Bragg." Some early reports from the battlefield quoted Taylor as having issued this order in a cool and calm voice as the artillery battery of Captain Braxton Bragg turned back a major Mexican attack during the battle's decisive moments. The phrase established a national reputation for Bragg and was successfully used during Taylor's 1848 presidential campaign. Bragg later said the first he heard of it was "by newspapers from the U.S." Taylor never stated it during the battle, Bragg averred, and added, "Many events and much reputation as they exist in the popular mind [in the States] had no other origin than in the same inventive faculty of the press and its correspondents." Regardless of what Taylor said, the *Picayune's* observation that the phrase "is a sure passport to historical distinction" proved closest to the truth. Whether fact or fiction, many newspaper readers apparently enjoyed the flood of Taylor anecdotes, and he was well on the way to the White House.[28]

Weeks after the battle had been fought, Americans in the States were still in the dark. Papers asked apprehensively, "Where is Taylor and his tiny army?" Had it been "cut to pieces" as the flood of rumors continually warned? In mid-March the *Picayune* observed: "The cry has been 'wolf, wolf' for so long a time that it is about time the 'wolf' should come."[29] And finally, in the third week of March, almost a month after the battle had been fought, the first accounts arrived. The cause of the long delay was similar to that following the battle at Monterrey. Taylor's army, exhausted and short of personnel after the costly victory, had taken several days to collect its wits, bury the dead, and regroup. Without regular newspaper correspondents at the scene, there was little sense of rushing to be "first with the news." Roads to the rear again were controlled by Mexican guerrillas. As a result, eight days after the battle ended, Taylor's first official accounts were still at Monterrey. In a letter later published in the *Delta*, John B. Butler, army paymaster at Monterrey, explained the American position was "too weak" to provide an adequate escort. On March 2, Butler hired a Mexican rider to go to Camargo. Butler wrote, "In the worst event that can happen, I lose my horse and a hundred dollars." It took nine days for the messenger to safely reach Camargo.[30]

From there, army doctor George F. Turner took over as courier for Taylor's reports, traveling to Matamoros. An occasional correspondent, army Lieutenant J. J. C. Bibb, prepared a synopsis of the battle and casualty reports and forwarded them to the *Picayune* by ship. An agent for the *Picayune* and the *Evening Mercury* boarded the ship as it entered the Mississippi River, obtained Bibb's report, and carried it by express to the city. As happened so often throughout the war, the newspapers had beaten the official government messengers, this time by two days. From New Orleans, the *Picayune*'s account was carried northward by the express riders and provided the excited country with the first authentic news of Taylor's surprising victory. Within ten days, the story blanketed the country.[31]

By March 14 the New Orleans papers agreed there had been a battle February 22–23 near Saltillo, adding Taylor "fell back in good order." Even this would be a victory, the *Picayune* and *Delta* reassured readers.[32] For another week, bits and pieces of the story trickled into New Orleans, until indications were too much for the *Delta*'s editors—they decided to take a chance. Their headline on Sunday, March 21, read:

VICTORY! Victory! Victory!
Good News from Gen. Taylor

This was followed by a cautious lead: "Although these reports are still vague and indefinite, enough can be gathered from them to give every assurance that Gen. Taylor has whipped Santa Anna."[33] The story was inconclusive, a careful restatement of known facts topped off with the unverified conclusion that Taylor had won a great victory. It was "a good guess," the *Delta* later admitted. True or not, the story had the ring of truth and was carried northward, where many of the papers used it along with headlines of the assumed Taylor triumph.[34]

Later that same day (March 21), the first authentic news reached New Orleans. An express rider carrying messages for the *Picayune* and *Evening Mercury* reached New Orleans at approximately 4 P.M. The *Mercury*, an evening paper, was able to get an extra edition out by 5:30 P.M., and the *Picayune*'s extra was available an hour later. It was only a momentary setback for the enterprising *Picayune*—even without a regular correspondent at the scene, the paper still became the country's main source of news about the critical battle.[35]

In contrast to the Americans' long delay, Santa Anna's distorted version that Taylor had been defeated reportedly reached Mexico City within four days. The Mexicans' intelligence system did not surprise Corydon Donnavan, a former Ohio newspaper editor who was imprisoned in Mexico during part of the war: "It is a remarkable fact that, although their facilities seem to be inferior, they always manage to compete with us in dispatching an express," Donnavan wrote. He credited Mexican law, which "authorizes the rider to supply himself with a fresh mule or mustang at every rancho, if necessary, and to always take the fleeted."

Confirmation of the battle simultaneously had reached New Orleans from Mexican and American sources. The Mexican account was considered more important because it was Santa Anna's official government report. It had been published in an extra edition of the Tampico *Sentinel* on March 11. Co-owner James R. Barnard personally carried the information to the New Orleans newspapers. The *Sentinel* obtained the news from a Mexican newspaper, *El Soldado de la Patria* of San Luis Potosi, where Santa Anna stopped after retreating from Buena Vista. His official version was misleading, claiming victory, but it contained more battle details than the American papers had been able to obtain from any other source. In reprinting it at length, the *Picayune* explained, "[Mexicans] sometimes meet with a sneer that [American] accounts are exaggerated and one-sided—that if the whole truth were known, that there would be less occasion for rejoicing. . . . We are determined that this time the Mexicans shall have all the benefit of their own statements, in all the copiousness that we are able to give them."[36]

Meanwhile, exhaustion, relief, and thankfulness prevailed at Buena Vista. Correspondent Rufus Arthur reflected, "Now that the excitement of the battle is over and we calmly reflect upon the consequences of war, we are almost ready to say it is uncivilized, barbarous, and inhuman." Albert Pike confessed, "So gloomy were my anticipations of the next day's battle, I never passed a more anxious night, nor was more rejoiced than when the cold, gray daylight . . . revealed . . . the enemy camp deserted." Josiah Gregg observed the battered American forces were "too weak" to pursue Santa Anna. William Osman rewalked the battlefield, watching as the Americans brought in abandoned Mexican wounded "whose groans are still ringing in my ears." The Mexicans' field hospital, he said, "shows that the surgeons found their offices anything but sinecures, for they left a cartload of amputated limbs . . . and from appearances the work was done up most unskillfully and cruelly." He watched as Saltillo residents buried the Mexican dead: "They dug holes a foot or two deep, and pitched them in helter skelter, first stripping them of every stitch of clothing." The battle's sights, sounds, and sensations also had an impact on the introspective Tobin, who closed his report of the two days to the *Delta* with the assurance, "We are acting on the advice of the 'Tuner of the Latin Lyre.' *Carpe Diem*." Live for the day.[37]

CHAPTER NINE

Siege at Veracruz

On the heels of Buena Vista came the news from Veracruz, a historic invasion route on the east-central coast of Mexico. Mexican and American newspapers had speculated from the first days of the war that the Polk administration would launch an expedition against the city.[1] A final decision to follow this route had been slow in coming, however, because the president could not accept the necessity of appointing either Winfield Scott or Zachary Taylor, potential Whig presidential contenders, to head the expedition. It finally became clear in late fall 1846, however, that Scott would have to carry out the assignment. Polk reluctantly appointed the general to the command, and by February 1847, Scott had assembled an invasion army of 10,000 men.[2]

The Mexican government had many indications the invasion was imminent.[3] There had been various attempts to strengthen Veracruz and its fortress, San Juan de Ulua, but without much success. It still was a substantial military obstacle when Scott landed 8,600 men on the beaches south of the city on March 9, 1847, in the first major U.S. amphibious landing. A twenty-day siege and bombardment followed, the invaders encircling the city and fortress. On March 28, following days of shelling by American guns, the city surrendered.[4]

Having long expected the Veracruz landing, the press was well represented when it occurred. Kendall, Haile, and Lumsden of the *Picayune,* Freaner and Peoples of the *Delta,* and two correspondents on the scene for the first time, William C. Tobey of the Philadelphia *North American* and Jane McManus Storms of the New York *Sun,* all reported the siege.

Kendall, with his usual energy, supplied the most extensive accounts and again made careful arrangements to have his reports and those of Haile and Lumsden relayed quickly to New Orleans. Kendall went ashore the first day, March 9, and spent much of the siege riding around the sand hills observing various American units. "It would take a page of our paper to give full effect to a description of the first landing of our troops," Kendall wrote to the *Picayune* after watching the unprecedented assault on March 9. "A more stirring spectacle has probably never been witnessed in America." More than seventy surf boats filled with almost 4,000 men were in the first wave, Kendall said. "Every man was anxious to be first—they plunged into the water waist deep as they reached the shore—the 'stars and stripes' were instantly floating—a rush was made for the sand hills and amid loud shouts they pressed onward." Why the Mexicans did not oppose the landing was "a greater mystery than ever," Kendall said.[5]

On March 13 he described a bombardment of the American lines by 13-inch shells from the Mexican fort: "I wish you could hear one of these huge projectiles in the air as they are coming, and see the scattering they make. The roar they make may be compared to that of a tornado, and every man within a quarter of a mile of the spot where they strike thinks they are about to fall on his individual head. The consequence is, there is a general scampering to and fro." Although it took two men to lift each shell, Kendall told the *Picayune* he was planning to send one to the paper "as a sample."[6]

On the beaches, Kendall found the American soldiers suffering from the hot sun, drinking bad water, and sleeping without tents. They were exhausted from marching in heavy sand, hampered by heavy, gusting winds from the north (Northers), and under constant fire from the Mexican guns. The Northers also washed a number of the American ships onto shore, leaving the beach strewn with debris. On March 23 the *Picayune* correspondent was getting ready to turn in for the night at one of the rear area camps when an alarm spread indicating that the Mexican cavalry was about to charge. "Seven full companies of the odds and ends of the camp—wagoners, hostlers, cooks, boatmen, clerks, servants and what not—were collected and armed, and every preparation was made to annihilate the 2000 cavalry aforesaid; but not an enemy appeared, and the whole affair ended in less than smoke."[7]

It apparently was not totally unpleasant for the *Picayune* editor, another correspondent reporting, "Your friend Kendall . . . found us in the afternoon and I opened my last bottle of brandy for him."[8] I. R. Diller, occasional contributor to the Philadelphia *Pennsylvanian,* wrote, "Lumsden and Kendall of the *Picayune* are here, and play the very mischief with the [snipe and plover], not only in killing them, but are not slow in eating them after."[9]

On March 24, Kendall watched as the American guns bombarded the city. "The conflagration was certainly the most grand I have ever witnessed," he reported as fires swept the city. The shelling continued the following morning, Kendall describing the roar as "Tremendous. . . . Every one of the guns are now keeping up an incessant firing upon the city."[10]

Haile traveled to Veracruz with troops under General William Worth. Writing from their camp as they waited for the ships to carry them to Veracruz, Haile described the scene about him: "[The troops] . . . appear to be as gay as children. Large fires have been lighted . . . and they are boiling their coffee, cooking their supper, and cracking jokes. Tattoo is now beating. Nothing is more stirring than the fife and drum well played. Half a dozen drums and as many fifes are now 'discoursing' merry music." The former West Point cadet was moved by the hardships and simple life the regular troops had to endure in the army of the 1840s. "I wish some of your quiet readers, who are at this moment quietly seated at their fireplaces, with their wives and children near them, could visit this spot for a few minutes tonight," he wrote. "The noble fellows now wrap themselves in their blankets, stretch themselves upon the ground, and whilst the cold night mist sweeps over them, dream, perhaps of *their* wives and children and mothers at home; of friends and homes that many of them, probably, are destined never to see." Haile took the moment to urge President Polk to take advantage of a new military appropriations bill about to be passed by Congress to reward the regular army: " . . . not just those who are fortunate enough to be the sons of powerful political men. I feel confident. . . . Tried merit, and long and zealous services will be remembered by him." Haile added: "This Mexican War is severe on all concerned in it—a dangerous, laborious, comfortless, and, I have some times thought, a thankless service."[11]

On March 7, Haile watched as Scott and most of the leading American officers at the scene made a firsthand inspection of the landing site and the city from aboard a small steamer. When it neared the castle, the ship was fired on, two shots just missing it, Haile reported. "Had they sunk her," he wrote, "it would have been the greatest windfall that Mexico has been or ever will be blessed with."[12]

On the afternoon of March 9 the troops began landing, Haile describing the surf boats as "moving off in gallant style and in the most perfect order." Haile watched as Worth jumped out of the lead boat and led the troops onto the beach without opposition. Three waves of the troops landed as Haile watched, the operation continuing past midnight. "The surf boats were manned by the sailors from the . . . fleet, who labored with right good will," he wrote. Haile did not go ashore for several days, remaining on the *Alabama* until the night of March 11, when he was told the ship was about to carry dispatches back to New Orleans. "It is now time to foot up the news to this evening," he wrote that night from the ship's deck, adding, "but I must do so by only giving the outlines . . . because the field of operations is too extensive to allow of my gathering particulars." The next day he was unable to accompany the troops: "I was prevented by circumstances from going into the field today, but felt the more easy about it as both Kendall and Lumsden were there."[13]

During the next week Haile traveled from unit to unit, compiling a detailed report of the American operations and the troops involved in the investment. The Mexican firing from the city "was incessant and their shot fell like hail upon our entrenchments," he noted.[14] Haile's first reports, together with Lumsden's and Kendall's, reached the *Picayune* the night of March 24. The next day the paper's headlines announced "Investment of Vera Cruz!"[15] In order to print all the letters from its three correspondents, the *Picayune* issued a supplement "at no extra cost to the public." The paper also interviewed the captain of the ship that had carried the mail back to New Orleans and described a map sent by Kendall, giving the position of the ships in Veracruz harbor and the troops on the beach.[16]

Lumsden, Kendall's *Picayune* partner, fully intended to join "the ball at Vera Cruz" and made careful arrangements to arrive early. He traveled with the command of General James Shields on the steamer *New Orleans,* departing from Tampico on March 7 with Kendall. He went ashore soon after the first troops reached the beach and spent the next two days riding across the sand hills as the Americans enlarged their beachhead. At night he stayed aboard the sloop *Albany* and wrote his letters for the *Picayune.*[17]

The heat and marching through the sand hills greatly fatigued him, Lumsden reported. When ashore, he enjoyed scouting with the advance units of the American forces, and on one occasion he participated in the capture of a Mexican soldier who was leading some horses.[18] Reading of the incident, the lighthearted St. Louis *Reveille* put a gag headline on the item: "Farewell to the Quill!"[19] Lumsden's exploits soon ended his war reporting, however. While on a scouting mission with some dragoons, he was thrown from his horse and broke a leg. Confined to bed, he wrote, "You would laugh could you see my position while writing. When I say I am screwed up, splintered up, bolstered up, tucked up and tied up . . . you can begin to imagine, though very imperfectly, what a figure I cut."[20] Lumsden returned to New Orleans three weeks after the city surrendered, and did not resume active reporting of the war.[21] His work was widely reprinted during his two brief stints in the field, many editors apparently expecting war correspondence similar to Kendall's due to the prominence of the *Picayune.* But, on balance, Lumsden's writing and analysis were limited and his overall contribution minimal.

The *Delta* had carefully prepared to give the *Picayune* stiff competition at Veracruz. Freaner and Peoples made arrangements to arrive early to witness the assault from the beginning. Peoples left Tampico February 26, but was on a slow-moving schooner carrying horses and military baggage, and the ship's leisurely pace cost him an opportunity to report on the siege. The boat arrived only a few days before the city surrendered.[22] Freaner believed Peoples had arrived first at the invasion site and assured the *Delta,* "Chaparral is with the advanced troops and will keep you advised by every opportunity of their movements."[23] After arriving, Freaner searched for Peoples in the U.S. camp. Unable to locate him, he wrote apprehensively to the *Delta*: "Great fears are entertained for the schooner *Ella,* 20 days out of Tampico with [Chaparral] aboard."[24] Peoples's ship eventually arrived, but he filed only one short summary article regarding the siege.[25]

Freaner had better luck. He departed New Orleans in mid-February and reached the U.S. Navy base at Brazos Island on February 23. At Tampico he found that most of the U.S. troops had already departed.[26] On the morning of March 7 he boarded the fast steamer *New Orleans,* the same ship carrying Kendall and Lumsden, and reached Veracruz on March 9, the day of the landing. He watched as the army and navy mounted a three-wave landing, gushing in his letter to the *Delta,* "This . . . was decidedly the most magnificent view ever presented to the eye of an American citizen."[27]

The New York *Spirit of the Times* correspondent "Truth" was another enthusiastic observer of the landing. "The excitement was intense," he wrote, as the small boats headed out for the beach "amid the cheers of thousands" aboard the U.S. ships. "The riggings were manned, every point from which an observation could be obtained was greedily sought after," he wrote. As the first small boats reached shore, "Every one's face paled with excitement and the heart throbbed audibly—pure unadulterated patriotism flowed at every pulse." "Truth" went ashore about midnight, 13 hours after the landing commenced. "I . . . was completely soaked wading from the breakers to the beach," as he carried the prescribed blanket and four days' rations. He found the beach "one mass of human beings, in anything but good order, on account of the confusion of landing in the dark." He soon fell "asleep from exhaustion."[28]

After going ashore, Freaner tracked down the camp of his old companions, the Texas Rangers. The second morning on the beach, Freaner found himself under heavy fire from the Mexican positions: "The balls came whistling through 'as thick as hail.'" He spent most of his day visiting American units and wrote that night: "The more I see of the investment of the city of Vera Cruz the more interesting and exciting it becomes. It is, indeed, a source of pride, and at the same time of pain, to see the gallant little army of ours marching and maneuvering about over the sand hills and through the chaparral." He continued,

> From morning until night they are exposed to the scorching rays of a burning sun, with the thermometer ranging from 90 to 100 in the shade; and while they are wading knee deep in sand, up and down the hills, with their arms, ammunition and day's rations on their backs, or chopping or digging out roads, they have been exposed to the fire of the heavy guns

of the town and Castle, but the greatest energy and enthusiasm prevails among them.

Despite the heat, fleas, deep sand, and enemy firing, Freaner said he heard no complaints, and he was happy to report there was "no evidence of anything like *vomito*."[29]

On March 19, after watching the start of the American bombardment, he predicted the city could hold out for only eight or nine days. That night he described the replacement of American troops in nearby trenches:

> The troops who returned from the entrenchments were literally covered with smoke and dust, and so much disfigured that they would not be recognized except by their voices. Shell after shell exploded in their midst, and shot after shot threw barrels of earth from the embankments over their heads as they lay in the trenches. Their escape seems to have been miraculous, indeed, and every person is surprised that at least one-half of their number was not slain.

Freaner noted after being relieved that the American gunners had immediately started a card game with "an old greasy pack" and "nothing but tobacco for stakes."[30]

On March 26 at sunrise, the Mexicans raised a white flag and asked for a parley. "The Mexicans will palaver until the vomito or millennium comes, if they are permitted, which I trust and feel assured will not be the case," Kendall wrote.[31] As he demonstrated at Monterrey, Veracruz, and later at Mexico City, Kendall opposed peace talks. At a later time he explained: "A Mexican can out-*talk* an American, an Indian can out-*talk* a Mexican . . . both or either of them can out-*talk* the—devil."[32]

When the Mexicans asked for the truce, Freaner expressed the same fear—that it was only a ruse to allow them to strengthen their positions. It was not the case at Veracruz, however, and the next day, March 27, the fighting ended. Later, when he entered the city with the first American troops, the *Delta* correspondent was surprised by the scene. "The destruction of the city is most awful," Freaner wrote. "One half of it is destroyed. Houses are blown to pieces and furniture scattered in every direction—the streets are torn up and the strongest buildings seriously damaged."[33]

Kendall agreed. After the siege, he reported the city "has been torn all to pieces—the destruction is dreadful."[34] Freaner had generous words for Scott following the surrender, writing that he "has certainly achieved a great, glorious and almost bloodless victory over an enemy in a position that was considered impregnable." In addition, Scott showed "coolness, courage . . . and humanity—the best evidence of a brave and competent officer," the *Delta*'s correspondent stated. He also had strong praise for the army's engineers and ordnance corps and the navy. Without the navy's "cooperation, in my humble opinion, we would not have been able to operate against Vera Cruz at all," he observed.[35]

On the day of the surrender, John Peoples of the *Delta* stood with the rows of American troops outside the city's gates as the disarmed Mexican troops marched out. He wrote,

> Women and children, old men and lame ones, hobbling off, preceded the column of the vanquished; and although they are, and should be, the enemies of every American, my heart bled for them. Their treachery and cruelty to our people was [*sic*] lost sight of in their humiliated looks, and although I was well aware that our magnanimity and respect would live but a moment in their memories, on my soul I could not help pitying them.

"No pen can paint to you the scene that was presented, and several occasions I imagined myself in a dream," Peoples reported. As the defeated troops marched by, a cannon went off, causing Peoples to look toward the fort,

> where the eye quickly fell upon the Stars and Stripes gradually ascending by the halyards to the top of the flag staff on Fort Santiago. Then . . . the sound of hundreds of cannon burst upon the ear, proclaiming that the city was ours. The bands struck up the 'Star Spangled Banner' and [all the troops] moved off in the direction of the city, each regiment wearing its colors, and bands performing the choicest of our national airs.

Carrying a special pass from Scott, Peoples rode into the city to view the damage. "I found that part of the city nearest our batteries very much battered down, and the doors and windows shattered by the bursting of our shells in the streets." Peoples estimated 175 civilians and forty soldiers had been killed in the bombardment. He noted almost every house was flying the flag of a neutral country "fearing the *voluntarios*" would break into them. "Bolts, bars nor walls" would prevent the volunteers from seeing the city they helped to take, Peoples said, but he noted Scott planned to camp them "some little distance from the city" to avoid problems.[36]

Haile also watched as the Mexican army marched out of the city, the scene reminding him of the earlier exodus from Monterrey. He accompanied the first infantry companies into the city, reporting, "The effect of the shells upon the city was now seen, and proved to be deplorable. Hardly a house had escaped, and a large portion of them were ruined. The shells had fallen through the roofs and had exploded inside, tearing everything into pieces— bursting through the partitions and blowing out the windows." The next day, March 30, Haile made an inspection of the city's huge castle, providing the *Picayune*'s readers a detailed description of its fortifications.[37]

Former editor Captain George T. M. Davis, corresponding for the Alton (Ill.) *Telegraph*, also had a closeup view of the departing Mexican forces: "I never before witnessed such a motley group in my life. . . . The soldiers were most miserable creatures." He estimated Mexican casualties in the city at 400, "which I am deeply pained to say, fell upon women and children." In one instance, he observed, a shell from an American gun "struck the Charity Hospital, penetrated the roof, bursting the room where the sick inmates were lying, and killed twenty-three. Thus rushing into eternity, in the twinkling of an eye, not only the invalid, but the innocent and unoffending." From the strength of their fortifications, Davis said, the Mexicans could have held out weeks longer if they had more food. In that case, "to have taken the city we should have had to take it *a la mode* Taylor, by storm."[38]

Kendall wrote a detailed account of the effects of the shelling on the city's houses, and estimated the dead at 150: "It is certain that women, children and non-combatants have suffered the most." Complaints by foreign residents about the American tactics were particularly irksome to the *Picayune* correspondent. "The actions of some of the foreigners," he wrote, "in not wishing to leave the city until their own dwellings were trembling about their ears, would indicate a doubt in their minds of the ability of the Americans to capture the place. They have found themselves mistaken, many of them when it was too late for either their safety or comfort." He doubted they would repeat the mistake.[39]

During the siege, William C. Tobey, a former writer for the Philadelphia *North American* and New York *Spirit of the Times*, became established as another of the war's important correspondents. Writing under the pseudonym "John of York," Tobey also compiled diary-type reports of the events and sent them off in batches to the *North American*. His accounts, although not as widely reprinted as those of the New Orleans journalists, still brought recognition from other papers, and before long his writing was being described in the press as "piquant," "able and patriotic," and "of great versatility and power."[40]

Tobey had been active in Philadelphia journalism for several years before the war. His background was well known to the editor of the Ottawa (Ill.) *Free Trader*. "Tobey affords a good illustration of the ups and downs of the life of a journeyman printer," the editor wrote. He related that Tobey was from Tonawanda, New York, and had made his way to Harrisburg, Pennsylvania, on foot and by canal boat after running away from an apprenticeship. "He was a funny little fellow—could tell a capital story—sing a good song, and write poetry, so that he soon became a favorite with the b'hoys and got a 'sit.'" Tobey went on to be a reporter for the *Pennsylvanian* and *Public Ledger* in Philadelphia, then legislative reporter and assistant editor at the Harrisburg *State Capital Gazette*. For a brief time he was a protégé of Senator Simon Cameron of Pennsylvania and studied law under him. He resumed his journalism career as editor of a penny-press daily, the Pittsburgh *Ariel*, but it failed, and Tobey became a general correspondent for New York and Philadelphia papers, using the nom de plume "John of York." "The war fever carried him off to Mexico," the *Free Trader* explained.[41]

Tobey joined a Pennsylvania volunteer regiment in fall 1846, along with a number of other Philadelphia journalists, including Robert F. Small and Montgomery P. Young of the *Public Ledger*. Small and Young became occasional contributors to their paper, but their work did not reach Tobey's scale. Tobey first served in a civilian capacity in the regiment's quartermaster section but later enlisted as a private and fought at Veracruz and Mexico City.[42]

The 29-year-old Tobey started his Mexican War letters while the Pennsylvania Volunteers were being outfitted at New Orleans. His regiment sailed south to Lobos Island, north of Veracruz, where the army was assembling. The scene on board the crowded ship was described in the Philadelphia *Pennsylvanian* by occasional correspondent I. R. Diller, who observed Tobey was "engaged as I am, in [editing] letters to some of your fellow editors in Philadelphia. This is . . . the way we spend our evenings."[43]

Camped out on the island's beaches in rows of white tents, Tobey reported the volunteers were looking forward to their first combat. "This going to war," Tobey wrote, "is so full of excitement and danger, that the laziest man on the face of the great plantation known as the 'world,' would, if here, forget his *penchant* for afternoon siestas and morning dreams." In a moment of reflection he wrote, "Fatalism, however mischievous in other 'professions,' is the true creed for the man who puts himself up as a target at seven dollars per month." He added, "There is not a man in our regiment who volunteered for patriotic motives, but *feels* that he is to play a conspicuous part in the bloody drama before him—who dreams of else than green laurels and bright honors." Regarding the more practical matter of making his daily ration of pork and beans "more agreeable," Tobey said he was spending twice the cost of the meal in "the purchase of good things." He also took time to assure the editors "that my letters are not dictated, in matter or manner, by any one," particularly any officers. "I write altogether from personal observation—knowing no favorite."[44]

Tobey went ashore during the main landing on March 9. The Pennsylvania regiment was assigned to Major General Gideon Pillow. "The day was the hottest I ever made acquaintance with, and climbing over the burning sand hills which yielded and buried our feet . . . made the march one of great labor and fatigue," Tobey recorded. At one point he informed his editors, "I have been soldiering the whole time in the ranks, and could not take notes like Messrs. Kendall, Lumsden, Haile, and a dozen others who are here riding from one part of the field to another."[45] Within a few days, Tobey was able to visit more of the American entrenchments, writing a letter almost daily during the siege. Receiving a batch of ten letters, the *North American* ran them during a three-day period under the headline:

ARMY CORRESPONDENCE
For the North American
History of the Siege
Incidents, Movements and Descriptions[46]

To this the paper added, "From Our Active Correspondent," and commented, "His letters need no apology, but to show the inconvenience under which he writes in camp, we may state part of his letters are written in pencil and part in ink which looks like gun powder and water, while other portions bear evidence of the hurry and bustle of the field of war."[47]

Tobey's extensive coverage had come about because he "obtained permission to doff my knapsack" and to tour the American lines. On March 15 he was at a sector of the American lines that came under fire from the Mexican guns. Crouching in a trench, he wrote,

But those shells—you have never heard them singing through the air under just such circumstances as I do now even while writing thus coolly. They make a most enchanting sanguinary sound. He that hears their music feels that there is death in it, but still will like it; and believe it or not, one often, when they have ceased for a time, wishes they would begin again their song of destruction.

Tobey added, "After six days of listening to them, however, the first impression [of fear] wears off." For several days, Tobey continued his walk north along the perimeter of the American lines, noting at one point that the New Orleans correspondents had "better facilities" for reporting than he did because they had horses.[48]

Ticks, ants, and sand flies "that poison the skin where they bite" were causing as much trouble for the "rank-and-file," he wrote, as the Mexican artillery. He also noted General Scott was "determined to preserve sobriety in the army," resulting in officers smashing several whiskey stills. "He will not have a great deal of trouble," Tobey thought of Scott's efforts, "for liquor is so dear and so bad, that few can afford to spare money and health." On the night of March 24, Tobey stood near the American batteries as they bombarded the city, observing,

> After dark the scene was awfully grand. I could follow the shells from our batteries as they went whirling round and then descended upon a roof or into the streets of the city, exploding with tremendous reverberations. Sometimes a shell would light on a stone roof and run around nearly a minute before exploding. Others would break through with a tremendous crash and burst inside. I saw one hit a large dome and pass through it. Another struck a light spire on a public building and shivered it to atoms.

The following morning he predicted the city would yield within 24 hours because "our batteries are utterly ruining" it. That same night a temporary truce was declared to allow the Mexicans to bury their dead. Tobey reported, "As I write multitudes are engaged in the sad office, which others may soon in their turn render them." If Philadelphians could see the death scenes "you would all turn Quakers," he wrote.[49]

Most of Tobey's letters dealt with the movements of the Pennsylvania Volunteers. He noted the *North American* could get general accounts of the fighting from the New Orleans papers. On March 27, when the city surrendered, Tobey closed, "Duty has kept me from getting a copy of the terms of surrender, but my watchful contemporaries here, who have more time to spare, and stronger incentives to activity in collecting the *materiel* of the transaction, will lay them before you through the New Orleans press, sooner perhaps than this letter will reach you."[50]

Tobey also watched as the Mexicans evacuated the city on March 29. "One glance would show how grossly wrong" it would be to direct the war at the Mexican people, he commented. "It would take ten years of unprofitable, wasting war to establish American authority over Mexico with any kind of permanency. . . . The field fighting would be nothing [but] the endless guerrilla system of warfare that would swallow up garrisons and beggar our treasury." The course to follow, Tobey argued, was to go after the Mexican government, although "it is difficult to see how peace is to be made with a country that has no responsible head." From his previous journalism experience, Tobey was able to combine description and analysis of the war's events; he remained an important reporter of the conflict until the American evacuation in summer 1848.[51]

***

As Tobey was starting his role as a war correspondent, Veracruz became the last story for two *Picayune* writers. Francis Lumsden, with his badly injured leg, went home and did not return to Mexico. Veracruz also marked the end of Christopher Haile's role as a civilian correspondent. In April 1847, he accepted a commission as a first lieutenant in the infantry, and at the end of May he was promoted to captain. He was named commander of a company in the newly organized 14th Infantry and spent most of summer 1847 traveling along the Mississippi River recruiting men for it. His unit arrived at Veracruz in August, en route to join Scott's army near Mexico City. On August 15, 1847, it fought a short but fierce engagement with Mexican irregulars at National Bridge, west of Veracruz, and was forced to fall back to the port city. Haile later served as a camp commander at Veracruz, was briefly in Mexico City, and ended his military career as a barracks commander at Baton Rouge, Louisiana. He was "honorably mustered out" of the service in July 1848.[52]

Although the war continued for more than a year after Haile ended his role as a reporter, his writing was among the most extensive and thorough of the campaign. In eleven months of service for the *Picayune*, he had filed more than 100 letters with the paper, covered two major battles—Monterrey and Veracruz—and spent many months in the various camps in southern Texas and Mexico. In addition to his straight reporting, he found time to record the "singular sights and scenes" of Mexican life, as he described it, and compose his unique "Pardon Jones" letters. He wrote from the bias of his professional military training at West Point, but this experience also allowed him to give detailed accounts of the operations, men, units, and military equipment in the engagements he witnessed. He was sympathetic toward key generals—Worth, Taylor, Scott—but also praised the "bone and sinew who carried the muskets," to use his words. He wrote in the elaborate, exaggerated antebellum style of the day yet appreciated the need to have his letters ready for the departing express rider, allowing the *Picayune* to be first with the news. On occasion he showed contempt and distrust of the Mexicans, particularly their army, but he also came to realize they had customs and a culture that were suited to their own society. Overall, the quality and quantity of his work are among the best of the Mexican War correspondents.

The contribution of all the correspondents was becoming more evident to the nation's editors. A new American newspaper at Veracruz, the *American Eagle*, spelled out what many other papers were starting to comment on: "The *corps editoriel* [sic] of the United States," the paper stated, "to our mind is much endebted to the [enterprise] of the New Orleans press since the start of the [war]." The *Eagle* said the *Delta* and *Picayune*, in particular, had "spared neither pains nor expense" to provide coverage. "When we landed at Vera Cruz we found [Kendall, Lumsden, Haile] as busy as bees setting down every item that would interest the readers . . . while on the other hand the indefatigable man of the *Delta*—Mr. Freiner [*sic*]—was hurrying from battery to battery, and one man says he saw him chasing a shell that was speeding through the air, with the expressed intention of seeing where 'that fellow would strike.' . . . Now are not such [papers] entitled to thanks from the press of the country?"[53]

CHAPTER TEN

Jane McManus Storms

Early in the summer of 1846, with the war just under way, Secretary of the Navy George Bancroft received an outspoken letter pointedly telling him how to reform the navy and fight the war. The signature read, simply, "Storms." "Who is Storms?" the perplexed Bancroft asked in a note to Secretary of War William L. Marcy. Marcy replied, "She is an outrageously smooth and keen writer for the newspapers in [New York]." Later, after meeting Jane McManus Storms, Bancroft wrote: "And do you suppose I could forget your visit at my office? Bright eyes and keen wit are not so common as to pass out of my memory in a moment."[1]

George Bancroft was not the first political figure to feel the sting of Jane McManus Storms, a well-known, if somewhat opinionated and controversial, Washington letter writer during the 1840s and 1850s. The Baltimore *Sun*'s Washington correspondent described Storms as "a very able writer." Influential Louisville *Courier-Journal* editor Henry Watterson believed "a braver, more intellectual woman never lived," adding she was "a born insurrecto and a terror with her pen." Her "courage, stability and perseverance" were attributes cited by another admirer, Aaron Burr. But Missouri's powerful senator, Thomas Hart Benton, complained of her "masculine stomach for war and politics." She had met President Polk on several occasions and had contacts with Marcy, Bancroft, Secretary of State James Buchanan, members of Congress, and Polk's wartime administration.[2]

Storms, through involvement in a secret peace mission to Mexico City by New York *Sun* publisher-editor Moses Yale Beach, became the only woman correspondent to provide firsthand coverage of the war and was the only correspondent to do reporting from behind the Mexican lines. Storms was 39 years old when the war broke out and had been active as a writer of political letters and essays for about six years. She first became interested in Texas and the Southwest when her father joined other investors, including Burr, to form the Galveston Bay and Texas Land Company. She lived in Matagorda, Texas, during the mid-1830s and became acquainted with Texas politics and political figures. Her father's colonization project failed, but the groundwork had been established for Storms's long interest in American expansion into Texas, Cuba, the Caribbean, and Latin America.[3]

She returned to New York City in 1839 and established herself as a writer, lobbyist, and propagandist for expansionist issues. Her interests primarily were political, but the writing provided her with a means of support. Her major newspaper writing was accomplished for Beach's New York *Sun*. The *Sun* was the country's first successful penny-press newspaper and had built its circulation rapidly in the 1830s and 1840s. During the war it claimed its circulation rose from 45,000 to 55,000, which would have made it the most widely read newspaper in the country. Although it claimed to be neutral, the *Sun* was a strong supporter of the Polk administration's war policies and aggressively called for annexing all of Mexico. The newspaper provided readers with extensive coverage of the war, but it relied primarily on reports from New Orleans newspapers and occasional letters from freelance correspondents in Cuba and Mexico rather than its own staff.[4]

During her journalistic career, Storms also contributed articles to the New York *Herald*, New York *Tribune*, Philadelphia *Public Ledger*, Washington (D.C.) *States*, and John L. O'Sullivan's proexpansionist *Democratic Review*, which first used the term "manifest destiny" in an 1845 editorial. Her pseudonyms "Montgomery" and "Cora Montgomery" were well established in the press by the time the Mexican War began. Storms's writing style was fluid and forceful, heavily laced with opinions, insight, predictions, and on occasion biting sarcasm. Her Washington letters to the *Sun* reflected considerable knowledge of the American political scene. The continuing major concerns in her *Sun* letters were national politics, Texas annexation, states' rights, American expansion, and U.S. relations with Mexico and Latin America. She generally praised the Mexico policies of Polk, Buchanan, and Marcy but did not hesitate to criticize the administration and did not particularly like the president.[5]

Her role in reporting the war started in November 1846, when Beach convinced Polk and Buchanan to send him to Mexico City on a secret peace mission. In the autumn of 1846, Beach, Storms, and the Catholic bishop of New York City, John Hughes, received messages from Texas contacts that the Mexicans were sending out peace feelers. Beach became convinced the time was ripe for a settlement, and Buchanan invited him to Washington to discuss the issue. Polk and his secretary of state listened with interest to Beach's view that a mission to Mexico might bring peace, not the least because it coincided with the administration's hopes the war could be ended early. Beach's son later wrote that Polk and Buchanan agreed with Beach's contention that personal conferences with leading Mexican government and church officials might end the war. They reportedly urged the New York editor-businessman to "accept the duty personally," and he did.[6]

The secret mission called for Beach to go to Mexico City and to seek a peace settlement if he found the opportunity. In return, as a broker's fee, Beach was to receive transit rights across the isthmus of Tehuantepec for a possible Atlantic-Pacific canal or railroad route. Beach also hoped to win a banking concession in Mexico City. His cover story throughout was to be that he was on a business trip. President Polk, Buchanan wrote Beach, "has full confidence in your patriotism, ability and discretion," adding, "The trust thus confided to you is one of great delicacy and importance."[7]

To conceal his mission, Beach decided to travel to Mexico by way of Havana. As a further concealment he was accompanied by his 26-year-old daughter, Drusilla, and by Storms, who was to be his interpreter as she spoke fluent Spanish and was Catholic. The trio left New York City in late November 1846, taking a circuitous route to Havana, where Beach and Storms conferred with Cubans who wanted to annex the island to the United States. At Veracruz the Mexican authorities were highly suspicious of the trio. The Mexicans apparently had received a warning from an agent in Havana; the party was delayed three days for questioning.[8]

During the delay Storms inspected Veracruz. Writing to the *Sun* from the Mexican seaport on January 13, 1847, she predicted the city would resist the pending American invasion, "or resistance will never be made by the Mexicans." She continued, "The citizens will prove themselves better soldiers than the regular army . . . for they are animated by a proud, inflexible Spanish resentment against their invaders." She also returned to one of her favorite topics—criticism of the U.S. Navy. "The deplorable inefficiency of the navy has added at least a year to the . . . war," she wrote. U.S. Commodore David Conner could easily have taken the city seven months earlier, she claimed, "before the scurvey [*sic*] decimated his men." In earlier letters she had charged, "The last refuge of despotic cruelty in our nation is in the sea service; and there the most horrid, disgusting brutality reigns. If our seamen were just black we would have anti-slavery societies and crusading lecturers active in arousing the nation to extinguish the wrong." As for the U.S. Congress, its various factions and failure to build war steamers were causing the war to "continue the same useless and costly burden to the nation."[9]

The party finally was allowed to proceed and on January 24, 1847, it reached Mexico City. Beach began a series of promising meetings with government, banking, and church officials, while Storms continued her correspondence to the *Sun*. They had arrived at the Mexican capital at an unusual moment. Santa Anna was in the north preparing to fight Zachary Taylor's forces at Buena Vista. The political blocs in the capital were in a state of flux. As part of the internal power struggle, on January 11, 1847, the Mexican Congress had passed new regulations greatly adding to the church's war taxes.[10] The church resisted, and in late February prochurch National

Guard units revolted, demanding a repeal of the "anti-religious laws." Fighting broke out and continued intermittently in the streets of Mexico City for three weeks. Beach claimed at one point he supplied $40,000 from his own funds to help pay the salaries of the prochurch troops. His peace mission had come to an unusual state of affairs: While the main Mexican army was in the north fighting Taylor's forces, and a smaller Mexican army was at Veracruz resisting Winfield Scott's siege of the city, the New York newspaper publisher was in the Mexican capital apparently assisting a civil war at the rear of both forces.[11]

Meanwhile, Storms continued her letters. Many reflected her major theme—that Mexico should "be transferred under the wing of the United States." On March 8, 1847, she wrote to the *Sun* from Mexico City, describing the political crisis. "Was ever a nation so determined on suicide?" she asked, referring to people fighting a civil war while under invasion. "The treasury is the god of these military adventurers and they have no creed, doctrine or party beyond the simple belief and practice that the people were created to be plundered," she wrote. Surveying the countryside around the Mexican capital, she observed, "It cannot in any sense be looked upon as a strong position . . . the city could be reduced to terms in a week." In reference to the street fighting, she noted, "[Mexico] is not true to herself, and even at this hour, she is doing more for the generals of the United States than they can do for themselves." She concluded that these events would leave Mexico "more than ready to receive an American government."[12]

The rebellion ended abruptly on March 23 when Santa Anna returned from his defeat at Buena Vista and quickly resumed control of the government. Soon afterward, Beach was warned that Santa Anna was going to arrest him. Leaving their baggage behind as a ruse, the publisher and his daughter fled the city and spent ten hazardous days traveling until they reached the American garrison at Tampico. A few days later a ship took them down the coast to meet General Scott at Veracruz.[13]

Storms left the Mexican capital before Beach, also under hazardous conditions. When news reached Mexico City in mid-March that Scott had started his assault on Veracruz, Beach asked Storms to undertake the difficult, 200-mile trip to the coast to apprise the American general of events at the Mexican capital. Traveling alone by stagecoach, Storms observed many "sorrowful and destitute families" fleeing the coast and "upbraiding the Americans as the cause of their ruin." She reached the American lines on March 20. Scott, stern and formal, is reported to have been disturbed to find an American woman in the battle area. Beach's son later wrote that Scott uttered an epithet regarding her presence in the war zone. Scott finally agreed to meet, and she provided him with information about the civil war, the peace possibilities, and conditions on the Veracruz–Mexico City invasion route. "Old Fuss and Feathers," however, still had reservations about a woman taking part in such affairs, and when Beach later arrived at Veracruz, Scott is reported to have cautioned him against sending important messages "by a plenipotentiary in petticoats."[14]

Storms's message to Scott may have been similar to the content of her letters to the *Sun*. In these she urged Scott to make war only on the Mexican military, not the Mexican people: "Gen. Scott can have the people with him—or at least passive—while he exterminates their old oppressors; he can march to Mexico [City] without the loss of a single man in battle, if he will pursue the wise, explanatory, protecting system of [General Stephen W.] Kearny; but if, like brave Old [Zachary] Taylor, he will use no argument but the sword, it will cost many lives, much treasure and still more precious time to conquer peace." The American public had overlooked Kearny's successes in the West, she observed sarcastically, because they did not "come in garnished with dead and wounded." Storms repeatedly blamed Santa Anna and other generals for Mexico's problems: "It is they who have betrayed and conquered their country. . . . Their leaders are traitors to their country, and inflicted upon the citizens more burdens and outrages than the Americans dare impose."[15]

Storms arrived at Veracruz before it fell to Scott's forces, and she had a front-row seat for the final days of the siege. She watched the conclusion of the bombardment from a U.S. ship in the harbor. On the day that Scott's forces occupied the city (March 29), she wrote, "Now . . . the United States has to decide whether it will save or destroy the last hope of the Mexican people." The need, she said, was for America to "act with firmness and liberality"; it must accept various portions of Mexico into the Union in order to preserve the freedom of Mexico's "long suffering and hardly-treated working classes." Such a plan would include, she noted, "a full and assured right of way" for the United States to build a canal or railroad across the Tehuantepec Isthmus.[16]

In addition to commenting on the political consequences resulting from the city's capture, she did eyewitness reporting about the events. She was highly critical of American merchant-ship captains for charging evacuees from the city—"even women"—high prices to ride out the siege on their ships, whereas British captains did not. She inspected the city the day after it was occupied by the Americans, reporting, "Vera Cruz presents a woeful aspect. Houses beaten in, with cannon shot, many disemboweled with the exploding bomb shells which fell through the roofs, then bursting and tearing the whole inside out, and in many cases setting fire to the buildings." Regarding the heavy bombardment by the Americans, she observed European accounts of it "will not flinch to tell you that there were more women and children killed in the taking of the city than soldiers, which unhappily is true—but they will not impute it to the hard necessity of war, which is equally true." Insensitive Mexican army officers, she charged, had remained safe behind the walls of the city's heavily fortified castle, San Juan de Ulua, while "a storm of shells poured destruction on the unarmed inhabitants, who saw, in helpless terror, their houses falling around them." The army decided to surrender only at "the moment the heavy guns were ready to play on the walls of the castle," she wrote.[17]

Although Storms consistently supported annexing all of Mexico, her letters clearly indicate she did not favor a battlefield solution. She was, in fact, quite caustic about the military. She called attention to the paradox of an American sailor in the Gulf fleet being hanged for insulting an officer, while an American army unit that plundered a Mexican village went unpunished. The sailor was hanged from the yardarm "for forgetting one day that he was a common sailor and remembering that he was a man capable of feeling and returning injury," she wrote. "Such is the natural tendency of discipline and justice in times of war that a rudeness to an officer is thought worthy of death, but the frolic of a party of soldiers making a playful visit to the Mexican village of Boca del Rio in which they burned some houses, outraged some women and committed some robberies, is not a matter of grave punishment." Mixing insight and biting comment, she continued, "In the race for glory there is little time to look after such trifles as justice or humanity. If a man fights with the promptitude of a tiger and the perseverance of a bulldog, he is entitled to such gentle relaxations as plundering houses and insulting women—they are usual in war."[18]

In another article, continuing her argument against a military solution to settle the dispute with Mexico, Storms wrote, "The sword is not the implement of republicanism. The shouts of victory hide the blood, ruin and desolation with which it is bought." Her solution was to annex those states of Mexico that showed interest in joining the United States (Yucatan and some in northern Mexico), then to seek a peace settlement through negotiation with the antimilitary factions of Mexico. She believed these groups would accept American rule because it would bring stability. She frequently laced her arguments with reminders about canals, rich mines, trade, and manufacturing possibilities for Americans in Mexico. She left Mexico in late April 1847, convinced it was "a rich and delightful country, soon destined . . . to enrich and be enriched by Anglo-Saxon enterprise and industry."[19]

Storms met with President Polk in Washington on May 13, 1847, two days after Beach met with him to report on the failed peace mission. That same evening, writing in his diary, Polk described her as "an intelligent woman,"

but added, "when she retired I did not feel I was enlightened by any information which she had given me." Storms did not actively report the events of
the war after this period, but she continued to strongly advocate the annexation of Mexico and Cuba.[20]

Storms's wartime letters are forceful and independent—an interesting
contrast with those of most other American correspondents in Mexico. She
was particularly independent in her views about the American military, the
most important aspect of her reporting from Mexico. Storms saw the U.S.
presence in Mexico from a political standpoint and was less sympathetic to
the military than her contemporaries, obviously not having a vested interest
in the presence of the American army as did a number of the other correspondents. And she did not disguise her attitudes—she was openly critical
of the U.S. Navy, called attention to soldiers looting Mexican citizens, and
questioned the wisdom of Zachary Taylor's penchant for battlefield solutions
instead of diplomacy to end the war. She also was highly critical of the Mexican military and urged compassion for the Mexican people, whom she considered oppressed by the generals who controlled the country's politics. Her
view of the war's outcome was clear-cut. She assured her *Sun* readers: "The
difference made by this war is only this; the commerce, manufactures, territory and power of the United States have gained that which else was destined
to swell . . . a European rival."[21]

CHAPTER ELEVEN

"I Am Requested by the President . . ."

Saturday, April 3, 1847, was a quiet, sunny day in Pensacola, Florida. John McKinley, editor of the local Pensacola *Gazette,* was preparing his weekly edition for the press when he was startled by the firing of heavy guns in the harbor. Puzzled, he rushed to the city wharf to investigate and discovered the firing had been a signal from an incoming navy warship. It was the *Princeton,* fresh from Veracruz with exciting news—the Mexican city had capitulated to the assault forces of General Winfield Scott. McKinley quickly boarded the ship, found the captain, interviewed him, and wrote out a day-by-day summary of the battle events. "Glorious News!" read a small headline in the *Gazette* that night, and unbeknown to McKinley, he had achieved a glorious national scoop.[1]

The race to be first with the news of victory again was close. *Princeton,* carrying Scott's official reports and the New Orleans newspaper correspondence, reached the Southwest Passage off the tip of Louisiana on April 2, eighty-two hours after leaving Veracruz. The *Picayune, Evening Mercury,* and *Delta* had arranged for expresses to the city, about 60 miles. The *Evening Mercury,* which did not have a regular correspondent at Veracruz but arranged for freelance reports, had the first extra on the streets. The *Picayune,* with the detailed accounts by its correspondents, soon followed.[2]

When the fighting ended at Veracruz, Kendall was ready almost immediately to send off the critical dispatches for the *Picayune:* "Not knowing what vessel is to sail first, I have written duplicates of this letter to send off by any and every conveyance." He learned that the *Princeton* was going to leave as soon as the battle ended to carry Scott's first official message to Washington. Kendall was waiting on the beach as a boat from the ship shoved off from the camp, and he placed the *Picayune*'s accounts on board.[3]

The *Delta,* in spite of elaborate arrangements, was late and had to reprint the *Evening Mercury*'s accounts in its first extra edition. Correspondent James Freaner had decided to personally deliver his reports about the surrender. But, as the *Delta* later recounted, "by one of those unforeseen accidents . . . or misfortunes, through which the best laid plans are sometimes frustrated," he missed his connections and the deadline. After arriving at the mouth of the Mississippi on the *Princeton,* Freaner failed to get on a smaller boat that carried the first news of the victory upriver. The *Delta* still published an extra edition, as well as a two-page supplement in its regular edition with his letters, which filled three and a half columns. As for Freaner, the paper reported, he was "in good health and well conditioned" from his month on the Veracruz beaches.[4]

Although the New Orleans papers had the best coverage, Veracruz was one instance in which they did not provide most of the country's papers with the first reports of the victory. After the *Princeton* stopped to unload the New Orleans mail with the correspondents' accounts of the battle, it went to Pensacola, providing the *Gazette* with its April 3 scoop. The next day, the *Gazette*'s report was reprinted in the Mobile *Herald and Tribune*. An express carrying copies of the *Gazette* and the *Herald and Tribune* reached Charleston April 7 and Baltimore April 10. The Baltimore *Sun*, Philadelphia *Ledger*, and New York *Herald* had organized the express run, and as a result papers in Philadelphia, New York, and Boston had summarized reports by April 10 and were able to rush out their own extra editions.[5]

The Baltimore *Sun* had been instrumental in bringing the news so rapidly to the North. Under a headline reading "UNPARALLELED EFFORT OF NEWSPAPER ENTERPRISE," the paper explained the feat had been accomplished by its pony express system, covering more than 1,000 miles: "We have at great expense and by a most extended effort been enabled to hasten the transmission of this intelligence to our anxious citizens; and eminently gratifying as it is to those national feelings which we are all proud to confess, we shall find an all sufficient reward for our enterprise, in the assurance we have again enjoyed an opportunity of presenting to the people of Baltimore, and a large portion of the nation, the first details of this most important and honorable achievement of American prowess and skill."[6] After opening its express packets from the South, the *Sun* sent a telegram to President James K. Polk in Washington. It was the president's first news of the outcome. In his diary, Polk wrote the telegram "was joyful news." Two hours later the president had a copy of the *Sun*, rushed to the capital by train, and after reading the account he commented, "It comes so well vouched for as to leave no doubt as to its authenticity."[7] Two days later, the *Sun* received a letter from J. Knox Walker, Polk's personal secretary, stating, "I am requested by the President to thank you for your obliging kindness."[8] But Polk was far from pleased about press coverage of the war. From the president's perspective, the year had been marred by a series of problems related to the press and his leading generals.

The first incident involved Winfield Scott and the controversial Spanish-language newspaper in New Orleans, *La Patria*.[9] *La Patria*'s editors seldom sidestepped controversy, and in January 1847 the paper became the focus of a national dispute after it published the Polk administration's purported official war plan. In the article, editor E. Juan Gomez presented what he believed to be the correct American plan of operations against Mexico. He carefully added, "These affairs are yet enveloped in the thick veil of mystery."[10] The plan he described was garbled but had some elements of truth in it. Administration officials feared that Gomez had somehow obtained the government's secret plan when General Scott stopped in New Orleans en route to Mexico to organize the Veracruz invasion. On the surface, the fear had a thread of credibility. Before Scott departed Washington in early December 1846, he had written to army officers in New Orleans asking them to recommend a man "of gentlemanly habits" to serve as an interpreter. They recommended Gomez, and when Scott arrived in New Orleans on December 21, he held a brief meeting with the editor. Apparently satisfied, Scott asked Louisiana governor Isaac Johnson to commission Gomez as a lieutenant colonel. The appointment drew immediate criticism. Influential New Orleans residents complained to Scott that Gomez could not be trusted. They charged he was "unAmerican" and "a Mexican at heart."[11] They further charged *La Patria* had repeatedly "abused the Polk Administration" and that the paper's policies were "almost treasonable."[12] Scott immediately rescinded Gomez's appointment, and the matter appeared to be a dead issue. On December 31, 1846, however, a few days after Scott had departed for Mexico, Gomez published his war-plan story, and the controversy broke.[13]

It became a national issue when Senator Thomas Hart Benton of Missouri, chairman of the Senate's military affairs committee, said it was the official plan.[14] New York senator John A. Dix complained, "Scott has made a perfect fool of himself by taking a Mexican into his military family and disclosing his plan."[15] "Excitement has arisen in some quarters in regard to [*La Patria's*] publication," the Washington correspondent of the New Orleans *Commercial Bulletin* wrote to his paper.[16] Scott employed Gomez for his staff, the administration-supported Washington *Union* told readers, "and the latter had thus become possessed of the plan of campaign against Mexico."[17] Even Polk apparently believed this to be the case, jotting anti-Scott comments in his diary after reading the *La Patria* story. "This could only have gotten to the public from General Scott," Polk wrote, blaming what he called the general's "inordinate vanity" for the supposed leak of the invasion plans.[18] Both Scott and Gomez strongly denied the allegations, but the coincidence of the editor's brief acquaintance with the general was too much for a number of editors to ignore.[19]

Most of what Gomez published had appeared in other papers long before Scott reached New Orleans. The nation's press had speculated for months that the military would attack Tampico and Veracruz. During the war, the government employed few precautions regarding secrecy, and civilians and officers who carried military dispatches often summarized them publicly for editors. One military officer observed, "The thousand prying eyes and brazen tongues attendant upon a free and uncontrolled press" often led to military operations being openly discussed before they occurred. Mexico did not need spies, the proadministration Mobile *Register and Journal* observed, because "everything intended by [our] government is demanded with fierce impatience to be published, criticized and assailed in the press."[20]

Gomez was not put off by the widespread press criticism, and he soon published a similar article, titled "Another Plan of Operation," which gave fairly accurate details of the Americans' pending landing at Veracruz. It was obtained from "reliable sources," Gomez assured readers. He jibed at Senator Benton by asking, "Will Mr. Benton say that this . . . new revelation is correct?"[21] The Missouri senator remained silent the second time, as did the administration and most editors, and the controversy passed.

Ironically, it was Winfield Scott who provided Polk ample warning about the next press issue that caused presidential ire—letters from serving officers to newspapers. Scott's concern was not new. In January 1846 an army officer, Adjutant General Roger Jones, had written to Zachary Taylor at Corpus Christi, noting that letters from officers complaining about hardships at the Texas camp were hindering recruitment. Jones asked Taylor to investigate and punish "conduct so prejudicial to good order and military discipline." Taylor replied he was "unwilling to believe" any of his officers were "guilty of such unmanly and mischievous statements," adding, "It is plain that I can institute no official investigation without exceeding the powers given me by law." The latter comment raised Scott's ire. When the correspondence was forwarded to Secretary of War William Marcy, Scott added an explanation that "it certainly was not intended that General Taylor should 'exert an energy beyond the law' in repressing the evils prohibited" by army regulations. Statute law and "a general's moral influence of persuasion" allowed Taylor to halt such letters, Scott argued. "But *indiscipline* prevails, to a considerable extent," Scott complained, warning, "It may soon become *the order of the day*." Scott asked that Marcy and the president consider the problem, but no action was taken.[22]

Then, unexpectedly, a Zachary Taylor letter renewed the controversy. Unhappy about Washington criticism of his Monterrey surrender agreement, Taylor unloaded his feelings in a private letter to General Edmund P. Gaines, who also had been rebuked by the administration earlier in the war. Taylor's letter included defense of the Monterrey terms, his personal views on how to fight the war, and complaints about poor War Department support.

The letter was given to the editor of the New York *Express* and was published on January 22, 1847. Newspapers everywhere reprinted the complaints, and although Gaines took responsibility, the administration blamed Taylor. Determined to take action against the flood of letters from the camps, Polk reinstituted an obscure paragraph from the Army Regulations of 1825. Paragraph 650 of that document prohibited officers from writing to the press, or face dismissal. Initially, Polk's action had impact, but the intent soon was blunted because it could not prevent civilians from writing letters on behalf of ambitious officers.[23]

Whig newspapers, in particular, railed at the administration's "gag order," as they labeled it. The New York *Express* called the ban "contemptible." "[Officers'] mouths," the paper said, "are to be closed in much the same manner as Mr. Polk hoped to stop free discussion by the press, by calling the plain truth 'treason.'" The paper correctly observed, "This attempt to gag the people will not succeed." The New York *Tribune* wrote, "The President will yet rue the day when the odious order was revived." In New York, only the superhawk *Sun* supported the president, calling officers' letters "injurious, if not dangerous to the cause . . . enabling [the enemy] to shape his course accordingly."[24]

For the press, there was a key victim of the President's decision—Captain William S. Henry—who had written regularly to the New York *Spirit of the Times*. Henry's reporting of the opening battles and from the camps had produced a shower of praise from the national press.[25] Henry was at Victoria in Mexico with Taylor's command when he heard he would have to curtail his letters. The *Spirit* expressed "regret" and "annoyance" at the government's decision, particularly as Henry was "acknowledged on all hands as *the* military historian of the campaign."[26] Henry immediately arranged for a replacement, who he described "as a friend accompanying the army *en amateur* like Kendall, Haile, Thorpe and others." Using the pseudonym "Truth," the new correspondent soon drew the *Spirit*'s praise as challenging the quality of Henry's reporting. For his part, "Truth," like many of the correspondents, explained, "My letters serve to kill many a weary hour." The new correspondent took time to explain the seriousness of the army orders: "[They] are of such a nature that no officer will be permitted to correspond about the events of the campaign without running the risk of the loss of his commission."[27] But it was an issue that would not go away, and by the end of 1847 it returned as a larger, even more controversial national dispute.

In the aftermath of Veracruz, a brief feud erupted in the press about the accuracy of some of the reporting. Kendall was at the center of the dispute, and most of the criticism came from Democrat newspapers. The Washington

Union's Thomas Ritchie led the attack, obviously speaking for Polk and his administration. One Kendall paragraph in particular upset the president. It read: "Only 10 mortars have landed so far—a heavy responsibility rests with the War Department in not having the ordnance here in due season—some 12,000 to 15,000 are completely paralyzed . . . such is the position in which General Scott now finds himself." Ritchie rebutted that he "had been favored with copious details from the proper department" that showed the supplies had been sent to Veracruz. "The public press and its correspondents," Ritchie lectured, "should be more careful before it raises a suspicion or gets up a clamor against the administration—every member of which has faithfully done its duty in the vigorous prosecution of the war." Displeasure with Kendall did not prevent the *Union* from reprinting the *Picayune*'s letters, and Ritchie observed that Haile's descriptions of the Veracruz amphibious landing gave "a clear and striking account."[28]

One measure of Kendall's influence at this time is that Polk, the incumbent president, and Taylor, who would be the next president, both were fretting about who was benefiting from the editor's writing and war analysis. Polk was convinced the *Picayune* and Kendall were promoting the presidential ambitions of Taylor and Scott, and he reacted quickly and defensively to articles in the New Orleans paper.[29] Kendall had good access to Taylor during the Monterrey campaign, but the general's feelings toward Kendall cooled when the *Picayune* editor accompanied Scott's command into central Mexico. Taylor was deeply bitter toward Scott and Polk for taking his regular army troops. When Kendall started sending articles Taylor considered complimentary of Scott, the general wrote to his son-in-law that they were "no doubt written by the direction or under the supervision of Scott, to laud him." Taylor accused Scott and Kendall of being "complete sycophants" of the administration. In truth, Kendall was critical of Scott and clearly was not a supporter of Polk or his policies.[30]

But the seeds of discord had been planted, and as the war continued there would be a wider, deeper dispute about the correspondents and their work. In addition to content, Polk also was irritated that the press reports beat the government's official messengers. Within a month, Polk received two more messages from the press informing him about Scott's march inland and subsequent victory at Cerro Gordo. "This should not be," the president wrote in his diary, "and moreover it might be vastly important to the government to get the earliest news." Polk discussed his concerns with his cabinet and directed that a government express be established between Mobile and Montgomery to beat the regular mail delivery by a day. The plan had only mixed success, however, and the president continued to jot notes into his diary throughout the summer of 1847 about his anxiety to hear directly from

Scott. It reached the point that in October the Washington correspondent of the New York *Express* observed, "If Mr. Polk does not hear from [Scott] soon, he will be compelled to draw up that part of his annual message to Congress [about Mexico] from the letters of Kendall of the *Picayune* and Mustang of the *Delta*."[31]

George Wilkins Kendall, ca. 1837. Photo made from oil painting by Thomas Hicks. (Courtesy of the Kendall Family Papers Collection, Special Collections, University of Texas at Arlington Library, Arlington, Texas)

"A LITTLE MORE GRAPE CAPT BRAGG"
GENERAL TAYLOR AT THE BATTLE OF BUENA VISTA FEB. 23RD 1847.

Although the caption "A Little More Grape Capt Bragg" was attributed to General Zachary Taylor at the 1847 battle of Buena Vista—and used successfully in Taylor's 1848 presidential campaign—Captain Braxton Bragg said later the first he heard of it was "by newspapers from the U.S." From color lithograph by Cameron; lithography and publication by N. Currier. (Courtesy Library of Congress)

Newspapers put out extra editions with surprising speed, despite their handicap of setting type by hand. New Orleans *Daily Picayune— Extra Edition*, vol. 11, no. 61: "Bombardment and Surrender of Vera Cruz and the Castle of San Juan de Ulua," New Orleans, Monday Morning, April 5, 1847. (Library of Congress archive; photograph by Manley Witten)

Thomas Bangs Thorpe, 1855. Engraving by J. C. Buttre, C. L. Elliot, delineator. Illustrated in Knickerbocker gallery, 1855. (Library of Congress Prints and Photographs Division)

War Supplement to the Philadelphia *North American*, April 9, 1847, with a report from Veracruz by William C. Tobey signed with the pseudonym John of York. (Courtesy Library Company of Philadelphia)

James R. Barnard and William Jewell began publishing the Tampico *Sentinel* on February 6, 1847. This extra edition is from August 31, 1847. (Tom Reilly, Mexico War collection, Oviatt Library Special Collections, California State University, Northridge)

James Knox Polk, unknown photographer, ca. 1847–1849. Daguerreotype with applied color, plate 6. (Courtesy Amon Carter Museum, Fort Worth, Texas)

AMERICAN STAR—NO. 2.

VOL. 1. PUEBLA, (*MEXICO*,) JULY 8. 1847. NO. 8.

THE AMERICAN STAR—No. 2,
Will be published on Thursdays and Sundays, during the stay of the American Army at Puebla, by
PEOPLES, BARNARD & CALLAHAN.

ARMY ITEMS.

We have been kindly furnished with copies of [illegible] N. O. Delta from the 12th to the 20th ult. in[illegible]sive. The following items of news relative to [illegible]my matters are extracted, and will be found of [illegible]:

The Returned Volunteers.—The First Tennessee Volunteers had a splendid reception on their arrival at Nashville. They were met on approaching the city by a large procession, headed by A. Ewing, who tendered them a welcome home in an eloquent speech. Lieut. Col. Anderson replied in behalf of the regiment—Col. Campbell being absent with his family. At night, a torch-light procession was formed, rockets were fired, and a general illumination attested the joy of the city at the return of its gallant sons from the war, in which they have reaped such a rich harvest of glory.

Orleans Battalion.—Three companies of this gallant body of men are now encamped at Carrollton, and we are informed that Capt. Warrington and Seefeldt's companies would have gone up on the 17th had it not been for the rain. Lieut. Col Fiesca received his commission, as Lieut. Colonel Commanding the Battalion, on the 16th ultimo. —— Guyot has been appointed Adjutant; David McDowell has been appointed Commissary of Subsistence, and R. F. Coates, Assistant do. The battalion is expected to leave for the seat of war some time next week.

A large amount of money, belonging to the U. S. Government, arrived here on the 17th, by Green & Co's. Express. This money is destined for public service.

The 5th Illinois Regiment has elected the following field officers: Capt. E. W. Newby, of Brown Co., Colonel; H. P. Boyakin, of Marion county, Lieut. Colonel; J. P. Donalson, of Pike county, Major. This Regiment will proceed to Santa Fé.

A letter from Fort Leavenworth, dated on the 3d ult., received at St. Louis, states that on that day an election was held by the *Bent Guards* for Lieut. Colonel. The entire vote of the company, eighty-five, was given for Alton R. Easton. This was the last company to vote, and the whole battalion have united in the election of Col. Easton. He left St. Louis for Fort Leavenworth on the 10th ult.

Embarked.—Companies B and D, of the 3d U. S. Infantry, in all 167 rank and file, under command of Lieuts. Sheppard, Trevitt and Schroeder, embarked on the 19th by the steamer McKim, for Vera Cruz.

Recruiting.—Capt. Haile, of the 14th Infantry, is recruiting soldiers for the army in this city. Lt. Cheney, of the same company, is also recruiting at Vidalia, opposite Natchez. The other lieutenant, Sandford, is beating up for men in the Northwestern part of the State.

Capt. Haile is a graduate of West Point, conversant with all the duties of the soldier. He is, too, a gentleman of refined feelings. Those who enlist in his company may rest assured that, while they will be taught the discipline of the soldier, they will also be treated with the kindness due to American citizens.

Arrival of Troops.—The steamer J. M. White, Captain Swon, from St. Louis, brought down from Jefferson Barracks, company B, of the 12th Regiment of Infantry, under the command of Capt. Holden, and Lieuts. Linn, Giles and Bronaugh, numbering 132 men rank and file.

From Monterey.—From Capt. Wilson, who arrived here on the [illegible]th directly from Gen. Taylor's camp, we learn that the troops at Monterey and Saltillo enjoy excellent health. Gen. Taylor's present force consists of the 2d Mississippi volunteers, the 1st Massachusetts volunteers, the North Carolina volunteers, and the Virginia volunteers; some three companies of Texan cavalry; the 16th and 10th regiments of infantry; a detachment of the 2d and 3d regiments of dragoons, with Bragg's, Washington's and O'Bryan's batteries of artillery. The health of the 2d Regiment Mississippi volunteers had greatly improved. No cases of the small pox were recently reported among them.

We learn that for the last one or two days the Paymaster's Department has been busily engaged in paying off the 3d Ohio regiment. The troops under Col. Doniphan will commence receiving their pay on the 21st of June. Each private who has been in service for a year will receive about $380, all told, besides their land scrip. Their gallant colonel will receive only about $2500.

From the Picayune of the 14th we learn that Col. Doniphan had an engagement with Indians between Parras and Saltillo.

The Washington correspondent of the Baltimore Sun says that Capt. Hughes, of the Topographical Engineers, has been appointed Lieut. Colonel.

The following additional items are taken from the Picayune of the 14th ult.

Massachusetts Regiment.—At an election of officers in this regiment, Lt. Col. Wright was elected Colonel, Major Abbott Lt. Colonel, and Capt. Webster Major. This regiment had left Matamoros for Saltillo.

Col. Curtis has received the appointment of Adjutant General to Gen. Wool.

The new regiment of Rangers elected, before leaving San Antonio, [illegible] C. Hays Colonel, I. A. Harper Lieut. Colonel, and James Boarland Major.

Departure of the Troops.—The brig Magnolia, Capt. Leslie, cleared from Savannah on the 29th ult. for Vera Cruz, with one hundred recruits. Seventy-eight of these soldiers (belonging to the 1st Regiment U. S. Voltigeurs,) were recruited in Georgia, many of them in Savannah, says the Republican of that city. The remaining twenty two recruits came from Charleston. They belong to the artillery and are under the charge of Lieut. Welch. The detachment of voltigeurs is under the command of Lieut. Forsyth, Lieut. McIntosh being detained at the barracks by sickness.

The Little Rock Gazette understands that a requisition has been made upon Arkansas for a company of mounted gunmen. A company already organized has offered its services, and the Gazette is of opinion will be ordered shortly to Santa Fé.

Another Requisition upon Illinois.—By letters from the Adjutant General's Office in Washington, to an officer in the U. S. Army, in St. Louis, says the Reveille, we learn that the War Department has called upon the Governor of Illinois for an additional regiment of volunteer infantry, and one company of mounted men. This is in addition to the regiment of infantry and the mounted company recently called for from that State.

The Texas Advocate of the 7th says that Major Ben. McCulloch left the Cuero settlement a day or two previous with a number of noble volunteers, to fill up his company now in service in Mexico. He also takes out with him quite a number of government horses, for the dragoon [illegible] service.

The Late Gen. Hamer.—The following is an extract from a very eloquent eulogy, pronounced on the death of Gen. Thomas L. Hamer, by David T. Disney, of Cincinnati:

"In the bloody streets of Monterey, when the death-storm was at its highest, and the shattering volley came pealing down—when the wild huzza, and the muskets' crash and the cannons' deadly boom told how the fatal work progressed—firm at his post he braved the terrors of the field. On a thousand wings came flying the messengers of death—the earth was bathed in gore—the star-spangled banner fluttered in the smoke, until the conquering power of the freeman's arm planted it on the topmost tower of the captured town. But not fated there to die, he escaped every danger of the day. Not among scenes of blood and carnage—not amid the groans of the wounded and the shrieks of the dying was his career to close—but when all was done, and the battle's strife had slept, the fiat came; and disease destroyed what the fight had spared. Unsearchable are the ways of God. Thos. L. Hamer has passed from among us—may we profit by the example of his life.

The Army Medical Board, which was convened in the city of New York for the examination of applicants for appointment to the Medical Staff of the Regular army, adjourned on the 25th of May. Of the candidates who were examined the following were found qualified for appointment, and were accordingly approved: Nicholas L. Campbell, N. Y. Samuel L. Barbour, Ga. George Edward Cooper, Penn. Ebenezer Swift, Ohio. P. G. Stuyvesant Ten Broeck, N. Y. John S. Battee, Md. Glover Perin, Ohio. John Campbell, N. Y. John E. Summers, Va. Charles H. Smith, Va. Washington M. Ryer, N. Y. Before the same Board, Surgeon John B. Wells was examined for promotion to that grade, and was fully approved.

The Mexican Pirates.—President Polk has issued orders, directing the steamship Princeton to be immediately got ready for sea. She is to go to the Mediterranean in quest of the privateer "Union," and any other vessels that may be insulting our flag there. The matter was formally laid before the President by Mr. Buchanan, and his action thereon was prompt and decisive. The Princeton was to be made ready to sail on or about the 15th of June.

From Rio Janeiro.—The Baltimore Sun of the 7th inst. says: "We received yesterday papers from Rio to the 25th April. There has been some warm correspondence at the Court there, between the Argentine Minister and the Minister of Foreign Affairs, in relation to the request of the Rio Government for England and France to interfere in the River Plate question. It is thought the Argentine Minister will demand his passports, and that question will finally lead to a war between Buenos Ayres and the Empire."

Mexican Artillery.—Major Clark, commanding the Missouri Volunteer Artillery, attached to Col. Doniphan's command, has, we learn, given up to the Quartermaster's Department the artillery belonging to the United States, but retains the Mexican pieces captured by him, which he will take with him as trophies to St. Louis.

Major Gen. Patterson arrived at his home, in Philadelphia, on the 8th ult., accompanied by several officers of the army and navy.

THE HONORED DEAD.

Yesterday morning, a meeting of the Committee of the General Council of the city of New Orleans took place, when the following resolutions were adopted:

Resolved, That Maj. Gen. Lewis and Col. H. Davis be invited to order the Louisiana Legion and Washington Battalion under arms to morrow (this day) at 3 o'clock, P. M., to escort the remains of Col. McKee, Lieut. Col. Clay, Capt. Willis, Lt. Vaughan and Private Trotter, from the steamboat Arsenal to the steamboat Ringgold.

Resolved, That Maj. Gen. Lewis and Col. Davis be invited to cause a gun to be fired every quarter of an hour, from the Place d'Armes and Lafayette Square, from sunrise till the arrival of the procession at the boat, and upon the vessel's leaving the wharf, to cause a national salute to be fired from the Place d'Armes.

Resolved, That the masters of vessels and steamboats in the port of New Orleans be requested to hoist their colors at half-mast throughout the day.

Resolved, That the citizens of New Orleans and all strangers, military and civilian, be requested, and are hereby invited, to join in the solemnities of the day.

Resolved, That the procession be formed in the Public Square, under the direction of Maj. Gen. Lewis, and move therefrom at 4 o'clock, P. M., precisely, and proceed to the State Arsenal in St. Peter street, there to receive the remains of the honored dead. From thence the procession will move up Royal and St. Charles streets to Poydras, and down Poydras street to the steamboat Ringgold.

Yesterday, the remains of these gallant soldiers were visited by hundreds of our citizens. Their coffins, with their mournful decorations and sombre ornaments, were exposed to view in the Arsenal. The stern soul of valor was unbended, and patriotism wept at beholding the noble relics of the honored dead. A year ago, when they were living, we gave them a fervent welcome, and now that they have returned embalmed in glory, it behooves us to give them a fitting escort from our shores. Their mortal remains may be wrapped in the silent sleep of death, but the memory of their glorious achievements can never die. The "Ringgold," named after one of the gallant pioneers of our country's glory, will bear the honored ashes of the dead to scenes once made joyful by their presence. Still, each American heart will be an urn in which will be preserved the memory of their virtues and their valor.—*Delta of the 12th.*

The Shamrock.—So closely interwoven, as a meaning emblem, is the Shamrock, or Clover, with all the heartfull feelings of Irishmen, that its poets and minstrels have drawn from the inspiration of such associations some of the most beautiful ideas. Moore's "Shamrock, the green, delightful Shamrock," may be named as a happy illustration of this, and even that bard might now be proud to have written Lover's touching little song, "I'll seek a four-leaved Shamrock." It is an innocent superstition of Erin that he who finds a sprig of this little herb, with four leaves, is endowed thereby with magical power, and can do as he lists while it remains fresh and green in his possession. Of this Lover has made beautiful use in the little ballad just named. Would he might indeed prove the possessor of the potent spell, for his suffering country's sake. For what says he?

Oh, I would use my magic art
To scatter bliss around;
And not a tear or saddened heart
Should in the world be found.

To worth I would give honor,
I'd dry the mourner's tears,
And to the saddened lip recal
The smile of happier years!

Revenue from the Mexican Customs.—In a late number of the Washington Union it is stated that the Government has already realized a half million of dollars from the custom houses in Mexico under the recently established tariff.

John Peoples and James Barnard published the *American Star* in Jalapa from April 25 to May 13, 1847. *American Star No. 2* was published in Puebla from June 12 to August 7, when the printers packed their belongings and joined General Winfield Scott's troops on the march to Mexico City. This issue of *American Star No. 2,* vol. 1, no. 8, is dated July 8, 1847. (Tom Reilly, Mexico War collection, Oviatt Library Special Collections, California State University, Northridge)

The New York *Sun* was the first successful penny-press newspaper, and its daily circulation claim of 50,000 during the war would have made it the most widely read newspaper in the country. (Library of Congress archive; photograph by Manley Witten)

Twenty-four Hours Ahead of the Mail.

By the arrival of our special express yesterday we are placed in possession of papers twenty-four hours in advance of the mail, containing one day's later proceedings in Congress and several items from New York, Baltimore and Charleston.

The New Orleans *Picayune*, which had started running expresses from the Northeast as early as 1838 to speed the delivery of news, established an express with the Baltimore *Sun* and other northeastern newspapers during the war that repeatedly beat the U.S. mail by 24 to 72 hours. (Library of Congress archive; photograph by Manley Witten)

CHAPTER TWELVE

Battle of Cerro Gordo

After Veracruz surrendered, Winfield Scott did not tarry long on the beaches to celebrate. He feared the *vomito* (yellow fever) season would set in before he could move his troops to the higher and healthier interior. His haste to move, and a decision by Santa Anna to try to block him, soon brought the two armies together again, this time at the strategic mountain pass Cerro Gordo.

It was a bold move by Santa Anna, who had lost to Zachary Taylor at Buena Vista in February and had to put down an insurrection at Mexico City in March. By mid-April 1847, he had positioned his army at the narrow pass along the National Highway, which the Americans had to use on their march inland. Again the Mexicans had a numerical advantage. But, as happened so often in the war, Scott's forces outflanked them and, in a two-day struggle, April 17–18, 1847, routed the defenders. The defeat was so complete that Santa Anna retreated to Mexico City, and Scott quickly followed up his advantage by occupying the inland cities of Jalapa, Perote, and Puebla, the latter but 75 miles from the capital.[1]

The American press did not anticipate a major battle so soon after Buena Vista and the fall of Veracruz. The printers accompanying Scott's army were busy with their favorite preoccupation—they had quickly started another newspaper in Veracruz. As soon as the city surrendered, John Peoples made an arrangement with Scott to establish an American paper, but one that differed somewhat from those previously started at Corpus Christi, Matamoros, Monterrey, and Tampico. The Veracruz *American Eagle* was to assist the army commander "in the promulgation of his orders, and in the establishment of good order and the government of the city." It was to be, in Peoples's words, "the army paper." He later explained, "Although the idea was original, to follow our . . . army with a press . . . the services rendered were not without . . . advantage to the army." Scott apparently agreed, and Peoples, working with various combinations of other printers, operated semiofficial papers with Scott's patronage at Veracruz, Jalapa, Puebla, and Mexico City over the next fourteen months.[2]

It was clear that Scott needed the New Orleans publications. The general was particularly proud of his innovative martial law order and took care to have it published in each city the army occupied. Although the order was controversial in some political and military circles, Scott gave it particular credit for the success of the campaign. Its publication was one of the first orders of business when each new paper was established.[3]

James Barnard and William Jewell from the Tampico *Sentinel* again associated with Peoples at Veracruz. Moving quickly into the captured city, Barnard, Peoples, and Jewell were able to find a print shop one block from the city's plaza. In their first issue on April 3 they printed Scott's official letters and documents regarding the city's surrender, with the response of the Mexican garrison commander. The items were widely reprinted by American newspapers. Their second paper three days later carried the list of American dead and wounded in the siege, and this too was widely reprinted. The *Eagle* was so popular with American troops that it published four times in its first week of operation. "We must acknowledge our friends stepped forward nobly in aid of our efforts," the *Eagle* stated on April 10. "The Yankees are a great people and must continue so whilst they sustain the independent press of their country," the paper said. "Two weeks ago the presses and types we possess at this time were hurling forth invectives at the United States . . . [but the type has been taught] to chronicle nothing but what is American to the backbone."[4]

Such a valuable news source drew wide attention. The *Picayune* noted, "These gentlemen deserve much credit for their enterprise." The Charleston *Courier* called the trio "enterprising pioneers of the press," and the New Orleans *Delta* commented, "we augur much for its success and popularity." One sharp-eyed critic of the paper, however, was Jane McManus Storms of the New York *Sun*, who shrewdly observed, "It is a spirited and well conducted affair but too devoted to the army to be entirely just. Truth always goes home from the seat of war dressed exclusively in robes of American manufacture."[5]

After the Veracruz siege ended, life for the correspondent quickly returned to normal. Kendall wrote that the weather was excessively hot until midday, when a sea breeze usually tempered "the fierce rays of the sun." There were also swarms of flies and mosquitoes to contend with. Kendall was not inactive long. Word came that Santa Anna was positioning an army in the mountains to the northwest in an effort to block Scott's advance. Kendall left Veracruz the night of April 13 to catch up with the forward units.[6]

Riding with Kendall was his special courier, Charles M. Bugbee. "Charley" Bugbee had gained a reputation in Boston in the early 1840s for enterprise and speed in boarding English steamers and selling the news they carried before American papers could issue extra editions. The Boston *Daily Mail* said, "Young Bugbee was one of the best specimens of a live Yankee we ever knew." The paper continued, "We will wager our best beaver that Bugbee will come back from the war worth $10,000 in cash, and twice that amount in 'glory.'" The *Picayune* described Bugbee as "a young man of spirit and energy, and the mainstay and support of his family." "Kendall's letters by 'Bugbee Express'" became a byword among the journalists in Mexico, the *Picayune* observing that Bugbee was "shot at again and again while riding express for Mr. Kendall."[7]

Kendall and Bugbee reached General Worth's headquarters that same night and found that the American troops had "suffered incredibly" on their march inland due to "excessive heat and fatigue." Kendall also learned a messenger had arrived from the forward unit with the news that Santa Anna was dug in ahead of them with 15,000 troops. Taking notice of Santa Anna's move, and the increasing guerrilla raids, Kendall observed, "The Mexicans are playing a bloody and at the same time bolder game than is usual for them."[8]

Kendall and Bugbee continued riding along with various American units as they advanced up the highway toward Santa Anna's reported position. On April 16 they reached the small town of Plan del Rio, 3 miles from Cerro Gordo. "I find all excitement and bustle here," Kendall reported after visiting the Americans' assembly area. With the main Mexican army to the front, and guerrilla bands to the rear, Kendall explained: "The road is now so much infested by small parties of the enemy that it is deemed imprudent for a single man to start, let him be ever so well mounted." On April 17, the opening day of the battle, Kendall accompanied Colonel James Duncan and other officers to view the fighting. Returning to camp at 5 P.M. he recorded, "I have just returned from the scene of conflict and a bloody one it has been." He gave a summary of the first day's events, concluding that the Americans "will have warm work tomorrow, if the Mexicans stand up as they did today." Kendall assured the *Picayune* editors he would relay reports of the battle as quickly as possible, "although one has little time or convenience in the chaparral for writing." By the next afternoon, April 18, the Americans had routed the Mexican defenders. Kendall led off his letter that night:

> The American arms have achieved another glorious and most brilliant victory. Outnumbering Gen. Scott's force materially, and occupying positions which looked impregnable as Gibraltar, one after another of their works have been taken today, five generals, colonels enough to command ten such armies as ours, and other officers innumerable, have been taken prisoners, together with 6000 men, and the rest of their army driven and routed with the loss of everything, ammunition, cannon, baggage train, *all*. . . . I write this in great haste, and with noise, confusion and everything else around me.

After giving a short summary of the day's major movements, he closed, "No time to say another word. I send this off by an express." The next day he resumed:

> The Mexican loss upon the heights was awful—the ground in places is covered with the dead! . . . Their loss in the retreat was terribly severe— every by-path is strewn with the dead. Had our dragoons been able to reach them in season, all would have been killed or captured. . . . I cannot now recollect one-tenth part of the instances of almost reckless daring displayed, but shall endeavor to pick them up. . . . At present it is almost impossible to get hold of anything.[9]

After dispatching his first reports to Veracruz, Kendall left the battle site on April 20 and rode forward to Jalapa, where the main American units had stopped. He spent the next week interviewing army personnel, assembling a recap of the two-day battle and a detailed list of the killed and wounded, which he pieced together by visiting the headquarters of various units. These follow-up reports appeared in the *Picayune* May 6–7. Exhausted from his work during and after the fighting, Kendall rested at Jalapa. He remained there for a month following the battle, sending a steady stream of war analysis and army news to the *Picayune*. From April 16, the day preceding Cerro Gordo, to May 21 he provided twenty-eight letters plus the detailed list of killed and wounded. The *Picayune* had so much news arriving from its correspondents at this time that on several occasions it printed two-page supplements containing only Mexican news. The Charleston *Courier*'s New Orleans correspondent observed these issues were enough reading to fill the whole day, "but it is a kind of reading that never seems to tire."[10]

The *Delta*, meanwhile, was not faring well. Freaner had returned to New Orleans with his reports after Veracruz fell and was not with the army when it moved inland, thus missing the story at Cerro Gordo. He did not return to the army until May 7, long after the battle.[11]

Peoples, however, provided coverage for the *Delta* and the *Bee*. Peoples was at the *American Eagle* in Veracruz on April 13 when he heard General Twiggs's advance guard had skirmished with enemy forces near Cerro Gordo. The correspondent rushed to Worth's Veracruz headquarters but learned the general had left for the front. In a hurried letter to the *Delta*, Peoples stated his belief Santa Anna wanted peace, but he predicted that "a terrible battle will be fought at Cerro Gordo." Peoples closed, "If I can buy, beg or borrow a horse I will leave for [the front] at daylight [and] will endeavor to make up for lost time." His efforts to reach the front in time were successful, and he witnessed the fighting in the central area where Tennessee and Pennsylvania volunteers under General Gideon Pillow suffered heavy casualties. The Mexicans had withheld their fire, Peoples wrote, until the American advance was within 40 yards of the defenders' guns: "Then the dogs of war were let loose with such fury that our men were driven from their positions with great slaughter." At other points of the battlefield "the scene was truly horrible," the correspondent reported, describing the large number of Mexican dead.[12]

The Mexican retreat intrigued Peoples, as had the one from Veracruz. He wrote a detailed account of paroled prisoners as they marched in "admirable disorder" from the battlefield in a column that stretched for more than 5 miles. Peoples rode alongside the straggling masses as they moved slowly toward Jalapa, weaving his horse back and forth "to avoid riding them down." He wrote:

> I felt much interested in the numerous camp women—those devoted creatures who follow them through good and evil—and it grieved me to see them, worn down with fatigue, moving at a snail's pace, with their heavy burdens almost weighing them to the earth. . . . These women, like the Indians, are the slaves of the men—a slavery they submit to under the all-powerful influence of affection. In addition to their bedding and wearing apparel, they pack upon their backs the food and utensils to cook it in, and worn out as they are by the toils of the day, whilst their husband or lover sleeps, they prepare his repast.

Farther down the road, Peoples came to the site where the American dragoons had caught up with the Mexicans fleeing the battle: "The road was lined with dead Mexicans and horses. They lay thick around and a more horrible scene would be difficult to picture . . . some [were] resting up against trees, others with legs and arms extended, and occasionally with a lancer laying with his arm upon the charger that received his wound from the same volley that ended the career of his rider." Arriving at the army's headquarters at Jalapa, Peoples tried to piece together a list of the American killed and wounded. "The list is much larger than first reported," he wrote, describing the difficulties he had getting correct figures. "The alterations in some of the report plays the devil with what I have."[13]

Peoples had another reason for wanting to arrive quickly at Jalapa. He and his partner, James Barnard, were anxious to get another camp newspaper under way. Their new paper, the *American Star*, started on April 25. Some of the most graphic reporting of the battle, written by Peoples, was published in the new paper. The *Picayune* used long portions of Peoples's account, calling it "the most connected history of the events . . . we have seen yet." In addition to Peoples's story, the first issue carried Scott's official orders. For

his part, Peoples was pleased to note a change in the government's policy under Scott: "In Scott's orders . . . you will note a long cherished principle of
mine—to live off the enemy—is about to be realized."[14] The new army paper
was quickly praised by the New Orleans press, but it bemused the New York
Tribune, which observed, "The types, presses and material have been borrowed from the Mexicans as the Fates *borrowed* Hector . . . *without any intention of returning him!* So we not only turn their cannons against them, but
their types also." The anti-war *Tribune* added sarcastically, "[This] must be
most gratifying to all interested in the extension of 'the area of freedom.'"[15]

William C. Tobey of the Philadelphia *North American* and George M. C.
Davis of the Alton (Ill.) *Telegraph* wrote detailed follow-up accounts of Cerro
Gordo. Davis wrote a particularly poignant description of the battlefield the
day after the struggle:

> Now, all was silent as the grave, with naught to break that silence but the
> flapping of the wings of the buzzard, and the carrion crow, who rose in
> countless numbers as I rode along, blackening the heavens as if with a
> dark cloud, and leaving with reluctance their banquet upon the bodies
> of both Americans and Mexicans, that every where covered the heights
> and the plains where I trod. Amid the unburied and unnoticed dead were
> many whom, but a few short days before, I had mingled with, all of whom
> were buoyant with hope and enthusiastic ardor, and who had panted to
> mingle in the fierce conflict. . . . There lay victor and vanquished who had
> wrestled even in the agonies of death, 'Man to man, and steel to steel.'
> There were strewn the bodies of others, who, having for a season survived
> their wounds, had perished beneath the scorching rays of this tropical
> sun, without even the consolation of having their burning and consuming
> thirst quenched by a single drop of water from some friendly hand.[16]

Other journalists at the scene had similar strong reactions. Tobey, the *North
American*'s "John of York," missed the fighting at Cerro Gordo but arrived
soon after. He had been assigned to help establish the American post office
facilities in Veracruz and remained behind after the Pennsylvania volunteer
units moved forward. In a letter to the Philadelphia paper, Tobey observed,
"It is said to be the hardest thing in the world for 'geniuses' to write without
pay . . . but in my way of thinking it is more difficult for any army correspondent to make up a readable letter when there is no fighting."[17]

Tobey left Veracruz on April 21, traveling with a small convoy taking mail
and money to the army. He carried two revolvers and a carbine for protection. He explained: "If a soldier straggles ten rods away from the train, the

lasso is around his neck and the knife to his throat before he can make an alarm." The group reached the forward camps on the night of April 23. The next morning he visited the army's field hospitals to see wounded friends, and that afternoon he reached the battlefield. He was shocked at the strength of the positions the Mexicans had held and lost. "The battle I knew had been fought and won by our troops; yet, it seemed . . . a dream. I could not shake off this feeling as I rode along the enemy's lines of entrenchments, entered dismantled forts and magazines, and looked from his chosen heights upon the paths up which our troops rushed into the jaws of death." Referring to the still visible scenes of death, Tobey wrote:

> While the fight is raging men can look upon death and shrink not from his bloody features; but to walk coldly over hundreds of human bodies, blackened and bloated by the sun, stretched around among broken muskets and dismounted cannon—the steed and rider offering inviting banquets to the foul birds that here battened upon them on every hand, sickens the senses and the soul; strips even victory of its gaudy plumage and stamps the whole with an unspeakable horror.

At one point he could not pass because of the tangled bodies of Mexican troops. "The gorge was choked up with the mangled bodies of the flower of the Mexican army. The wolf dog and the buzzard howled and screamed as I rode by, and the stench was too sickening to endure." After the battlefield visit, Tobey went to Jalapa. The road still was strewn with corpses of the Mexican stragglers who had been run down by the American dragoons. "Almost every man's skull was literally split open with the sabres of our horsemen and they lay stretched on the ground in ghastly groups," he recorded.[18]

The news of the Cerro Gordo victory reached Veracruz on the eve of Jane Storms's departure for the States, in time for her to send another letter to the New York *Sun*. She called it "the most scientific . . . splendid and decisive victory that has yet attended the American arms, and the world will have another conclusive evidence of Gen. Santa Anna's military incapacity. . . . The truth is Santa Anna is no soldier . . . he is always defeated in battle [but not in diplomacy] and Gen. Scott's promptitude deranged all his plans." Storms claimed "the higher priesthood" wanted peace, the "great mass" of Mexicans were indifferent to the war, and many states wanted to join the United States. She predicted Santa Anna's opponents would not accept "a treaty of his making" and would probably make "one more effort for their country." If peace efforts failed, she counseled, "the United States must take so much territory as she decides upon" and leave the rest for Europe.[19]

The *Picayune*'s careful planning and enterprise once more resulted in beating its competitors with the story. As soon as he had completed his accounts, Kendall gave them to his express rider Bugbee. Bugbee set off immediately for the port city, evading several guerrilla bands on the six-hour, 50-mile trip. At Veracruz Bugbee boarded the steamer *McKim.* Ten days later, as the ship slowly made its way up the Mississippi, Bugbee left it, obtained a horse, and rode the final 30 miles into the city. The *Picayune* quickly set Kendall's letters in type and issued an extra edition the same day, April 30. The paper noted it also interviewed two government messengers carrying General Scott's official battle reports to Washington; they "furnished all the information desired of them."[20]

The *Picayune* was once again the country's main source of the news. The *Picayune*'s extra of April 30 reached Mobile May 1 and Charleston May 4. There was a mix-up with the U.S. mails at Charleston, delaying the news. The Charleston *Courier* explained, "The mail boat did not arrive preventing our friends of the press who are associated with us at the north from availing themselves of the advantage of the express which has been established at such great cost and trouble." The express also faltered on another route. The Augusta (Ga.) *Chronicle and Sentinel,* which did not publish the news until May 6, blamed "the most culpable negligence and carelessness in the post office at Montgomery [Alabama]. . . . The letters containing the news were detained 24 hours at Montgomery . . . and came in the regular mail."[21]

For the first time since the opening days of the war, the telegraph managed to beat the ponies to the North, although its reports were brief. On April 21 the line had been extended 60 miles from Washington to Fredericksburg, Virginia. A copy of the *Picayune*'s April 30 extra reached Fredericksburg on the morning of May 7, and a summary of the news was telegraphed to Washington, Baltimore, Philadelphia, New York, and Boston. Many papers in those cities had extras on the street by noon.[22]

The express, with the fuller account, was close behind. After rushing out an extra the morning of May 7 with the short summary from the telegraph, the Washington *Union* reported two pony express deliveries, including a messenger from the *Picayune* with a complete copy of the April 30 edition. "Again the country has been indebted to the enterprise and foresight of Kendall and his partners," the St. Louis *Reveille* wrote. In Washington, a New York *Sun* correspondent added praise for the battle details "which the editors of the New Orleans *Picayune* and *Delta* have so carefully collected and transmitted. Indeed, the government and the people are greatly endebted to those journals for the most authentic accounts of events which have occurred during the war."[23]

CHAPTER THIRTEEN

"Mustang" of the *Delta*

Mustang—the name is common, but there's magic in it. . . .
As an army correspondent [he] has no superior.
—New Orleans *Daily Crescent*, March 5, 1848

The war stood still for four months following Cerro Gordo. Scott, short of supplies, funds, and troops, halted at Puebla during summer 1847, until he could reinforce his army for the advance on Mexico City. In the meantime, Nicholas P. Trist, the State Department envoy, attempted to establish peace negotiations with the Mexican government. Relations between Trist and Scott were strained at first, but gradually they became friends, and by the end of the summer lull they were working closely in an attempt to end the war with a treaty.[1]

During the summer the newspaper competition narrowed to a battle between Freaner of the *Delta* and Kendall of the *Picayune*. The *Delta*, in a light moment, described them as the "Homer of the *Delta*" and the "Hesiod of the *Pic.*"[2] John Peoples, who had written for the *Delta* for more than a year, ended the association and concentrated on his occupation newspapers. The *Picayune* forces also were reduced, Haile having joined the army and Lumsden returning to New Orleans after breaking his leg at Veracruz.

Freaner, writing under his popular pseudonym "Mustang," continually expanded his efforts during the summer, and his name and reporting gained in national recognition. "Scott cannot advance beyond Puebla without reinforcements," Freaner explained, "and I'll divide my time between Puebla, Jalapa and Perote." He assured the *Delta*, "I will write you from every camp ground en route and send an express if there is another battle." In Veracruz and on the trip to Jalapa, Freaner cemented a fateful friendship with Trist. "I have had an eye on him for several days and unless I am very much mistaken his mission is" more important than that of a messenger, Freaner wrote. Trist's knowledge of the people, language, and country will allow him to perform "with more ability and dignity than many of those who have preceded him to Mexico," the correspondent told his *Delta* readers. Trist became an important source for Freaner, and their new friendship would have consequences for the writer that he never could have imagined.[3]

Trist trusted Freaner from their first meeting. He later wrote that Freaner was "one of the truest men I have ever known, and *every* way one of the noblest—the very type of the American *Man,* in all the dignity of his, in many respects so peculiar, *Manhood:* . . . no better ever sat in a saddle, or carried a 'shooting iron.'"

Trist expanded:

> No lie found there—I will stake my life upon it. I have never read [his] letters; not so much, perhaps, as one column of them in all. But I knew the man; and, on the strength of this knowledge—nothing like a lie. Nay, more, I would stake my life upon no "President-making" being found there; no "Available" manufacturing. In a word, nothing but the information which the country wanted, . . . nothing but the truth, so far as he could get at it. And, to this matter, he got at more of it than anyone I know there; and, I verily believe, than all of them put together.[4]

Such qualities were recognized by many people who met Freaner in Mexico. General Persifor Smith, writing several years after the conflict, observed:

> I have perfect confidence in Freaner's honesty & trust worthiness. He is exceedingly intelligent and untiring in his industry & attention to business. He is cool & courageous, never daunted, and [capable] of as much bodily labour [*sic*] & of undergoing more fatigue than any one I know. I think from his ardent temperament & confidence in himself he would be apt to rush into extensive & intricate speculations, attracted by their very difficulties.

General Ethan Allen Hitchcock, writing in 1851, praised Freaner's "cheerfulness & high spirits" and "his perfect confidence in himself." Freaner and Kendall were called "gentlemen of great ability" by Major General John A. Quitman, who added they "bore a gallant part in the various engagements and then described them with rare fidelity and eloquence."[5]

Such high opinions of Freaner were shared by many of his journalism contemporaries. James R. Barnard, who helped operate many of the American newspapers in Mexico, said, "If energy and industry with self-confidence 'large' are elements of success . . . have no fear for Mustang." John Warland of the Boston *Atlas* wrote of Freaner: "I know him very well. It is no secret" that Trist and Freaner had a close working relationship, Warland wrote. "Mr. Trist [wrote]—or, at least dictated and furnished material—for quite a number of Mustang's letters from Mexico." Warland had the highest regard for Freaner's work. "Mustang is a lucky fellow and quite a pet with the government officers of every grade. He would procure letters from different officers, and items of news or gossip, wherever he could find them." Freaner condensed these items "into the shape of a correspondence" and "spared no expense" to get them to the *Delta* as soon as possible. Usually Freaner sent off duplicate copies via different riders. "Thus one of the letters would be sure to reach its destination," Warland explained. The rival *Picayune* paid him perhaps the highest compliment when it hired him a year after the war to be a correspondent in California. The paper noted, "He acquired a reputation during the Mexican War for spirit, intelligence, and discretion which point him out as one of the best men in the country for a correspondent."[6]

During the summer lull, Kendall and Freaner used a variety of sources for news: their own correspondents in various towns; verbal reports and newspapers from Mexico City; interviews with passengers, particularly Europeans, on stagecoaches from the Mexican capital; and interviews with American civilians and military personnel. Even freed American prisoners in Mexico City provided information to the journalists about conditions and battle preparations at the Mexican capital.[7]

Another important source was the American newspaper at Puebla. On June 12, Peoples, Barnard, and Charles Callahan, a former printer for the New Orleans *Picayune*, had started the *American Star No. 2*. The rapid establishment of the paper led the *Delta* to comment, "It is a locomotive concern and will keep with the advance of the army." The *Picayune* was happy Callahan was involved, noting, "Mr. Callahan is a new proprietor and a very efficient (partner) he will prove. . . . These wars seduced him from us." The paper continued publishing until Scott's departure on August 7.[8]

Freaner, meanwhile set up two courier systems at Puebla—one taking his dispatches back to Veracruz for forwarding to New Orleans, the other traveling through the Mexican lines to Mexico City to seek news at the capital. On June 14 he wrote, "I start a courier to the city of Mexico tonight—he will return if he succeeds in passing the guerrillas and robbers in about two days, when I will forward the [newspaper] files to the coast." Freaner hoped the relay could operate at least once a week. He also arranged to have the Mexico City papers translated before forwarding them to the *Delta*.[9]

In addition to receiving Mexican newspapers, Freaner forwarded files of the *Delta* and the Washington *Union* to Mexico City. His cousin was associated with him in the two-way courier system. Among the regular users of Freaner's express system were Trist, Scott, Major General Gideon Pillow, and other prominent officers. Writers were encouraged to use thin tissue paper for messages. Trist explained he preferred Freaner's express because it was fast and efficient. When Freaner's packets with the letters of the government officials reached New Orleans, *Delta* editors would place them in the regular U.S. mail service for forwarding to Washington.[10]

One Freaner letter to the *Delta* detailed how he received and forwarded his news. "The 'Diligence' is about to leave" for Veracruz, he explained, "and I write to give you the latest up to departure. The 'Diligence' from Puebla is looked for momentarily which will give us the correct position of affairs at the capital. If it should arrive in time to overtake the line towards Vera Cruz, I shall send an express to overhaul it." This information was in a letter with the dateline "Jalapa, May 21, 11 1/2 A.M." An accompanying letter, dated "Jalapa, May 21, 12 o'clock," added, "There was nothing of value on the 'Diligence' from Puebla." Freaner included information he obtained from the passengers on the stagecoach, however, as well as a summary of letters he received from other American units, and sent off an express rider to catch the Veracruz-bound stage.[11]

Because Freaner moved frequently and the mails were hampered by guerrillas, there were many interruptions in his reporting. At the end of July, the *Delta* noted it had not heard from its correspondent for three weeks: "This to our readers as well as ourselves is an absolute deprivation." When at last Freaner was able to get some letters through, the *Delta* commented, "His friends particularly, and our readers generally, will no doubt be gratified to hear that their long-lost-friend is found, that he is alive and kicking and has made arrangements by which in the future the long delays which have tortured us for some weeks past will be avoided." At the capital, the Mexican army guarded the gates, forcing Freaner's couriers to attempt ingenious methods: "To-day [one] tries it dressed as a woman, almost in rags, driving asses, which pack in charcoal and I only send you a line or two, plaited inside his whip lash." Several Mexican newspapers also were smuggled out on the same trip "by stuffing one in each ear of the jackass he was driving, and the other tied round a sore leg." Freaner added: "I cannot send them to you to-day by the present courier, on account of the bulk—it might be the means of his being arrested."[12]

Some Democrat newspapers saw Freaner's reports as a preferred alternative to Kendall. But Freaner often showed independence from the proadministration *Delta*, occasionally moving the paper to explain their relationship. When Freaner praised the military performance of Scott, a Whig presidential possibility, the *Delta* commented, "We do not feel disposed to impose any limits to the expression of opinions and feelings of our correspondent, even where we may differ from him. We say this in order that our readers may understand our relations." On another occasion, the *Delta* explained: "We need not add we are not prepared to subscribe to Mustang's opinions, but as we aspire to make our paper perfectly impartial, we take pleasure in publishing the opinions and arguments of those who take very different views from ourselves on the [war]." In general, the paper did not interfere with Freaner's performance, and as the war continued his national reputation grew.[13]

Kendall also was strengthening the *Picayune*'s reporting and express system. He reached Puebla on May 27 and found the city isolated from the outside. The stagecoaches from Mexico City were not running, he reported, and there was no indication of what General Scott planned to do. Kendall already had lost several express packages to the guerrillas. He closed one *Picayune* letter: "I send this off hap-hazard by the diligence to Jalapa, but it is doubtful whether it will reach New Orleans." He ended another: "For fear my letters may be overhauled by the Mexicans I cannot say half I otherwise should."[14]

Most of Kendall's letters at this time were analytical regarding political conditions in Mexico City, Santa Anna's movements, and the prospects for peace. There was a peace movement at Mexico City, he said, but "to defeat the Mexicans in every encounter is easy enough—to settle all differences and disputes with them will be found an entirely different matter." The time was wrong for Trist's peace efforts, Kendall wrote. "I believe that the hard blows of 10,000 regulars will have more effect in bringing these people to their senses than all the soft words of an equal number of diplomats." After the rout at Cerro Gordo, Kendall summarized the Mexicans' situation: Their country was broke and blockaded, the army shattered, the people and government "disorganized, disunited." He asked, "Poor, and most unhappy Mexico! and what is to be the end of all this? . . . If this war continues another year, and is prosecuted with that vigor which it becomes the United States to press it, there will be nothing left of Mexico but a name, and that not of the proudest." Mexico, he concluded, should not "shut [its] ears against all proposals of an honorable" peace.[15]

From the Americans' view, Kendall wrote, "I can see no other result than the subjugation of [Mexico] entirely—or at least in bringing it under the protection of the United States." He urged that "an honest and well meaning [Mexican]" be chosen as president and given "the assistance of a few thousand [U.S. Army] men to keep down revolutions." In an apparent reference to Trist's efforts, Kendall added, "He who thinks that a lasting and beneficial peace can be made with Mexico, or believes that the American troops are soon to be withdrawn, is someone who has not been over the country—he starts in his belief from false premises, and judges a race of people by the ordinary rules which govern human nature." The Mexicans, Kendall contended, did not follow such rules.[16]

Although Trist had a close relationship with Freaner, it is clear he did not confide in Kendall. Kendall was mostly silent on the initial dispute between Trist and Scott. When Trist arrived at Jalapa, Kendall reported, a bit pointedly, "Mr. Trist is going on with the army, but in what capacity it is best known to himself. He has certainly had no personal communication with Gen. Scott." In another letter, Kendall observed, "I can say one thing for Mr. Trist: if the Government . . . instructed him to keep his mission secret, he has preserved a most commendable silence." Kendall's comments were so cryptic that the *Picayune* noticed the omission: "In the letters we have . . . there seems to be studious care not to touch upon the difficulties between the general and Mr. Trist."[17] Kendall was quite aware of their dispute, however, and later said that the "disgraceful" incident "brought out the weaker point in the character of Gen. Scott in bold relief." It started, Kendall explained, because a sealed envelope Trist carried from Secretary of State James Buchanan to the Mexican government reached the general "in an evil hour when he was in a bad humor."[18]

For his part, Trist strongly resented advice from "G. W. Kendall and the like." In camp, Trist said he did not believe a treaty could be made, while privately believing it could. He sarcastically classified Kendall and his friends as "wise and practical men" who are convinced they "understand men" and "possess a thorough knowledge of Mexican character." Trist felt Kendall "and such like" saw Trist as "a simple sort of body; a noodle that could be made to believe anything, and whom any Mexican could twist around his thumb like a piece of red tape." Such low opinions of him "*went to help the cause*" of making the eventual treaty, Trist said. But his need for secrecy misled the correspondents and, as a result, much of the American public.[19]

Kendall was critical of almost every action of Santa Anna but expressed some reluctant admiration, too. In early August, as the U.S. Army prepared to march to Mexico City, Kendall wrote:

There is no such thing as foreseeing what such a man as Santa Anna can do—look what he has done since his terrible defeat at Cerro Gordo for example. No one but he would have dared show his face at the capital after such a reverse; but with a miserable remnant of an army he boldly entered the city, and since, with an empty treasury and with obstacles that seemed insurmountable, he has collected and appointed a numerous force, inspired the hopes of a people he has a thousand times deceived, and for the time being at least rides rough shod over everything.[20]

Kendall wrote, "There are yet strong reasons to believe that the English legation is exerting every influence to keep the Americans out of the capital."

Britain was trying to limit the Americans to northern Mexico, Kendall argued, in order to "come in at the southern extremity and lay hold of territory to her heart's content." Kendall strongly favored Scott immediately attacking the Mexican capital. "Another battle in my humble opinion, will be of immense advantage to the United States [because if] there is no more fighting, the enemy will contrive to come out of the war conquerors." The Mexicans would contend the Americans were "fearful of risking a battle at their principal city [and] sue for peace. . . . In the eyes of the world they will be able to make a tolerably clear case," Kendall wrote. Kendall asserted he would not be surprised "if English influence and American gold were now at work at the capital and that bribery was endeavoring to take from the bayonet its legitimate office"—strong words, yet not far from what Scott and Trist were in fact attempting to do. "The idea of purchasing a peace of these people," Kendall argued, displaying his own feelings, "must be repugnant to every true lover of his country—it would be dishonorable on the very face of it, and would be far from proving lasting in the end."[21]

One issue sure to rankle Kendall was the contention in the Washington *Union* and other proadministration newspapers that Scott had a force of more than 22,000 troops. Kendall called the number "paper troops," manufactured in Washington. With rampant illness, deaths, and expiring terms of volunteer units, Kendall said the actual number available to Scott was close to 8,000. Scott would be able to take Mexico City with even that small number, the correspondent contended, if he had sufficient transport and troops to garrison rear towns and keep open communication lines. Kendall fumed, "Had our government laid out a few extra dollars and called but a few more men in the outset, this war would have been over by this time; but greatly to our cost the 'penny wise and pound foolish' system of economy must prevail, and millions are added to the national debt as a consequence." Kendall asked, "And where is blame to attach for all this?" Not with government bureaucrats, he observed, "for with them responsibilities are so easily shuffled off." Requests are always referred "to the next grade above . . . until it reaches the President, who will very likely refer the whole thing back to the people. In this respect our government is weak." When the proadministration New York *Sun* accused Scott of delaying at Puebla in order to "suck oranges," Kendall scolded, "It ill becomes writers at home snugly and safely ensconced in their sanctums, to criticise [*sic*] and censure movements they have no means of understanding."[22]

Regarding the precarious situation of the Americans at Puebla, Kendall asked his editors, "Has it ever occurred to you that there are other Americans in Mexico besides those [prisoners] in the capital, who are certainly so far confined as to be utterly unable to leave?" A list would include "your humble servant in the number, who have seen quite enough of Mexico, and are anxious once more to breathe the fresh air of the United States, but to all intents and purposes we are prisoners here." It was unsafe for Americans to go beyond the camp's sentries, Kendall wrote, so "the largest liberty is here compressed to the smallest possible space." In September, after Mexico City fell, Kendall reminded his readers that Scott had so few troops that "he does not hold a foot of land between [here] and Vera Cruz outside the range of a 24-pounder, nor will he until reinforced."[23]

Getting mail past the guerrillas, then through the shipping jam in Veracruz harbor and the U.S. post offices in Veracruz and New Orleans, had become a major problem. William Tobey of the Philadelphia *North American* described the New Orleans postal facility "as the worst run grocery I have ever seen." John Warland of the Boston *Atlas* visited the Veracruz facility and found all the stateside newspapers thrown into "a promiscuous heap" and all soldiers "refused . . . the privilege of digging through it for newspapers." Only generals and colonels could get their papers. "Whether they are too lazy or too dignified to sort the newspapers I do not know," Warland complained of the post office staff.[24]

In an attempt to handle the news and mail problems at Veracruz, Kendall recruited two former New Orleans printers, William Jewell and Daniel Scully, to be *Picayune* correspondents in that city. They reported regularly for the paper and handled the *Picayune* expresses when they arrived from the interior. Scully defended the quartermasters, who handled the mail and military supplies: "Who is there who has ever been across the gulf since the war commenced, be he officer, soldier, Jew or Gentile, speculator, newspaper correspondent, idler, or loafer that has not cursed the quartermaster?" Scully asked. "I have indulged in my full share of blaming them, yet the more I have seen of their endless duties, and the killing labor that is imposed upon them, the more do I feel convinced that they are a thousand times more sinned against than sinning, and that the press should at least protect them against the numerous unjust complaints . . . by anonymous writers."[25]

The *Delta* also appointed trusted correspondents at Veracruz, and for a short period in summer and fall 1847 A. H. Hayes, a former co-owner of the *Delta*, assisted with handling correspondence, mail, and newspapers from the Mexican port. Hayes was another journalist who decided to "go see the elephant." Selling his interest in the *Delta*, he made his way to Veracruz and joined up with Christopher Haile's infantry company, which was preparing to march inland. A *Delta* correspondent at Veracruz reported, "He is well mounted with a pair of holsters in front. He is determined to see the elephant and prays for a chance to [fight]." After ten years as the editor of a daily newspaper, Hayes was seeking "the health and recreation which he stands so much in need of," the *Delta* explained. He wanted to see Scott enter Mexico City, as did Haile. Their hopes ended at the National Bridge, near Veracruz, where their small convoy of three infantry companies was ambushed by guerrillas and driven back. Haile's company performed well in covering the retreat but lost all its baggage, wagons, and mules. Hayes saw the action he desired. The Veracruz *Sol de Anahuac* reported he commanded a detachment in the fight, but Hayes asked for a correction: "I merely performed the usual routine of duty . . . and do not want credit for acts of others." Hayes stayed at Veracruz for several months after the engagement, supplying the *Delta* with articles and newspapers.[26]

Assignment in Veracruz generally was difficult for the correspondents during the American occupation. A *Delta* correspondent summed up the situation: "I have not a particle of news. . . . The guerrillas are getting bolder and bolder every day, and all communication is cut off. . . . The yellow fever is still raging." Among the more popular hangouts were "coffee houses," a combination bar and gambling parlor. "There are very few coffee houses . . . without a gambling table," a *Delta* correspondent explained. Another *Delta* correspondent in Veracruz described their boredom: "There is neither amusement nor excitement here, and the spare moment a poor devil has he [melancholy] walks the streets looking occasionally at the senoritas as they pass gracefully smoking their cigaritos." A *Picayune* correspondent observed, "A fellow who is fortunate enough to get . . . papers [from the States] has to hide them. . . . [Later] he slips off to some obscure place where undisturbed he reads the news *which passed by his own door two weeks before,* so true is it we get most of our army and Mexican news from New Orleans."[27]

A key source for the correspondents and U.S. officials at Veracruz was Rafael Beraza, the courier who brought official British government reports from Mexico City for forwarding to London. Beraza often supplied off-the-record information about events in Mexico City. An observer wrote, "The information from the courier it seems may be relied on—still it is important that it should not be known that it is derived from him." With a sense of amazement, the observer concluded, "It is said this man is nearly seventy years old and makes the ride from Mexico in two days." The English courier was widely considered "the only safe and reliable means of information" from Mexico City, the *Delta* told readers, and George T. M. Davis observed in a letter to the St. Louis *Republican* that it took an escort of forty Mexican troops to protect him from the guerrillas.[28]

The New Orleans papers also were helped by several U.S. officials at Veracruz, particularly F. M. Dimond, the port collector; Captain B. F. Whittier, the army quartermaster in charge of the main supply dock; A. J. Clifton, the harbormaster; and Sebastian Allis, the former *Picayune* office worker who had fought at Monterrey and served as assistant postmaster in the Mexican port. The 26-year-old Allis was a special favorite of the New Orleans press. In order to expedite the mail handling at Veracruz he was given an early discharge from the Louisiana Volunteers by General Scott. With his understanding of the newspapers' desire for speed, Allis worked out a system for placing their mail directly in the hands of ship captains, bypassing post-office bottlenecks.[29]

The guerrilla bands were the most difficult problem for reporters. The army and the press had become more isolated than they first realized. There were enough American troops to hold the four principal cities—Veracruz, Jalapa, Perote, and Puebla—but in between, the guerrillas and bandits had free rein. The army described them as "atrocious bands called *guerilleros* and *rancheros,* who, under instructions from . . . Mexican authorities, continue to violate every rule of warfare observed by civilized nations." Unit commanders were told, "No *quarters* will be given to known murderers or robbers . . . whether serving under Mexican commissions or not. They are equally pests to unguarded Mexicans, foreigners or small parties of Americans, and ought to be exterminated." Flagrant violators were to be punished with death or up to fifty lashes. Despite the directives, however, the guerrillas continued to effectively disrupt the Americans' line of communication until spring 1848.[30]

Freaner, Kendall, and Peoples tried to break the blockade with express riders; they frequently used Mexican riders, occasionally Americans. Dependent on their own devices, the correspondents operated private mail services from the Battle of Cerro Gordo in mid-April 1847, until March 1848, when the army finally established reliable deliveries between Veracruz and Mexico City. Freaner and Kendall each kept four to six Mexican riders in their employ at all times and arranged for relays of fresh horses at each city the Americans held. When the news warranted, the correspondents wrote duplicate copies of letters and started riders for Veracruz at intervals of several hours. The toll in riders was heavy, however. At least twenty-five express riders were captured and killed, wounded, or tortured by the guerrilla bands.[31]

The Mexican view of the express messengers was different. On one occasion the *Boletin de Noticias,* a pro-Mexican paper published at Jalapa despite its occupation, reported, "A Mexican acting as a spy for the Americans was arrested in the vicinity of Jalapa" by guerrillas and was to be tried speedily. "Upon the spy were found twenty-five or thirty letters—among them various articles for the papers of the United States," the Jalapa paper reported. Although it published a number of the captured letters, the paper called them "exaggerated" and "absolutely ridiculous." Freaner and Kendall letters that were captured found their way into the Mexican press. John Warland notified his paper, the Boston *Atlas,* that some of his letters had been intercepted and published by the Mexicans, adding, "I pity the ranchero who first endeavored to read it in manuscript. You well know that my chirography [*sic*] is none the best."[32]

Kendall's desired solution for the guerrilla problem was the Texas Rangers. As more express riders were cut off, Kendall wrote, "Never was there a time when the services of a regiment of well mounted Texans was as much needed as the present—were they here, on the road, the Mexicans would become even more sick of the guerilla [*sic*] system than they now are of regular fighting." The guerrillas intercepted so much of the newspaper mail that there was at last one serious suggestion that they be bribed to let it pass. The *Picayune*'s correspondent at Veracruz, Daniel Scully, proposed the arrangement. "Considerable commerce is now carried on with the interior," he wrote the editors. It was allowed through payment of "a fee" to the guerrillas. "I think if your agents could but *hold* a parlay with the chief, they might make a contract at a very moderate price to have your letters from (Kendall) brought through regularly." There is no evidence, however, that the *Picayune* took the suggestion seriously.[33]

CHAPTER FOURTEEN

The Northern Occupation

There was no major fighting on the northern front after Buena Vista. Taylor, his army stripped by Polk to bolster Scott's forces, remained in camp near Monterrey and gradually turned his attention to his developing prospects for an 1848 presidential nomination. During the war's final sixteen months, the troops in the north had to be content with the dull garrison life of an occupation army.[1]

Another of the war's important correspondents, John E. Durivage, became active during this time. "Jack" Durivage, a former Boston and New York newsman who was working as an actor and writer in New Orleans when the war broke out, was hired by the *Picayune* to provide coverage from Taylor's army. The paper made the assignment when Haile, Kendall, and Lumsden followed Scott to Veracruz. The paper anticipated there would be more major fighting on the northern front, but Durivage arrived too late for Buena Vista and spent most of 1847 reporting about camp life and scouting missions.[2]

Durivage left New Orleans on March 20, 1847, at the height of the rumors about Buena Vista, but it was mid-May before his reports started arriving. The *Picayune* explained he was "having trouble sending his letters out" because of guerrillas.

Mail deliveries from Monterrey remained disrupted for most of the summer due to guerrilla raids. When a packet of letters from Durivage arrived a month late, the *Picayune* commented unhappily: "Their contents so far as regards news, had been anticipated by a thousand channels." Writing from Taylor's camp, Durivage described the problem: "Although there is no regular or considerable force of the enemy on the road, there is a sufficient number of disaffected Mexicans ready to pounce upon small parties or stragglers, and it is fool-hardy for smaller parties than six or eight mounted men to go any considerable distance alone or ahead of trains." When finally settled into camp, Durivage took time to describe "a torment" he felt. It was not the occasional rattlesnakes, centipedes, tarantulas, repeated mail failures, lack of iced drinks, or mosquitoes, he explained. And it was not the loose flagstone steps found everywhere, which when stepped on were "apt to squirt filthy water over your white pants and elegantly polished boots." The torment was, he explained, "myriads of flies." Every house and tent was infested with them, he complained. "The air seem filled with them—they buzz about and settle on your person, they dart into your eyes, insinuate themselves into your nostriles [*sic*] and gambol in your ears. . . . They dispute every mouthful of food a person puts into his mouth, are mixed upon every dish he eats and his drink is converted into a tincture of flies."[3]

Durivage also was having another problem endemic with Americans new to the war zone—within days of his arrival he became sick with what he described as "typhus fever." He was bedridden for a week and lost considerable weight. The *Picayune* editors would be "shocked and surprised" if they could see him, Durivage wrote, because of his weight loss. He explained:

You would have seen a lank, attenuated individual astride of a diminutive mustang pony, in front of an enormous pair of saddle bags stuffed almost to bursting; a haversack containing the entire contents of a Saltillo [shop] and a very suspicious looking black bottle hanging from the saddle-bow; an enormous pair of holster pistols and a two-quart canteen . . . [all belonging] to an individual whose blue Attakapas pants were "a world too wide for his shrunk shanks."[4]

Durivage spent considerable time at Saltillo, the southern anchor of Taylor's defensive line. In May 1847, following a hard, hot ride to reach the city, Durivage wrote, "Well, I have penetrated this far into the country of the enemy without seeing anything like fighting or even skirmishing, or seeing an armed Mexican." Durivage was surprised at the appearance of Saltillo. "The streets are all clean and in good repair and in every door and at every window were señoras and señoritas," he commented. But the garrison of Ohio Volunteers appeared to be the most "ragged, woe-begone set I [ever] saw." He added, however, "I was delighted to find the place had not suffered in the slightest degree from the occupation of our forces."

After recovering, he visited the Buena Vista battlefield, explaining, "A long tedious eight days' fever having partially left me I am able to write you again with some little idea of what I am doing." One of his first reports dealt with the growing concern about the volunteers' misbehavior. In April Durivage wrote to the *Picayune*, "You will be no less shocked to hear that an equally sickening piece of outrageous barbarity has been perpetrated . . . by persons calling themselves Americans." The murder of an Arkansas volunteer led to his comrades deliberately murdering twenty-four Mexicans "who have been assured that they should be respected and protected." He continued, "This is a fact, a melancholy, incontrovertible fact." The search for the attackers, Durivage said, had "proved fruitless . . . and they will never be discovered probably." The murders were committed by "lawless and irresponsible persons," he said, who discredited the American volunteers.[5]

Problems with the volunteer units were common. Two officers were mortally wounded during a duel, Durivage wrote in one letter. In another, he said several officers "were roughly handled" by volunteers refusing to obey orders. "Muscal was the cause," Durivage observed. In August Durivage reported on a brief mutiny by volunteers in the camp. Members of North Carolina and Virginia regiments protested the discipline ordered by Colonel Robert Treat Paine of the 1st North Carolina Infantry. About thirty men gathered in front of the officer's tent and started throwing stones. The colonel arrived on the scene and drew his sword to disperse them, only to have them refuse. He finally drew two pistols and fired, killing one of the soldiers. "This prompt and decisive step quelled the mutiny," Durivage reported. In September there was more trouble in the camp when two lieutenants and nineteen men of a Texas volunteer company deserted. "They have been so much trouble that General Wool did not think them worth sending after, and suffered them to go their way in peace," Durivage wrote.[6]

William Osman, editor of the Ottawa *Free Trader,* who was serving in the Illinois Volunteers, observed of the volunteers, "It is a fact, sufficiently humiliating," he wrote, "it must be confessed, that there are few volunteers that can with any degree of safety be left to garrison a town. Those that have been tried here have made such a hand of it that [General Taylor] made it his first business to get them away. The men appear to become perfectly reckless, and run into every kind of excess, from which the officers, if they had the power, manifest little disposition to restrain them." When the murder of the Arkansas volunteer occurred, he wrote, "for the honor of the American name, I regret to have occasion to mention" it. The Mexicans were unarmed, he noted, and their slaughter indiscriminate. A letter from General Taylor was read to the troops calling "the act atrocious and cowardly and the perpetrators as murderers." Even though the unit was to be banished to a rear area, Osman believed there were "mitigating circumstances in favor of the accused." Their captain was a prisoner of the Mexicans, he explained, and three of them "within the last four weeks have been lariated by Mexicans and two of them murdered and all robbed of their horses and arms . . . [and] the perpetrators so often have been sent away scot free for want of proof, if not a proper investigation." This tempted the volunteers "to take the law into their own hands," Osman believed. The unit's character was a factor, too, Osman explained: "It is made up of the hardiest kind of backwoodsman, who love the largest liberty" and "can little brook the absolute submission demanded by so punctilious a disciplinarian as Gen. Wool." Wool refused to call them soldiers and always referred to them as "these Arkansas people." Osman, however, defended them: "And as to bravery, they are madly brave—utterly reckless of danger—every man would single-handed, engage a host."[7]

Another widely reprinted writer critical of the incident was Albert Pike of the accused Arkansas Volunteers. Pike had a reputation in his company as a "strict disciplinarian," and his letters to the *Arkansas State Gazette* frequently reflected his unhappiness with the performance of the Arkansas unit and its commander, Archibald Yell.[8] Pike got into a protracted public dispute with several other officers of the regiment and was challenged to a duel when he wrote a letter to the *Gazette* exposing the massacre of the unarmed Mexicans by Arkansas volunteers. Pike explained: "I am anxious that the information should so go to the world, that those only who *deserve* the shame may bear it." Pike was not an eyewitness to the incident but got information from an army teamster who had participated and later was assigned to Pike's company: "His account was that they found the poor wretches unarmed, drove them in a huddle like sheep, and shot them down."[9]

The murders also drew criticism from George Tobin of the *Delta,* who tried to soften it, noting, "It was certainly unchristian-like, but they kill us when they meet us at a disadvantage." In a similar incident, Durivage reported, "I have alluded . . . to the murders committed at Saltillo by Mexicans upon Americans. They have killed one too many." After another member of the Arkansas Cavalry was fatally stabbed and his horse stolen, two Mexicans were arrested as suspects. Durivage reported that after a trial was "deemed inadvisable" by local authorities, "a party of men demanded them, and they were taken out and shot. . . . I regret to state that many Mexicans were killed that day—some say seventeen, and some more. Comment is unnecessary."[10]

Josiah Gregg wrote to the Louisville *Journal* that "it is painful to feel compelled to confess that the volunteers . . . have given much cause for the dread in which they are held by the Mexican citizens." He reported being an eyewitness to "depredations [that] have been a disgrace to the American name." The writer asked his editors: "Can you explain this?" Politics at home was Gregg's explanation. "When an officer neglects to punish a soldier or a subordinate for an outrage or a dereliction of duty, have we not a right to suppose that it is for fear of his influence at home?" The Mexicans, Gregg contended, "have no great right to complain at these outrages while they confess that their own troops treat them no better; and while, in fact, it is well known that more murders and more robberies . . . were constantly committed by their own highwaymen" as well as by Indians in northern Mexico. The Americans had ended that, Gregg said, but it still did not justify the volunteers' actions, particularly because the U.S. Army had guaranteed to protect Mexican civilians in occupied areas.[11]

Gregg also occasionally criticized the regular army and what he called the "modus operandi of the war." Gregg explained he did not agree with the army's policy of paying "high prices" to Mexican civilians for animals and supplies. It was not justified, the merchant-turned-writer believed, because many Americans had suffered "outrages" and "the name of our Government in its inefficiency . . . had become a scoffing by-word instead of a terror to the Mexicans." Gregg also criticized the army for later abandoning Mexican cities it occupied, leaving people "well disposed towards us . . . to a barbarous persecution for their partiality to us; so that all our conquests amount to nothing, except perhaps to inflict an injury upon the friends of liberty." The writer added, "In many other regards, I find my humble views to differ from those . . . in command." Particularly appalling to Gregg was General Wool's habit of riding to church and through the streets of Saltillo with an escort of twenty dragoons with drawn sabers. Gregg criticized "the parade and pomposity of his 'suite' especially when compared with the very unostentatious style of Gen. Taylor."[12]

George Davis, an Illinois volunteer officer, contended that regular army officers forced the volunteers to remain in undesirable rear areas "to rot like sheep" and do "all the drudgery and menial service of the army." Their purpose, he contended, was to break "down entirely the volunteer system," to increase the standing army, and to "create a new batch of drones to flourish about our cities in gold lace and broad cloth, at public expense." Davis, formerly editor of the Alton (Ill.) *Telegraph,* also explained why few volunteers were willing to reenlist, even for short terms: "Few are willing to reenlist, solely for the reason, that they consider they are basely and ungenerously treated and frequently made the scapegoats of the marauding conduct of the men in the regular service, many of whom are fugitives from justice." Davis was refreshingly outspoken in his letters. "Such are the fruits of war," he wrote while observing U.S. troops burn down a village of about 800 people after a skirmish nearby with Mexican guerrillas. "A few miles beyond *this scene of triumph,*" he noted sarcastically, the troops looted but did not burn a Mexican whiskey distillery. "There were no volunteers *now* to [blame]. . . . They were perpetrated by those models of *military discipline and deportment,* the regulars." Davis concluded, "Such is the discrimination of an invading army. *Spare a distillery! but burn a town!* The act speaks volumes."[13]

Davis brought a critical eye to many of the practices in the army. During a stop in New Orleans he observed: "The way Uncle Sam is skinned in this city is curious. A faithful history of the fitting out, and carrying on this Mexico campaign would not redoubt much to the credit or honor of many of those who have had a finger in the pie. . . . The day will come when the *expose* will be made, and the participators will have to submit to public indignation unsparingly expressed." Davis was continually appalled at the volunteers' high death rate along the Rio Grande, and in December 1846 he estimated more than 1,600 already had died of disease. He noted, "We are suffering seriously from the want of medical stores, and hospital tents; and so far this goes, we have great cause of complaint, as . . . the lives of many of our men were wantonly and unnecessarily [sacrificed] for the want of them." The unit officers could not be blamed: "A serious responsibility rests somewhere, and a neglect to furnish shelter to the sick, and medicine for their relief will be visited upon . . . those who are at fault." Later in the campaign, at Jalapa in central Mexico, Davis returned to this issue, when he observed "the mortality among the sick and wounded still continued to be very great" despite the healthy climate. He wrote:

> It is not to be disguised, that the treatment and attention the wounded generally receive in the hospital, is very far from being calculated to aid in their recovery. . . . I am only astonished that as many live as do. This, I suppose, is one of those irremedial hardships attached to a war, for which there is no redress. Many and many is the life that has been lost during this campaign, which a very little kindness and attention could have saved; and, in my judgement, there is manifest neglect, and, I might add, *cruelty*, attached somewhere.[14]

Durivage described Monterrey and Saltillo as filled with "peace rumors." But the correspondent refused to believe them: "I have so little confidence in *anything* Mexican." Instead, Durivage was sure that Taylor was preparing to march south to Mexico City. "I have, therefore, a fair prospect of 'revelling in the halls of the Montezumas' . . . and if I live through the campaign and return via Vera Cruz I shall have seen quite as much of the country as I care about." Within weeks, however, more of Taylor's troops were withdrawn to support Scott's forces in central Mexico. "Now everything is knocked in the head," Durivage wrote about his hopes of marching to Mexico City. "This leaves Taylor utterly powerless," he explained to the *Picayune*, predicting, "This second attempt to paralyze the movements of the old general will but endear him more to the people."[15]

Without army activity, Durivage reported little hard news. Finally in July he had an opportunity to break the monotony of camp life by making a two-week reconnaissance with a unit of dragoons. "When we'll return or the purpose of the expedition . . . I haven't the remotest conception. . . . It is sufficient for me to know that I'll have a chance of seeing something and that it promises variety and adventure." Following several days on the road, Durivage wrote, "After a hard ride of twenty-five miles over a rough, rocky road, a good nap and glorious camp dinner if a person does not feel in the humor for writing I pity him." Durivage returned to the army's camp at Buena Vista, where he liked the weather and the discipline: "The discipline of General Wool is extremely strict and enforced; and discipline is nine points in the game, especially where volunteers are concerned." Durivage was disturbed at the high rate of illness among the volunteers. During July, deaths in the volunteer regiments averaged three a day, he reported, laying the blame to overeating of fruit. "It really does seem as if they required as much looking after as children," he said of the volunteers. Durivage also was bothered by the army's system of purchasing food. The camp's corn, flour, and cattle were obtained from an English company in Parras, a small town on the western flank where the Americans kept a token force. For their protection, most of the town's Mexican merchants would not sell to the "Yankees," Durivage explained. An English firm would "go into the market and buy up everything we want, forestalling us completely, [and] immediately demand higher and unreasonable rates . . . amounting to exorbitance such as our Government never ought and probably will not pay." Durivage recommended that the army seize the goods if the Mexicans would not sell at reasonable rates.[16]

Durivage's reports often were laced with deprecating remarks. In one letter he noted, "Two American soldiers were arrested last night, charged with having committed a rape upon a Mexican female. I hardly think it is a possible case in this country, but the accused will be tried for the offense nevertheless." Citing a high number of robberies in the area, Durivage observed, "Since the *guerrillos* confine their exertions exclusively to robbing Mexicans, I do not know that we have any great reason to complain." On another occasion he wrote, "We had a great circus here last night," and he described the interrogation of forty Mexicans arrested after the murder of an Arkansas volunteer. After watching the questioning, Durivage noted, "Mexicans certainly can lie with the best face of any people in the world." He continued, "When we [begin] to civilize the people of this country, the precept of the venerable and excellent matron, Mother Goose, should be inculcated in every juvenile mind, and the familiar verse which holds up the terrible fate in stone for liars painted [*sic*] up in every domocil throughout the land."[17]

In August 1847 Durivage was appointed as a civilian aide on General Wool's staff. The official order indicated the correspondent had "tendered his services." Although the general gave him the pay and privileges of a major, he did not have the authority to give Durivage the actual military rank. This did not prevent the *Picayune* from commenting good-humoredly, "The major is hereafter to be 'obeyed and respected' accordingly." Until receiving the appointment, Durivage had been planning to organize a party of civilians to travel to Mexico City, reporting from a number of the towns in northern Mexico that American forces had not captured.[18]

One use Wool made of his friendship with Durivage was to push his claim that he was the officer who had selected the Buena Vista battlefield. Wool mounted a modest public relations campaign during summer 1847 in support of his claim. Wool identified the defensive position as early as December 21, 1846, two months before the battle. He later exchanged several letters on the topic with an aide, Captain James Henry Carleton, who supported the general's claim. Wool turned copies of the letters over to Durivage, who forwarded them to the *Picayune*. The *Delta*'s George Tobin also wrote letters from Buena Vista supporting Wool's claim about selecting the battlefield. Publication of the claim led to a spate of newspaper letters from other officers seeking some of the honor. Following the intense public clamor about the victory at Buena Vista, a friend wrote to Wool asking for battle anecdotes, sketches of the battlefield, and a daguerreotype of the general for artists to copy. "Editors and Authors are ready to pay just tribute, but want details," the friend wrote. "I find an occasional talk with some of them quite acceptable to them. And now and then I have to supply an article." In another letter, the friend urged, "I wish some of the officers would take the pains to do as General Taylor's friends are constantly doing—send anecdotes—sayings—or incidents respecting you. . . . The Taylor anecdotes are coming in thick and fast."[19]

By the middle of October 1847, with fighting clearly over and Taylor making plans to return to New Orleans, Durivage decided to end his assignment. Durivage's final letters told of numerous army disciplinary problems, hangings and shootings of Mexicans, freezing conditions in the camps because "tents and pantaloons are made of cotton," and depredations in Monterrey by the Massachusetts Volunteers. As a native of Boston, Durivage was particularly rankled by the latter. "I am very sorry to say that the Massachusetts Regiment have [*sic*] left a very bad name behind them, but trust they may be able to retrieve it upon the other line for the credit of the Old Bay State." Durivage left Monterrey on November 8 with Taylor's party but went ahead when he grew impatient with its slow pace. He reached New Orleans November 28, ending eight months of reporting events of the occupation in the north.[20]

Tobin of the *Delta* also was active in the northern area until the war ended, but his reporting was sporadic and his style often whimsical. After Buena Vista, Tobin remained with his Texas Rangers unit. When it was disbanded in June 1847, Tobin told the *Delta* he was "in for the war" and joined another advance scout unit stationed at Parras, on the Americans' western flank.

When it heard Tobin was staying with the army, the Philadelphia *North American* said he reminded the editors of the words from an old song: "How happy the soldier who lives on his pay, and spends all he gets though sixpence a day." In summer 1847 Tobin was promoted to first lieutenant and for a time commanded Ben McCulloch's old company of Texas Rangers, although his published articles continued to carry the title "Captain Tobin."[21] Tobin regularly mailed files of the Mexican papers to the *Delta*, but because his letters contained little hard news, the paper often delayed publication. On one occasion it noted, "The impatient friends of Capt. Tobin must excuse us for deferring the publication of his letter one day longer." Most of Tobin's reports included lighthearted anecdotes about the Texas volunteer units, such as this example:

> We're in a starving condition out at the Texas camp—nothing to eat except beef, pork, bacon, mutton, hams, venison, bearmeat, snipe, ducks, plover, etc.; and for dessert, only mangos, apples, pears, peaches and delicious grapes. If the war be brought to a premature close—which Heaven forbid—I don't know what we will do for a living; as they say the penitentiaries at home have shut up for want of business; and we'll be too lazy to work.

Although such whimsical writing appears to have amused many editors, the antiwar New York *Tribune* saw it differently, commenting, "The paragraph opens a vista for reflection."[22]

Tobin's letters from Buena Vista in February 1848, a year after the battle, presented a vivid description of the problems faced by the occupation army. "We had a bungling sort of execution lately," he reported. A private in the Arkansas company was to be shot, and twenty-two soldiers were detailed to carry out the sentence. "And at the word 'fire,' he went head over heels across the coffin. Everyone supposed him dead, and the detail was marched off. . . . After a while he rose, sat on the coffin, and asked for a drink of water. The water was given him and the detail was sent for, when he was killed, *really*, over again." Twenty soldiers had agreed to fire over the prisoner's head, Tobin reported, and the other two wounded him. They apparently hoped to spare his life. "It was misplaced friendship, he had to die and he deserved to die," Tobin wrote.[23] Soon after, "Another Arkansas man was hanged in the Plaza for wantonly shooting an old [Mexican] man in the streets of Saltillo. He died like a brute—drunk as a *cup*," Tobin recounted. This incident was soon followed by the execution of three Mexicans for killing three discharged volunteers. "They died with great firmness," Tobin noted, "one fellow put the rope around his own neck, and they all swung off the cart with cigars in their mouths." One survived the hanging and an officer was sent for, "and Mr. 'Greaser' soon 'ceased to exist'—a favorite expression among the rangers when they send another citizen to Hades."[24]

Tobin returned to New Orleans in mid-July 1848, and the *Delta* greeted him as the "Hero of Letter Writers." When he stopped at its office, the paper noted, he was "a burly figure of a fierce looking half-sailor, half-soldier looking individual, in a check shirt, with a Mexican cavalry roundabout, a Texas Ranger's pantaloons and a U.S. infantry cap on." Tobin was, the *Delta* insisted, "the best scholar, readiest wit, happiest poet, and most genuine good fellow and gallant Ranger, whom this war has called from the walks of private life."[25]

CHAPTER FIFTEEN

Contreras and Churubusco

> *See, here's the very last invented news!*
> *From Mexico, from Texas, and the South,*
> *By telegraph, epistle, word of mouth.*
> *Here is the "Be all and the END all"*
> *Of "Montezuma's Hall," Prescribed by Kend-al.*
> —From a poem in *Spirit of the Times*, January 8, 1848

The summer lull ended on August 19–20, 1847, with the battles at Contreras and Churubusco near Mexico City. After receiving reinforcements in early August, Scott started moving his army of 10,700 men from Puebla toward the Mexican capital. Faced with the tactical problem of which approach to take, Scott made a flanking move to the south, around large Lake Chalco. The move bypassed the Mexicans' strongest fortifications and brought the smaller American army up against less formidable defensive positions on the southern approach to the city.[1]

On August 19 an American frontal assault on the Mexican positions near the town of Contreras was costly and unsuccessful, and by the end of the day Scott feared he might have lost as much as half his army. That night, in a heavy rain, a force led by American General Persifor F. Smith found a ravine leading to the rear of the Mexican position, and the next morning the force routed the defenders in a swift attack. In retrospect, Kendall wrote no defeat of the war was "more crushing and [disastrous]" for the Mexicans than Contreras. On August 20 the Americans followed up their advantage. The retreating Mexican forces suffered heavy casualties; Santa Anna, bringing up reinforcements, attempted to block the American advance at the fortified convent of Churubusco. Scott launched another frontal assault and after a costly struggle sent the defeated remnants of the Mexican army fleeing into the capital. Many of Scott's officers wanted him to continue the attack and take the city at once.

Instead, he halted. The Americans had suffered more than 1,000 killed and wounded in the two-day battle. Scott had reports there were still 20,000 Mexican defenders inside the city, and he feared Santa Anna's government would collapse completely and end all possibility of a negotiated peace. A controversial two-week armistice ensued while Trist and Scott resumed the work of trying to bring peace by diplomacy.[2]

In New Orleans, meanwhile, a severe yellow fever epidemic and a disruption of mail shipments to and from Mexico had slowed the news. The epidemic was described as New Orleans's most severe outbreak in a decade, and the weekly death toll soon climbed past 500, including a number of journalists and printers. Shorthanded, several daily papers, including the *Courier*, *Commercial Times*, *Commercial Bulletin*, and *Bee*, reduced publication to three times a week. In addition to affecting the newspapers in New Orleans and other Gulf Coast cities, the epidemic slowed construction of the telegraph line through the Deep South, effectively preventing that line from being completed by the end of the war. The disease continued to interrupt life in New Orleans until mid-October.[3]

In addition to the normal difficulty of carrying the news past guerrillas, the pressure of moving reinforcements and supplies for Scott to Veracruz forced the government to divert troop transports. The *McKim, Telegraph, Alabama, New Orleans*, and other ships that made the regular weekly runs to the Mexican port were utilized in the more urgent military project, resulting in a seventeen-day delay in mail deliveries to New Orleans. At Veracruz, the *Delta*'s correspondent reported gloomily that at least five more express riders, three for the *Picayune* and two for the *Delta*, "had been cut off" between Veracruz and Jalapa.[4]

Freaner, Kendall, and the other journalists, meanwhile, were advancing with Scott's army. Freaner had departed Puebla on August 8 with General Worth's division. Resting in the army's camp prior to the resumption of fighting, Freaner noted, "The division I came up with had a very fine and agreeable march." He added he had many other army items he wanted to send to the *Delta*. "I have always with me four horses for my own use and eight extras, and four Mexicans, faithful and good riders, who accompany me and are always on hand to ride expresses." The editors approved of the arrangements, noting, "It is a source of great mortification to us that the expensive arrangements we made to keep up our Mexican correspondence have been sometimes defeated by the success of the guerrillas."[5]

Freaner's hard work and preparations were to pay off, and his extensive accounts of the Contreras and Churubusco battles arrived at the *Delta* at the same time Kendall's reached the *Picayune*. Freaner moved with several different units during the two days of fighting, traveled over all the battlefields, and conducted extensive interviews afterward. Following his established practice, he also asked several officers to "write out memorandums" with their impressions for him. "The Mexicans were still burying their friends when I passed over the battlefield two days ago," Freaner wrote on August 26, commenting on the large number cut down by the American guns. So much had happened during the two days, he noted, that the *Delta*'s readers would probably get the best information from the official "reports of the several commands." He continued, "I find that if I were to attempt to record the entire details of the achievements of [August 20] I would not be able to conclude it in time enough to be of any interest to your readers." As it was, Freaner's summary account, together with an extensive list of killed and wounded he compiled, filled more than six columns in the *Delta*. "It is more full than that furnished by the *Picayune*," the Augusta (Ga.) *Chronicle and Sentinel* noted, and before long a number of the country's papers were again praising "Mustang's" efforts.[6]

Kendall had been concerned about the condition of Scott's small army even before it left Puebla. "No man in the United States could believe for one moment the straits to which our army has been driven for want of cash," he wrote to the *Picayune*. It had become necessary for officers of the quartermaster and commissary units to pay as much as 15 percent interest to borrow money to defray the expenses of marching to Mexico City, he reported. When General Twiggs's division led off the departure of Scott's army on August 7, Kendall joined it. "The coming fortnight will come to us burthened [*sic*] with news, and whether it be peace or war to the knife, I shall give you the intelligence as early as possible," he wrote on the eve of departure.[7]

Kendall started August 19 by observing Scott as the battle unfolded: "If the eye was buried in taking in this exciting panorama, the ear was deafened with the sound of the conflict." Kendall observed, "No soldiers are as bold as the Americans before battle." He particularly praised the work of the engineers and called Captain Robert E. Lee "an officer of stubborn will and iron endurance." It was impossible to keep up with Churubusco's many incidents, Kendall admitted. As he advanced with the troops, he witnessed "the shouts, groans, cries of despair, the bayonet at work." When the battle came to its climax, Kendall stated, "the defiant yells of the enemy as they still held their works, amid the groans and shrieks of the wounded as they lay writhing or were run over in their agony, all presented within a narrow [view] a full measure of the excitement as well as the horrors of war."[8]

John Peoples joined up with Kendall on the second day, and they rode to various parts of the battlefield to witness the American attacks. Both spent part of the day serving as volunteer aides to Major General Pillow. As the two days of fighting came to a climax, they stood near the artillery battery of Major James Duncan and witnessed the final bloody attack on the key

Mexican position, the Convent of San Mateo at Churubusco. Kendall believed the fighting at Churubusco was the bloodiest of the war.[9]

Among the 1,200 Mexican prisoners at the convent were seventy-two foreign members of the San Patricio artillery unit. Their capture caused excitement, strong emotions, and controversy in the American army and press. On August 25, a few days after the battle, Kendall reported that the prisoners included seventy-two "deserters and other foreigners" who were members of the battalion that had fought against the Americans at Monterrey, Buena Vista, and Cerro Gordo. A court-martial was under way for "this precious set of scoundrels," Kendall reported, "and it is to be hoped they may have full justice done them." John Riley, the captured San Patricio commander, "openly makes his brags of what he has done, and says he expects no mercy."

When the fighting ended, Kendall quickly assembled the rough details of the two days. His first account was an overall sketch of the fighting. He followed this up a day later with a detailed story. "To describe the fierce conflict even now that two days have elapsed, or to give an account of the part taken by the different regiments, [is] impossible," he stated. Kendall also assembled an extensive list of the killed and wounded.[10]

Freaner and Kendall had their express riders under way soon after the battles ended. The first word of the two victories reached the United States by a much more unusual route, however. On the morning after the defeat, the official Mexican newspaper at Mexico City, *Diario Official del Gobierno*, carried a summary of the fighting and the armistice. A copy of the paper was taken by a Mexican express rider to the city of Orizaba, halfway between the capital and Veracruz. An American representative in the city forwarded a summary to F. M. Dimond, the U.S. collector at Veracruz. Dimond received the report on August 26 and made it available to reporters. They in turn dispatched it to New Orleans, and on the morning of September 3 a *Picayune* extra proclaimed:

American Arms Again Victorious!
The Mexicans Defeated by Gen. Scott in
Two Distinct Engagements
The City of Mexico at our Mercy[11]

Express riders again headed north. On September 4 the telegraph line from the North reached Petersburg, Virginia, 20 miles farther south than previously. On that day an item in the Washington *Union* asked the editor of the Petersburg *Republican* to make arrangements for a competent reporter to "transmit at once" any important news from Mexico via New Orleans, "and we will cheerfully meet any expenses which it may incur."[12]

The *Union* had a chance to pay off five days later, September 9, but the telegram came from Fredericksburg, not Petersburg. "The mails and the telegraph to the South" had failed, a reporter in Fredericksburg wired the *Union*, but John R. Martin, the mail agent there, had received a brief summary of the *Picayune*'s September 3 report. Martin telegraphed the news to Postmaster Cave Johnson (who presumably notified the administration) and at the same time made it available to the press. The Philadelphia and Baltimore papers had it the same day, September 9, and the next morning it reached New York.[13]

The eyewitness reports from Kendall and Freaner reached New Orleans about 2 A.M. on September 8. Both papers rushed out extras, basically condensed versions of their correspondents' many long letters; the full documents ran the following day. Freaner's reports filled six columns of the *Delta*, and Kendall's letters and the casualty list filled more than nine columns of the *Picayune*. Despite the volume of Kendall's letters, the *Picayune* did not attempt to cut them. "We make no attempt at a summary," the paper said. "We are persuaded that every word of them will be read with interest."[14]

The same morning the news arrived at New Orleans, Trist's official messages to the State Department also arrived as part of Freaner's packet and were dispatched by special messenger for Washington. The same courier took a copy of the September 8 *Picayune*, with three columns about the battles, and it was delivered to the Baltimore *Sun* on the evening of September 14—covering the distance in six days and a few hours. The *Sun* had the *Picayune*'s report reset and on the streets before the regular mail arrived from the South.[15]

Scott's truce agreement at the end of the fighting greatly aggravated Kendall. Because of his previous imprisonment and experience, Kendall deeply mistrusted Santa Anna, the Mexicans generally, and the British. He was in Scott's camp at dusk on August 20 when a coach arrived from Mexico City carrying Edward Thornton, secretary to the British embassy, and Ewen Mackintosh, the British consul-general. Kendall's friend, Lieutenant Thomas Pitcher, had watched the correspondent and other officers immediately after the fighting: "The excitement of the battle being over the wise ones commenced racking their brains with eyewitnesses as to the result of the day's operation. Of these there were not a few, and all different." When the British diplomats arrived, Pitcher said, Kendall feared "there was 'cheating in the game.'" A U.S. Navy lieutenant, Raphael Semmes, who was staying in camp with Kendall, later recorded that the correspondent was highly upset at the sight of Mackintosh. "When they had gone, Kendall, with the bluntness and frankness which characterize him, exclaimed: 'It's no use, we're humbugged—McIntosh [*sic*] is among them!'"[16]

After a short time Mackintosh appeared again, this time to talk to General Worth about sparing the lives of the mostly Irish and European immigrants who had deserted to the Mexican forces. Kendall recorded the scene: "With eyes flashing the impetuous American general told the Englishman that the rules and articles of war in the British army, in relation to deserters, were the same as those of the United States, were short, and he would repeat them: 'He who deserts to the enemy in the time of war, shall suffer death.'" With that the English representative left.[17]

In letters to the *Picayune,* Kendall expanded on his apprehension about the truce: "The armistice has finally been settled and signed and I do not tell half the story when I say that it has produced universal dissatisfaction in the army—in the entire army." He continued, "The whole affair, on the face of it, looks like one of Santa Anna's old tricks to gain time and plan some new scheme of trickery—and as he had British influence to back him he will be likely to carry out what he undertakes." The Mexican defenses were so weak at the end of the battles on August 20, Kendall said, "that one of our weakest regiments could have entered the Grand Plaza with but little opposition . . . and driven every soldier out of the city." As the cease-fire neared its end, Kendall wrote, "If peace be made it will be purchased of Santa Anna—regularly bought—and this against the wishes of nine-tenths of the [Mexican] population." Most of the political factions hated the Americans, Kendall explained, but Santa Anna still had the army behind him, and his greed might lead him to sign "with the hope that he will be able to put down the revolution which must immediately be raised against him." Fear of the political opposition would force him to put greed aside, Kendall contended, "and another battle must ensue." As the treaty violations and delays grew, he also vented his frustration at Polk's administration: "I wish Gen. Jackson was alive and President."[18]

Kendall never forgave Scott for declaring the armistice. "Many good and brave men had fallen," the *Picayune* editor recalled twenty years later, "and all through the stupid armistice granted the crafty and contemptible Santa Anna. . . . Gross blunders and mistakes have been made in war, but few as flagrant as this." The cause, Kendall said, was Scott's presidential aspirations and ignorance of Santa Anna's "cunning and duplicity." Scott "had his own way," Kendall wrote, and "the useless sacrifice of over a thousand men" followed. The general "thought he was macadamizing a plain and smooth road to the White House," but in the end he failed to get the quick peace treaty he felt would assure his election. Scott's "own feelings" as he read the list of "brave men killed" in the following battles well "may be imagined," Kendall wrote.[19]

In contrast, the proadministration *Delta* was a bit embarrassed by Freaner's praise for the Mexicans' resistance and Scott's leadership in the battles. The Mexicans resisted at every point and "fought us as they never fought before," he wrote. Scott, Freaner noted, was wounded slightly during the fighting yet told no one until it was over. "Those who have not seen him in battle cannot form any just conception of his abilities," Freaner believed. "His cool consideration of everything around him—his quick perception—his firm resolve and quick execution—equal if they do not surpass those of any of the great generals whose deeds have been made so conspicuous in history." The editors at the *Delta* were somewhat cautious but supportive of Freaner's strong words for the general. "Some allowance must be made for the warmth of the language natural to the excitement of so great a victory as that related by our correspondent," the paper explained. Freaner, the *Delta* continued, "has never been suspected of flattery, toadyism or favoritism towards any of our officers." Scott, the paper observed, "has been made at home the subject of vilification and abuse, the most unprecedented and infamous on record."[20]

After Scott had reached the temporary armistice, John Peoples unexpectedly found himself leading the first American journalists to enter the Mexican capital. Having signed the truce agreement, Scott wanted to have copies printed for his troops. Peoples volunteered to accompany several Mexican officers secretly into the city at night and print the document. Arrangements were made through Santa Anna to use a Mexican newspaper office to set the English-language message, and the copies were struck off on the paper's press. Accompanying Peoples on the dangerous trip were James Barnard, Charles Callahan, and John H. Warland, an experienced Massachusetts editor serving in the New England (9th) Volunteer Regiment. Warland recalled the group went "well armed and in citizen's dress [as] it was dangerous . . . the armistice still pending and no U.S. troops having taken up quarters in the 'Halls of Montezuma.'" Accompanied by Mexican officers, the group retraced its steps through the city streets, which Peoples noted "were filled with excited people," and delivered the printed proclamations to Scott.[21]

Kendall reported that on another of the several trips Peoples made into the Mexican capital the printer and two companions were detained overnight "in the guard house at the National Palace." It was for their protection, they were assured. However, "they were counted every fifteen minutes [and] they certainly did not enjoy the largest liberty," Kendall wrote. Peoples recalled that the trio passed the night singing "The Star Spangled Banner" and killing a bottle of cognac. They were released the next morning after being assured again that they had not been prisoners.[22]

Following the battles of August 19–20, Freaner and Kendall had fateful encounters involving the controversial Gideon Pillow. Freaner, making his usual rounds to various unit headquarters, asked a number of officers, including Pillow, for written statements about their battle experiences. When he received Pillow's report, Freaner immediately doubted its accuracy, but he took it with no intention of using the contents. He decided to save the unused letter, a decision that later put the correspondent in the middle of a bitter, protracted court-martial proceeding involving Scott, Pillow, and an incensed Polk administration (see Chapter 20).

In his official army report, Pillow praised Kendall for "promptly bearing and delivering orders" for him during the battles. Kendall's assistance to Pillow turned out to have ironic overtones, because in the months that followed, the reporter was attacked extensively in Democratic newspapers for understating Pillow's reputed role in the victories. The Boston *Post*, Nashville *Union*, and Washington *Union* led the criticism. The *Post* printed a letter that charged Kendall "had suppressed the truth" regarding Pillow's contribution. The letter also charged Kendall had not done justice to Generals Franklin Pierce and James Shields because they, too, were Democrats. It cautioned Democrats around the country "not to confide in the representations of Mr. Kendall when democratic officers are interested."[23]

"A viler slander was never penned," the *Picayune* rebutted. The *Picayune* noted it was "being censured for attempting to injure General Pillow *by [our] silence in regard to him*." The New Orleans paper went on to point out it had reprinted every account of the two battles it had been able to obtain, including the official military reports from the *Union*, "partially because of the interest and importance of the battles themselves, and partially from a desire to justify the original report we gave from the pen of Mr. Kendall." The *Picayune* noted it had also "incurred" the additional expense of engraving and printing maps of the battles "to render the different narratives clear." It added, "The report of Mr. Kendall has been confirmed by every report we have seen yet from military authority."[24]

The Washington *Union* also attempted to discredit Kendall by accusing him of attacking Scott. The administration paper took a line from Kendall's letter that said the armistice "has produced universal dissatisfaction in the army" and charged it represented "a slur against Scott." The *Union* concluded, sanctimoniously, "We are unwilling, until we receive fuller and official accounts, to discuss the question, or to cast any slur upon the general, whose military services are receiving the thanks of the people."

In rebuttal, the *Picayune* stated: "We did not understand . . . Mr. Kendall as censuring General Scott himself on account of the armistice, nor do we think the language used by him will justify . . . [criticism] by the *Union*. Our colleague aims faithfully to narrate the occurrences in the army and the opinions [of] . . . officers and men connected with it. He has no prejudices against the commanding general to gratify."[25] The dispute simmered for a while, but it did not die. After the fighting resumed, and new reports came from the battlefield, Kendall faced another round of political attacks from proadministration newspapers about his reporting and analysis.

CHAPTER SIXTEEN

Disaster at Molino del Rey

The pressure to be first to report the fall of Mexico City led the press to publish a number of false alarms and mistakes during the summer of 1847. On July 30, ten days before Winfield Scott started for the Mexican capital, the New Orleans *National* issued an extra edition stating he had taken the city without a fight.[1] The next morning the *Delta* agreed with the report, but the Spanish-language *La Patria*, the *Commercial Times*, and the *Picayune* strongly disagreed. The *National*'s editor, Thomas Bangs Thorpe, was sincere in reporting the surrender, the *Picayune* said, "but we are unable to arrive at the same conclusion." It obtained the same news two days earlier, the *Picayune* said, "but did not believe it and did not use it."[2] Newspapers in many other cities, however, did believe the *National*'s report. The New York *Tribune* was fooled, and in Philadelphia it was reported "flags were flying . . . from the *Ledger, Inquirer, Sun, North American, Pennsylvanian* and other newspaper offices" after the story arrived. The St. Louis papers also used the story but "with doubts," as the *Missouri Republican* reported. It was another week before a letter from Kendall came through the guerrillas' blockade, confirming Scott was still at Puebla.[3]

In September the New York *Sun* ran an alleged eyewitness report of a battle to capture Mexico City, which fooled some papers but was criticized by many others. The false report was published in New York on September 14, the very day the real battle was being fought at Mexico City. "The [story] is not worth publishing even as a joke," the Washington *Union* scolded. "It is said to have been received by their swift courier Baron Munchausen," the *Picayune* joked, referring to the eighteenth-century book full of bizarre tall tales. The Washington *National Intelligencer* and New York *Journal of Commerce* were more direct, stating flatly the letter had been written in New York. The New Orleans *Delta* criticized the *Sun*'s effort yet still printed it: "It's a fancy sketch even if fictitious."[4]

At the time, truth was scarier than fiction. "The rumors from the seat of war are certainly alarming," the New York *Herald* observed, "and if they are founded on truth, our gallant little army is indeed in a precarious situation." The Philadelphia *North American* told its readers: "The position of the army in Mexico is one calculated to produce the deepest anxiety in the breast of every American—anxiety all the more [harassing] from the mystery which surrounds it, and the wild, vague, exciting rumors of battle and carnage, amazing victories and terrible perils, which come to us through Mexican channels." During the confusion of the conflicting reports, the Charleston *Courier* explained, "we proceed to give all the intelligence received by Express, leaving our readers to draw their own conclusions."[5] Thus, in an atmosphere heavy with rumor, mystery, and mistake the press and public waited for news from Mexico.

In truth, Scott's situation *had* grown more precarious. The renewed peace negotiations first looked hopeful, but as the shock of the August 19–20 defeats diminished, the Mexican position hardened. Nicholas Trist stood firm on the American demands for California, New Mexico, and the Rio Grande boundary. Santa Anna, his power further weakened by the disgrace of the defeats, decided to fight the smaller American army again. He hoped it might be reduced even more and, perhaps, put in such a perilous position the Americans would reduce their terms in order to save it. Scott now had 8,000 troops to Santa Anna's estimated 20,000. Scott broke off the talks on September 6, after the Mexicans violated the armistice by reinforcing their key defensive site, Chapultepec, which guarded the western approach to the city. A half mile to the west of Chapultepec was El Molino del Rey ("The King's Mill"), an intricate arrangement of low stone buildings. Scott incorrectly believed cannons were being forged there and at nearby Casa Mata and that a quick American raid would destroy the works. The assault plan was enlarged, and on September 8 fighting resumed. It was a costly disaster. The Americans suffered almost 800 casualties and found no forge or military value in the position. Despite the heavy losses, it was immediately abandoned.[6]

When the fighting resumed, Kendall decided to stay with Worth, who directed the American assault. Before dawn on September 8, the *Picayune* correspondent accompanied the field artillery battery of Lieutenant Colonel James Duncan to the front line. Duncan later wrote that Kendall "executed an important and exceedingly hazardous" reconnaissance in the predawn light that allowed Duncan's artillery to distinguish between the Mexican lines and the Americans advancing across the field "in the imperfect light of the morning." The *Picayune* correspondent spent most of the battle relaying information and orders by riding back and forth between Worth and his field commanders.[7]

It was a day of horror. "For some time the result was doubtful," Kendall wrote to the *Picayune* that night. "The air was filled with balls. . . . There was no safety on any part of the field." At one Mexican strongpoint, when it appeared the defenders were winning the battle, Kendall observed the "Mexicans shouted with frantic joy. With savage yells [some charged] and bayoneted the [wounded] Americans. By pretending to be dead some of the soldiers saved themselves." The Mexicans seemed to send "a perfect sheet of molten iron and lead" into the American charge, Kendall recorded. "It required Anglo-Saxon stamina to stand steadily up to such slaughtering work. It was cool, calm, determined, unfaltering iron energy that won the battle."[8]

He reported, "Our small force's . . . dauntless courage carried them over every obstacle, and notwithstanding the Mexicans fought with a valor rare for them, they were finally routed from one point or another until all were driven or dispersed. The defeat was total." He was quick to add, "To gain this victory our own loss has been uncommonly severe—it has been purchased with the blood of some of the most gallant spirits of the army." As soon as the fighting ended, Kendall tried to assemble a casualty list. "Knowing the deep anxiety felt in the United States by the families of all, this shall be my first care," he wrote. It was a difficult task, made more difficult when the Mexicans shelled some ambulances picking up the American dead from the field. General Scott and Nicholas Trist were riding across the battlefield when this occurred, Kendall reported, and an officer standing next to the correspondent "with a sarcastic expression of countenance asked whether Mr. Trist had any new peace propositions in his pockets." Kendall was happy to note that Mackintosh and the other British diplomats "did not come out after the battle to gain more time for Santa Anna, nor worm out fresh intelligence on the strength and movements of our army."[9]

James Freaner also had a good view of the assault. When the day was over, he was appalled: "We were deceived in reference to the character of the buildings," as there was no foundry or even a resemblance of one, "and after blowing up some of the buildings, and bringing off our killed and wounded, we evacuated the place, as the occupation of it would give us no advantage. Our loss was 800 killed, wounded and missing."[10]

Freaner pointed out the American force advanced across an open plain that sloped toward the Mexican position. The infantry was "far in advance of [our] artillery . . . and consequently . . . was exposed to a most terrible fire of musketry from the Mexicans behind the houses, walls and fortifications, which mowed down our men like grass before the scythe." After heavy losses, the position fell. "But," Freaner wrote, "you can imagine our astonishment when we discovered that these buildings, which had cost us so much, contained not the slightest appearance" of a foundry, "we having watered the field with the blood of our best troops." The position was immediately abandoned, Freaner reported. He ended his report on the battle emotionally: "The name of Molino del Rey will never be forgotten by us, nor the veterans who there fell, and whose names will be engraven upon our memory as long as life endures."[11]

Freaner also put together a long casualty list, noting, "Many a tear will be shed on its perusal, and many a heart will bleed for the noble souls, and the old and firm veterans who fell in the assault." Freaner's meticulous list of killed and wounded, which clearly indicated the extensive number of casualties the Americans sustained, filled four columns in agate type in the *Delta*.[12]

The difficulties of the assault also were graphically described by an army officer, Captain William S. Henry, in a report he wrote for the New York *Courier and Enquirer* several months after the battle. At the Molino, he noted, "The fighting was desperate, but our men overcame all difficulties." It was at the Casa Mata and Hacienda, 500 yards to the northwest of the Molino, that the American attack faltered. "The plain over which the attack was made slopes towards the work, and is as clear of any obstructions as the palm of your hand." As a result, the attacking brigade "composed of the 5th, 6th and 8th regiments of Infantry, were completely, you may almost say, annihilated." The column advanced "under a destructive fire" but finally reached the front of the stronghold, when a "fatal order to retreat was given." Henry continued, "It is unknown who gave that unfortunate order, [disastrous it was in every sense,] for in the retreat the 5th and 6th suffered more than in the advance. It was here that the lancers dashed out and lanced our dying and wounded without a particle of mercy." With hindsight, Henry concluded, "I think the manner of the attack upon Casa Mata caused useless and terrible effusion of blood." Since the Molino was taken first, he explained, "Casa Mata was at our mercy, either by shells from the Molino, or by turning it."[13]

Few Americans would know of the Molino del Rey disaster until months later. It was a bloody, costly day for both sides, particularly the smaller American force, though it received little recognition at the moment. The more important events of the next few days quickly eclipsed the coverage. As is often the case in journalism, timing affects the coverage an event receives. This was clearly the case for the fighting at Molino del Rey and Casa Mata. Although it was one of Scott's worst blunders—costing almost 800 dead and wounded for an objective he immediately abandoned—it received little press attention in the heat of the moment. The successful battles for Chapultepec and Mexico City four days later were more decisive to the outcome of the campaign. The correspondents barely had time to assemble their Molino articles and casualty lists before the larger, climatic fighting started. When the Molino news accounts finally reached the press at home, they were buried under the weight of the more dramatic events that followed on September 13–14.

CHAPTER SEVENTEEN

The Halls of Montezuma

On the morning of September 12, Kendall watched as American artillery started a daylong bombardment of Chapultepec. That night he wrote, "[Our movements] indicate that the strong works up on the crest are to be stormed early tomorrow. . . . I have little time to write."[1] General Scott had little time, as well. As Santa Anna hoped, the Americans' strength was further weakened by the losses at Molino del Rey. Scott's army was reduced, it had to guard its wounded and supplies, and it had incomplete intelligence as to the size and placement of the Mexican defenders. After conferences with his generals and engineers, Scott decided to attack Mexico City from the west, directly at the formidable Chapultepec and its military academy. On September 13, American forces assaulted the hilltop fort from several directions and took it by midday. By nightfall the army fought to Mexico City's northwestern and southwestern gates. During the night Santa Anna, his troops demoralized, funds and supplies low, and urged by city leaders to spare further assault, evacuated. Early the next morning, September 14, Scott's troops marched in, raised the American flag, and started a nine-month occupation of the Mexican capital.[2]

The correspondents were spread thin during the final climatic days of fighting. Peoples, Tobey, Warland, and Barnard were on hand but only slightly involved in the reporting. Freaner and Kendall, with their competing papers, provided the major coverage.

On the morning of the September 13 assault, Kendall rode toward the wall surrounding Chapultepec with his friend Lieutenant Colonel Paul Hébert of Scott's staff. On a road north of the approach to the position, the *Picayune* editor saw young Lieutenant Thomas J. Jackson (the legendary "Stonewall" Jackson of the Civil War) commanding a section of Captain J. B. Magruder's artillery. "A Mexican shell burst directly in the battery," Kendall wrote, "killing or crippling some eight or ten men and as many horses. I never saw a man work as hard as did young Jackson, tearing off harnesses and dragging out dead and kicking horses." Kendall recalled vividly, "A brogan which hummed by us, containing the foot of one of . . . Jackson's men, and which, cut off by the shell, had been hurled against the wall" and "bounced down into the road under our horses' feet, the flesh still quivering."[3]

Two nights later, after witnessing the fall of Chapultepec and additional heavy fighting to capture the city, the *Picayune* correspondent excitedly began his letter: "Another victory, glorious in its results and which has thrown additional lustre upon the American arms, has been achieved today by the army under General Scott—the proud capital of Mexico has fallen into the power of a mere handful of men compared with the immense odds arrayed against them, and Santa Anna, instead of shedding his blood as he had promised, is wandering with the remnant of his army no one knows whither." Regarding Chapultepec, Kendall continued, "The apparently impregnable works on Chapultepec, after a desperate struggle, were triumphantly carried. . . . The daring and impetuosity of our men overcame one defense after another . . . although at great loss."[4]

Kendall provided only a rambling summary of the final assault in his first *Picayune* letters, but he later wrote in detail about Chapultepec's controversial conclusion: "The work of slaughter still was not over when resistance was nearly at an end; for the maddened assailants, many of whom remembered . . . a long catalogue of cowardly outrages, allowed the bayonet a great play that the officers found difficulty in averting. Into the interior of Chapultepec the infuriated Americans pushed their way, those who still resisted being instantly [cut] down." When the defenders retreated to the rear of the facility, Kendall described the scene: "Here the descent was precipitous, yet down the cliffs in the extremity of their fright, the staggering defenders (went), pitching and tumbling, many of them head long in their haste, and meeting death by being dashed to pieces to avoid the bayonets of their incensed assailants."

After Chapultepec fell, Kendall advanced with Worth's troops along the San Cosme Causeway leading toward the city's northwestern gate. The Americans came under heavy fire from the Mexican artillery, which "commanded and completely swept the street along the aqueduct," he wrote. So intense was the fire, Worth had to revert to "the old Texas plan" he had learned at Monterrey, "boring and burrowing through the [walls of] houses" in order to advance. It succeeded, the Americans advanced, and a final "dash carried the [Mexicans'] works without great loss." Concerned that Scott might impose another halt on the advance into the city, Worth, with his "usual chafing and unquiet disposition," anxiously wanted to push on, Kendall said. "But how and where?" The Americans did not know the city, and dusk was starting to fall. Suddenly, a "little, fat, pursy, pot-bellied Englishman" in a blue dress coat with brass buttons walked into their midst. He operated a brewery next door and "appeared quite anxious to help." His anxiety was accelerated, Kendall suggested, because Worth was allowing his troops to sack San Cosme since they had taken it by assault. "His men were at it," Kendall noted, and the Englishman apparently thought his brewery might be next.

Worth discovered the brewer knew the city well and asked him to point out several locations: the National Palace, the Grand Plaza, the archbishop's cathedral, and "where the rich people lived." As the man helpfully pointed in the various directions, Worth and his gunnery officers stood behind him making sightings. The Americans drank the man's beer and his knowledge, Kendall explained. By the time the helpful Englishman realized what was occurring, Worth's guns were set up and ready to fire. "But you are going to bombard the city," the Englishman protested, just as the first volley went off. The unhappy informant continued "jumping and skipping about" in protest, the bombardment continuing unabated, until "a deputation" from the city government "came hurriedly down to San Cosme to report that Santa Anna had evacuated the city bag and baggage and that it was at our mercy."[5]

Early on the next morning, September 14, Kendall watched as Scott "entered the city a conqueror . . . mounted on a horse some eighteen hands high, rigged out in full regimentals, with military hat and yellow feathers." The commander "loomed up like a steeple" above everyone, Kendall thought, presenting a sharp contrast to the other Americans. "They had been camping out all night" and "were shabby" and "begrimed." Scott's appearance did not surprise the *Picayune* editor. "It was nothing but vanity that induced Gen. Scott to thus make himself conspicuous; it was characteristic of the man, and he could not help it." Kendall wrote that Scott "always richly deserved" his nickname "Old Fuss and Feathers." Kendall sat on horseback with General Worth and his staff watching the flag-raising ceremonies in the Grand Plaza. The correspondent was disgusted to hear Scott refer to the Mexican crowd as "our Friends." Convinced the fighting was over, Kendall told Worth that he "was done with glorious war's alarms. . . . It was not my vocation." When Worth expressed doubt that Kendall could resist the excitement, the editor vowed "never again [to] put myself in the way of whistling bullets in foreign countries." Within moments, however, Kendall and the other Americans were under attack again, this time by mobs of criminals and *leperos* (beggars) who had been released from the city's prisons by the fleeing Santa Anna.[6]

The result was sporadic, daylong street fighting against the Americans, forcing Worth to have dragoons, infantry, and cannon fire sweep through the city's streets and into buildings. "Many innocent people have doubtless been killed during the day," Kendall reported, "but this could not be avoided." Several more days of "assassinations" followed before American control was completed. "The fault lies partially with our own men, who straggle from their quarters and get intoxicated at the first . . . grog shop," Kendall wrote. The fact these men were being murdered "shows that a feeling of revenge and deep hatred [remains] against us."[7]

After the war, Kendall praised the final Mexican resistance. "Piles of dead among the rank and file, found behind many of the ramparts they had unsuccessfully defended gave evidence that they had resisted to the last," he wrote. But, in the final analysis, he believed, "The bayonet, which tries the stuff that soldiers are made of, found them wanting . . . for with this weapon many victories in Mexico were gained." At Chapultepec, he observed, the Mexicans' strong position and "passive courage" allowed them to hold off a day of heavy American bombardment. "But when the determined opponents scaled [Chapultepec's] walls, and jumping in among them put the bayonet to its work, their resistance was over."[8]

James Freaner also witnessed the daylong bombardment of Chapultepec on September 12. He reported the Mexicans' guns at first answered with "much rapidity and precision." As the day wore on, however, the American shells destroyed the castle's edifice and parapets, exposing most of the defending troops. "Our guns proved to be very destructive," Freaner related, "as we found after the work was taken 500 dead men unburied but thrown in ditches. The building was completely riddled." On the same day, Freaner watched as the army engineers scouted the Mexican defenses in order to provide information for Scott. The correspondent gushed, "The Engineers, throughout all operations, have performed a most dangerous and laborious duty. They have proved themselves to be men of sterling worth—of masterly ability, and bright ornaments of their profession."

When the early-morning assault on Chapultepec started, Freaner was with General John A. Quitman's division, which attacked from the southeast. He described the scene as Quitman handed an American flag to the officers leading the first assault unit. The general explained that it had been used to "conquer Seminoles, Black Hawks and Mexicans," urging that it be planted on Chapultepec. "Those colors were the first that waved over the Castle of Chapultepec," Freaner claimed. The assault was so intense and involved, the correspondent could only note, "A thousand heroic deeds were acted at all points, to refer to which I have no space, nor could words have power to describe them." After Chapultepec fell, Freaner advanced with Quitman's division as it battled along the southwestern aqueduct toward the city. At one point he was standing with Quitman, Generals James Shields and Persifor Smith, and other officers when a shell burst over their heads, knocking them all to the ground. "No one received any injury except by the fall," Freaner reported, "among them . . . your humble servant."

By early evening the Americans reached the city gates, Freaner accompanying Lieutenant P. G. T. Beauregard (later of Civil War fame). It was a hectic day for both, particularly as Beauregard was in the engineers and frequently had to scout Mexican defenses before the American forces attacked. At one point Freaner reported, "I saw [Beauregard] complete his reconnaissance of the [main city gate] after he had received two severe contusions." This vantage point also put Freaner in harm's way. At one spot a spent bullet struck his horse's saddle but caused little damage. Again he was knocked "head over heels" by an exploding shell. "Being in a hurry to pick myself up I trod on an officer, who said I had no business being there anyhow."

On the afternoon of September 13, as the Americans pushed toward the city from two directions, Freaner reported they "met with a decided and stubborn resistance . . . so hot that they were compelled temporarily" to halt. Again, the American batteries "hurled the shot and shell about the ears of the enemy a little hotter than they desired," and the advance resumed, Worth taking the northwestern gate and Quitman the southwestern gate. Freaner witnessed the final assault at the southwestern gate, where the Mexicans' "firing was so heavy, both from small arms and artillery, that it was deemed prudent to carefully reconnoitre [sic] before attacking." The correspondent watched Beauregard and two other lieutenants go forward, then report the situation to Quitman. American infantry were sent forward "for the purpose of picking off the artillerists, which they did . . . with the same success and accuracy as one of our southern or western men would shoot squirrels." When the Mexicans attempted to move their cannons back from the firing, they were rushed and overwhelmed, the *Delta*'s correspondent wrote.

Early on the morning of September 14, Freaner entered the city with Quitman's and Smith's units and marched to the central Grand Plaza "under a fire directed upon us from the tops of the houses." Freaner beat Kendall into the heart of the capital because Quitman ignored Scott's orders and marched to the plaza and was first to raise the American flag over the National Palace. Worth, following orders, stopped short of the plaza. He was almost shot at that point as he, Kendall, and others in his command came under sniper fire. Soon after, Freaner watched as "Gen. Scott and Staff, in full feather, escorted by the Cavalry, entered the city, amidst the huzzas of the soldiery on all sides." An army band added "Hail Columbia" and "Yankee Doodle" to the general's arrival, Freaner noted. But the fighting resumed. "Throughout the 14th, and on the morning of the 15th, the Mexicans continued to fire from the corners and tops of the houses, killing some and wounding many," Freaner reported. The U.S. artillery was "ineffective" in this situation "owing to [the Mexicans'] concealed position." Finally, "the deadly fire of the [infantry] picked them out from their hiding places when they least expected it," Freaner wrote. "The Mexicans were very much mistaken when they came to engage the [infantry] on the house-tops."[9]

From their descriptions, it is clear Kendall and Freaner were under frequent fire, and both suffered minor injuries in the final assault. Kendall did not mention the incident, but Freaner filled in the details. Kendall's injury was not considered serious, Freaner wrote, "as the ball struck him right plumb in his horse's ear and at the present he looks to be in as fine health and spirits as I have ever seen him and as well as a 'war-torn soldier' might expect to be." After the *Delta*'s account appeared, the *Picayune* explained, "[Kendall] was slightly wounded . . . by a musket ball in the knee, but the injury was so slight that we would not have mentioned it if [the *Delta*] had not."[10]

General Worth's official Mexico City battle report to the War Department noted Kendall was wounded while carrying orders during the fighting and said he "exhibited habitual gallantry, intelligence and devotion." Worth, increasingly mindful of presidential prospects at home, also cited Kendall in his official report about the fighting at Molino del Rey. Dated September 10, the general's comments included, "I have to acknowledge my obligations to . . . G. W. Kendall, Esq., of Louisiana . . . who came upon the field, volunteered [his] acceptable services and conducted [himself] in the transmission of orders, with conspicuous gallantry."[11] During the fighting at the city's gates, Worth's attention also was attracted by the sharpshooting of another man. When the general rode over to compliment him on his shooting, he asked, "What regiment do you belong to?" "None sir," replied Charles Bugbee, Kendall's express rider. "I belong to the press."[12]

With all of his reports of the fighting from September 8–14 completed, Kendall supplemented his packet of letters to the *Picayune* by including Mexican newspapers, captured documents, and a daily diary he had kept since August 30. "In the main I believe I was correct in my surmises, although not always right," he closed. The battles over, Freaner also settled down in camp: "Now, having taken a bath, brushed off the smoke and dust of battle, and between good liquor, good segars and a moderate share of the balance of the good things of the world 'am as comfortable as might be expected under the circumstances.'"[13]

With the fighting ended, both correspondents faced the difficult problem that occurred frequently after the war's major battles. The American forces were so exhausted and stretched thin that they could not immediately organize courier escorts to the rear. Sending single riders, or small groups, was too dangerous. As a result, Kendall and Freaner prepared duplicate copies of their letters. Their fears were justified: Freaner lost at least two dispatches that contained his first detailed letters regarding the fighting at Molino del

Rey. Kendall lost four riders. Freaner's Molino article finally reached the *Delta* seven weeks later through a chain of circumstances. His messenger, carrying it to Veracruz, was captured by guerrillas and the letters taken. They turned up in a Mexican paper, *Nacional*, at Atlixco. They were reprinted in the *Arco Iris* at Veracruz. The *Delta* commented, "Our Mexican friends are welcome to them; they have read a better account of the battles than any furnished by their own [people]." Freaner, the paper noted, had sent a duplicate summary of the battle. The road to Veracruz was so hazardous for the express riders that a number of officers in Zachary Taylor's northern army believed the news of Scott's Mexico City victory would get to New Orleans faster by way of Monterrey than Veracruz. The *Picayune*'s Jack Durivage, stationed at Buena Vista in the north, had so much confidence in Kendall's express system that he won a new hat by betting who would win the race with the news. He wrote to the paper's New Orleans office, "You will be kind enough to give the *Chapelerie Parisiene* an order for a hat as I intend to appropriate my winnings to that laudable purpose . . . if I succeed in bringing home a head to put it in."[14]

After the long wait and anxiety regarding the outcome at Mexico City, the New Orleans papers were not sure they had the verification when it finally arrived. The first Mexican rider with news of Scott's victories reached Veracruz on September 18. This report appeared in the Spanish-language Veracruz *Sol de Anahuac* on September 20, but it was garbled.[15] Meanwhile, F. M. Dimond, the American collector at Veracruz, received a message regarding the victories via an express rider from the city of Orizaba. Following the same pattern by which Dimond was first to learn about Contreras and Churubusco, the three-paragraph message said simply that Scott had taken Chapultepec and Mexico City. Vouching "for its authenticity," the *Picayune*'s Veracruz correspondent Daniel Scully packed the short message into a bundle of Kendall's prebattle letters, which he forwarded to the paper. At the same time, the *Delta*'s Veracruz correspondent, identified only as "Alpha," also forwarded Dimond's report. Both shipments reached New Orleans on September 25. The newspapers immediately issued extras; they followed with more complete accounts the next morning. Each paper used caution in presenting the reports of victory, the *Picayune* explaining: "They are brief, but sufficient to satisfy the public curiosity and allay the anxiety for the fate of the army."[16]

A number of factors complicated the issue for the New Orleans press: The city was still recovering from the severe yellow fever epidemic; ship arrivals from Veracruz had been infrequent for more than a month because of heavy military shipments; and a large tropical storm had blanketed the Gulf of Mexico. "The great news from Mexico City came . . . just when it was least looked for," the Charleston *Courier*'s New Orleans correspondent explained. "In fact, the only reliable basis for it is the [Orizaba] letter [to Dimond] which consists of a half dozen pithy lines."[17]

Also confusing the New Orleans editors were the numerous incorrect, misleading, or partial reports they had been receiving for more than a month. Additionally, there was the traditional pattern of handling news, which led the papers to print verbatim almost every item they received, using little explanation, interpretation, or follow-up. Further, the contemporary method of presenting news chronologically—regardless of an item's importance—often buried critical events. Finally, in the same September 25 shipment, the *Picayune* and *Delta* received long, detailed reports from Kendall and Freaner regarding the earlier fighting. The eyewitness reports, as usual, received preferential treatment. As a result, the Dimond letter and the Mexican newspaper reports recounting the fall of Mexico City were buried by both papers in an entire page of Mexico news.[18]

The *Picayune* extra was soon in the hands of the express riders and reached Charleston on October 1. "It is still very disjointed news," the *Courier* complained. This time the telegraph worked from Petersburg northward, and the Washington *Union* and other northern papers ran a telegraphic summary from the September 26 *Picayune* in their editions of October 3. "This bulletin flew about with the velocity of lightning throughout the city," the *Union* observed. For the people and papers in the North it now became a case "of watching nightly for the *Sun*'s ponies."[19]

On October 5 the *Picayune* carried another letter from Daniel Scully at Veracruz that stated, "The information which I sent you [previously] that Gen. Scott has entered Mexico has been fully confirmed today, but with few additional particulars." Scully closed the letter by informing the paper that "Mr. Kendall has sent down four other couriers since he left Puebla, none of whom have reached here." On October 7, after a week's delay due to storms, the steamer *Fashion* finally was able to clear Veracruz, carrying with it the eyewitness Mexico City battle reports from Freaner and Kendall. The mail reached the *Picayune* and *Delta* in time for them to publish extra editions on October 13. They printed fuller accounts October 14 and 15.[20]

The news reached Charleston October 18 and Petersburg on October 20. A telegraphic report from Petersburg dated "October 20, 8 A.M." informed the northern press that confirmation had arrived. It was put on the wire by the Baltimore *Sun*'s express rider, who stopped long enough at Petersburg to wire the paper the main details. The express, with full accounts from Kendall and Freaner, reached Baltimore that night, and by the next day their letters had been distributed throughout the Northeast.[21]

CHAPTER EIGHTEEN

Backlash

*In order to discriminate justly, he who reads the descriptions of
the battles should bear in mind constantly that these accounts are
written by partisans, officers, lovers of war—and the accumulated
horrors of a battlefield are glossed over by fine phrases and
sonorous military technicals* [sic].
—Claremont (N.H.) *National Eagle* editorial,
September 24, 1847[1]

With the arrival of the Mexico City coverage by Kendall and Freaner, a new round of quarreling broke out in the political press over who had done the best job. For the most part it was limited to a handful of proadministration papers, principally the Washington *Union*, Boston *Post*, Nashville *Union*, and the *Delta*, with the *Picayune* defending Kendall. The *Union* renewed the attack on October 21, the same night Kendall's letters arrived in Washington. The paper noted it was running Kendall's reports ahead of Freaner's because they arrived first: "We take this occasion, however, to enter a caveat against those portions of Kendall's letters which do gross injustice to the Administration. We are sorry to see his party feelings prompting him to misrepresent its course." What rankled the *Union* most was Kendall's comment that the administration had offered Santa Anna a "bribe" in order to open peace negotiations: "He is grossly illiberal in attributing 'bribery' to the Administration."[2]

Kendall made only a passing reference to a bribe attempt in his letter, but the allegation became a national issue a month later through a letter printed in the St. Louis *Republican*. The letter was from the *Republican*'s Mexico correspondent, "Gomez." Former Illinois editor George T. M. Davis used the pseudonym while serving on the staff of General James Shields of the Illinois Volunteers. In the controversial letter, Davis reported Scott and Trist proposed to offer Santa Anna a $1 million payment to speed peace negotiations. Following the advice of British diplomats, they felt it was justified if it ended the war without more casualties. At a secret meeting, Scott polled his generals for their opinions. They split widely; Shields strongly opposed the idea and later was assumed to be the source for Davis's account of the meeting.[3] Although written in early August, the letter was delayed by the guerrilla disruptions and did not appear in the St. Louis paper until November 22, 1847. Its publication came at a time of great tension between Scott and the administration and added to their political dispute.[4]

Shields vehemently denied he was Davis's source. At an army court of inquiry in June 1848 Shields gave a weak defense for Davis, telling the judges, "I have no knowledge that he is the author." Shields continued that he had written to Davis "charging him with being the author—pointing out the dishonorable light in which it placed his character." Shields said he told Davis the letter also "implicated [Shields] in some degree" regarding leaking the information. Davis replied, Shields said, "that he had neither written or forwarded the article."[5]

Davis's source was not Shields, however, but Nicholas Trist; after the secret session Trist had shared his views with Davis. When he later learned of the "Gomez" letter, Trist said he did not know Davis "was one of the class called 'our correspondent.' Else I should have been more reserved on that occasion." Despite the generals' mixed support, Scott and Trist proceeded with the proposal, but it failed after a preliminary payment of $10,000 when Santa Anna changed course.[6]

In the meantime, the Washington *Union* continued its criticism of Kendall's letters. The administration's allegation centered on Kendall's association with General Worth. He was "one of the most industrious" of the army correspondents, "but a whig" and "not as impartial as he might have been," the *Union* complained. In particular, the paper charged, he ignored the contributions of General Gideon Pillow, and his "description of the battle of Chapultepec [was] singularly [meager]." By contrast, the paper pointed out, "Mustang's letters . . . supply many of the omissions and do justice to all the gallant officers." In closing, the *Union* had one more knock for Kendall: "We leave the public to judge of the propriety of these partisan statements. We regret to see it in a gentleman who is a man of letters, and a man of talent, and from whom we expected all the impartiality of a faithful historian of the events he describes."[7]

Noting Kendall's criticism of the government, the New York *Herald*'s Washington correspondent observed, "No man can object to Mr. Kendall's writing them out providing he thus elicits the truth." The *Herald* correspondent charged that President Polk had written a note to *Union* editor Thomas Ritchie directing him not to publish Kendall's letters. Ritchie denied the allegation, stating, "We received no such note, nor such a request in any other form from the President." The Boston *Daily Mail* believed Ritchie was trying to influence national opinion by printing "an extraordinary puff for the letters of 'Mustang,' in which they were pronounced the most graphic and faithful of any written from the Army." In the article Ritchie had argued Freaner's accounts were "more forcible and strike us as even more correct than Mr. Kendall's." Ritchie advised others "to read again and again from the *Delta*" because Freaner's letters covered "the achievement of all generals."[8]

One appreciative reader of the attacks on Kendall was Gideon Pillow. The general called a letter defending him in the Washington *Union* on October 29, 1847, "very energetic and manly." He continued, "It is written with great ability & is withering & blasting to Kendall's character as a chronicler of events. The truth is, that he is a *vindictive Partisan* of forgeries and prejudices so violent that he is incapable of doing anyone justice *except* Worth & I am right glad to see him so *skinned*, & that the public begins to understand him."[9]

In early October the Boston *Post* ran a commentary attacking Kendall:

> As the smoke clears away from the late battlefields of Mexico . . . it will be well to review the works of the *historians* of those battles. . . . It is pretty well known [the army] has had in its train a corps of letter-writers mainly, if not entirely, attached to the New Orleans press. This corps of letter-writers are indeed a novelty in the history of modern warfare, and may be regarded as one of the results of modern civilization, or perhaps an anomaly peculiar to American civilization in its present state of development. But while it is a novel element of modern armies, it would be an interesting and useful one, if the individuals constituting the corps of letter writers, were all impartial, high-minded, and truth-telling men.

They were not, the author contended, and implied this included Kendall. The commentary's author cautioned readers not to believe "the *Picayune* correspondent attached to the army" or regular army officers, who "exhibit their jealousy of their rivals . . . belonging to the volunteers." The *Post*'s attack demonstrated a vexing problem for Kendall—efforts by proadministration papers to link his reporting to the antiwar stance of many Whig newspapers. When the *Picayune* correspondent, in his Contreras and Churubusco account, made only occasional references to Pillow, Shields, and Pierce, all Democrats, the Washington writer for the *Post* claimed it was part of "a systematic plan on the part of the [Whig] press to misrepresent . . . and libel distinguished democrats who have joined the army." However, the weakness of the attack on Kendall was illustrated by the writer's next point: "Such ungenerous calumny upon brave and honorable men, is equalled in atrocity only by their traitorous support of the cause of Mexico." Although the Boston *Post* article criticized Kendall and accused him of suppressing the truth about Pillow, it conveniently ignored the correspondent's long and consistent support of the war.[10]

In November, another commentary in the Boston paper renewed the conspiracy allegation against Kendall. It was "an attempt unworthy of the writer to injure" General Pillow, the paper contended. The Nashville *Union*, which used long portions of Kendall's letters throughout the war, reprinted the attacks from the Boston and Washington papers, the editor adding, "probably every reader of the army correspondence of the *Picayune* has come to the same conclusion. And we take occasion here to say that the 'Mustang' letters of the Delta are not only the best written letters . . . but they are also the most reliable."[11]

In December another attack on Kendall in the Washington *Union* called him a "camp follower . . . without a glimmer of military knowledge." The writer admitted Kendall's letters "have attained a degree of popularity and many have considered him oracular in all matters of fact and opinion about which he has chosen to write." Thus, "his editorial correspondence from [Monterrey onward] began to attract attention; but however it may have increased the *money* receipts of the Picayune, it added little to his reputation as a candid writer." This was because Kendall lived at the headquarters of a specific general (Worth, without being named) and represented the "sentiments and peculiar prejudices of [an army] clique." The writer continued, "It was notorious that his letters [were] to pay back the flatteries which had been lavished upon him, and to compensate the favors and familiar attentions he has received." As a result, "Kendall's letters have long been looked upon by the army as fictions—sometimes amusing enough, but not to be fully relied upon." They were part "of a system of persecution" against Pillow. "Through General Pillow the enemies of his administration seek to wound Mr. Polk." The criticism concluded, "It remains to be seen whether the fame of a gallant *American,* won on desperate and immortal battle-fields, can withstand the puny assaults of the venal and prostituted pen of a scribbler in his Camp."[12]

The *Picayune* provided a strong defense of Kendall. On October 21 the New Orleans paper stated it had run Kendall's letters exactly as he had sent them, had republished "almost every line" the *Union* had printed about the Mexico battles, and had incurred extra expense to have engravings made of the battlefield maps for its readers. The paper said it republished many letters about the battles from other papers "from a desire to justify the original report we gave from the pen of Mr. Kendall. . . . Yet we are charged with the suppression of the truth." The *Picayune* presented a number of rebuttals to the *Union*'s charges, arguing repeatedly the official military record sustained Kendall—and that history would, too.[13] "We are not required to come to the rescue of Mr. Kendall's character as a historian," the *Picayune* retorted, contending his battle reports "stand, in the main, side by side" the army's official reports. The *Picayune* pointed out the "Gomez" letter vindicated Kendall's earlier report of the bribe proposal. Kendall did not deny being a Whig, "far from it," the *Picayune* reported, "but he does deny that he allowed his party predilections" to warp his judgment about the war. "He has been accused of unfairness and partisanship because he could not discover any astounding military genius in Gen. Pillow," the paper noted. Not only did the Polk administration want Kendall to support its war policies, "but he must endorse and swallow Pillow, too, a gulp we opine even the editors of the Union and the Boston Post by this time have found it difficult to digest."[14]

In truth, both Kendall and Freaner received considerable national recognition for their letters. Many editors did not buy the administration's contention that Kendall's work was politically inspired. Leading penny-press editors used his reports extensively and quoted his opinions about the war and peace prospects. "He writes those admirable letters from Mexico," the Cincinnati *Enquirer* observed, "and appears to be at every point there is a battle, on hand for any thing of interest to be gathered." The Albany *Argus* said Kendall's letters "furnish a complete history of the war," explaining why it was using "somewhat copious extracts." "His letters abound in interest," the *National Intelligencer* commented. After quoting his opinion on how to end the war, The Boston *Daily Mail* added, "Mr. Kendall . . . is a keen and generally very correct observer of the events and phases of the campaign." In a moment of insight, an editorial item in the Philadelphia *U.S. Gazette* observed, "Lucky, rich and generous, [Kendall] is uneasy. . . . There is nothing good going on, good for others, that Kendall does not contrive to get ahold of, or into."[15]

Freaner's strong performance in reporting the August and September battles also brought widespread comment in the press. After New Orleans *National* editor Thomas Bangs Thorpe praised Kendall's work, the *Delta* countered, "with no desire to detract from the consideration and praise due to Mr. Kendall for his zealous and active efforts . . . [we have been represented] by a correspondent just as active and authentic." The *Delta* continued: "We appeal to the press of the whole country . . . on the question [if] the *Picayune* has throughout this war exceeded the *Delta* either in the fullness, authenticity or early publication of its Mexican intelligence."[16] Whether in response or not, many editors during fall 1847 and spring 1848 complimented the quality of Freaner's work. The Philadelphia *Public Ledger:* "The best accounts yet published . . . clear and connected. . . . In perusing them, even the reader uninitiated in military terms and movements, can clearly understand the various operations." The Cincinnati *Daily Commercial:* "The [*Delta's*] account is ahead of all others for clearness." Louisville *Journal:* "His letter contains the most intelligent and fullest description of the . . . victories . . . that we have yet seen." Boston *Daily Mail:* His "graphic accounts of the operations of our troops have been read all over the country." The Galveston *News:* "There are some manifest [discrepancies] between [Freaner's] account and that of Mr. Kendall, yet, on the whole, we have thought this to be the most systematic, comprehensive and satisfactory." The Boston *Atlas:* "[Freaner is] the intelligent correspondent of the Delta" and his articles "will be read with deep interest."[17]

Although the *Delta's* most passionate feelings were expressed for the work of Freaner, the New Orleans daily occasionally chimed in on the charges that Kendall was not giving sufficient credit to Pillow. The *Delta's* defense of Pillow was so strong in the eyes of some editors that they referred to the New Orleans publication as "the organ of a certain general." The *Delta* later rebutted "this is a stale calumny" and that other papers "could not say anything more offensive to our feelings." By the end of 1847 the *Delta* and many other proadministration newspapers would have bittersweet feelings about their earlier defense of General Pillow.[18]

For his part, Kendall was preparing to leave Mexico. "The whole seems like a dream," he wrote two weeks after the fighting ended, "yet here in Mexico we are, and masters." Kendall compared the Americans' conquest of Mexico City to that of the Spaniards, concluding "the deeds of Cortes, brave and vigorous as they were, must suffer by comparison." Cortes had better science for his time, Kendall argued. Kendall also was concerned about the best U.S. policy to end the war. Holding a line in northern Mexico, as Freaner advocated, would not work, Kendall believed. Although "preferable to our past milk-and-water policy, [it] will never do, to my humble thinking—we shall be at war with the Mexicans for all time." He wanted Scott reinforced with 50,000 troops. "Then real war should be declared against Mexico, not a quasi, half-and-half state of hostilities as at present . . . follow up blows *with blows*, not with soft words—leave peace commissioners and peace propositions at home . . . let every hard fought battle have a result, which has never yet been the case, and we shall soon have a peace."[19]

Kendall gave this summary of Mexican public opinion: "To nine-tenths . . . the war, as carried on, has been a pastime—to many a harvest. While those immediately on the lines occupied by our troops have made themselves rich by it, it [has not] made them our friends. They, from policy and a species

of patriotism, wish to see the war continued. The people remote from the
. . . strife, in their blind pride and over-weening [*sic*] self-confidence, have no
desire for peace, because they think that any peace would be ignominious."
Additionally, "The rabble of Mexico—of nine-tenths nearly of the population—useless, worthless, abandoned, yet with a happy self-sufficiency that
renders them blind to every disgrace and indifferent to every disaster. With
this population we have to make peace."[20]

Regarding the future of Mexico, Kendall cautioned against speculation:
"A Mexican future in many respects is the darkest of all, and he who can look
into and fathom it must read other stars than those that now shine in her
firmament." Kendall concluded, "You in the United States cannot be made
to feel and appreciate all that stern and unflinching courage has effected . . .
words are inadequate to give even a faint picture of the brilliant [victories]
which have ended in the subjugation of this proud capital." He promised, "If
I live to get home, full and most complete justice shall be done to all [Ameri-
cans] who took part in the glorious achievements."

He left for New Orleans on November 1 in the first military wagon train
to the coast following the fall of Mexico City, ending his direct participation
in coverage of the war.[21]

CHAPTER NINETEEN

The Yankee Press in Mexico City

Nothing is more remarkable or more indicative of the intelligence and education of our people, than the fact that newspapers have been established in every town of importance which has been captured from the enemy. . . . American journals have been busy in imparting information, in combatting crime, in inculcating virtue, in fostering all of the attributes of humanity in the bosoms of the American soldiery and in striving to extend over the benighted territory conquered by our arms, the ameliorating influences of our civilization.
—Secretary of the Navy John Y. Mason, 1847[1]

With the fighting over, important news from Mexico slowed down. "We are sadly deficient in the great staple article and 'staff of life'—news," complained the Charleston *Courier.* The army settled in for a nine-month occupation of the Mexican capital while the diplomats tried to find a peace table. For the Americans it was a frustrating occupation. Mexico's political factions, although they detested the foreign invaders, remained deeply divided by their complex fight for control of the weak, disorganized government. American aspirations, including those of the correspondents, were divided as well: Some hoped for permanent occupation of all of Mexico, some for reform of Mexican institutions, others for withdrawal to a northern Mexico boundary favorable to the U.S. war goals, and most for an early peace and departure. It was clear there would be no major fighting, at least for a while, but the issue of peace or war remained uncertain.[2]

In less than a week after the fighting ended, the printers were again doing what they had gone to Mexico to do—gather news and publish newspapers about the army and its personnel. Scott helped Peoples start another *American Star,* this time in the Mexican capital. By September 20, 1847, six days after the fighting ended, Peoples's first issue was published. "The flag of our country had not yet become easy in its new position on the National Palace before our *Star* was out announcing the success of our arms," Peoples wrote. The new paper started as a biweekly, then became triweekly, and on October

12 a daily. Working with Peoples was James Barnard, his associate from the other war papers. Scott's support came in the form of official printing contracts and supplying army personnel to help publish the paper.[3]

The army still needed paperwork, Peoples found. He reported, "For one month we worked incessantly to furnish the different departments with blank forms and other printing." Despite this income the *Star* never was financially secure, and at one point Peoples and Barnard had to appeal to their subscribers and advertisers to pay $2,500 to $3,000 in back bills to allow the paper to continue. Compared to the many other "war papers," however, the *Star* was the top example of the genre, publishing several thousand copies a day.[4]

One of the first stories to appear in the new *Star* was a first-person account of the hanging of fifty deserters from the American army and the whipping and branding of fifteen more. The story in the *Star* appears written by John Warland, a former Massachusetts editor who had been assigned by Scott to work on Peoples's staff. Warland, also a correspondent for the Boston *Atlas,* was the only major American correspondent to witness the execution of the San Patricio Battalion deserters. One of the war's memorable and controversial events, the hangings occurred soon after the American flag was raised over Chapultepec on September 13. Most of the deserters, primarily Irish immigrants, had accepted cash and land bounties to jump the American army before and after the start of the war in 1846. Their exploits in the Mexican army in the highly effective San Patricio Battalion artillery unit had been a continuing story in American papers throughout the war. Their battalion had been captured, after a desperate stand, during the battle at Churubusco on August 20. Under military regulations of the day, Scott decided those who deserted after the war broke out should be hanged. Those who crossed over prior to the start of the war received fifty lashes, were branded on the face with a *D*, imprisoned wearing an iron yoke until the American army left Mexico, and then drummed out of the service.[5]

The hangings, the *Star* reported, were scheduled at the same time the assault on Chapultepec began. The officer in charge delayed the execution until the American flag was spotted flying over the Mexican stronghold. "In a few moments our colors were raised, and after it was shown to them they were launched into eternity," the *Star* stated. As for their leader, former American army Sergeant John Riley, who had received extensive stateside coverage about his turncoat role, his fifty lashes "were well laid on by a Mexican muleteer," the paper reported. "He did not stand the operation with the stoicism we expected," the *Star* added. Soon after the hangings, Warland interviewed Riley in prison. "He was then confined with others, half striped, and engaged in bathing the red and blue stripes on his back, having just received several hundred lashes." The letter *D* branded on each of Riley's cheeks "gave him an exceedingly unpleasant appearance," Warland wrote. He described Riley as "a tall and very stout man, having a decided military air when in uniform." The deserter was immensely strong, according to the correspondent, "and when under the lash and branding iron remarked, 'Well one thing is certain, no man can bear it better than I.'"[6]

Of all the American correspondents, Kendall was the most outspoken about the hangings. He reported the number hanged at fifty, adding, "and well did they deserve their fate." The prisoners, he noted, "were compelled to stand upon the gallow until the flag they had deserted was flying over Chapultepec, and were then all swung off at the same time. Not one of them complained that his fate was undeserved." Another deserter was recognized among the Mexican prisoners at Molino, Kendall wrote, and "was summarily dealt with" when a former comrade, "to save the trouble of a court martial, at once pitched him into the mill flume and he was crushed . . . by the wheel."[7]

Besides supplying advertising, job printing, and printers, General Scott assigned Warland, quartermaster sergeant in the 9th Regiment (New England Volunteers), to the *Star* as an associate editor. This freed Peoples from the day-to-day editorial responsibility and allowed him to concentrate on the business and production of the publication. Warland, an 1827 graduate of Harvard College, was from Lowell, Massachusetts. He had served on New Hampshire and Lowell and Boston newspapers before joining the volunteers headed for Mexico.[8]

Warland spoke Spanish and was an accomplished writer. Often reflecting his New England perspective, his letters to the Boston *Atlas* during spring 1848 are some of the best of the wartime reporting. They were similar to William Tobey's—long, thorough, descriptive, filled with observations about Mexican culture, daily life, politics, and institutions. Warland felt the occupation would have a liberalizing effect on Mexico, and he urged its government to establish free schools, allow freedom of religion, trial by jury, and to limit the power of the Catholic Church. He later told the *Atlas* he was "not aiming to communicate news, but such political speculations, sketches of manner and other matters . . . I thought might possess interest or novelty for your readers. If I have succeeded in my purpose, I have not written in vain." Warland described himself as a prowar or "Mexican Whig." He was conscious of the growing North-South rift in the American army. There was constant tension over this issue, he said, because so many of the officers were southerners, whereas many enlisted personnel were from northern states. This caused problems for Warland, an outspoken New Englander. When

Peoples arranged with Scott to have Warland assigned to duty at the *Star*, it was handled as a verbal order. Later, when Warland's unit was moved to Pachuca, 70 miles away, the sergeant-editor argued his editing duties relieved him from accompanying it. His commanding officer, Colonel John M. Withers, a West Pointer from Virginia, disagreed. Warland described Withers as "very aristocratic and overbearing, as officers are apt to be, who suddenly find themselves raised to a position in which favoritism alone has elevated them." The dispute reached a climax when Warland wrote a long poem for the *Star* titled "Break New England's Lion Spirit." No one could break the spirit of a New Englander, the poem contended. The colonel apparently got the point. He had Warland reduced in rank, listed as a deserter, and sent troops to arrest him. Warned by friends, Warland managed to be "out of the way" before they arrived. The regiment's southern officers attempted to arrest Warland several times until Scott finally intervened and gave the editor's position official sanction.[9]

Taking advantage of the Americans' resumption of press freedom, the respected Mexican daily, *El Monitor Republicano*, returned on September 28. By the next day the city had a second American newspaper. With its support from Scott, and with Peoples's own political leanings, the *Star* was mildly pro-Whig. It concerned Democrats in the army that they would need a newspaper, too. On September 29 the pro-Democrat *North American* began publication, edited by the talented William Tobey. Though it attempted a daily schedule, the *North American*'s appearance was less regular; it published seventy-seven times between September 29, 1847, and March 31, 1848, when it terminated. It survived long enough, however, to conduct a running six-month editorial war with the opposition *Star* and to fire constant barbs at the municipal government of the occupied city.[10]

The two American papers in Mexico City were an instant hit with the press at home. The New York *Herald* claimed they contained "the romance and the reality of the war." The *Star*, the *Picayune* proclaimed, "is edited with intelligence, spirit and judgement."[11] The Philadelphia *North American* was obviously pleased with Tobey's new publication: "Its looks do great credit to the typographical arts in our sister republic. Mr. Tobey has the ability to make a good paper and we wish him all success." Another Philadelphia newspaper, the *Bulletin*, added its praise: "These papers give us a better idea of the present social, moral and political condition of the Mexican capital than we have been able to obtain from all the army correspondence which has yet appeared in print." The Philadelphia *Pennsylvanian* said Tobey was "an able editor" and "a most intrepid writer." When it received a file of the newspaper from Tobey, the St. Louis *Reveille* praised him "as an enterprising and vivacious fellow . . . a utilitarian." The New York *Spirit of the Times* observed the paper's "typographical appearance and contents do great credit to Tobey's enterprise and literary ability." The Albany *Argus* credited the new paper's appearance to the "spirit and ability" of Tobey, whose "effusions . . . have rendered him somewhat widely and favorably known."[12]

The new papers also proved convenient to the correspondents in Mexico City. The *Picayune*'s Daniel Scully sent batches of clippings from the *Star,* explaining, "you will find in the enclosed extracts from the *Star* all the news worth mentioning."[13] As a result, the New Orleans dailies reprinted large portions of the *Star* and the *North American,* and in turn the rest of the nation's press reprinted portions of that material from the New Orleans paper. Another important feature of the *Star* was its Mexican news. Peoples made arrangements to receive copies of Mexican papers published in cities where American troops were not quartered, in order to gauge the "war or peace" sentiment. This also made the *Star* popular with the American press, and Tobey was careful to add similar coverage to the *North American.*[14]

The *Star* and *North American* found common ground on many issues: reform of local government, improvement of the city's cleanliness and police service, defending treatment of the San Patricio prisoners, urging free education for Mexico's masses, supporting a crackdown on the city's *lepero* population, lifting of taxes on Indians entering the city to sell their goods—and, most of all, defending actions and policies of the occupying army. Like their counterparts at home, the editors also squabbled, criticized and exchanged barbs about their ability, ownership, loyalty, politics, U.S. government policies, Mexico's future, and the U.S. Army and its officers. The editors frequently expressed confusion and doubt about the progress of the peace treaty, even after it was completed. To this was added another contentious issue for the editors: the deepening political rift in the army, which threatened to pull down the generals, their officers, and possibly even some journalists.

Throughout the occupation Tobey remained a distinctive voice on the pages of the Mexico City *North American.* Although continually in financial trouble, the *North American*'s style was more literary than that of the *Star.* One of Tobey's regular items was a feature column called "Sidewalk Musings" in which he related his impressions of the Mexican city. It was written in the personality sketch–style popular with the Philadelphia papers. James Freaner called the column "a literary gem." Tobey also created a fictional character, Reuben, whom he used as the centerpiece for small commentaries he wrote each day about the city's social and political events. "Rube" often had a humorous or satirical observation to make and may well have served as Tobey's alter ego.[15]

Assisting Tobey with the editing chores for a period was Captain Mayne Reid of the New York Volunteer Regiment, later noted as a writer of children's literature. Freaner was offered an editor's position and part ownership, but when he asked to include a friend, Tobey broke off negotiations. He later explained he feared "three would eat up all the income." In February Tobey had a falling out with Freaner, apparently related to the generals' dispute, and they briefly exchanged allegations in public. Also associated with Tobey was his younger brother, Edwin, who operated a bookstore in the same building that housed the paper.[16]

Tobey made his politics clear in a number of letters to the pro-Whig *North American* in Philadelphia. He was not so much pro-Polk or pro-administration as he was pro-army, in the same manner as the New Orleans correspondents. He feared the outspoken campaign against the war by Whig politicians and newspapers would endanger the army. "We care nothing for Mr. Polk, as a man, and if he does wrong we shall not be behind any in avowing it when the proper time comes," he wrote. But, he continued, "whether the war is right or wrong this is not the time to discuss it." The problem, as Tobey saw it, was that the antiwar and "ultra abolitionist Presses and people in our Eastern states give [the Mexicans] great confidence . . . and extravagant notions." As a result, he said, the war was being prolonged. This was wrong, in his opinion, because the army was being endangered by what the Mexicans conceived to be strong opposition in Washington to Polk's policies. The answer, Tobey believed, was for the country to pull together until the war was won, the troops brought safely home, then "if you want to flog Mr. Polk go ahead, but do not cut our throats in the doing of it."[17]

Tobey warned his Philadelphia readers to be careful of reports that the Mexicans and Americans were getting along well in the occupied capital. "Our gentlemen correspondents," he wrote, "with a complacency that is really enviable destroy something of truth, and a great deal of foolscap, in describing [Mexican affairs] yet draw all their materials from fancy." Only the lower classes of the Mexican people were dealing with the Americans, Tobey wrote, and that was primarily for business purposes. As for himself, he told his editors, "I shall portray *Mexico as it is.*" Tobey considered the war an "eccentric war," with the Americans advancing steadily into Mexico holding out an olive branch that no one would accept. The "hand of friendship . . . has always been rejected," Tobey observed, followed by more defeats for "the vainglorious enemy." A "remarkable" and "pleasureable" feature of the war, Tobey believed, was the American newspapers that followed the army. They had "opened the flood gates of light and civilization for the Mexican people," Tobey contended.[18]

* * *

The *Star* and *North American* welcomed the resumption of the Mexican newspapers in the city. "The liberty of the press is the shield of freedom," the *Star* editorialized, "and when Santa Anna endeavored to crush it he made a bold strike at destroying entirely the liberties of the people." The *North American* wrote: "One of the most promising features of occupation by *los Americanos*" was freedom of the press. But both American papers were a bit startled at the aggressiveness of the Mexican editors. "They indulge in the largest sort of liberty, too," the *North American* commented, "and feeling it for the first time revel to their hearts content." The paper urged restraint: "There would be great suffering among the press gang were our army to leave suddenly." Many of the American correspondents were cautious about using the highly political papers as a news source, even though most published portions in English. Nicholas Trist, the U.S. peace negotiator, described it as "a venal Press . . . ever at work to smother the truth, to confound the public judgment, and to cheat our country into believing that the reality, apparent to all eyes here, had no existence."[19]

The Mexican editors did not need lectures from the Americans. They were seldom subdued during the occupation, unless forced by the American authorities. Their tone clearly demonstrated their spirit was not broken, even if the country was occupied, the army defeated, and the political leadership weak. Throughout the occupation the Mexican press tried to influence the Mexican government's decisions, openly criticized their occupiers, attempted to unite the Mexican masses, provided news and regulations of the occupation, served as an outlet for various complaints against the Americans, including alleged mistreatment of the San Patricio prisoners, and added spice to the situation by occasionally reprinting U.S. government documents and correspondents' letters that were captured by the roving guerrilla bands. There were limits to the Americans' tolerance, however, and a number of the papers were closed before the occupation ended.[20]

CHAPTER TWENTY

"First Impressions": Gideon Pillow and the American Press in Mexico

We are our own trumpeters, & it is so much more easy to make heroes on paper than it is in the field. For one of the latter you meet with 20 of the former, but not till the fight is done.
—Robert E. Lee to John MacKay,
from City of Mexico, October 2, 1847[1]

In early March 1848, James Freaner—now nationally known as "Mustang of the *Delta*"—arrived in the busy newsroom of the popular New Orleans newspaper. He was headed to Mexico City, but he needed to retrieve the original copy of a controversial letter that had been sent to the paper from Mexico. He had twice written to assistant editor John McGinnis asking that the original copy be held for him. Dubbed the "Leonidas Letter," it became the central issue in a bitter dispute at Mexico City among the army's principal generals—a dispute that involved presidential ambitions, military honors, the press, and in particular, Freaner, and Major General Gideon J. Pillow.[2]

The letter had appeared in the *Delta* on September 10, 1847. Signed "Leonidas," it was mostly a colorful invention, falsely giving Pillow, President Polk's friend and political associate, full credit for the critical American victories at Contreras and Churubusco the previous month. Before the war, Pillow had been active in Tennessee politics and claimed credit for Polk's 1844 surprise presidential nomination. He participated in battles at Veracruz, Cerro Gordo, Contreras, Churubusco, and Chapultepec, twice was wounded, but overall had a controversial record in the war.[3]

What was left of his reputation in the army was further eroded by the Leonidas Letter. It wrote Commanding General Winfield Scott out of the story. Among its exaggerations was this one:

> During this great battle, which lasted two days, Gen. Pillow was in command of all the forces engaged, except Gen. Worth's division, and this was not engaged; except in taking the last work—(Gen. Scott gave but one order and that was to re-inforce Gen. Cadwalader's brigade.)

Continuing its misrepresentations, some bordering on the absurd, was a description of Pillow allegedly fighting a hand-to-hand battle with a Mexican officer. Pillow reportedly said:

> "Let the honor and prowess of our respective countries be determined by the issue of this combat." The Mexican, a large and muscular man attacked with lance and sword, handled his arms with great vigor and skill but our general was his superior in dexterity and coolness. At last the Mexican made one terrible charge at our general with his lance, which the latter evaded with great promptitude and avidity, using his sword, tossed the weapon of the Mexican high into the air, and then quietly blew his brains out with his revolver. Both the American and Mexican armies witnessed this splendid effort.[4]

How the letter reached the *Delta* was a mystery, and the issue of its authenticity touched off a monthlong dispute in the nation's press. Among the central figures were Pillow, Freaner, and Alexander Walker, newly appointed editor of the *Delta*. Walker, an outspoken Democrat, gave conflicting versions of how the letter found its way into the *Delta*. At first he claimed he had purposely used it to hoax the other New Orleans editors. Months later he said that he had printed the letter "due to public anxiety" for news about the battles at Mexico City. The letter reached the *Delta* early on September 8, 1847, in the same package with Freaner's eyewitness accounts of Churubusco and Contreras.

McGinnis, handling the copy for the *Delta*'s morning edition, set aside the unusual item for Walker's review. Walker decided not to print it, but later changed his mind, believing it contained some new battle details. He also admitted to making some insertions in the copy, which magnified Pillow's role even beyond what already was claimed. Although it clearly was not written by Freaner, Walker said, "We believed it was from Mr. Freaner who had never before misled or deceived us." As a result it appeared in the *Delta* the day following the publication of Freaner's eyewitness battle accounts.[5]

What made the letter contentious was a long-running dispute the *Delta* and the *Picayune* had been conducting about Pillow's military abilities. The argument started in April 1847, after Polk promoted Pillow to major general. The *Picayune* wrote the promotion "was not indicated by the confidence of the army nor the display of any great military abilities." The paper repeated a story that haunted Pillow throughout the war alleging he constructed faulty defensive trenches at Camargo in northern Mexico. "They were the laugh of the service," the *Picayune* stated. After the battle of Cerro Gordo in April 1847, the *Picayune* attempted to be objective about Pillow's wound and reported "personal gallantry." It stated, "We have endeavored to give the facts as we believe them to have occurred and shall willingly modify this statement if it be in any degree erroneous." A request for modification soon came in the form of a letter signed by seventeen officers of the 2nd Tennessee Volunteer Regiment. They charged, "The truth is, the general was ignorant of the grounds and of the enemy's strength and preparations for defense." The embarrassed *Picayune* apologized: "The sympathies of the people were excited on account of a wound which was reported to have nearly severed [Pillow's] sword arm in twain, whilst in fact he carried the ball that hurt him in his breeches pocket." The *Delta*, Nashville *Union*, Washington *Union*, Philadelphia *Pennsylvanian*, and other papers loyal to Polk's administration vigorously defended Pillow.[6]

The appearance of the Leonidas Letter in September renewed the dispute. The *Picayune* attributed Leonidas to Pillow. "We know not who the author may be, but to our minds it bears the indelible impress of Gen. Pillow's genius. We believe as sincerely as we believe anything where the evidence is not direct and positive, that if not written by himself, it was written at his dictation or suggestion."

The *Delta* countered there was no proof that Pillow was involved. A. M. Holbrook, coeditor of the *Picayune*, and William L. Hodge, editor of the New Orleans *Commercial Bulletin*, claimed that they had seen the proof—the original letter to the *Delta*. It had been shown to them by a friend of Walker's. Further, they wrote, Walker reportedly told a number of people that the original was indeed from Pillow and was so wild in its self-praise that Walker toned it down.[7]

Walker attempted to close the dispute in a signed editorial, claiming Leonidas was a hoax: It was all "a very laughable hoax to which the *Picayune* editors fell easy victims." Walker also denied he said the letter was genuine. The editors of the *Commercial Bulletin* and *Picayune*, Walker concluded, were "a pair of editorial sap-heads." In reply, the *Picayune* called Walker's hoax claim a "disgraceful transaction. . . . The scheme was conceived in iniquity and carried through by unscrupulous means and repeated falsehoods." Hodge of the *Commercial Bulletin* was equally outraged. The "miserable and contemptible piece of manufacture" had earned the *Delta* the community's "contempt," he asserted. The *Picayune* flatly rejected the idea of a hoax: "We will not believe that [the *Delta*], the trusted guardians of his fame, have acted so faithless a part towards him as to lend their aid to perpetrate a hoax, the effect of which has been to hold Gen. Pillow up to his countrymen as a mark for their scorn and derision."[8]

Scorn, derision—and political defense of Pillow—followed for months afterward, as newspapers everywhere debated the content, authenticity, origin, and consequences of Leonidas. It became, as the antiwar New York *Tribune* could not resist noting, a case of a general whose "pen is mightier than his sword."[9]

Most Mexican War generals saw the obvious value of working with the army correspondents. George Kendall was favorably mentioned in two of General William Worth's official battle reports and in one of Pillow's. Writers often worked from a commander's headquarters, where there would be better food, tents, and care for horses. Kendall usually camped at the headquarters of Worth, a career officer who became more presidential-minded as the war progressed. The generals were aware of, and some openly discussed, the speculation that they might be presidential candidates. In the three presidential elections following the war—1848, 1852, and 1856—four of the six leading candidates were Mexican War officers, and two, Zachary Taylor and Franklin Pierce, were elected president.[10]

Many commanding officers apparently assigned letter writers, as an officer in the Pennsylvania Volunteer Regiment explained in a letter to a friend. His commander, Major General Robert Patterson, was so incompetent, the officer alleged, that he probably would face charges for "ignorance & tyranny." However, the officer continued, "he has two letter-writers with him, who will blazon his conduct to the people of the U.S. in most flattering language, but he has only adopted the example of Worth, who has Kendall as his eulogist, and Pillow, who, it is tho't, has been written into a political and military death by 'Mustang' and 'Leonidas.'"[11]

At different points of the war, General John E. Wool, second in command to Zachary Taylor in north Mexico, appointed correspondents Josiah Gregg and John E. Durivage as civilian staff aides with pay and privileges equivalent to a major. Colonel Henry Wilson, military governor at Veracruz, was accused of appointing a correspondent as one of his staff clerks "and telling him to bear light" on the colonel's occasional mistakes. A letter from Captain George T. M. Davis, the Illinois editor serving as an aide to General James Shields of the Illinois Volunteer Regiment, demonstrates how letter writers worked. He wrote to the Alton (Ill.) *Telegraph*, "I have no doubt that Gen. Scott's second report . . . to Washington, will do Gen. Shields something like justice; all previous ones having fallen very far short of it."[12]

Polk's peace envoy, Nicholas Trist, scoffed at the practice of Worth and Pillow praising Kendall in their official battle reports. The generals, he noted, did not mention "that he was the correspondent of the Picayune, nor of the 'services' rendered by him in *that* capacity." Trist charged the generals were attempting to obtain popularity "that is fabricated by the process founded on the *first* impression theory, and the staple of which consists of

'Leonidas' stupidity" or "adroitness" in relations with correspondents such as Kendall. In a letter to Secretary of the Treasury Robert J. Walker, Jefferson Davis, a colonel in the Mississippi Volunteers, complained, "We have too many new generals, seeking a reputation for other [political] spheres, as you must have seen by the puffs direct [*sic*] which have filled the news papers in the form of a correspondence, & which bear on every feature the impress of a Mexican atmosphere." Captain Braxton Bragg, later a Civil War general, told South Carolina Governor J. H. Hammond that half the reputations made in the war were from false reports and newspaper misrepresentations. Second Lieutenant Ulysses S. Grant observed, "I begin to see luck is a fortune. It is but necessary to get a start in the papers and there will soon be deeds enough of [one's] performances related."[13]

Not all officers wanted the attention. Captain E. Kirby Smith explained in a letter to his wife: "In truth, there is much discord, all are quarreling about the honors. . . . It is said the generals, too, utterly disagree in their reports, each claiming for their own commands the deeds done by other troops." Smith feared Scott would not be able to "sift the truth from the whole mass of discrepancies . . . indeed, I am induced to believe from what I have already heard that much injustice will be done by his" official battle reports. Regarding the generals' dispute, another officer stationed in Mexico City observed, "Each as I understand it is attempting to get all the glory. Hence each has their letters writers, puffers & each wants to be President—But while they are quarreling Old Rough and Ready will run away with the bone."

When Captain Robert Anderson, an artillery officer, learned that a *Delta* correspondent had mentioned him in a letter to the paper, he told his wife, "I am sorry that he mentioned my name at all, as the custom of recording everyone's deeds has become so common, that it is almost more creditable *not* to be among the distinguished." "Indicator," a naval officer who wrote regularly for the New Orleans *Tropic*, observed that military officers "talked a good deal" about newspaper letter writers. Such writers, he reported, lavished praise on "individuals whose *Military spirit* and *high qualities*" existed primarily in newspaper articles. But "Indicator" believed newspaper articles influenced government decisions on promotions. "The really modest and meritorious . . . officers will not permit their names to be dragged forward in newspaper articles," but they would have to accept the consequences, "Indicator" wrote. "I have observed in the navy that it costs very little to make a man a hero, particularly if *he* be disposed to aid the effort." In wartime, the writer contended, such behavior "is extremely natural."[14]

Kendall and Freaner, in particular, with their well-known newspaper affiliations, faced such approaches. Frederic Hudson, managing editor of the New York *Herald* during the war, later noted, "Kendall's letters, with their 'plunging fire,' were copied every where, and made the reputation of many a gallant officer and soldier, whose name and fame would have been smothered in the musty reports of the War Department." Kendall made no apology for operating from Worth's headquarters. He believed it made his war reporting better.[15]

Cut off from the outside world by the guerrilla forces to its rear, Scott's army in Mexico City remained ignorant of the monthlong feud in the nation's press about the Leonidas letter and its authenticity. On October 22, an explosion of sorts occurred, however, when the Mexico City *American Star* reprinted the letter. The rival *North American* soon followed, and the appearance of the document touched off a bitter dispute among the army's top generals. The dispute, which had presidential ambitions at its roots, pitted Scott, the Whig possibility, against two of his division commanders, Pillow and Worth.[16]

Another root cause was the unsettled issue of army officers' letters reaching the newspapers. After each of the war's major battles, many officers wrote to friends, relatives, and editors at home, describing the participation of the writer or his unit in detail. Secretary of War William L. Marcy and President Polk revived a military order that had not been used for twenty-two years in an attempt to stop the letters. Initially their action was aimed at Zachary Taylor. The order, No. 650, stated:

> 650. Private letters or reports relative to military marches and operations are frequently mischievous in design, and always disgraceful to the army. They are therefore strictly forbidden; and any officer found guilty of making such reports for publication, without special permission, or of placing the writing beyond his control, so that it finds its way to the press within one month after the termination of the campaign to which it relates, shall be dismissed from the service.[17]

Enforcement of the regulation was left to local commanders, who ignored it for the most part. But Scott, not noted for good humor in such situations, was deeply disturbed by the implication inherent in the Leonidas Letter—that credit for the Mexico City victories might not go to him. These concerns became more evident on November 12, when Scott issued his own version of Order No. 650, aimed at barring the letter writing practice:

GENERAL ORDERS—No. 349
Headquarters of the Army
Mexico, November 12, 1847

The attention of certain officers of this army is recalled to [Regulation No. 650] which the general-in-chief is resolved to enforce so far as it may be in his power.

As yet but two echoes from home of the brilliant operation of our arms in the basin have reached us; the first in a New Orleans, and the second through a Tampico newspaper.

It required not a little charity to believe that the principal heroes of those scandalous letters alluded to did not write them, or especially procure them to be written, and the intelligent can be at no loss in conjecturing the authors—chiefs, partisans and pet familiars. To the honor of the service, the disease—pruriency of fame, *not* earned—cannot have seized upon half a dozen officers [present], all of whom, it is believed, belong to the same two coteries.

False credit may, no doubt, be obtained at home, by such despicable self-puffings and malignant exclusion of others; but at the expense of the just esteem and consideration of all honorable officers who love their country, their profession and the truth of history. The indignation of the great number of the latter class cannot fail, in the end to bring down the conceited and the envious to their proper level.

By the command of Maj. Gen. Scott:—

H.L. SCOTT, A.A.A.G.[18]

It was an unusual army general order, to say the least. The second letter to which Scott referred was the "Tampico Letter," so named because the version that reached Mexico City was from the American newspaper *Sentinel* published in Tampico. It had been printed originally in the Pittsburgh *Post* on September 25, 1847. Although quite different in tone from Leonidas, it praised General Worth and Colonel James Duncan for their roles in a key campaign decision to lead the army south around Lake Chalco, near Mexico City. It mildly implied Scott would have taken the wrong road to possible disaster. It was strong enough, however, to rankle Scott. He quickly relieved Worth and Duncan of their duties and ordered a court-martial.[19]

Although he accepted full responsibility for the letter, Duncan was not the author. John Sanders of Philadelphia, a political friend of Worth and Duncan, wrote a campaign narrative based on material in private letters sent to him by Duncan and Lieutenant James Louis Mason and another lieutenant. Sanders sent his rewrite to a friendly editor in Pittsburgh, and the controversy followed. Sanders said the Chalco decision material came "exclusively" from the other lieutenant's letter, adding, "It never in a moment entered my brain that it would be in direct opposition with the subsequent narrative of the same fact in [Scott's] official reports." Sanders told Duncan, "But if your only offense was writing about military operations & allowing the writing to get beyond your control, others are equally implicate—Genl. (Franklin) Pierce's letter to Editor of the Boston Post is a similar offense—Major (William) Turnbull's & Capt. (Robert E.) Lee's letters which were published in the (Washington) Union *before* yours was, are (worse) infractions of the regulation" as they "doubtless" knew of Scott's restrictions.[20]

John Peoples mildly rebuked Duncan on the pages of the *American Star* and criticized the officer's standard defense that such letters were written only for friends and not for publication. When unsuspecting friends published such items they contributed to the errors, Peoples argued, because they "vouched for their correctness" and added "their weight and influence" to the author's contentions. The Tampico Letter dispute, Peoples explained, was "in everyway hurtful" to both Scott and Duncan, "for as every person knows, the first impression is always the strongest and hardest to eradicate." He urged they end the dispute. William Tobey provided Duncan rebuttal space in the *North American,* explaining, "the question had been better settled out than in the newspapers, but when a press assails a citizen he has an undoubted right to defend himself." Duncan responded that he believed he had enough evidence to convince anyone, including Peoples, "whose errors . . . doubtless are only the results of mistaken impressions." Duncan also had a letter he solicited from Kendall verifying the officer's movements at Churubusco. Scott's case against Duncan was dropped and he did not need to make the document public; after the issue died down in summer 1848, Worth advised his artillery officer to "return the Kendall letter."[21]

Another unhappy party in Mexico City was James Freaner. Totally unprepared, the correspondent had received the *Delta* with the Leonidas Letter and a critical letter from his editor, Walker, expressing "dissatisfaction and disgust" that the letter had been included in Freaner's personal mail packet. Freaner reacted indignantly. He immediately went to his friend Trist and "denounced in strong terms" Pillow's attempt to use him. Freaner held the trump card in the official investigation that followed. There were two originals of the published Leonidas Letter, and though proving he had not been involved, Freaner was able to produce both. Freaner recalled having seen the Leonidas Letter, which the *Delta* published. When he went to Trist, he asked for some old papers the diplomat was holding for him. Searching his papers Freaner found the similar Leonidas Letter, complete with Pillow's handwriting on it. It had been given to him by Pillow in August 1847, following the battles, Freaner told Trist. He handed it over to the diplomat. Trist, realizing the political importance of the letter, passed it along to Scott. At that point the commanding general relieved Pillow and ordered a court of inquiry.[22]

* * *

The Leonidas Letter published in the *Delta* on September 10, 1847, became the most famous, but there were, in fact, at least eight Leonidas Letters, seven of which were published. The first six were printed in the Philadelphia *Pennsylvanian*, an ardent champion of the Polk administration. The *Pennsylvanian* letters were all from someone in Pillow's command, giving detailed facts, travel arrangements, and predictions about the division's movements.

The *Pennsylvanian* letters that praised Pillow use the overkill language that characterizes the *Delta*'s Leonidas Letter. One, from Tampico, February 27, 1847, read in part: "[Pillow] is quite a favorite with the army, and beloved by all who have formed an acquaintance with him. He is eager for the contest which is rapidly approaching, and mark the prediction, he will nobly acquit himself in the fight." The second fulsome letter, written April 30, 1847, from Veracruz, following the battle at Cerro Gordo, observed: "In regard to General Pillow's appointment as Major General, the President could not have made a better appointment, or one more acceptable to the Army. . . . His two recent brilliant fights . . . afford the completest proof of his high military talents and eminent qualifications to lead our army."

The writer went on to contend Pillow's charge at Cerro Gordo "was the most daring made in the war with Mexico." Pillow only made the dangerous charge, the writer noted, because General Scott ordered him to do so "and there was no alternative left him but to make the charge, (desperate as it was), or disgracefully retreat and break up the whole order of the battle. General Pillow was not the man to retreat before the enemy." The writer added that the charge turned the tide of the battle, causing the Mexicans to "run up the white flag and surrender." The Philadelphia paper never provided a clue as to the author and did not make a connection between its Leonidas Letters and the *Delta*'s more controversial one. But the language, content, dates and places of origin, and partisan nature of the *Pennsylvanian* suggest a connection. And when the controversy broke, the *Pennsylvanian* was among Pillow's strongest and most consistent defenders.[23]

The eighth and unpublished Leonidas Letter spells out Pillow's motives a bit more clearly and confirms that Major A. W. Burns, Pillow's divisional paymaster, signed the *Delta*'s letters. The unpublished letter was sent to the *Delta* sometime between late September and October 22, 1847. It is signed "Leonidas" and dated Mexico City, September 25, 1847; the content clearly indicates it was written without knowledge of the stateside dispute over the *Delta*'s September 10 Leonidas Letter. Burns added and signed a footnote asking that his name not be used on the published version. The letter started by crediting "the Storming of Chapultepec" to Pillow. "These victories will stand unparalleled in the history of the world," the author wrote, claiming

Pillow and Worth were ready to take Mexico City "but for an order from Gen. Scott . . . to halt." After Santa Anna took advantage of Scott's "ill timed" armistice, "many a brave and gallant spirit in our devoted army paid the forfeit," the letter continued. Then Scott reportedly assigned Pillow to take the Mexican stronghold at Chapultepec, saying "that the safety of our army depended upon it." Pillow is said to reply, "I will take it, Sir, or die upon the field." The letter ends: "Still further honors await him, and the Democracy of the country will, as with his great prototype, the immortal Jackson, render to him that reward which his gallantry and skill so richly merit." And so the fictional Leonidas finally gets to the point, suggesting Pillow, like Jackson, receive the Democrats' presidential nomination.[24]

In addition to his own letters, Pillow wrote to political friends throughout the war urging them to send supportive letters to the *Ohio Statesman* in Columbus, the Washington *Union*, Nashville *Union*, and New Orleans *Delta*. "An article from your pen . . . for the *Union* would do a great deal of good," he told one friend. Letters from another, he said, "would produce an admirable affect upon the public mind." To a third he explained, "You are removed from the scene of excitement & neither your position will attract observation, nor your feelings be suspected." He urged the friend to use material from the official army reports about "the successful and daring assaults upon Chapultepec." He closed, "The columns of [these papers] are all open to you as I am persuaded, & the enemy will quail under your vigorous pen."[25]

When he realized the embarrassing Leonidas story was about to break in Mexico City, Pillow attempted damage control. He invited John Peoples of the *American Star* to his headquarters and denied all involvement. The editor was reminded that Pillow would be in charge of the army if Scott went home. The statement was an indirect threat, as Peoples well knew, because the editor was dependent upon Scott's army patronage. However, Peoples rejected Pillow's attempt to influence him and published the letter. Pillow's situation grew complicated as more and more officers were shown copies of Freaner's original Leonidas Letter with Pillow's handwritten additions on it. In a meeting with Major General John Quitman, who asked him about rumors that the writing on the letter was his, Pillow replied vaguely that he had never denied his own handwriting. He changed the subject by asking Quitman to intercede for him with Scott.[26]

In a letter to Polk, Pillow complained that Scott's charges "are one tissue of slanderous and [scandalous] falsehoods, which he knows he can't prove unless he proves *lies*." Pillow told the president, "[my] only offense consisted in having indiscreet friends whose partiality betrayed them into the folly of giving us more credit than was *pleasant*" to Scott. Pillow insisted Scott's charges occurred because he was defending the honor of Polk and the country. Apparently forgetting Polk had reinstituted Regulation 650, Pillow wrote:

"Even if I had written [the letters], it is no offence [*sic*]which can be punished because that provision of regulations is clearly and manifestly in violation of the Constitution and Bill of Rights. Congress itself has no power to prohibit a man or officer from writing the truth about *anything* and *everything*."

In a letter to another friend, Robert Reynolds, Pillow explained, "It all grows out of Scott's infamous Genl. Order No. 349 in which he adopted & acted upon the Slanderous comments of the Picayune." Despite all his troubles, Pillow found time to write to Polk seeking a commission for William Tobey, editor of the Mexico City *North American* and one of his key supporters. In the letter, Pillow explained: "[He] is a man of fine talent and sound judgement & *principles*. . . . He now edits, with unusual discretion & ability, the *North American*, which is the only check we have here against the slanders & factious assaults of the dirty sheets. . . . I do not make this application as a mere matter of form. *I desire it*."[27]

Writing from Mexico City on October 29, George Kendall of the *Picayune* reported Pillow's reaction to Leonidas. The general denied any involvement, Kendall wrote, and "says distinctly that he had no hand in the precious document." The correspondent pointed out that all of the other generals appointed about the same time as Pillow—Quitman, Shields, Persifor Smith, Pierce, and George Cadwalader—all "get along smoothly," yet Pillow "is eternally involving himself in difficulties" and "has made himself . . . the laughing stock of the army." Why is that, Kendall asked, then answered:

[Pillow] has the vanity to believe himself a great and most astounding military genius and the impudence to trumpet his own exploits; it is because he has a grasping ambition and a dishonest one—an ambition which diligently seeketh to build a reputation for himself even at the expense of others; it is because he has the effrontery, time and again, to pester not only his own officers but editors with stories of his prowess, and with bold requests that they might assist in spreading his deeds before the world; in short, it is because he has a restless and feverish desire and craving after all the honors of a campaign . . . with the insufferable weakness to believe that he is deserving of them.[28]

In another twist, the *Picayune* received a letter in which paymaster Burns took responsibility for the Leonidas Letter. He stated, in part: "I am the author of the letter as it originally appeared in the Delta. Gen. Pillow never saw the original, certainly never corrected it, nor did he ask me to write it. He is in no way responsible for it."

Burns implied he was late making this admission because he thought Pillow's earlier denial of involvement would end the issue and that he did not realize the Leonidas Letter was part of Scott's official charges against Pillow. Burns added he did not intend to take credit from other officers and that "the great fault which has been found with the production" was because it was the "first echo" from the army after the battles. The *Picayune* explained it published Burns's letter in fairness to Pillow but that the court in Mexico City would have to decide the general's innocence.[29]

The court finally convened on March 15, 1848, with Freaner as a key witness. He gave his account: On about August 23, 1847, several days after Contreras and Churubusco, he was compiling a list of killed and wounded when a message came inviting him to Pillow's headquarters. Arriving there, Freaner met Pillow and General Pierce. Pillow introduced him to Pierce as "our friend." Pillow then told Pierce he was "going to make the *Delta*" with its coverage of the battles. Freaner replied no one person could make a newspaper's reputation. Unperturbed, Pillow invited Freaner to have a drink and ordered an aide to prepare a casualty list for the reporter. Pierce departed and Pillow offered the correspondent dinner, a bed for the night, and a place to keep his horse. It was all a great temptation, Freaner admitted, because of the day's rain and the general difficulties of gathering accurate details after a battle.

At this point Pillow produced the Leonidas document. Freaner glanced at it, then told Pillow he was sending off only a general summary of the battles with the first courier and would send a more detailed story later. Pillow replied that he had prepared the letter for the reporter and was "anxious" that it go off with "the first impressions." Freaner told the court he again looked at the document and saw many misstatements in it. Without making a commitment to use it, Freaner offered to take the letter, and Pillow turned it over.

Freaner put the letter aside and did not see it again until receiving the *Delta* with the Leonidas Letter in it. He dug out Pillow's original and found "they were twin brothers."[30]

Trist also received a note from Pillow at about the same time, with the same paper, ink, and handwriting as Freaner's copy of Leonidas. Signed by the general, the message read: "Will Mr. Trist do me the favor of having the enclosed letters go by the morrow's courier. I have a *direct interest* in their going." An appended sentence added, "But do send them if possible. They are *all for my benefit*."[31]

After receiving the *Delta* with the published letter, Freaner told the court, he was summoned again to Pillow's headquarters. The general asked him if he still had the original letter. Freaner said he did, and Pillow asked him to return it. He reminded the correspondent that the editors of the *Delta* had told Pillow "that [Freaner] was a man who could be relied on." Pillow said he "should deem it a violation of friendship" if Freaner did not return it.

Freaner said he would contact Pillow later; that night he sent a note to the general stating that he had decided to keep the original. At the same time Freaner wrote asking the *Delta*'s editors to save the copy of the published version for him.[32]

Peoples also testified. He told how Pillow had approached him regarding the *American Star*'s republication of the Leonidas Letter at Mexico City. Peoples had wondered why Pillow often "had attempted to cement" a friendship between them. Nevertheless, he did consider the general a friend and was not surprised when he received a summons to go to Pillow's headquarters. "He solicited, aye, even sought to purchase our aid in giving credence to the romancing" of the Leonidas Letter, Peoples later wrote. Pillow told Peoples, "I never forget my friends or forgive my enemies." Peoples refused the request, however, and when the editor "treated the production in the manner it merited," he was not disappointed it "severed the bond of friendship" with Pillow.[33]

Because of his testimony, Freaner was criticized in a number of proadministration newspapers. The correspondent did not appear too disturbed, but after reading critical remarks in the Vicksburg (Miss.) *Sentinel,* he wrote: "Let them call me anything that suits their vivid imaginations, unless they say *whig*—if they call me a whig 'give them jessie,' for that's what I won't stand." As for his relationship with Pillow, Freaner said, realistically, "General Pillow has not forgotten the value of the press nor the press the value of General Pillow." Showing its irritation with the attacks on Freaner, the *Delta* stated: "The difference between Mr. Freaner and many other of our heroes, is, that he has received nothing for his services, whilst they have been well paid in money, as well as in public consideration and popular applause." Regarding the court investigation, the *Delta* stated, "Whatever proceeds from James L. Freaner 'will be the truth, the whole truth and nothing but the truth.'" It added, "The issue of veracity being raised between General Pillow and Mr. Freaner, the latter very properly and prudently" kept the letter, which served as his defense.[34] The Boston *Daily Mail* observed that President Polk "seems to have taken special pains" to have Pillow meet Freaner and "enlist his pen, so that the first and graphic accounts of the battles, which ever make the strongest impression, should not all redound to the glory of Gen. Scott." Pillow found "'Mustang' was not to be bought." Instead, the paper explained, Freaner's "object was to give a faithful and truthful narrative [because] he was a gentleman of probity and honor."[35]

The hearing dragged on for weeks. Scott and Pillow called numerous witnesses to counter each other's claims. Pillow admitted he had handed Freaner a copy of the Leonidas Letter and had written some corrections on it. He denied original authorship, however, or putting it into Freaner's mail. Two members of Pillow's staff supported the general's version. A clerk, Jacob D. Heistand, claimed he was the author of the first draft, which he said he wrote from rough notes about the battles he found on Pillow's desk. Major Burns said he had found and copied Heistand's version, and signed it "Leonidas." Both Heistand and Burns said Pillow did not author or see their versions. Under cross-examination by Scott, Burns refused to say if he had written other letters to newspapers about Pillow, on the grounds it may "tend to criminate [*sic*] me." The court upheld his refusal to answer the question.[36]

John Warland, writing to the Boston *Atlas*, observed, "Major Burns claims the authorship of the letter, but there are many who doubt whether he has the capacity enough even for the composition of so [sophomoric] an essay as that." Warland believed Heistand was the probable author. Pillow's orderly, a friend of Warland's from the New England Volunteer Regiment, said that Heistand admitted that he had written the letter and that "*Major Burns requested the favor of copying it.*" Thus Burns "could very well swear that he *wrote* 'Leonidas,' and yet after all be a mere transcriber of another's composition." By copying Heistand's original, Burns also could swear Pillow "never saw *his* letters." Warland said Burns's motive was to get Pillow's help in obtaining a promotion.[37]

Peoples was an intense observer of the hearings. He wrote, "It is all rich, rich, rich; and it will all tend to give the 'Modern Gideon' a notoriety which he doubtless thinks a man had better have than to have nothing at all." Scott had won on the battlefield, but he could not beat Pillow in the courtroom. Pillow was continuing his efforts "to create an *impression* at home," Peoples reported. The American public has "been gulled once by a 'first impression,' from [Pillow] and they should be careful that the dose is not repeated," Peoples cautioned.[38]

There never was a clear explanation of how the Leonidas Letter got into Freaner's mail parcel. The *Delta*, perplexed, said it must have been "hocus pocus." Burns claimed that he managed to get it into Freaner's mail bag in the guise of a private letter.[39]

In another contradiction, Burns and the *Delta*'s Walker each insisted on having made the same additions to the published Leonidas. On the question of the insertions, Walker explained, "[They] were made by the editor of this paper in exercise of the prerogative which all editors claim and exercise" to improve correspondence. After Walker testified, Peoples wrote from Mexico City: "The Army people don't understand Walker of the *Delta* admitting to putting in the interlineations, because he put down one event which [Pillow] introduced evidence to prove did take place—and right lustily did his witnesses swear to it too." By the time the court finished its hearings, Walker had a different view of Pillow. He wrote to Nicholas Trist:

Pillow had it all his own way. Gen. Scott should have insisted on personal cross-examination. Pillow is in high feather; and, backed by the office holders and many toadies (in New Orleans), has cut quite a dash. I have no more doubt that he was the author of Burns' letter than I have that I am the writer of this. They say that the examination of any of the Burns' private letters will show that it was a moral and physical impossibility for him to have written Leonidas.[40]

The various parties stuck by their conflicting statements. The court returned to the States for more testimony, and dragged on into the summer of 1848, finally acquitting Pillow of all Scott's charges. A satisfied President Polk hosted Pillow at a White House dinner, while Scott returned to his New Jersey home ill and without public celebration of his achievements in Mexico.[41]

The Leonidas dispute was a dark chapter of the Mexican War for the press and the military. Pillow's attempts to influence the reporters with offers of aid and favors foreshadowed a practice that became more widespread during the Civil War. But for Pillow, the effort failed. He did not achieve the reputation as a war hero that he sought, and his later attempts at political and military achievement also failed.[42]

The Leonidas Letter is instructive about the press at the time. The emerging penny press responded aggressively to reporting the war's events, but the political press also was a factor in shaping the public's understanding of events. Although Pillow attempted to gain the help of Freaner, Kendall, and Peoples, they resisted his heavy-handed and blatant efforts to take credit from other officers. As they had seen the battles firsthand, the correspondents easily recognized and reported about the general's misleading and self-serving letters. At home, however, the political press reported the Leonidas dispute along party lines. Pillow was criticized or defended based on a paper's political view.

For the penny press, standards such as objectivity and fairness were emerging but not yet fully defined or established. Thus, correspondents in the Mexican War could benefit from a general's hospitality, friendship, and access to information yet not feel there was professional impropriety in the relationship. The country's ongoing press-military relationship also needed refinement and definition. Influenced by the prevailing practices of the political press, and their own ambitions, many of the politically appointed officers wrote, or had someone else write, laudatory letters for them. Supportive editors of political newspapers at home printed such letters; penny-press editors were less inclined, preferring to hear from their own correspondents at the scene. The lesson for all in the Mexican War was that first impressions *do* count—but they are not always positive.

CHAPTER TWENTY-ONE

Stereotypes

The American correspondents made frequent comments about Mexican customs and culture. Strangers in a foreign land, much of what they saw was new, different, even exotic from their cultural frame of reference. Priests and Catholic churches often came under critical scrutiny of the writers. Many regularly attended church services and described Mexico's various cathedrals and religious practices at length. Thomas B. Thorpe visited the Matamoros cathedral and observed, "The priest is . . . celebrating mass, the worshipping congregation is impressing, and tempts the heart to join in the solemn service." Most of the worshippers, he wrote, were women, "many of them quite handsome. . . . They kneel gracefully and accidentally as possible expose a fine foot, tastefully set off with a small slipper." Twenty U.S. servicemen in uniform were at the same service, Thorpe reported, "on their knees in prayer, among the most devotional in the house."

John Durivage was more caustic. "Your Mexican cutthroat will murder the victim, and walking into church a few hours after, pop down on his knees, cross himself a few times, mutter a few prayers of which he does not understand the meaning, and come out with the priest's blessing and a conscience as clear as a whistle, ready for the next customer." Durivage continued, "I do not mean to say anything against the true Catholic religion, but against those who only use it as an instrument to encourage evil and keep men in woeful ignorance. Heaven save the country that is ruled by such priestcraft as Mexico."[1]

John Warland of the Boston *Atlas* argued the influence of the church would be diluted by free public education for the masses. What Mexico required "for the establishment of her prosperity upon a solid basis, is the education of the people," he wrote. "Let something like the free American school system be introduced, and another generation . . . will learn to think for themselves, and priestcraft must fall to the earth. Religious toleration will follow." He also advocated trial by jury, religious freedom, and introduction of a "republican impulse."[2]

Mexican women frequently drew the attention of the American correspondents. One night, Christopher Haile, an interested and sensitive observer of Mexican customs, decided to attend a midnight wedding at a

Camargo church. "Will they invite one to kiss the bride?" he wondered. "And if invited, ought a fellow to profit by the privilege? But we will see the bride before we decide these momentous questions." She turned out to be "tall, awkward and plain-looking." Haile concluded, "Nobody, fortunately, was called on to kiss the bride." Haile also wrote, "These Mexicans are a primitive people in their habits," as he described plowing of fields, tortilla making, and washing clothes and drawing water at the river. "I am told by some of my bachelor friends, on whose taste I can rely, that there is always 'a right smart sprinkling' of pretty feet and ankles to be seen on such occasions," he wrote.[3]

In one of his letters, William Tobey described the Mexican women at a fandango (dance) in Jalapa. "The 'ladies' were not remarkable for their beauty, nor were their costumes such as to indicate that they were above the grade called by the Texans, greaseritas." He also was surprised that both men and women smoked "sigaritos" during the dance. "Indicator," the naval officer who wrote to the New Orleans *Tropic* during most of the war, observed, "Their women have a shyness very closely resembling modesty, and some show a soft style of beauty, peculiarly interesting to the stranger. They are said to be less modest than they seem!" Thorpe also made some specific observations about Mexican women: "In the whole of Mexico, in fact in all the Spanish American countries, the women are superior to the men, both in body and mind. . . . It seems, however, to be in the order of Providence, that these women, so justly to be admired, are to become wives and mothers of a better race."[4]

Durivage noted, "There is a peculiar grace in a Mexican lady's manner that cannot be excelled by the French even." Durivage believed Mexicans to be a mix "of good and bad qualities." He rated highest "the great respect and veneration shown by children to their parents . . . and to all appearances they are honestly hospitable people." They were good at bargaining in the market, he noted, and the girls "quite equal ours in their delight at meeting each other. . . . As laborers, the men are proverbially indolent, and behind the age in everything of a labor-saving character." After observing that the Mexican women spent as much time in church straightening their clothes as praying, Durivage added, "They do look most bewitching, sometimes, I can assure you, and when at one portion of the service the poor creatures thump their well developed bosoms . . . it is really quite affecting." He continued, "The women, the lower classes particularly, are always sluttish and slovenly. . . . Beauty among the women . . . is not common." He ended the insult by comparing them to horses with "good gait and small feet."[5]

Most of the correspondents believed Americans had misjudged the Mexicans' character. Former journalist Edward F. Fletcher of the Illinois volunteers, writing to the Alton (Ill.) *Telegraph* at the beginning of 1847, predicted, "The beginning of the end of this war is not yet seen!" He explained, "The character, as well as the country, of the Mexicans is misunderstood—indeed, I may say, unknown—in the United States; and to this fact alone may be attributed many of the errors which have marked the movements of our armies in Mexico." The American government and armies had moved too slowly, Fletcher contended: "Cowardly as the Mexican nation is known and admitted to be, yet it possesses an obstinacy of character, that while yielding, will never submit. The country has to be entirely overrun by our troops; it has to be *occupied* as well as *invaded*, and absolutely *forced to complete subjection*, before terms, such as becomes a nation like ours, to accept, will be offered."[6]

John Peoples, who spent many months in Mexico City observing peace negotiations, wrote, "The Mexicans are diplomists by nature, unscrupulous as to truth, and consequently likely to get the better of men who, fair themselves, believe others to be so. They believe in all probability, that if they can get into another discussion with the *yanquies*, they can best them talking, if they do come out second best in the fighting." He continued, "They are a queer people, these greasers. One hour the political horizon will look bright and clear, and the next dark clouds will obscure it, keeping us, who are unused to such changes, on a constant look out to catch even an idea of what is coming. The same may be said of the press of the country." James Freaner supported this position, noting in one letter, "These people are so fickle that it is impossible, with any degree of certainty, to calculate by their actions today [*sic*] what will be their determination and their policy tomorrow."[7]

Tobey also had strong attitudes about the Mexicans. "They are a queer people," he wrote, "very different from the idea one would form of them by reading their newspapers and the pronunciamentos of their military chieftains." This was because "the masses are ignorant, indolent, barbarous, treacherous and superstitious; given to thieving, cheating, lying, and most other accomplishments that adorn civilized as well as savage humanity; though, if anything, 'a little more so.'" Tobey was particularly unhappy with the letters he read by some of the New Orleans correspondents about the Mexicans' "love for Americans." Nothing was further from the truth, he asserted. Only a small group of businessmen, who "are growing rich upon the money our army is scattering through the country," would deal with the Americans. "While we respect their persons and property they seize every opportunity to plunder and destroy us," Tobey wrote. Inoffensive Americans, he said, "are waylaid and murdered whenever they venture beyond the jurisdiction of our guns." The Mexicans, Tobey informed his readers, "when apparently the most friendly are the most dangerous." Their hatred "is to all

Americans, and they as quickly murder a friend as an enemy, so that he be but an American." People were not sincere about liking "Americans or their institutions," Tobey said. "It is all fudge, and is put forth for objects as unworthy as the intimations are groundless."[8]

Such widespread negative attitudes spilled over to other aspects of the war correspondence. The creation of "villains" was one, particularly Santa Anna and other Mexican generals. After Samuel C. Reid Jr., occasional correspondent for the New Orleans *Commercial Times,* accompanied American officers to meet Mexican General Pedro de Ampudia, he wrote:

> On our presentation to him he merely bowed, standing with his hands in his breeches, with a white jacket on, and an unlit cigar in his mouth, and asked what we wanted, without even extending to us the courtesy of a seat. . . . He was evidently drunk, and no doubt had been, from appearances, beastly so the night before. He is a large man of full six feet, inclined to corpulency, with little shrewd, cunning black eyes indicative of deceit, intrigue and libertinism. . . . There was nothing in his manners prepossessing or pleasing, but, on the contrary, you become disgusted with the man, and feel he is a villain, a tyrant, and a coward.[9]

The term *greasers* was used occasionally by almost all the correspondents. In June 1846, Kendall noted "the Texans have given the Mexicans the cognomen of *Greasers.*" Reid, a New Orleans lawyer who was a friend and traveling companion of Kendall, explained its use: "It was difficult to tell a *mocho* from a *greaser,* or in other words, a soldier from a friendly Mexican. . . . *mocho* is a low Spanish word for foot soldier and the term *greaser* we suppose is a corruption of the word *grazier,* the class of peons or labourers of the country." Kendall indicated the term may have originated from the buckskin clothing worn "by Mexicans of the lower order," which appeared greasy to the Americans.[10] Whatever the source, the term increasingly took a negative tone in the correspondents' letters. In one example, Charles Callahan, who reported for the *Picayune,* wrote from Mexico City in November 1847:

> This afternoon . . . a greaser was whipped in the plaza. He had attempted to kill one of our soldiers, and was sentenced to receive one hundred lashes—twenty-five on every Monday for a month. Nearly ten thousand Mexicans were in the Plaza, and as soon as the whipping commenced they began to throw stones. About a dozen of our dragoons, however, charged upon the mob, when they dispersed in all directions. The greaser was then whipped and taken back to the guard-house.

A similar incident at Mexico City caused John Peoples to comment, "These greasers will have to be taught a severe lesson yet. . . . the best thing for them is a dose of ball and buck, not over the head, but put in straight."[11] Such name calling occurred on both sides. In one letter Kendall noted, "You must have noticed in the Mexican papers of late that the editors have ceased to term the Americans barbarians, infamous usurpers, land robbers . . . and have settled down upon the epithet of *Yankees* as the most approbrious of all." Added Kendall: "This is funny enough."[12]

The correspondents also did not like the Mexicans' guerrilla tactics. John Warland called guerrillas "a cowardly, dastardly mode of warfare, recognized by no other nation—certainly by none which has any claim to civilization." He urged that wars be fought "under recognized rules, with some regard to honor and manliness." An editorial in the Mexico City *American Star* charged, "It cannot be denied that the mode of warfare pursued by Mexico . . . has been barbarous, unchristian and uncivilized in the extreme. . . . They have paid but little regard to the rules which govern all nations in carrying on hostilities." The *Star* also charged the Mexicans with killing wounded on battlefields and violating their paroles as prisoners.[13]

Scholar Raymund Paredes has observed many early American travelers "regarded the Mexicans as obstructions in the path of progress, to be quickly removed so that the important business of civilizing the continent could proceed undisturbed." A clear expression of this feeling came from the pen of Captain William Henry of the *Spirit of the Times,* when he wrote from the Rio Grande: "It certainly never was intended that this lovely land, rich in every production, with a climate that exceeds anything almost the imagination can conceive, should remain in the hands of an ignorant and degenerate race." In one of the most interesting sentences written by an American correspondent during the war, Henry expanded,

> The finger of Fate points, if not to their eventual extinction, to the time when they will cease to be the owners of the soil, and when the Anglo American race will rule with republican simplicity and justice, a land literally "flowing with milk and honey,"—who will, by their superior mental and physical abilities, by their energy and *go-a-head-i-tive-ness,* that no sufferings or provocations can retard . . . will populate the country with a race of men who will prove the infinite goodness of our Maker, in creating nothing but what is for use and some good purpose.[14]

CHAPTER TWENTY-TWO

Mustang Delivers the Treaty

On the night of February 19, 1848, Secretary of State James Buchanan was working in his study when he heard a commotion at the front door between his porter and another man. Going to the scene he was confronted by what he thought was "an old salt." The man before him wore a blue denim jacket and pants, one leg of which was strapless while "the want of suspenders displayed a fold of check linen over the waistband"; a broad-brimmed tarpaulin hat was on his head, and his face was covered with "ranchero looking whiskers." The man, tired and dirty from seventeen days of continuous travel, was James L. Freaner, "Mustang" of the *Delta*. To Buchanan's further surprise, Freaner handed him the proposed treaty to end the Mexican War.[1]

President James K. Polk had told the American public that the war was being fought "to conquer a peace."[2] In the end, a peace settlement proved almost as tough to conquer as the Mexican armies. Mexican War historian Justin Smith noted, "Nobody could have imagined the extraordinary course of events that was to bring [peace] about, and for a long while it seemed impossible." The peace treaty also set off an extraordinary course of events for the press, events that saw Freaner undertake a 1,700-mile trip to deliver the document to the president, even while the competing *Picayune* was covering the same ground to deliver the news to the public.[3]

After the capture of Mexico City, Nicholas P. Trist, whom Polk had sent to Mexico to work on a peace treaty, could not find a stable Mexican government with which to negotiate. In this atmosphere, the U.S. movement to annex all of Mexico, aided by outspoken eastern penny papers, gained strength. Trist opposed annexation, which he considered inevitable but premature, and that only his continued efforts at an early treaty could prevent it.[4]

In mid-November 1847, as Trist was beginning to make progress, word arrived from a dissatisfied, impatient President Polk relieving him of his assignment. Because the next military train to the coast was not scheduled until December 4, Trist decided to keep trying and, finally, to defy Polk's recall. For another two months he persisted against a number of obstacles, until the Mexican government agreed to the American terms. On February 2, 1848, in total secrecy, Trist met with Mexican representatives at Guadalupe Hidalgo, a Mexico City suburb, and signed the tentative agreement. He then turned the official American copy over to his trusted friend, Freaner, for delivery to President Polk.[5]

Freaner found himself in the awkward position of delivering the treaty after spending months encouraging Trist to persist with the negotiations, despite the recall order. Trist later gave Freaner credit as "the only man who had been in any way instrumental in determining [me] to make the attempt." Trist, after long months of close association with Freaner, had arrived at the conclusion that the correspondent was "an honest man of unusual sagacity . . . [with] a strong, sympathetic character."[6] Trist wrote to his wife that Freaner's friendship was marked "by unswerving uprightness & love of truth, generosity, kindness of heart, courage *a toute epreuve* and a host of other noble qualities." To Buchanan, Trist described Freaner as a man with "high integrity of character." Against this background of friendship, trust, and shared views on ending America's involvement in the war, Freaner encouraged Trist to continue the peace talks. When the negotiations concluded successfully, Trist asked Freaner to undertake the difficult job of delivering the agreement to the unsuspecting, impatient, perplexed president in Washington.[7] Ironically, although Trist had handed him one of the news scoops of the war, the *Delta* correspondent was bound to secrecy, and in the chain of events that followed his paper was scooped by the *Picayune*.

Long after Kendall had returned to the States, Freaner was sending detailed, almost daily accounts from Mexico City. His national reputation had grown considerably as a result of reporting the battles at Mexico City. Freaner had much to write about. Earthquakes had become a common occurrence, he reported to the *Delta*, noting they produced "much fright." The growing arguments among the American generals bothered him greatly, and he supported Scott in a number of his letters, fretting, "These disputes will no doubt be a fruitful theme for some of the political papers at home."[8]

Freaner took steps to obtain reports on the activities of the Mexican government at Querétaro, where it fled after the Mexico City evacuation. He arranged for a Mexican journalist to write to him twice a week and for express delivery to Mexico City. The Mexican Congress was attempting to convene, Freaner noting "their proceedings will be of a highly important character to the American people." Referring to the difficulties of forwarding his stories regarding the final battles, he urged the *Delta* to take steps to see that his letters were not detained at Veracruz. Freaner also made arrangements to receive letters from correspondents at other Mexican cities in an effort to gauge public opinion.[9]

Freaner's letters openly supported Trist in his efforts to conclude a peace.

Trist also continued as a major source for Freaner. At one point Freaner fell ill and Trist covered for the journalist, sending the *Delta* clippings from the Mexico City papers. "I considered this a slight return to Mr. Freaner for many acts of kindness received from him in bringing me intelligence," Trist later explained.[10]

So the friendship that had started at Veracruz the previous May came to a fateful high point on the morning of December 4, 1847. Full of anxiety and doubt, Trist turned to Freaner for advice. For the diplomat, their discussion became "an event that stands alone in history and is not likely ever to have a parallel." When it was over, Trist had made up his mind to stay and he credited Freaner. Trist later admitted he had previously thought about disobeying Polk's order, but now he was thoroughly swayed by the strength of Freaner's appeal. Trist said he was moved by "the fire from as true an American heart as ever beat," from the "gush of real, honest, genuine patriotism, fresh and pure from the heart of a man." The diplomat impulsively replied, "I will make the Treaty, and you stay here to carry it home."[11]

Writing to the *Delta* on the same day that Trist made his decision, Freaner said, "I contend, let the instructions be what they may, if any opportunity offers to Mr. Trist of negotiating peace, he should assume the responsibility at all hazards, and the country will sustain him." Further delays would so stall a treaty, Freaner argued, that the United States would be forced to mount a new army of 75,000 men to occupy Mexico. Trist's progress warranted the "belief that the treaty, if made, will be confirmed by the Mexicans," the *Delta* correspondent wrote. Reporting that the Mexican commissioners had come to Mexico City in mid-December to meet with Trist, Freaner said, "I hope for the interests of our country, that he will . . . go home with the treaty in his pocket."[12]

Freaner was aware of the danger of keeping a large American army deep in a foreign country. He noted it took only an army of 12,000 to conquer Mexico, but it would require up to 100,000 men, "with all the dangers of dull garrison life," to hold it. If the Mexicans failed to negotiate, he said, "let's set up our own boundaries, man them, and let any aggravated power drive us from our position if they can." The *Delta* correspondent also believed a large standing army would be a threat to "American republicanism" and would "endanger our existence as a nation." He contended, "Beyond all doubt or question the Anglo Saxon race will eventually possess and govern Mexico. The fertile land, rich mines and good climate are enough to ensure this. . . . Progress will determine this eventually."[13]

Strong opinions characterized Freaner's reporting during this period. Compared to the writing of the other American correspondents in Mexico, however, it is not unusual. Most were firm in their conviction that the

Americans should be tough in the peace negotiations. But to some, Freaner's statements sounded moderate and sometimes embarrassed the *Delta,* which favored keeping all of Mexico. When Freaner called Polk's annual message of December 1847 "lame and inferior" to his previous messages, the *Delta* quickly explained, "Our readers will make all due allowances for this opinion of our correspondent when they bear in mind that he is a warm advocate of taking a defensive line and of the withdrawal of our troops from the interior of Mexico."[14]

Slowly, but steadily, Trist pushed the negotiations forward. The diplomat's effort culminated on February 2, 1848, with the Treaty of Guadalupe Hidalgo. The terms required the United States to pay Mexico $15 million, assume numerous claims of American citizens against the Mexican government, and take responsibility for Indian damages. In exchange, Mexico ceded the United States more than 500,000 square miles, including New Mexico and California, and accepted the Rio Grande as the southern boundary of Texas. Within hours Freaner had packed the documents and was on his way to the coast, carrying the historic treaty in his saddlebags.[15]

Trist and Freaner had started making their plans in mid-January for delivery of the treaty. Mindful of the need to travel light, Freaner sketched out a plan for Trist to pass along to the military authorities. Freaner wrote,

> I would suggest . . . that thirty of the Texan mounted men be sent immediately to Rio Frio, there to wait my arrival . . . taking with them no other arms than their pistols.—One company of Texans to be dispatched to Oja de Agua. Taking with them all their arms and one extra horse. Neither of these commands to take any more baggage than their blankets. . . . By this arrangement I would be enabled to reach Vera Cruz in less than three days from the time of starting.[16]

Trist also asked General Scott to have "the *swiftest* vessel" available waiting at Veracruz "to start at a moment's warning."[17] With the recommended arrangements in place, Freaner outran his escorts along the route and reached the port city in less than three days, traveling through without sleeping. But he was not the first to reach Veracruz with the news—the British courier beat him—and the *Delta* would not be the first paper to break the story in New Orleans.[18]

After Freaner's departure the other correspondents in Mexico City and Veracruz continued to know little of the treaty's details. The *American Star* noted Mexican journals were the only source of news regarding the secret document. The *Star* was particularly vexed that the Mexican newspaper *Eco* had broken the story in Mexico City and continued detailed follow-up reports. The *Star* sarcastically wrote, "Will the editor have the goodness to state in his next article . . . what time he thinks the American army will leave the country . . . we should like to have a few days notice."[19]

The lack of precise details did not stop the correspondents from speculating about the document. The *Picayune*'s Daniel Scully, writing from Mexico City, noted, "The only topic here now is Peace. At every meeting the question is 'Will we have Peace?'" Everyone had a different view, Scully said. "In this conflict of feeling, ambition and interest it is next to impossible to find an unbiased opinion." He then demonstrated his own bias. "Mexico wants peace—craves for it, and, if this treaty is not ratified by her it is because of the stupidity and ineptness caused by the oft and repeated blows received by her within the last two years." Scully expressed doubts. The person behind the treaty, he contended, was Ewen C. Mackintosh, the British counsel-general. Trist had been offered similar terms by the Mexicans after the battles of Contreras and Churubusco the previous August, Scully claimed, but that settlement had been thwarted by Mackintosh. Scully wrote mockingly of the treaty's terms, which he considered too light in view of the American battle casualties. "This thing of being killed or wounded must be a delicious pleasure when we are willing to pay dearly for it."[20]

Scully extended his opposition in another letter. "It is humiliating. . . . The United States were a mere puppet, and the interests of Mr. Trist, Mr. Mackintosh and Mr. Davidson, the agents of the Rothchilds in this city, were of paramount consideration," he contended. They would all benefit, the correspondent claimed, by speculation in Mexican bonds, which would rise in value when the treaty's terms were announced. Having accused Trist, Scully then backed away: "There is no positive evidence of the truth of the statement in regard to Mr. Trist's connection with the speculation in my hands, but it is affirmed that he is, by officers of high rank—men who would scorn to rob a man of his reputation, and whose political sympathies would lead them to shield him, did not the honor of the country demand his exposure." Scully's motives in making the charge are fairly clear. "The whole army," Scully wrote to the *Picayune*, "is indignant at buying a peace and paying for territory that was conquered at the very opening of the war."[21]

For its part, the *Picayune* did not oppose the treaty, assuming it would be accepted by the U.S. government. But it refused to edit or tone down Scully's opinions. "So far as we can judge of the sentiment of the army in Mexico," the paper observed, "our correspondent speaks them much more nearly [*sic*] than the press at home." But the difference in opinion was important. The reporters in Mexico, close to the front lines and the army, still favored strong action against the Mexicans. The press at home, with a better view of American public opinion, knew the country had grown weary of the war.[22]

Freaner later somewhat defended Trist in a detailed account of the Mexican politics involved in the acceptance of the treaty. He credited Manuel de la Peña y Peña, the interim Mexican president, as "strong and popular" and "distinguished and influential," and this accounted for the delicate negotiations being steered past many political obstacles. "In Mexico," Freaner wrote, "money is a very essential element in all politics" and "unhappily Pena y Pena's treasury was" empty. Trist could not provide money, so agents for English and German merchants put up the funds the Mexican president needed, Freaner wrote, because they would benefit financially from the treaty's terms.[23]

"Mustang," meanwhile, was carrying out his assignment. He had changed roles, at least in his own mind, and now considered himself a government courier rather than a correspondent. For the *Delta* this proved to be an unfortunate circumstance; in his effort to maintain secrecy, Freaner did not notify the paper that a peace agreement had been reached. The *Picayune*, not bound by such restrictions, pursued the story with its usual energy and ended up breaking the news to the nation.

At Veracruz the army had made arrangements for the steamship *Iris* to carry Freaner to Mobile. The authorities also arranged to have the steamship *New Orleans*, bound for New Orleans, held in port for forty-eight hours. This was an attempt to prevent private reports reaching the States before the government courier. It was a wise precaution, from the government's point of view, because the *Picayune*'s express reached Veracruz soon after Freaner. *Iris*, however, lost a two-day lead due to a storm in the Gulf of Mexico. When the steamship *New Orleans* finally was allowed to leave, the captain responded to the challenge and pushed his ship to capacity power. The effort allowed them to reach the Mississippi Saturday afternoon, February 12, about the time *Iris* reached Mobile with Freaner on board. An extra issue of the *Picayune* was soon on the streets, and not long after express riders were headed northward carrying copies of the paper.[24]

The next morning, February 13, the *Delta* and the *Picayune* repeated the story that the peace treaty had been concluded. The *Picayune*, in a carefully worded statement, said the news was from a highly reliable source. The *Delta*, at first indicating Freaner had notified the paper in advance regarding his mission, held its comment to one paragraph: "Though we have no definite advices to that effect, we see no impropriety in stating our confidence that Mustang has with him the treaty of peace." Two days later, however, the paper noted ruefully, "Our correspondent, having been unfortunately for us, the bearer of despatches [*sic*] to Washington, has omitted to write us and we are therefore deprived of our most reliable source of information."[25]

Although Freaner was attempting to keep his mission secret, the press everywhere was reporting his whereabouts. The American papers in Jalapa and Veracruz announced his arrival and speculated he was on an important mission. The *American Star*'s Veracruz correspondent reported that "Mustang was quite mysterious" and "maintained a 'dogged silence.'" The reporter added everyone knew his documents were important, "but nothing transpired respecting the nature of them." In Mexico City, the *North American* observed Freaner had left "clothed in a great swad of mystery."[26]

Iris reached Mobile February 12 and Freaner immediately was spotted by reporters. The Charleston *Courier* reported, "He was in great haste and seemed to be full of important matter. Attempts were made to 'pump' him, but they failed." One of the reporters who failed to pump Freaner was from the Mobile *Daily Advertiser,* but he reported that "Mustang" boarded a steamboat that same night bound for Montgomery, Alabama. The New Orleans *Bulletin* stated, "It was pretty much understood [he carried] the treaty of peace or . . . the basis for one."[27]

Freaner reached Charleston on February 17, the same day as the express carrying the *Picayune* extra with the treaty news. Ironically, the Charleston *Courier* of the following morning (February 18) carried the *Picayune*'s scoop and another story that Freaner passed through the city "yesterday . . . and we understand expressed the opinion that there was a strong probability of peace being soon concluded." Freaner, after seventeen days of hard travel, reached Washington "after dark" Saturday, February 19. The New York *Tribune* reported it "was probably the fastest trip ever made between the two cities."[28]

News of the treaty took an unusual, somewhat confused, route at this point. John Forney, an experienced Washington correspondent for the Philadelphia *North American,* wrote to his paper on Sunday, February 20, that "Mustang and the news reports via telegraph from the South reached Washington at the same time." This would have been possible, because the northern telegraph link from Charleston opened on February 16. But no telegraph messages went north from Washington for the next two days. The New York *Sun,* in an angry editorial printed February 22, blamed the two-day blackout on the government. The paper implied it was done in the same fashion that the government had delayed the peace news at Veracruz for two days. The *Sun* further claimed the U.S. Post Office was involved. The *Sun* editorial continued that such expresses were "run at a cost of nearly one thousand dollars" and in this instance "we were robbed of all benefit by them."[29]

Instead, the New York papers, like other papers on the Eastern Seaboard, first received the treaty news via the Baltimore *Sun.* The pony express messengers carrying the *Picayune*'s reports reached Baltimore on February 20, the day after Freaner reached Washington. The next morning the *Sun* broke the news. The Baltimore telegraph moved a summary of it, and most of the major eastern papers carried that short summary on February 21. Recounting the events, Forney, in a letter to the Philadelphia *North American*, noted, "The telegraph has a fashion of getting out of gear just at the time of most importance to public interests."[30]

Freaner, meanwhile, had an interview with the president and met other leading figures at Washington. The Washington correspondent of the Boston *Atlas* reported that "the redoubtable Mustang . . . has been quite a lion here." The Washington *Union*'s editor, Thomas Ritchie, held a long session with Freaner, expressing pleasure at meeting the man "whose letters . . . have been read with so much gratification by the country at large." The Mexico City *American Star* had predicted he would be popular in Washington: "Everyone is a lion in the North who has seen the elephant in Mexico, and we expect when 'Mustang' gets among them there will be a perfect stampede. He can beat George 'blowing.'"[31]

In a fulsome letter of introduction to his wife, Trist wrote of Freaner, "Take him all in all—education, or rather want of education included, & want of all advantages of culture—I don't know but he is the most remarkable man I ever knew . . . he is one of *nature*'s nobles, of the very finest stamp." Trist urged his wife to care for the journalist while he was in the capital. "The whole cabinet at Washington, President included, have not a tithe of the *soul* that is in this man," Trist assured her. "His *love of truth* (added of course to his strong, clear, manly sense & quick sagacity, and his perfect fearlessness & extra ordinary activity) is the great secret of the success of 'Mustang.'"[32]

Trist wrote on behalf of Freaner a similar fulsome letter of introduction to the secretary of state, Buchanan. Trist explained Freaner had planned to leave Mexico City on the December supply train but accepted Trist's request to stay on and deliver the treaty when it was ready. "I consider him, therefore, as having been in the employment of the government as a special Bearer of Despatches from [December 9]. . . . he would be perfectly content with the consciousness of having been useful to our country, without any other reward."[33]

Forney, the Philadelphia correspondent, talked to Freaner, calling him the writer "that Mr. Trist has made a hero." Forney discovered during their conversation that while in Veracruz Freaner had met the government courier carrying the president's order relieving Scott of his command. "What rare extremes do sometime meet!" Forney marveled. "Here were two messengers at the same time in the same city—one bearing to Washington the happy result produced by [Scott's] services and skill, and the other bearing to Mexico, the highest mark of disgrace his Government could inflict." Forney, however, criticized Trist's letter to Buchanan praising Freaner's role. "His laudation of Mr. Freaner (Mustang), however well deserved, is the most extravagant production I ever saw. . . . Our ambassador is truly an extraordinary one and is most certainly a little damaged in the upper story, as the public will see ere long." Kendall, visiting East Coast cities on vacation prior to leaving for Paris to start a history of the war, also met Freaner in Washington, as did influential W. E. Robinson of the New York *Tribune*. Freaner's eventful stay in the capital ended February 25, when Polk appointed him to carry government messages back to Mexico City.[34]

Although he was deeply unhappy with the circumstances surrounding the Trist treaty, the president decided to pass it on to the Senate for consideration. It was expected that body might turn it down, but on February 23 House member John Quincy Adams, the former president, died, and the atmosphere in the capital changed. The country and Congress were caught up in the drama of the death, and by the time the Senate resumed its deliberations, the initial mood of hostility toward Trist's document changed. On March 10 the Senate ratified the agreement, 38–14.[35]

Although the treaty was supposedly a secret, the terms were generally known and widely debated in the American press. In Washington the agreement was somehow disclosed to a reporter for the New York *Herald*, John Nugent, who broke the story after the Senate ratified it. The *National Intelligencer*, the outspoken critic of the war, shaped the position of the Whig press by stating there was more to lose than gain if the treaty was rejected. Other strong Whig voices, Horace Greeley of the New York *Tribune* and Thurlow Weed of the Albany *Evening Journal*, backed this position, and a number of the nation's papers, Whig and Democrat, agreed. Even the *Picayune* was ready to join the rest of the nation in peace, writing: "There is something cheerful in the sound of peace. . . . We have heard so much of the cannon's roar that the tinkling bell is a welcome change."[36]

The method chosen to deliver the treaty to the president provides a window into the state of journalism at the time. James Freaner's decision to take the role of courier was regrettable for the *Delta*, but it was understandable given that values like personal integrity, duty, and mission were important in that day, and evidence points to Freaner's having been a person who believed in them. His editors, however, might have wished for at least a hint from him about the story. They were left to their own devices in obtaining the news, and they reported the circumstances as best they could. Yet the *Picayune*, not bound by secrecy, successfully carried out its journalistic role. Mustang delivered the treaty—but the *Picayune* delivered the news.

CHAPTER TWENTY-THREE

Withdrawal Pains

That we are in a State of War, few among us realize.
— *United States Magazine,* December 1847

With the peace treaty delivered, events in Mexico quickly passed from public interest. Revolutions in Europe became the leading story in many American papers. The New York *Herald* explained, "The great news from France [has] thrown a damper over every other subject . . . and we even believe the march of events in Mexico will now excite but little interest, and be hardly worth publishing in our columns." By mid–April 1848 even the *Picayune* admitted "the astounding events passing in Europe have so completely monopolized that faculty of the public minds that rejoices in news, and doats [*sic*] upon wonders, that the staple excitements of journalism [have] lost their savor." The paper noted particularly the interest in the French Revolution: "Everybody, every place, everything is full of it."[1]

One formal step remained for the war to end: ratification by the Mexican Congress of the treaty as revised by the U.S. Senate. The American correspondents in Mexico City were caught in limbo, waiting to see if it would be peace or renewed war. They continued a steady flow of letters to their publications—Freaner to the *Delta;* Peoples, once again using his familiar pseudonym "Chaparral" for a new New Orleans daily, the *Crescent;* John Warland to the Boston *Atlas;* William Tobey to the Philadelphia *North American;* and Charles Callahan and Daniel Scully to the *Picayune.* As before, they remained a key communication link between the government and people in the United States and the affairs in Mexico.

When Kendall departed for New Orleans he made arrangements with former *Picayune* employee Charles Callahan to provide the paper's coverage from the Mexican capital. Callahan, a native of New York City, had joined the paper as a printer in 1841 and later became a city reporter and finally a war correspondent. He was the paper's primary correspondent at Mexico City from late October 1847 until January 1848, when he joined William Tobey in running the *North American.* After the *North American* folded in

March, Callahan resumed writing for the *Picayune* as a backup correspondent for Scully. Callahan was well liked by the other correspondents, particularly for his eloquence and personality. He was an ardent supporter of Manifest Destiny. Americans would continue their expansion southward, he predicted on a later occasion, in order to aid "oppressed people . . . in establishing those principles of Republicanism which, as Americans, it was their mission to diffuse over the earth."[2]

Callahan was less experienced than Kendall and not as well connected with the army's leaders, and his letters were less analytical. During fall 1847 he reported that clashes continued between the American troops and the civilian population in the streets of the Mexican capital. Most of these incidents involved only small numbers of people, often robbery attempts or quarrels over gambling incidents. Callahan also had an eye for the brighter side of life in the occupied city. He attended the opera and was amazed at its quality, writing exuberantly, "I do not believe [it] has ever been equalled on this continent. . . . It would open the eyes of a New Orleans audience—but I think the expense of getting it up would rather frighten a New Orleans manager." On a Sunday in November he went riding through the city streets and observed, "The fair damsels are fast losing their fear of the 'barbarians of the North.'" As a result, Callahan noted, "about one-half of our army was also there." After attending a meeting in Mexico City in January 1848, at which a number of U.S. army officers urged a railroad be built between Veracruz and the Mexican capital, Callahan wrote, "It remains for the strong-minded and enterprising descendants of the Anglo-Saxons to confer upon this benighted people the benefits of civilization; first of which is the proposed railroad." His letters often revealed his bias. "The Mexicans are certainly the coolest thieves in the world," he commented on one occasion. In another letter he claimed, "I have never been in a church in Mexico without having my pocket picked." Although he wrote regular voluminous letters filled with army news to the *Picayune*, Callahan also worked as a printer. When the opportunity came to join Tobey as a partner at the *North American*, he quickly accepted. The *Picayune* wished him well, noting that his letters had been "copied extensively throughout the United States."[3]

At this point another important reporter of the war came on the scene—Daniel Scully of the *Picayune*. During the final six months of the American occupation, the influential *Picayune* relied on the outspoken and strong analytical writing of Scully for its primary coverage of events. Scully was another former New Orleans printer who had followed the armies to Mexico, serving briefly in the Louisiana Volunteers at the start of the war. His opportunity to report regularly came in January 1848, when Callahan resigned. The *Picayune* made arrangements to receive letters from Scully and gave him the title "Special Correspondent." Following the example of Kendall and Haile, Scully refused to be tied to the garrison cities and took to the field with American units. In January 1848 he accompanied General Joseph Lane on a three-week mission that almost succeeded in capturing Santa Anna. In May 1848 he was the only American reporter to witness the exchange of the final peace agreement at Querétaro.[4]

Scully's writing style was graphic and strongly pro-American in the vein of the other correspondents. The *Picayune* observed that he wrote in a "bold and independent tone." The paper had occasional problems handling all the materials he sent from the Mexican capital, once noting: "His narrative is intensely interesting, but is so long we cannot possibly find room for it (all)." Following its established pattern, the paper usually printed Scully's letters over several days. At times the *Picayune* disagreed publicly with Scully's observations but allowed him free rein. When the correspondent called for the United States to keep all of Mexico, the *Picayune* declared, "We would rather agree with our correspondent in his conclusion, if we could—at all events we are glad there are others who hope better things (than we)." Scully strongly believed the United States should annex Mexico. "I can see no other course to pursue but to retain the country we have conquered, and at once enact laws for its government, which will ultimately fit it for becoming a part of the Union, upon a footing of equality with the present States." The *Picayune* correspondent concluded this appeal with a good example of the Manifest Destiny philosophy of the day:

> Never was there a more erroneous idea than the country is not worthy of our efforts to elevate it. Leaving aside that its immense mineral resources, the soil and climate combined . . . are equal to any I have ever seen or experienced . . . our commerce and manufacturers would be vastly benefitted by [keeping Mexico]. The introduction of our liberal system of commerce and just laws, and the immigration of our people and enlightened Europeans, would stimulate commerce and teach the inhabitants new wants which we, as the cheapest manufacturers of . . . fabrics, would be called upon to supply.[5]

Of the remaining correspondents, only James Freaner clearly opposed full annexation. The U.S. occupation eventually would be "full and permanent," William Tobey prophesized. Also using the best Manifest Destiny language of the day, he argued, "The word is onward. The spirit, the heart of the [Mexican] people calls for it. . . . And some would have it. The great Ruler of the nation ordains, as we believe, that the descendants of the Saxons shall retrieve this country from its ruin. May they fulfill their mission."

The popular army officer William S. Henry, now a major newly returned to Mexico after his tour in the recruitment service, supported these arguments. Assigned to a unit in Mexico City, he corresponded to the New York *Courier and Enquirer* and the *Spirit of the Times*. Writing to the *Spirit*, Henry commented, "Having advanced, would it not be madness to retire? If we give up the capital and withdraw to a line, I question whether the coming generation will be witness to a treaty." Henry favored making the Mexicans pay to support the U.S. army: "That the time is not far distant, when the whole country will be under the rule of the *Anglo Yankeeano* blood, is as certain as two and two are four."[6]

In March, when Scully opposed the terms of Trist's peace treaty, the *Picayune* again disagreed publicly but explained, "Agreeably to our custom, we allow him full scope for the expression of his views—adopted not hastily nor without deep consideration." Generally the paper had strong praise for Scully's work. After his day-to-day account of General Lane's attempts to capture Santa Anna arrived, the paper observed it had had "nothing more graphic" since Kendall's reports on the fall of Mexico City. Noting Lane cited Scully's participation in his official report about the mission to the War Department, the *Picayune* expressed pride that "Mr. Scully is honorably mentioned."[7]

During the twenty-two-day march by Lane's command, which covered almost 500 miles, Scully filed eight long reports to the *Picayune*. To assure that these reports reached the paper as soon as possible, he hired special messengers to carry them to Veracruz, and although the normal communication problems delayed them about three weeks, the paper praised Scully's resourcefulness and gave the letters extensive space. Scully wrote in excited tones about his experiences in the field. On January 21, after the American units had broken camp in a heavy rain before daylight, Lane passed the word Santa Anna was reported nearby. Strict secrecy about this mission had been maintained, Scully wrote, "in the full hope the wily Mexican would soon be within our grasp." The hope was not fulfilled. "The command did not travel with the celerity the general designed," Scully reported. Santa Anna apparently was warned by scouts, Scully noting, "We had the mortification to learn the great object of our search had fled two hours before we arrived." The correspondent amused himself along with the rest of the troops by poking through Santa Anna's captured possessions. These included "his best military wardrobe, two of his costly canes, his field glasses, an elegant writing desk and three trunks of his lady's clothing." The American officers split up the captured goods, Scully assuring the *Picayune*, "His military property was taken as legitimate spoils." Scully occupied most of this time writing about the countryside, describing various towns the troops occupied, usually contending that the local inhabitants wanted the Americans to occupy them permanently, and speculating whether various areas could support U.S. manufacturers. A small clash with Mexican troops occurred on the next-to-last day of the expedition. Scully, accompanying a dragoon unit headed by Major William H. Polk, was personally involved in the action. It ended after an exchange of shots, Scully reporting eighteen Mexicans killed, three captured, and only one American injured. Scully concluded the expedition had proved that "the country may be considered conquered from one extremity to the other."[8]

Scully's trip with Lane's troops was the last incident of combat reporting for the American reporters. For the most part they were suffering the pains of deep boredom. On March 9 Scully complained, "This is the dullest place imaginable and will continue so during the armistice." The slow treaty deliberations by the Mexican Congress irritated John Warland, who told Boston *Atlas* readers, "We are beginning to lose all patience." Peoples, writing to the New Orleans *Crescent,* observed the Americans in Mexico City "were rusting away." Expressing the mood of the reporters, Freaner wrote wistfully, "To you, all my old sweethearts, married and unmarried, or want to be married, or do not want to be married. Mustang wishes (you) all, a merry and happy May Day."[9]

Social activities for the reporters centered on the numerous saloons, cantinas, and coffeehouses, or private clubs, such as the Aztec Club, which catered to high-ranking American officers. And there was considerable gambling, though the reporters generally frowned on it. Callahan observed, "Probably no place in the civilized world has the vice of gambling been carried to a greater extent than in this city within the last three months." Scully complained, "Gamblers are a species of scoundrels with which this city is infested." He was particularly concerned with the number of American and Mexican soldiers who were "being corrupted" by the gamblers' activity. "I'm afraid the Monte and Roulette tables . . . licensed by [our] government and patronized by [our] army have been the death of many a gallant spirit who could not resist the temptation," Warland wrote to the Boston *Atlas.*[10]

Another amusement for the Mexico City garrison was horseracing. Races were held in March, April, and May 1848. Peoples, writing to the New Orleans *Crescent,* reported, "All of the [Mexico City] editors and the . . . correspondents from New Orleans have been presented with [passes] by the club." Peoples complained he was so busy covering the Pillow court of inquiry that he could not take advantage of his pass. However, he, Freaner, and Callahan found time to supply detailed accounts of the race result. Scully was upset with social conditions in the occupied city. He noted poverty was so widespread that "Indians carry ice down from Popcatapetl on their back for a half dollar to a dollar." These trips, which involved two or three days' work, were made to provide ice for the drinks of the Americans, he wrote. When walking in the streets of the city, Scully said, "one is beset with the lame, the blind and the deformed in every possible manner [all begging]. . . . A great number of them are soldiers who were wounded in the [war's] battles, and I have observed they never ask a Mexican for charity, but prefer begging from Americans." In addition to the former soldiers, numerous children were involved as professional beggars, Scully reported.[11]

Freaner, after his role in delivering the peace treaty, resumed writing letters to the *Delta*. One day he ran into his old friend, Captain Christopher Haile, the *Picayune's* former correspondent: "They say the Captain doesn't speak to common folks now-a-days, such as correspondents, reporters and editors of newspapers, but I am inclined to think this is a mistake—for, although the straps sit very well upon his shoulders and he looks as well as captains generally do, there is a sort of unnatural appearance about him, which I do not think can be corrected until they take the soldier's clothes off him and put a quill in his hands." Freaner had more serious thoughts about the army as well. In a detailed essay titled "Reforms in Our Army," he argued for "1st, a refuge for the sick, wounded, and the soldiers disabled while in the service; 2nd, promotions from the ranks for gallantry in the field; and 3rd, a 'Retired List' for officers who are incapacitated for active service by age or injuries, such as wounds or disease incurred . . . in the service." He urged Congress to establish veterans homes and improve benefits for officers and their widows; and he pointed out that President Polk already could make battlefield promotions but was not supporting most recommendations from the field commanders.[12]

In a bittersweet moment, Winfield Scott hurriedly left the Mexican capital on April 21. He departed, Freaner wrote to the *Delta*, "not with his victorious divisions following him . . . but escorted by a single company of Dragoons—disarmed, but not dishonored." Freaner reported:

EDS DELTA—He is gone! and the blessings of the whole army go with him. . . . This morning Gen. Scott set out for Vera Cruz whence he will sail directly for New York. I have never seen such a sensation produced in the army as his departure. . . . It really seemed like the breaking up of the 'Old Homestead,' and the departure of the parental Head . . . , leaving the unprotected household to take care of itself. Almost every man in the army so felt it. . . . But all this time, while he has been overthrowing the enemies of his country in the front—exalting our national character, redressing our national injuries and adorning our national history—his "enemies in the rear," have been working to tarnish his fair fame and destroy his just claims. . . . In the very face of the enemy he has routed and defeated, and in the capital he has conquered, he has been placed in the humiliating attitude of one scrambling for justice with his inferiors—inferiors in rank, in talent and in the high traits of character and education which make the great and successful warrior, the statesman and the logician.[13]

Major William S. Henry returned to his journalist's role during the late spring, when the army assigned him to Mexico City. Writing for the daily New York *Courier and Enquirer* and the weekly *Spirit of the Times,* he easily resumed his descriptive and opinionated observations of Mexican life and politics. After attending a bullfight, he expressed strong praise for a female matador. "She was much bolder and more fearless than the male matadors," Henry asserted. Speaking generally of Mexican women, he wrote, "The women have thrice the bravery of the men!" Henry was appalled that three women, wives of lancers in a troop of Mexican cavalry he accompanied, trotted the entire 32 miles the group rode in order to serve their husbands lunch: "I was disgusted with this remnant of . . . barbarity. . . . The poor devils did not walk but trotted like dogs at the head of the column."

Henry rode over the major battlefields near the city and described the incidents, even criticizing Major General John Quitman's successful attack on the capital's gates as "ill advised" and "excessively improper," because "that distinguished and gallant officer ignored orders." He reported on the treaty deliberations of the Mexican Congress, cautioning, "If any one knows the Mexican character, they must feel assured that, until the *vote* is taken, nothing can be certain." He did assure the *Courier and Enquirer* editors, "The army will move immediately after the . . . ratification."[14]

As peace drew near, the correspondents started to notice changes in the city. Early in April, Peoples reported, "The greasers are getting particularly saucy since the armistice, and chuckle whenever they think that the man they feared so much [Scott] has been suspended from the command." John Warland recalled that long days at the *American Star* often caused him to return home through darkened streets after midnight, but he "went well armed with sword and pistol, besides having a good dog as a companion." In addition to the problems with the city residents, Peoples noted the army's morale and discipline were slipping. "Robbery seems to be the order of the day just now," he commented, reporting on several armed holdups committed by American military personnel. "Many soldiers have recently deserted from our army, and have taken to robbing for a living," he wrote. Gambling was the cause behind it, Peoples reported. After detailing robberies of an American priest and the American library, he added that the thieves "committed the unpardonable sin of relieving one of the collectors of the American *Star* of ninety odd dollars." As he also was the owner of the *Star,* Peoples was able to observe the theft "came very heavy . . . as it was the evening preceding pay-day. . . . I can trace this bad conduct on the part of some belonging to the army to nothing but the insatiable appetite for gaming that exists in this city. Men lose their money, then their credit, and self respect."[15]

The American community and the correspondents turned their attention to the peace prospects. "When I got up this morning," Peoples wrote on April 25, "I found the peace market flourishing, and the stock about as high as it has been yet." Even the Mexican press "had changed its tune" and expected the country's congress to settle the issue, he observed. The outcome "heaven only knows," predicted Peoples, adding, "You must not forget my advice to be prepared to chronicle either peace or war."[16]

CHAPTER TWENTY-FOUR

The Last Story

When the U.S. Senate approved the peace treaty with Mexico in March 1848, it made several changes that required ratification by the Mexican Congress. To carry out this final step of diplomacy, President James Polk chose Senator A. H. Sevier of Arkansas, chairman of the committee on foreign relations, and Nathan Clifford, the U.S. Attorney General. In mid-May, after procedural delays, the Mexican Chamber of Deputies and Senate accepted the treaty as amended. On May 30, 1848, Sevier and Clifford exchanged the ratifications with Mexican authorities at Querétaro; the war was officially ended. The American forces moved quickly to evacuate the occupied territory, and by August 1, 1848, the last troops sailed from Veracruz, bringing the occupation to a close.[1]

During the final months, Freaner, Peoples, Warland, Scully, and Callahan provided detailed coverage of peace prospects and Mexican politics. They also arranged with Mexican correspondents at Querétaro to report on the efforts to assemble the Congress and its deliberations. Peoples observed, "To Queretaro alone the eyes of all are fixed."[2]

It was six months after the capture of Mexico City before the American correspondents could rely on their letters arriving safely at Veracruz. In the months immediately following the fall of the city, they had to use the irregular deliveries of the army or private express riders, who still faced roving bands of guerrillas and bandits. In March the army put mail service on a two-a-month basis, but the size of the writers' bundles of letters and newspapers was restricted. In late March regular stagecoach service was established between the capital and the coast. "We will not have to make our packages so small now," Peoples informed the *Crescent*.[3] It was an excellent service, Scully of the *Picayune* wrote, noting the regular delivery of papers and mail relieved "the monotony of inactivity."[4] The regular stage did not completely end the robberies, however. The only safe means of sending a message to Veracruz, the correspondents noted with regret, was with the British legation courier, who always went through unmolested, or with an American army detachment of at least fifty men.[5] In an attempt to overcome the mail problems, all the New Orleans daily newspapers continued to use express riders between Mexico City and Veracruz for breaking news. They continually strived to cut the transit time to New Orleans; the *Picayune,* on one delivery in May, hit seven days and seven hours, claiming "the shortest time on record."[6]

Freaner and Peoples, realizing the importance of the concluding treaty story, established daily communication with stringers at Querétaro. If important news came, Freaner notified the *Delta,* "I shall put it through by extraordinary express or go with it myself as far as Vera Cruz."[7] Peoples sent John Warland, his Spanish-speaking associate editor, to Querétaro to provide coverage for the American *Star* and the *Crescent.* Warland found it a busy assignment, covering and reporting the proceedings during the day, and at night preparing editorials "to censure the Mexican papers."[8]

By late April "the all absorbing topic" in Mexico City, Freaner reported, was "will we have peace?" and "what is the news from Queretaro?" Freaner felt it safe to predict "the present state of affairs incline us to believe it is favorable [for peace]." Even Mexico City's robberies and murders appeared suspended, he wrote, "until the affairs of state are settled by the Mexican Congress."[9]

The treaty's progress was Scully's main topic, too. In a letter to the *Picayune* in mid-March he said, "We suppose the great question with you now is 'Will it be ratified by the Government at Queretaro?'" With this, Scully launched a series of letters analyzing the long process of political and government action that eventually led to the Mexican Congress's acceptance of the revised treaty. Mexican enemies of the United States and the "military plunderers were all opposed to the treaty," Scully warned his readers. He explained, "The friends of the United States, or, as they are termed here, 'annexationists,' are composed of the poor, honest, intelligent and industrious portions of the citizens of the country, who have experienced the benefits of our Government, military though it be, who have struggled again and again to strip the church of its overwhelming power—who have struggled also to pull down the military, and who . . . look to American occupation as the only remedy for the innumerable evils they are suffering." In Scully's estimation "friends" favored American annexation, whereas "enemies" and "military plunderers" opposed the treaty terms as too stiff.[10]

Scully also made arrangements for a Mexican journalist to provide regular coverage from Querétaro. The journalist forwarded letters in Spanish to Scully at Mexico City; after translating them, he included them in his packets to the *Picayune.* By mid-April Scully reported increasing signs the treaty would be approved. One such sign, he said, was the support of British agent Ewen Mackintosh, whom Scully (like Kendall) frequently criticized. Scully explained: "It is true . . . [for] if he has the shrewdness he has credit for, he will see in the rejection of this treaty that the occupation of the country by Americans is inevitable, and his national prejudices, as well as his [mercantile] interest would prompt him to work against the events." Mexican factions were leaning the same way, Scully believed.[11]

On May 22 the American commissioners, Sevier and Clifford, left Mexico City for the 145-mile trip to Querétaro and the final ceremonies. Scully joined them. Heading their military attachment was Major William H. Polk, the president's brother—and Scully's friend from earlier missions against the guerrillas. On May 25 a large crowd turned out to view the Americans' entrance into Querétaro, crowding "streets, doorways and roof tops," Scully reported. But the reception was slightly deceptive, because after reaching their quarters the American troops had stones thrown at them. "It was feared that a collision would take place between our troops and the people," Scully reported, but Major Polk took steps to have the local authorities maintain order.[12]

The next day Scully watched as the American representatives presented their credentials to the Mexican president, Manuel de la Peña y Peña, and his cabinet. His report included verbatim copies of the formal addresses presented by each side. One day later, May 27, the entire American delegation met the Mexican president. Looking over the proceedings, Scully observed, "They were received in a very plainly, indeed I might say meanly, furnished room in a private house near the suburbs of the city." The Mexican president shook hands with all the Americans in the delegation and talked with them for about fifteen minutes, both sides expressing hopes for "a speedy peace and long harmony between the two countries." Although the only step remaining was to exchange the final treaty ratifications, a two-day delay followed. The cause, Scully explained, was that the Mexican government's national seal was in Mexico City and the president and his cabinet felt it was needed to make the document official.

While waiting for the express riders to return with it, Scully spent his time touring Querétaro and gathering information about the large number of American army deserters, now members of the Mexican army, who were camped nearby. "As well as I can learn there are about one thousand deserters, or men whose terms of services in the American army expired . . . enrolled in the Mexican army," he wrote. "These men have been the preservers of Pena y Pena from revolution," Scully claimed. Reminding his readers of the volatility of Mexican politics, and the fact many politicians could not support peace, he reported the American deserters already had suppressed one insurrection against the Mexican government. "The Mexicans, soldiers and citizens, have the greatest fear of them," he claimed, putting a unique twist on the correspondents' constant theme that the Mexicans always feared American troops, apparently even deserters. The official seal arrived on May 30 and Scully closed his letter that night: "Half-past 7 P.M.—The treaty has just been signed . . . and peace is made."[13]

At Mexico City the correspondents were well prepared to forward the final story. The *Delta*, *Picayune*, and *Crescent* had arranged with their Mexican representatives in Querétaro to forward the news by express. The riders usually covered the 145 miles between the two cities in 24–26 hours, depending on bandit and guerrilla activity.[14] The final story broke in three parts: the important vote by the Chamber of Deputies on May 19; the Mexican Senate vote on May 24, which was considered by the American press as the terminating event; and the ratification exchange on May 30. The British courier was the first to reach Veracruz with the news of the two votes and thus the source of the initial reports in the New Orleans papers. The newspapers' own sources brought the final news. The three concluding stories appeared in the New Orleans press May 31, June 4, and June 8.[15]

James Freaner had taken double care that his articles would get through to the *Delta*, sending off two express riders separately each time news arrived. The *Delta* may have felt a bit of disappointment at the speed of the British courier, for it later heard from Freaner that his express with the final ratification news had been the first to arrive at Mexico City from Querétaro. The British agent, however, traveled directly to Veracruz, without the stop at Mexico City made by American messengers. The news of the Mexican Senate's vote reached New Orleans late the night of June 3, and the next morning the *Delta* reported "the highly important intelligence of the FINAL RATIFICATION OF THE TREATY."[16] With Scully at Querétaro, Callahan handled the story and express arrangements in Mexico City for the *Picayune*. When Callahan's follow-up reports on the Senate vote arrived, the *Picayune*, under a small one-column headline reading "Later from Mexico," announced, "*Peace is considered made.*"[17] Long expected, the final treaty ratification rated only one or two paragraphs in most American newspapers, but, as Mexican War historian Justin Smith later noted, "With all speed it ran from, city to city, from town to town, from vale to vale; and everywhere it was greeted with quiet but heartfelt rejoicing."[18]

With the treaty settled, the Americans moved rapidly to leave the country. John Warland reported the city's peace celebration. "The crowd on the Boston common on the night of the Fourth of July may give you an idea of the immense collection in the Plaza," he told the *Atlas*, describing rockets, illuminations, and music by American military bands. Mexicans, he added, still cursed "deep and loud . . . against *Los Yankees*. . . . I shall long remember it." When John Riley and other San Patricio prisoners were released on June 2, Peoples wrote to the *Crescent*, "they will be great lions amongst the Mexican people after we leave." Reprisals against Mexicans who had cooperated with the Americans started in the outlying areas as soon as the withdrawal started. Women who were friendly to the Americans had their hair cut, their houses sacked, and some were branded on the cheek with *US*. As the troops packed for the trip to the coast, Peoples wrote, Mexican women "who had got a *particular* friend among the Americans . . . were running around the wagon yards begging the teamsters to take them" out of the city. The cause of their fear, Peoples believed, was the "hatred," jealously, and "brute" nature of Mexican men toward foreigners who admired their women. The correspondent added, "Many of the gamblers, the only Americans who carry home any wealth, have left in coaches drawn by mules, their money packed before, behind and on top of their coach, and themselves and their native *lady* seated inside."[19]

The *American Star*, after publishing daily for eight months in the occupied capital, closed on May 30. Departing troops could buy a complete set of the paper for $30, Warland noted. The New Orleans *Crescent*, which carried Peoples's correspondence, stated there should be "no regrets" when the *Star* closed "because with the end of the war ends the mission of the *Star* and its efficient editor." Instead, Americans should praise Peoples for his "pioneer work" and the quality of his Mexico newspapers, the *Crescent* stated. Because of Peoples, the paper added, "The history of the war will be much better understood and misrepresentations less likely to go [uncontradicted]." In the final issue Peoples wrote, "The *Star* has advocated an honorable peace—it has been brought about. We are satisfied—our country is satisfied—Mexico is satisfied—may peace rest continually with all." As for his role, Peoples wrote, "If the gallant soldiers think occasionally of him who followed you from battle to battle and raised his *Star* to chronicle your needs of glory, it will be consolation enough."[20]

Peoples had anticipated the closing of the *Star* for some time. In mid-May, as it became increasingly obvious the American army would soon depart, Peoples became involved in "another adventure," as he described it. It was a proposal to help organize an "army of from one to five thousand" of the disbanded Americans to help rule Mexico until the regular government was on its feet again. Foreign interests in Mexico City were to pay the army's salaries in the interim, in return for protection. "It was not intended for me to organize and command that force," Peoples explained, "but to publicize it among our officers and men." The idea failed, however. Peoples next tried to organize an expedition of discharged soldiers to settle in California. The plan fell through when word came health conditions and the availability of ships on the western Mexican coast were uncertain.[21]

He next flirted with organizing an expedition of discharged U.S. troops for Yucatan. Interested people were urged to see him at the *Star* office for details, Peoples stating that an army of 400–500 men would be raised. He wrote to the New Orleans papers asking for their support, and some editors responded by printing announcements about the plan. A Yucatan committee was organized in New Orleans and the editors of *La Patria*, the New Orleans Spanish-language paper, became involved, supporting the project.[22]

At Mexico City Peoples proceeded with his plans, and several U.S. Army unit commanders joined him. At first the American commander, Major General William O. Butler, told Peoples soldiers could muster out voluntarily at Mexico City, which would allow them to join the expedition. Enthused, Peoples distributed a handbill under his own name with the Yucatan information, and as a consequence Butler was swamped with applications for resignation. Faced with a new problem, the general decided to follow U.S. government orders that all personnel would have to return to the United States for discharge. Peoples called Butler's decision a "severe blow," but he did not give up on the expedition. After leaving Mexico City June 6, Peoples made stops at Perote, Jalapa, and Veracruz in an attempt to recruit army volunteers. Finally he decided to go to Yucatan to check the prospects for the proposed expedition; he went "on a Republican mission," as another *Crescent* correspondent described it.[23]

At Merida, the capital of Yucatan, Peoples found chaos. "The government is in a most deplorable condition," he wrote to the *Crescent*. Whites, he reported, "feel foreign intervention necessary to save themselves from the Indians."[24] Peoples later explained he went thinking it was a struggle for independence, only to find the peninsula would revert back to Mexico if the Indians were defeated. Additionally, he found "that the Indians were more than half right in opposing . . . the Spaniards." He was deeply disappointed. "I was in search of . . . excitement, for which [my] appetite had grown by what it had fed on in Mexico," he explained.[25]

Nevertheless, he entered into an agreement "to land an American expedition in Yucatan." But in a letter to the *Crescent* he said he feared "it will be of little avail" as the American officers most interested did not get their discharges at New Orleans. In the end, the project never materialized. Peoples returned to Veracruz on July 21 and found the city "literally deserted." Recalling his wartime experiences, he wrote, "To me it is almost impossible to realize the efforts and labors of the past 15 months—they are too dreamy—too felicitous to be apparent as a 'sure enough' fact."[26]

At Mexico City, Freaner also was packing to leave. Reflecting the mood there, Freaner wrote:

> In 10 days or less the army will be on the move to the coast . . . [soon] they will be among you—you will then see the boys who "have been baptized in blood and come out steel"—they have "conquered a peace" at the point of a bayonet, and for the sake of humanity and justice, let them revel for

one night in the "Halls of White Settlements" before sending them down to Yucatan to be eaten by mosquitos [*sic*] and sand fleas.[27]

In a final letter from Mexico City, written June 9, Freaner closed his two-year career of reporting the war with the results of an investigation he conducted. An English firm with close ties to Santa Anna had been the chief provisions contractor for the U.S. Army at Mexico City. It was being suggested, Freaner said, while expressing his disillusionment, "that Santa Anna has been enjoying a portion of the profits [from the American contracts]."[28]

Freaner apparently was the last American correspondent to leave the capital. Callahan went first, Peoples noting the rest were "waiting to see the performance to the end." He added, "For myself, I saw the Flag put up, and I will endeavor to see it hauled down." Peoples changed his mind, however, and left for Yucatan on June 6 with General Twiggs's division, "which I have been with ever since it left Monterey."[29] Before departing he made arrangements with a Mexican journalist to continue the *Crescent*'s correspondence from Mexico City, as did the *Delta* and *Picayune*. John Warland also left on June 6 and decided to walk the entire route to Veracruz, taking twenty-four days before ending the trip by plunging "into the surf of the Gulf [of Mexico]," which he said was more "refreshing and delightful" than any other "bathing on earth." He summed up his experiences for the Boston *Atlas* by writing, "It has been a year of interest, adventure and peril—but I have seen the world under a new aspect and . . . I have learned, above all, to set a high value upon my own country, its institutions, and the high moral character of its people."[30]

From the correspondents' view, the occupation of the Mexican capital had represented a mixture of opportunities—possible advancement for themselves, for their friends, and for their country. Such hopes ended with the evacuation. The last story had been filed; all that remained for the correspondents was the trip home.

Epilogue

In late July 1848, the *Picayune* put a symbolic ending on the war's coverage when it confessed, "The pressure of European news upon our columns compels us to cut short Mexican affairs." In Veracruz the remaining handful of correspondents—James Freaner, Charles Callahan, S. D. Allis, John Peoples, and Antonio Yznaga, Peoples's Spanish-section editor on the Mexico City *American Star*—prepared to view the handover and catch the last departing army ship. Peoples noted the Americans' final night in the port was somewhat restrained after local authorities "inconveniently" closed the coffeehouses. "The consequences of this wise precaution were that no disturbances occurred," a *Picayune* correspondent reported. At 8 A.M. on August 1 a crowd gathered in front of the city palace to witness the final event. Many had come to see "the pulling down of the American stars and stripes," the *Picayune* correspondent wrote, but were disappointed because it had not been raised that morning. Instead, "the Mexican flag—red, white and green, with the eagle and serpent embroidered on the white—was hoisted on the flag-staff of the Palace [while] the officers saluted and the soldiers presented arms." In his final letter of the war, Peoples wrote, "There was no public reaction. Not one shout or huzza was heard." Church bells rang, an American army band played and cannon salutes were fired from the city's forts, the *Picayune* reported, but "not a single shout or cheer was heard (from the crowd) when their country's flag was flung to the breeze." Late that afternoon the correspondents boarded the steamship *Alabama* and departed for New Orleans: "An hour more and . . . the town gradually faded from our sight; and so ended the last day of American rule in Vera Cruz."[1]

Although many of the correspondents seemed reluctant to let go of the war, they soon scattered to their various fates. At least nine died in the short time before the start of the Civil War. Charles Bugbee, the express rider who had eluded so many wartime guerrillas, was shot and killed in a stagecoach robbery near Jalapa, Mexico, in April 1849, reportedly working as an agent of the New York *Sun*. Christopher Mason Haile, the *Picayune*'s first full-time civilian correspondent and author of the "Pardon Jones" letters, returned to northern Louisiana and became editor of the Plaquemine *Sentinel*. He died on September 10, 1849, at age 33, at Indian Village, Louisiana, near

Plaquemine, from the lingering results of yellow fever he had contracted while at Veracruz. The *Picayune* observed that Haile was "endowed with a fertile fancy, and was as remarkable for the vigor of his style as for his genuine humor. . . . All honor to his memory." Major William S. "Guy" Henry remained in the army and wrote occasional articles to the New York *Spirit of the Times* from frontier posts. He died on March 5, 1851, at age 34, while on army duty in New York City.[2]

Six were attracted by the goldfields and the promise of California, and three died there. The indefatigable John Peoples, famed as "Chaparral" and founder of American newspapers in Mexico, initially returned to Corpus Christi, Texas, where the army had camped prior to the war. He started the Corpus Christi *Star* in September 1848, but left the paper in the hands of Charles Callahan in February 1849 to go to the California goldfields. Callahan ran the paper until August 1849, when he, too, left for California, turning the paper over to James R. Barnard, their wartime partner. Peoples's party had a difficult trip to California and arrived in San Diego in June 1849, "having suffered much from hunger and thirst." In fall 1849 the California military governor, Persifor F. Smith, appointed Peoples as chief aide in distributing relief and help to those arriving on the Lassen Trail in northern California. Early in 1850, Peoples joined an expedition seeking the mouth of the Trinity River, at the time thought to be on the northern California coast. On March 27, 1850, he drowned when a small boat carrying members of the group overturned in rough surf near the present-day site of Crescent City.

After the battle at Buena Vista, Josiah Gregg remained in Saltillo, working as a doctor and continuing his botanical studies. In 1849 he started on a business and research trip to the West Coast, going first to Mazatlan, Mexico, and then by ship to San Francisco. He died of illness on February 25, 1850, near Clear Lake, California, while exploring the state's northern coastal region. James L. Freaner, "Mustang" of the *Delta*, was hired as an auctioneer by the army in the war's closing days to help sell off military surplus at Veracruz. After returning to New Orleans he was hired by the *Picayune* to serve as its California correspondent. In June 1852, while surveying a wagon road under a state contract, he was killed, together with three companions, during an Indian attack as they crossed the Pit River in northern California.[3]

John E. "Jack" Durivage returned to the *Picayune*, then spent two years after the war as part owner and coeditor of the popular *Alta California* in San Francisco. He sold his interest and returned to his native Boston in October 1851. Charles Callahan of the *Picayune* and George H. Tobin, "Captain Tobin" of the *Delta*, also spent time in San Francisco, but eventually both were attracted to filibustering in Latin America. Tobin joined expeditions to

Yucatan and Central America, still writing his popular letters for the *Delta*. Callahan was killed on September 14, 1856, at San Jacinto, Nicaragua, while fighting as part of filibuster William Walker's forces. Callahan traveled to the Central American country to cover Walker's invasion for the *Picayune*, then joined the filibuster army and died in its failed attempt to capture the country.[4]

John H. Warland, who had corresponded to the Boston *Atlas* and coedited the Mexico City *American Star*, returned to his newspaper career in Massachusetts, editing the pro-Whig Lowell *Courier*. In 1858 he suffered recurrence of a mental illness, which afflicted him before the war, and he was institutionalized. He died in 1872 at the Lowell Mental Asylum. William Tobey resumed work as a political reporter in New York, Washington, and Pennsylvania; he died at Harrisburg on August 1, 1854, from consumption. Correspondent-poet Albert Pike resumed his Little Rock law practice, continuing his feud with fellow Arkansas volunteers about his Buena Vista battle reports. He later served as a Confederate brigadier general and was a prominent leader in the Scottish Rite of the Masonic Order. Daniel M. Scully of the *Picayune* returned to New Orleans and resumed his career as a printer. Thomas Bangs Thorpe completed two anecdotal books about the war after his brief stint with the army. He worked for Zachary Taylor's successful 1848 presidential campaign and continued his career as a newspaper editor, artist, and freelance writer.

Of all the Mexican War correspondents, only Samuel Chester Reid Jr. carried over his reporting experiences to the Civil War. Writing first for the *Picayune*, and then for other southern newspapers, he became one of the South's most prolific and best-paid war correspondents. Jane McManus Storms continued her editing, writing, and lobbying efforts for Cuba annexation after the war. She married William L. Cazneau, lived in Texas, and together they promoted Caribbean issues as special agents for presidents Franklin Pierce, James Buchanan, and Andrew Johnson. She drowned on December 12, 1878, in a shipwreck off North Carolina.[5]

Francis A. Lumsden, George Kendall's friend and coeditor at the *Picayune*, drowned in September 1860, when the excursion ship *Lady Elgin* sank in a storm on Lake Michigan. Although he made only two brief trips to the field during the war, Lumsden later made an informed observation about the correspondents and the journalism of 1847: "We hope to see the day when the press shall be regarded as an avenue to distinction, as eligible as the learned professions. It affords opportunities which other professions do not for the exercise of the largest talent and highest attainments in a direction to sway the minds of the people, to enlighten their ignorance, and uphold and elevate public morals." But, he added, "It will not reach its full capacity of doing good till it insures those who embrace it" a fair salary and recognition for their efforts.

Kendall departed Mexico in November 1847, pledging "full and most complete justice shall be done to all [Americans] who took part" in winning the war. He immediately started work on an illustrated history, *The War between the United States and Mexico, Illustrated*, completed in 1851 with the collaboration of artist Carl Nebel. Kendall spent many years working on a massive, factual history of the war but died before concluding it; his family also was unsuccessful in finding a publisher following his death. He did not report about or participate in the Civil War, turning his energy to family life and attempting to develop a large sheep ranch near New Braunfels, Texas. He died there of lung congestion on October 21, 1867, at age 58.[6]

In an 1854 letter, reflecting on the American experience in Mexico, Kendall defended the importance and necessity of civilian war correspondents. "Honesty and character" were their required attributes, he believed. He urged military authorities to cooperate with journalists to assure the quality of their reports. It was dangerous work, he noted. If a correspondent "happens to leave a leg or an arm behind in his anxiety to push forward and obtain reliable facts" and "exact truths" about a battle, they received no special promotions or benefits, Kendall wrote. He concluded: "Had our own people, during the Mexican War, received no other intelligence than . . . the reports of Gens. Scott [and] Taylor . . . they would have been kept in a disagreeable state of suspense."[7]

Afterword

Having researched American news coverage of the Mexican War for more than twenty-five years, Tom Reilly commanded a scholarly expertise based on an exhaustive examination of primary sources. Reilly's primary research question was, How did the New Orleans newspapers report the Mexican War? In addition, he answered the questions, Who were the Americans who witnessed portions of the war? and What did they write?

He also considered the following: What were the lessons of reporting in the Mexican War? And do the words of the Mexican War correspondents still hurt, more than 150 years later?

Reporters who witnessed the Mexican War had no training in covering military excursions in a foreign land. They were influenced by the spirit of adventure in existing literature, which portrayed Mexicans in a negative light. In addition, the military experience of some reporters and the access that all reporters had to U.S. military leaders contributed to the glorification of the American objective. Although coverage included critical comments on aspects of the American army such as a shortage of supplies and poor sanitary conditions, it contained a basic bias that was anti-Mexico, proexpansionism, pro–Manifest Destiny, and pro–American army.

Reporters became the prime source of information for the American public and contributed to the understanding, attitudes, and support for the distant conflict. The penny press responded to the opportunity presented, met the public's needs, and emerged stronger than ever from the war period.

The major contribution of reporting the war was in news transmission. The ability to deliver a story from a distant battlefield to the people at home, often before the government couriers, positioned the New Orleans newspapers, particularly the *Picayune* and the *Delta,* among the best in the country in the 1840s. Nine of the eleven principal correspondents reported for the New Orleans press, with six of them writing for the *Picayune.* The influence of the New Orleans newspapers was strengthened by the news exchanges they created. The Mexican War was a story that helped to carry the American press into the modern era.

Manley Witten

Notes

Introduction

1. Frank Luther Mott, *American Journalism, a History, 1690–1960*, 3rd ed. (New York: Macmillan, 1962), chap. 12; Edwin Emery, *The Press and America*, 5th ed. (Englewood Cliffs, N.J.: Prentice Hall, 1992), chap. 11.

2. Mott, *American Journalism*, 242–243.

3. *New York Herald*, May 15, 1846.

4. *Charleston Courier*, May 25, 1846.

5. *New York Sun*, May 16, 1846. The *Sun* claimed a daily circulation of 45,000 at the start of the war, 55,000 when it ended in summer 1848.

6. *New York Tribune*, May 14, 15, 1846. The *Tribune* had three regular editions daily: 6 A.M., 1 P.M., and 3 P.M.

7. *New York Herald*, May 14, 17, 1846.

8. *New Orleans Delta*, May 3, 1846.

9. *Charleston Courier*, May 25, 1846.

10. *New Orleans Picayune*, September 20, 1845.

11. Quoted in ibid., October 15, 1846.

12. Ibid., November 3, 1846.

13. *Delta*, October 13, 1846.

14. *Washington Union* extra, October 21, 1847.

15. Ibid., April 1, 1847.

16. *Philadelphia North American*, April 3, 1847.

17. *Picayune*, April 13, 1847.

18. Ibid.

19. *Philadelphia North American*, May 12, 1846.

20. Joseph J. Mathews, *Reporting the Wars* (Minneapolis: University of Minnesota Press, 1957), 54.

21. Robert Selph Henry, *The Story of the Mexican War* (New York: Frederick Ungar Publishing, 1950), 1.

22. For examples of war predictions, see *New York Tribune*, March 25, April 20, 1846, and *New York Herald*, February 2, 3, 6, 28, and April 8, 9, 10, 17, 1846.

23. Quoted in *New Orleans Picayune*, December 9, 1846.

24. Ibid.

25. *New Orleans Delta*, November 2, 1847.

26. *Picayune*, December 21, 1847.

27. Ibid.

28. *Augusta (Ga.) Chronicle and Sentinel*, February 2, 1847; also see January 5, 1848.

29. *New York Herald*, May 21, 1848.

30. *Claremont (N.H.) National Eagle*, June 5, 1846.

31. *New York Tribune*, January 5, 1846.

32. Ibid., May 8, 1846.

33. Ibid., April 20, May 11, May 20, May 28, 1846; March 25, April 14, 1847.

34. Ibid., May 12, 1846.

35. Ibid. For other examples of Greeley's editorials against the war, see ibid., July 17, November 24, December 1, 27, 1846; October 24, 1847; February 22, March 4, 13, 1848. But Greeley's words failed, and it would be two years before he could praise the treaty ending the war. See ibid., June 5, 1848.

Chapter 1. The War Press of New Orleans

1. The latter reference was to Zachary Taylor's presidential prospects. An earlier version of this chapter, Tom Reilly, "'The War Press of New Orleans': 1846–1848," appeared in *Journalism History* 13, nos. 3–4 (Winter–Autumn 1986): 86–95. For consistency in this study, most New Orleans newspapers are cited with full title in first use and by the paper's name only in subsequent uses.

2. Thomas Ewing Dabney, *One Hundred Great Years: The Story of the* Times-Picayune *from Its Founding to 1940* (Baton Rouge: Louisiana State University Press, 1944), 4–5; Harold Sinclair, *The Port of New Orleans* (Garden City, N.Y.: Doubleday, Doran & Co., 1942), 195–197; Fayette Copeland, *Kendall of the* Picayune (Norman: University of Oklahoma Press, 1943), 143. Copeland, *Kendall of the* Picayune, and Dabney, *One Hundred Great Years*, provide excellent information on the Mexican War period. For a colorful description of New Orleans and its press in the late 1840s, see A. Oakey Hall, *The Manhattener in New Orleans* (New York: J. S. Redfield, Clinton Hall, 1851). Also valuable is Carl R. Osthaus, *Partisans of the Southern Press: Editorial Spokesmen of the Nineteenth Century* (Lexington: University Press of Kentucky, 1994).

3. *New York Sun*, May 3, 1847; *Louisville Daily Journal*, March 16, 1847; Hall, *The Manhattener*, 23; Sinclair, *The Port of New Orleans*, 195.

4. Most of the research for this chapter was obtained by reading New Orleans newspapers for 1846–1848. Included were the *Bee, Commercial Bulletin, Daily Crescent, Daily Delta, Evening Mercury, Louisiana Courier, Picayune*, and *Tropic*. Other Louisiana newspapers read include the *Baton Rouge Democratic Advocate, Baton Rouge Gazette, Franklin Planter's Banner*, and *Plaquemine Southern Sentinel* (1848–1849).

5. Frederic Hudson, *Journalism in the United States, from 1690 to 1872* (New York: Harper, 1873), 491; Hall, *The Manhattener*, 163; *Mobile Alabama Planter*, December 21, 1846.

6. For various citations to these papers, see Copeland, *Kendall of the* Picayune; Dabney, *One Hundred Great Years;* John S. Kendall, "Early New Orleans Newspapers," *Louisiana Historical Quarterly*, 10 (1927): 383–402; B. H. Gilley, "'Polk's

War' and the Louisiana Press," *Louisiana History* 20 (1979): 5–23. Also see Raymond R. MacCurdy, *A History and Bibliography of Spanish-Language Newspapers and Magazines in Louisiana, 1808–1949* (Albuquerque: University of New Mexico Press, 1951); and Edward Larocque Tinker, *Bibliography of the French Newspapers and Periodicals of Louisiana* (Worcester, Mass.: American Antiquarian Society, 1933). According to Tinker (5, 12, 81), there were as many as sixteen French-language newspapers in Louisiana during the war. New Orleans has a rich history of Spanish-language newspapers, including the country's first-known publication, *El Misisipi*, dating to 1808. See Felix Gutierrez, "Spanish-Language Media in America: Background, Resources, History," *Journalism History* 4, no. 2 (Summer 1977): 34–41, 65–67; and John S. Kendall, "The Foreign Language Press of New Orleans," *Louisiana Historical Quarterly* 12 (1929): 363–380. The 1840s and 1850s were the most active period for the Spanish-language press in New Orleans, with twelve new newspapers and magazines started. MacCurdy, *Spanish-Language Newspapers*, 20, attributes this to "accelerated immigration of Spanish-speaking nationals and filibustering activities." "Marksman" quote is in Robert Clemens Reinders, *End of An Era* (New Orleans: Pelican Publishing, 1969), 232.

7. Milton Rickels, *Thomas Bangs Thorpe, Humorist of the Old Southwest* (Baton Rouge: Louisiana State University Press, 1962), 109–110.

8. The sketch appeared in the *Pensacola Gazette*, July 24, 1847.

9. *Charleston Courier*, June 10, 1847; *Philadelphia North American*, July 17, 1847; *Georgian*, quoted in *New Orleans Crescent*, April 24, 1848; *Republican*, quoted in the *New Orleans Bee*, June 24, 1848.

10. Copeland, *Kendall of the* Picayune, 36.

11. *New York Herald*, April 30, 1846.

12. Dabney, *One Hundred Great Years*, 15, 65–68; Copeland, *Kendall of the* Picayune, chaps. 11–12; Osthaus, *Partisans of the Southern Press*, chap. 3. A *picayune* was a Spanish silver coin, the half real, valued at one-sixteenth of a dollar. See Copeland, *Kendall of the* Picayune, 23n.

13. Dabney, *One Hundred Great Years*, 60–61; *Picayune*, May 1, 1846.

14. Greeley in *New York Tribune*, August 6, 1846; *New York Sun*, January 17, February 4, 1848; *Charleston Courier*, January 21, May 15, 1847.

15. Copeland, *Kendall of the* Picayune, chaps. 1–3. Quote from George Wilkins Kendall, *Letters from a Texas Sheep Ranch*, ed. James Harry Brown (Urbana: University of Illinois Press, 1959), 123; Osthaus, *Partisans of the Southern Press*, 50–59.

16. Copeland, *Kendall of the* Picayune, chaps. 13–18; Francis Brinley, *The Life of William T. Porter* (New York: D. Appleton, 1860), chap. 9.

17. Editorial, *Picayune*, August 23, 1845; also see July 1, 25, 1846.

18. A collection of his writing is in Denis Corcoran, *Pickings from the* Picayune (Philadelphia: Carey & Hart, 1846).

19. *Delta*, October 12, 1845, and December 24, 1846, for examples; editorial, November 2, 1847; May 9, 1848.

20. Ibid., September 29, October 13, 1846, January 5, 1847; new press quote January 5, 1848. The paper ran two-page news and advertising supplements on eight

dates during the first three weeks it had the new press. For circulation, see ibid., January 19, 1848; for Veracruz, see ibid., March 21, 1848. The agent had the paper printed in Veracruz because of the delay in boats leaving for New Orleans. Express, ibid., November 10, 1847, March 31, 1848. The arrangement grew out of the friendship between *Delta* correspondent James L. Freaner and government peace negotiator Nicholas Trist and the Polk administration's preference for an arrangement with a pro-Democrat paper. Trist Papers, Library of Congress.

21. Gilley, "'Polk's War,'" is an excellent summary of editorial positions of Louisiana newspapers during the war. Quotes are from *Delta*, January 7, March 27, May 3, 23, July 2, 1846. Also, October 14, 1845; also see March 27, May 10, June 13, 16, 25, December 16, 1846; January 6, 26, July 28, 1847; February 9, 1848.

22. Ibid., January 17, 1847; "All of Mexico," December 30, 1847.

23. Tom Reilly, "American Reporters and the Mexican War" (Ph.D. diss., University of Minnesota, 1975); Jimmy L. Bryan Jr., comp., "Correspondents of the U.S.-Mexican War (1846–1848) from the *New Orleans Delta*" (Arlington: Center for Southwestern Studies and the History of Cartography, University of Texas at Arlington, 1998).

24. *New Orleans Crescent*, March 5, 9, 1848. The *Crescent* sold for 5 cents per copy, 15 cents for a weekly subscription. "It is beautifully printed and arranged and forms to our taste the model of a daily paper," the *Mobile Register and Journal* observed (March 7, 1848).

25. *Crescent*, May 4, 8, 1848. Walker, who later gained notoriety as leader of Latin America filibuster expeditions, is discussed in Albert Z. Carr, *The World and William Walker* (New York: Harper & Row, 1963), 15–35. It is interesting that Whitman was hired at the prowar *Crescent*, as he apparently lost his job at the *Brooklyn Eagle* in January 1848 because he cooled on that paper's strong support of the war and Mexican annexation. Later in 1848, after leaving the *Crescent* in a dispute over money, Whitman went to work as editor of the *Brooklyn Freeman*, a free-soil newspaper. See Thomas L. Brasher, *Whitman as Editor of the* Brooklyn Daily Eagle (Detroit: Wayne State University Press, 1970), 20; Frances Winwar, *American Giant* (New York: Tudor Publishing Co., 1941), 120.

26. *Commercial Times* prospectus is printed in *Delta*, October 13, 1845. Rickels, *Thomas Bangs Thorpe*, chap. 1. J. J. Hawkins was assistant editor; Lewis Haylinger, an experienced New Orleans journalist, served as commercial editor and was co-owner with Charles Black and David Bravo; *Delta*, October 13, 1845; *Picayune*, April 25, 1848.

27. *Delta*, April 1, 3, 1846. There was wide use of the *Tropic*'s war news by other papers. For examples, see *Baltimore Sun*, May 13, 14, June 8, 26, July 1, 14, 18, August 25, October 10, 19, 22, 24, 30, November 23, December 7, 23, 1846; *Delta*, September 18, 1846, May 29, June 9, 1847; also *Baton Rouge Gazette*, May 29, June 19, 1847.

28. *Delta*, November 1, 3, 10, 26, 1846. Cessions, a former *Picayune* reporter, took full control of the *Mercury* in June 1847. *Franklin (La.) Planter's Banner*, June 24, 1847; *Picayune*, November 10, 1846; *Crescent*, April 24, 1848.

29. Reinders, *End of an Era*, 232.

30. See Tom Reilly, "A Spanish-Language Voice of Dissent in Antebellum New Orleans," *Louisiana History* 23 (Fall 1982): 325–339; MacCurdy, *A History and Bibliography*, 19, 20; *Picayune*, January 13, 1846; *Delta*, June 3, 16, July 12, September 3, November 27, 1846, January 5, 1847; *Mobile Register and Journal*, March 24, 1847; *New Orleans Bee*, July 23, 1847; New Orleans *La Patria*, October 25, 1847, quoted in MacCurdy, *A History and Bibliography*, 20.

31. *Picayune*, May 22, 1847. Treatment of American prisoners in Mexico was a special concern of the *Picayune* because its editor, George Kendall, had been a prisoner in Mexico after being captured with the Santa Fe Expedition in 1841. See *Picayune*, May 27, June 4, 8, 1847. *La Patria*'s editors were threatened with violence many times during the war and were involved in a number of editorial disputes with their prowar newspaper neighbors. See Reilly, "A Spanish-Language Voice."

32. Complaints about *La Patria*'s coverage can be found in *New York Tribune*, October 14, 1847; *St. Louis Reveille*, September 26, 1847; *New Orleans Bee*, September 16, 1847; *Boston Daily Mail*, September 9, October 14, 15, 1847; *Charleston Courier*, August 3, September 22, 1847; *New York Herald*, September 24, October 14, 1847; quotes in *Mercury*, September 16, 1847; *Republican*, September 24, 1847; *Courier*, July 10, 1847.

33. *New Orleans Tropic*, May 20, 1846; writer quoted in *Picayune*, July 24, 1847; Monterrey (Mexico) *American Pioneer*, May 13, 1847.

34. Greeley, *New York Tribune*, March 4, 1848; *Courier and Enquirer*, quoted in *Delta*, November 26, 1847.

Chapter 2. The Corps of *Scribendi*

1. The epigraph is from a writer who used the initial "T," most likely John G. Todd, identified in the *Delta*, May 19, 1846, as formerly with the Texas Navy.

2. *New York Spirit of the Times*, March 21, 1846. For a concise summary of this prewar period, see Seymour V. Connor and Odie B. Faulk, *North America Divided: The Mexican War, 1846–1848* (New York: Oxford University Press, 1971), chap. 1; also Robert H. Thonhoff, "Taylor's Trail in Texas," *Southwestern Historical Quarterly* 70, no. 1 (July 1966): 7–22.

3. Quote is in Edward S. Wallace, "The United States Army in Mexico City," *Military Affairs* 13, no. 3 (Fall 1949): 158–166. Two valuable studies of life in the army are James M. McCaffrey, *Army of Manifest Destiny: The American Soldier in the Mexican War, 1846–1848* (New York: New York University Press, 1992); and Richard Bruce Winders, *Mr. Polk's Army* (College Station: Texas A&M University Press, 1997).

4. *Niles' National Register*, July 25, 1846, quoting from the *Louisville Journal*.

5. *New York Tribune*, May 19, 1847.

6. Quoted in ibid., May 28, 1847.

7. Justin H. Smith, *The War with Mexico*, 2 vols. (New York: Macmillan Co., 1919), 1:156–180; John S. D. Eisenhower, *So Far from God: The U.S. War with*

Mexico, 1846–1848 (New York: Random House, 1989); Henry's letter is printed in the *Picayune*, May 3, 1846.

8. Ulysses Simpson Grant, *The Papers of Ulysses S. Grant*, ed. John Y. Simon (Carbondale: Southern Illinois University Press, 1967), 1:86.

9. Henry, in *Spirit of the Times*, May 23, 1846.

10. Tom Reilly, "American Reporters and the Mexican War" (Ph.D. diss., University of Minnesota, 1975).

11. *Picayune*, January 1, 1848.

12. *Washington National Intelligencer*, October 1, 1846.

13. *North American*, January 16, 1847.

14. *Niles' National Register*, November 21, 1846, 180.

15. *New Orleans Tropic*, June 22, 1846.

16. *New York Spirit of the Times*, January 9, 1847.

17. Letter (Newton Curd) given to Gales and Seaton, March 12, 1848, Mexican War Collection, Special Collections Division, University of Texas at Arlington Libraries.

18. George Meade, *The Life and Letters of George Gordon Meade*, 2 vols. (New York: Scribners, 1913), 113, 131.

19. Emma Jerome Blackwood, ed., *To Mexico with Scott: Letters of Captain E. Kirby Smith to His Wife* (Cambridge, Mass.: Harvard University Press, 1971), 121. Smith felt the way officers got promoted was by toadyism, favoritism, or luck rather than merit.

20. *Arkansas State Gazette*, January 23, 1847.

21. *Pensacola Gazette*, October 17, 1846.

22. *New York Tribune*, May 10, 1847.

23. *Alton (Ill.) Telegraph*, February 12, 1847. Robbins had claimed Colonel John J. Hardin was not popular with the Illinois volunteers.

24. See letters from Colonel W. B. Campbell to D. C., Monterrey, December 7, 1846, cited in Justin H. Smith Collection, Benson Latin American Collection, General Libraries, University of Texas at Austin, vol. 16.

25. *Boston Daily Mail*, May 27, 1846.

26. See F. B. Marbut, *News from the Capital: The Story of Washington Reporting* (Carbondale: Southern Illinois University Press, 1971).

27. *Delta*, November 7, 1845.

28. Ibid., February 1, 1847.

29. *Baltimore Sun*, September 24, 1846.

30. *Washington Union*, November 2, 1846.

31. The sarcastic term "the corps of *scribendi*" was in *Niles' National Register*, November 21, 1846, 180.

32. Quoted in *Charleston Courier*, October 27, 1846.

33. Ibid.

34. Ibid.

35. *Philadelphia North American*, January 16, 1847.

36. Ibid.

37. *Picayune*, November 16, 1847.

38. Ibid., April 14, 1847.

39. *Washington Union*, September 14, 1846.

40. *Picayune*, January 20, 1847.

41. *Philadelphia Public Ledger*, quoted in *Picayune*, December 15, 1846.

42. *Picayune*, July 9, 1846.

43. *St. Louis Reveille*, April 9, 1847.

44. *Delta*, May 13, 1846.

45. *New Orleans Commercial Bulletin*, May 6, 1846; *National*, quoted in *Mobile Register and Journal*, November 4, 1847.

46. *New Orleans Louisiana Courier*, May 5, 1846.

47. *Tropic*, quoted in *Mobile Register and Journal*, May 7, 1846.

48. *Baton Rouge Gazette*, May 9, 1846.

49. *New Orleans Bee*, May 4, 1846.

50. *Delta*, May 23, 1846.

51. Ibid., May 29, 1846.

52. *Baltimore Sun*, October 30, 1846.

53. *Delta*, January 26, 1848.

54. *Picayune*, August 9, 1846.

55. *Delta*, June 5, 1846.

56. *Picayune*, June 14, 1846.

57. *Niles' National Register*, May 23, 1846, 179.

58. *Cincinnati Enquirer*, May 18, 1846.

59. Ibid., May 7, 1846.

60. Stringer's sentiments are in the *Delta*, May 23, June 19, 1846.

61. *Delta*, August 7, 1846. Quotes from Larue are in ibid., July 7, August 6, 7, 1846.

62. Ibid., August 7, 1846.

63. Quoted in *Niles' National Register*, September 26, 1846, 56.

64. *Little Rock Arkansas State Gazette*, July 13, 1846. Borden remained and fought at Buena Vista in February 1847. Ibid., April 24, 1847.

65. *Ottawa (Ill.) Free Trader*, January 22, 1847.

66. *New Orleans Bee*, May 29, June 20, 1846.

67. *New Orleans Commercial Times*, July 30, 1847, in *New York Tribune*, August 9, 1847.

68. *New Orleans Crescent*, March 5, 1848.

69. *Delta*, March 27, 1847.

70. *Picayune*, April 28, 1848.

71. Ibid., July 7, 1846.

72. *Washington Union*, November 2, 1846.

73. *Delta*, February 1, 1847.

74. *New York Sun*, September 24, 1846.

75. *New York Herald*, June 25, 1846.

Chapter 3. "Mr. Kendall of the *Picayune*"

1. Kendall wrote at least 214 reports for the *Picayune* during the war, including special battle histories and related sketches and anecdotes. See George Wilkins Kendall, *Dispatches from the Mexican War*, ed. and with an introduction by Lawrence Delbert Cress (Norman: University of Oklahoma Press, 1999). For a biography of Kendall's varied career, see Fayette Copeland, *Kendall of the* Picayune (Norman: University of Oklahoma Press, 1943). Copeland (150) calls Kendall "the first modern war correspondent." Also highly valuable are the introduction by Ron Tyler in George Wilkins Kendall's *The War between the United States and Mexico, Illustrated*, with illustrations by Carl Nebel (1851; reprint, Austin: Texas State Historical Association, 1994), vii–xxviii; and Walter Prescott Webb, H. Bailey Carroll, and Eldon Branda, eds., *The Handbook of Texas*, 3 vols. (1952; reprint, Austin: Texas State Historical Association, 1976), 1:945.

2. See editor's comments in George Wilkins Kendall, *Letters from a Texas Sheep Ranch*, ed. James Harry Brown (Urbana: University of Illinois Press, 1959), and also 10.

3. Copeland, *Kendall of the* Picayune, 295.

4. Kendall quotes in George Wilkins Kendall, *Narrative of the Texan Santa Fe Expedition*, 2 vols. (New York: Harper & Bros., 1844), 1:13–14, 66. For detail on the start of the expedition, see Copeland, *Kendall of the* Picayune, 42–80. See also Richard Bruce Winders, *Crisis in the Southwest: The United States, Mexico, and the Struggle over Texas* (Wilmington, Del.: SR Books, 2002), for Kendall's Santa Fe experiences and the connection between Texas's earlier conflicts and the Mexican War.

5. Copeland, *Kendall of the* Picayune, 95.

6. Kendall, *Narrative of the Texan Santa Fe Expedition*, 1:294.

7. Ibid. Quote on i; because of the book's emphasis on the Mexicans' cruelty and its impact on American opinion, historian Carey McWilliams referred to Kendall's narrative as "the *Uncle Tom's Cabin* of the Mexican War." Carey McWilliams, *North from Mexico* (reprint, New York: Greenwood Press, 1968), 117. Raymund Paredes, "The Image of the Mexican in American Literature" (Ph.D. diss., University of Texas, Austin, 1973), 94, observed, "The 'Narrative' was at once popular and influential, stirring up wells of outrage against the Mexicans, a rage which would soon find release in outright warfare." Other strongly critical views of Kendall's *Narrative* are in Janet Lecompte, "Manuel Armijo, George Wilkins Kendall, and the Baca-Caballero Conspiracy," *New Mexico Historical Review* 59, no. 1 (January 1984): 49–65; Paredes, "The Mexican Image in American Travel Literature, 1831–1869," *New Mexico Historical Review* 52, no. 1 (January 1977): 5–29; and Cecil Robinson, *With the Ears of Strangers: The Mexican in American Literature* (Tucson: University of Arizona Press, 1963). Robinson observed, "Kendall was unhampered by any notions of scholarly objectivity. With all his prejudices intact, he was pristine America caught in the maze of a complex and totally alien culture" (18).

8. Kendall, *Letters*, 10; see his letter from North Hampton, Massachusetts, in *Picayune*, August 30, 1843. Kendall also had an office slave at the paper. Copeland, *Kendall of the* Picayune, 145n5.

9. First quote in Copeland, *Kendall of the* Picayune, 15; Frederic Hudson, *Journalism in the United States, from 1690 to 1872* (New York: Harper, 1873), 494–495; contemporaries quoted in *Picayune*, November 10, 1867; Raphael Semmes, *Service Afloat and Ashore during the Mexican War* (Cincinnati, Ohio: William H. Moore, 1851), 412.

10. Copeland, *Kendall of the* Picayune, chaps. 1–2; *Picayune*, October 27, November 10, 1867; quoted in Marilyn McAdams Sibley, *Travelers in Texas, 1761–1860* (Austin and London: University of Texas Press, 1967), 11.

11. Quaife's comments are in George Wilkins Kendall, *Narrative of the Texan Santa Fe Expedition* (Chicago: Lakeside Press, 1929), xxiv–xxv. See Copeland, *Kendall of the* Picayune, chap. 14; and F. Lauriston Bullard, *Famous War Correspondents* (Boston: Little, Brown, 1914), 351–374.

12. Russell is discussed in Rupert Furneaux, *The First War Correspondent: William Howard Russell of The Times* (London: Cassell & Co., 1944); and Phillip Knightley, *The First Casualty* (New York: Harcourt Brace Jovanovich, 1975), 3–17. See 4 for the definition.

13. For examples, see Bullard, *Famous War Correspondents*, 352; James Melvin Lee, *A History of American Journalism* (1917; reprint, Garden City, N.Y.: Garden City Publishing, 1923), 259–260; Frank Luther Mott, *American Journalism*, 3rd ed. (New York: Macmillan, 1962), 248–250; Edwin Emery and Michael Emery, *The Press and America*, 7th ed. (Englewood Cliffs, N.J.: Prentice Hall, 1992), 113–114; Robert Rutland, *The Newsmongers: Journalism in the Life of the Nation, 1690–1972* (New York: Dial Press, 1973), 157–158. Kendall's views are in an undated *Picayune* clipping (from Paris, June 19, 1854) in the Kendall Family Collection, Special Collections Division, University of Texas at Arlington Libraries.

14. Copeland, *Kendall of the* Picayune, 148–150; Kendall in *Picayune*, May 30, June 1, 3, 14, 1846.

15. Kendall in *Picayune*, June 14, July 7, 1846. A *New York Herald* correspondent, who met Kendall in Matamoros, wrote, "If no other advantage to the country is derived from his enlistment in this just and holy war, literature will receive a valuable addition [as] Kendall will write a book of mostly army news." *Herald*, July 25, 1846.

16. Kendall in *Picayune*, June 26, 1846; *New York Tribune* quote dated June 27, 1846.

17. *Picayune*, July 8, 17, 1846.

18. Ibid., June 24, 26, 1846.

19. Ibid., July 17, 1846. In general, Kendall ignored the issue.

20. Peoples reprinted in *Niles' National Register*, August 1, 1846, and *New York Post*, August 6, 1846. See also *Bee*, July 27, August 28, 1846.

21. Undated *Picayune* clipping, written from Boerne, Texas, May 5, 1861, in Kendall Collection, Special Collections Division, University of Texas at Arlington Libraries; Kendall, *Mexican War Illustrated*, 13.

22. *Picayune*, June 20, 26, July 19, 1846.

23. Ibid., June 5, 1849. This was written from Paris after the war.

24. Ibid., August 15, September 6, 1846. One hundred lashes were occasionally prescribed, although usually twenty-five, thirty-nine, or fifty were ordered. On

one occasion, General William O. Butler remitted another officer's sentence of 500 lashes. See John Porter Bloom, "With the American Army into Mexico, 1846–1848" (Ph.D. diss., Emery University, 1956), 166–167.

25. *Picayune*, July 7, 1846. "To see the elephant" was a slang term commonly used by soldiers in their first combat experience referring to "seeing the world." Kendall, *Narrative of the Texan Santa Fe Expedition*, 1:108–110, defined it in civilian terms: "There is a cant expression 'I've seen the elephant,' in very common use in Texas . . . and when I first heard one of our men say that he had seen the animal in question, I was utterly at a loss to fathom his meaning. . . . When a man is disappointed in anything he undertakes, when he has seen enough, when he gets sick and tired of any job he may have set himself about he has 'seen the elephant.'"

26. *Philadelphia North American*, August 28, 1847; *Baltimore Sun*, June 28, 1847; *New York Tribune*, September 17, November 30, 1847.

27. *Picayune*, May 19, 20, August 8, 1847.

Chapter 4. Pardon Jones Goes to War

1. Taylor's problems are discussed in Justin H. Smith, *The War with Mexico*, 2 vols. (New York: Macmillan Co., 1919), vol. 1, chaps. 11–12. Also see Chester L. Kieffer, *Maligned General: The Biography of Thomas Sidney Jesup* (San Rafael, Calif.: Presidio Press, 1979), chaps. 10–11.

2. *Thayer Memorial Edition, Register of Graduates and Former Cadets of the United States Military Academy, 1964* (West Point, N.Y.: West Point Alumni Foundation, 1964), 266–267; *Picayune*, September 16, 1849; letter to the author from Dr. Herbert Leventhal, Chief, U.S. Military Academy Archives, West Point, July 6, 1977. Among Haile's classmates at West Point were William Tecumseh Sherman; George Henry Thomas, the Civil War's "Rock of Chickamauga"; his future brother-in-law, Paul Octave Hébert, governor of Louisiana from 1853 to 1856, a colonel in the Mexican War, and a Confederate brigadier general; Richard Stoddard Ewell, Confederate lieutenant general; and Bushrod Rust Johnson, a Confederate major general. Also see Fayette Copeland, *Kendall of the* Picayune (Norman: University of Oklahoma Press, 1943), 158, 160.

3. *Delta*, February 2, March 5, 19, May 22, 1846; *Picayune*, May 30, 1844, September 15, 1849.

4. *Delta*, July 22, 1846. Another contemporary, John E. Durivage of the *Picayune*, described Haile as "an amiable, kind-hearted and talented gentleman." *San Francisco Alta California*, December 10, 1849.

5. *Picayune*, May 30, 1846.

6. Haile's quotes in ibid., June 14, July 7, 8, September 8, 11, 1846. Privates were paid $7 per month. The many challenges of serving in the army are described well in Richard Bruce Winders, *Mr. Polk's Army: The American Military Experience in the Mexican War* (College Station: Texas A&M University Press, 1997), chaps. 7–8; and James W. McCaffrey, *The Army of Manifest Destiny: The American Soldier in the Mexican War, 1846–1848* (New York: New York University Press, 1992).

7. *Picayune*, June 14, 20, July 7, 1846.

8. Ibid., June 14, 16, 1846.

9. Ibid., February 18, 1847.

10. Ibid., July 7, September 6, 1846.

11. *Philadelphia North American*, May 4, 1847.

12. *Picayune*, January 27, February 4, 1847.

13. Ibid., January 27, 1847.

14. Ibid., June 20, 1846; the later trip is reported February 3, 1847.

15. Ibid., July 11, August 15, 1846.

16. Ibid., June 16, 1846.

17. Ibid., July 7, September 6, 13, 1846. Taylor was an avid newspaper reader and frequently said his most reliable information about the war came from the papers. But he was generous in loaning them out "& I had as well look for a needle in a hay stack as to recover them," he once complained. Zachary Taylor, *Letters of Zachary Taylor, from the Battle-fields of the Mexican War* (Rochester, N.Y.: Genesee Press, 1908), 22, 125. Taylor's favorite newspapers appear to have been the *Picayune* and the *Louisville Journal*, which he called "ably conducted . . . and devoted or will be to my interest for the presidency." Ibid., 104. With a long, unreliable communication line behind him, Taylor often learned about actions of the American and Mexican governments by reading the papers. For examples, see *Messages of the President of the United States . . .* , Exec. Doc. 60, 30th Congress, 1st Session (Washington, D.C.: Wendell & Benthuysen, Printers, 1848), 98, 122, 334, 397, 444, 550, 690, 1179. Also see David Lavender, "How to Make It to the White House without Really Trying," *American Heritage* 18, no. 4 (June 1967): 78–86.

18. *Picayune*, April 14, 1842. At least forty-seven prewar Pardon Jones letters appeared in the *Picayune* between December 1840 and April 1845.

19. Three additional Pardon Jones letters appeared in the *Picayune* late in the war, long after Haile had joined the army and returned to Mexico as an officer. They were in the same basic style but subdued in comparison to his earlier work. *Picayune*, March 16, April 1, 27, 1848. For a good study of this style and its influences, see Norris W. Yates, *William T. Porter and the* Spirit of the Times (Baton Rouge: Louisiana State University Press, 1957), particularly 100.

20. *Picayune*, July 16, 1846.

21. Ibid., November 11, 1846.

22. For Old Southwest School humor, see Walter Blair, *Horse Sense in American Humor* (Chicago: University of Chicago Press, 1942), 102–122; John Q. Anderson, *With the Bark On* (Nashville: Vanderbilt University Press, 1967), 9–10, 113; Bruce R. McElderry Jr., ed., *The Realistic Movement in American Writing* (New York: Odyssey Press, 1965), 546–601.

Chapter 5. Meeting the Demand

1. Henry's father, John V. Henry, was a well-known Albany, N.Y., lawyer who died in 1829. Van Buren wrote to Eaton, "If you can consistently appoint his son

... I am confident you could do no act on the same scale which would be more grateful to public sentiment of many parts of that state." Martin Van Buren to John H. Eaton, November 25, 1829, in *U.S. Military Academy Cadet Application Papers, 1805–1866*, National Archives Microfilm Publication no. 688. Henry's middle name appears frequently in the literature spelled Seaton. The author has taken the spelling Seton from a letter his older brother and guardian, James V. Henry, wrote to Eaton from New York City, November 23, 1829, nominating William for admission to West Point. Ibid. Henry's biographical information is from *Official Register of the Officers and Cadets of the U.S. Military Academy* (1832–1835); and George W. Cullum, *Biographical Register of the Officers and Graduates of the U.S. Military Academy at West Point . . .* , 3rd ed. (Boston and New York: Houghton, Mifflin, 1891), 618; Francis B. Heitman, *Historical Register and Dictionary of the United States Army, from Its Organization, September 29, 1789 to March 2, 1903*, 2 vols. (Washington, D.C.: Government Printing Office, 1903), 1:524. Also see William Seton Henry, *Campaign Sketches of the War with Mexico* (New York: Harper & Brothers, 1847); William Starr Myers, ed., *The Mexican War Diary of George B. McClellan* (Princeton, N.J.: Princeton University Press, 1917), 48; Robert Johannsen, *To the Halls of the Montezumas* (New York: Oxford University Press, 1985), 153; *Picayune*, July 18, 1847. Henry's West Point classmate George Meade called him "a very good fellow." George Meade, *The Life and Letters of George Gordon Meade*, 2 vols. (New York: Scribners, 1913), 1:167–168. Another classmate, William T. H. Brooks, called Henry "a warm . . . useful friend." Letter, Brooks to his mother, April 5, 1847, in William T. H. Brooks Papers, U.S. Army Military History Collection, Carlisle Barracks, Pa.

2. The Matamoros report, dated May 23, 1846, is reprinted in *New York Tribune*, June 13, 1846.

3. *Spirit of the Times*, April 25, May 16, 30, October 24, 1846.

4. Henry quotes in the *Spirit of the Times*, March 28, May 20, July 4, August 1, 29, December 26, 1846; January 9, 1847.

5. *Delta*, November 7, 1847; the pronunciation of Freaner's name is in a letter from Nicholas Trist to his wife, dated Mexico City, February 2, 1848, Trist Papers, Library of Congress.

6. Lt. George B. McLellan referred to volunteers as "mustangs" because of the lanky Mexican horses they often rode. See Winders, *Mr. Polk's Army*, 218n. The term was considered scornful and was also applied to commissioned officers who served previously as enlisted personnel. For Freaner's background, see Thomas J. C. Williams, *A History of Washington County, Maryland* (Hagerstown, Md.: John M. Runk & L. R. Titsworth, 1906), 241, 281–282; Fayette Copeland, *Kendall of the Picayune* (Norman: University of Oklahoma Press, 1943), 157–158, 179n8; William A. DePalo Jr., "James L. Freaner," in *The United States and Mexico at War*, ed. Donald S. Frazier (New York: Simon & Schuster Macmillan, 1998), 165. The "Mustang" anecdote is in the *Delta*, November 6, 1847; J. F. H. Claiborne, *Life and Correspondence of John A. Quitman*, 2 vols. (New York: Harper & Bros., 1860), 399–400; and James Kimmins Greer, *Colonel Jack Hays* (New York: E. Dutton & Co., 1952), 141. Freaner did not mention it in his wartime correspondence.

7. *Delta*, June 16, 1846.

8. Ibid., January 24, August 6, 1847.

9. Ibid., May 12, 1847; April 27, 1848. Tobin may be the "Ben Tobin" described by Samuel E. Chamberlain as "one of the best fellows in the world, son of a Irish gentleman, [who] was sent to Maynooth College to be educated for the Priesthood, was expelled, came to America, and was now the wild rollicking Texas Ranger." See Samuel E. Chamberlain, *My Confession* (New York: Harper & Bros., 1956), 102.

10. According to Tobin's military records, he served as a captain in the Louisiana Volunteer Regiment May 6–August 6, 1846. He rejoined the army as a private in the Texas Rangers in January 1847. When it reported the latter, the *Delta* (January 24, 1847) observed it would always call him "Captain Tobin" for the simple reason "he is one although he has never worn an epilet." Tobin later became orderly sergeant in Capt. Ben McCulloch's Texas Ranger company (*Spirit of the Times*, May 13, 1848) and was elected second lieutenant in another Texas Ranger company in March 1847. See *Albany Evening Journal*, November 6, 1846; *Delta*, April 30, 1847; *Spirit of the Times*, May 13, 20, 1847; Heitman, *Historical Register*, 2:70; Orderbook, "Army of Chihuahua." Centre Division Orders No. 251, March 23, 1847, 234, in John E. Wool Collection, New York State Archives, Albany.

11. *Delta*, September 23, 1846; *Spirit of the Times*, October 10, 1846.

12. *Philadelphia North American*, December 8, 1846; *Baltimore Sun*, October 8, 1846; *St. Louis Reveille*, March 28, 1848; *Spirit of the Times*, February 6, 1848.

13. See Milton Rickels, *Thomas Bangs Thorpe, Humorist of the Old Southwest* (Baton Rouge: Louisiana State University Press, 1962). The Washington *National Intelligencer* (May 18, 1847) praised Thorpe as "one of the most vigorous and spirited writers of which our country can boast."

14. *Delta*, April 1, 1846; Rickels, *Thomas Bangs Thorpe*, 267.

15. Rickels, *Thomas Bangs Thorpe*, 119–123; Thorpe also carried military messages to Gen. Taylor, assuring himself free transportation. *Tropic*, May 21, June 2, 1846. *Baton Rouge Gazette*, May 23, 1846. "Of course he will use his perceptives and reflectives while there," the *New York Tribune* noted tartly, June 1, 1846.

16. All quotes from *Tropic*, June 2, 1846.

17. Thorpe items quoted from *Tropic*, July 1, 1846; *New York Post*, July 8, 1846; *Nashville Whig*, July 22, 1846.

18. Quoted in Rickels, *Thomas Bangs Thorpe*, 156–157.

19. For examples, see *Baltimore Sun*, June 8, 26, 1846; *Charleston Courier*, June 11, 1846; *New York Tribune*, June 13, 24, 1846.

20. Rickels, *Thomas Bangs Thorpe*, 123. Neither book was a commercial success, however. Also see Eugene Current-Garcia, "Thomas Bangs Thorpe and the Literature of the Ante-bellum Southwest Frontier," *Louisiana Historical Quarterly* 34, no. 2 (April 1956): 199–222; and David C. Estes, ed., *A New Collection of Thomas Bangs Thorpe's Sketches of the Old Southwest* (Baton Rouge: Louisiana State University Press, 1989).

21. Rickels, *Thomas Bangs Thorpe*, 151–156. Thorpe's letters generally were unsigned, although some ended with the initial "T." Most had the small headline, "Editorial Correspondence."

22. *Picayune,* July 21, 1846. Lumsden's background is in Copeland, *Kendall of the Picayune,* 20, 155, 165, 185–188. See also Mitchel Roth, "Journalism and the U.S. Mexican War," in *Dueling Eagles: Reinterpreting the U.S. Mexican War, 1846–1848,* ed. Richard V. Francaviglia and Douglas W. Richmonds (Fort Worth: Texas Christian University Press, 2000), 110.

23. *Picayune,* August 16, September 10, 1846.

24. Ibid., September 6, 1846.

25. See Samuel Chester Reid Jr., *Scouting Expeditions of McCulloch's Texas Rangers* (Philadelphia: G. B. Sieber & Co., 1847); also J. Cutler Andrews, *The South Reports the Civil War* (Princeton, N.J.: Princeton University Press, 1970), 48–49, 52–53. Greer, *Colonel Jack Hays,* 41–42, notes that the rangers traveled light and it was not easy to meet their requirements. Members had to supply their own weapons, saddles, blankets, similar equipment, and usually the horses. They were often selected for character, courage, and skill in horsemanship and marksmanship.

26. Reid, *Scouting Expeditions,* 120. Quote about letters on 6.

Chapter 6. Battle of Monterrey

1. Quoted in James T. McIntosh, Lynda L. Crist, and Mary S. Dix, eds., *The Papers of Jefferson Davis* (Baton Rouge: Louisiana State University Press, 1981), 3:55, also 56n7. The *Picayune,* October 14, 1846, printed the list of officers killed or wounded at Monterrey, but it was another month before the full army list was published. Monterrey is spelled with one *r* in this citation according to the common American usage at the time. It should be noted, however, Monterrey, Mexico, is spelled with two *r*'s, and will be used here with two *r*'s, unless it involves a direct quote from the reporters' letters. Monterey, California, also referred to in this study, is spelled with one *r.*

2. *Philadelphia North American,* October 15, 1846. For examples of such Monterrey coverage, see *Washington Union,* October 11, 1846; *Baltimore Sun, New York Sun, Philadelphia North American,* all October 12, 1846.

3. For details of the battle, see David Lavender, *Climax at Buena Vista* (Philadelphia and New York: J. B. Lippincott, 1966), chap. 6; Justin H. Smith, *The War with Mexico,* 2 vols. (New York: Macmillan Co., 1919), vol. 1, chap. 12; K. Jack Bauer, *Zachary Taylor* (Baton Rouge: Louisiana State University Press, 1985), chap. 6; John S. D. Eisenhower, *So Far from God: The U.S. War with Mexico, 1846–1848* (New York: Random House, 1989), chaps. 11–13; Joseph E. Chance, *Jefferson Davis's Mexican War Regiment* (Jackson: University Press of Mississippi, 1991); Edward S. Wallace, *General William Jenkins Worth: Monterey's Forgotten Hero* (Dallas: Southern Methodist University Press, 1953); *New York Tribune,* July 31, 1846.

4. Lavender, *Climax at Buena Vista,* 120. President Polk, appalled at Taylor's generosity, ordered the armistice ended, but by then it was too late. Taylor, *Letters,* 46, 50, 54.

5. *St. Louis Reveille,* October 3, 1846. The paper did not know the battle already had been fought; *Delta,* September 26, 1846; *Washington Union,* September 14, 1846; *Picayune,* October 18, 1846.

6. George Wilkins Kendall, *Letters*, 102; Fayette Copeland, *Kendall of the* Picayune (Norman: University of Oklahoma Press, 1943), chap. 15. For Reid's experiences at Monterrey, see Samuel Chester Reid Jr., *Scouting Expeditions of McCulloch's Texas Rangers* (Philadelphia: G. B. Sieber & Co., 1847).

7. For an example of Kendall's letters as used by other newspapers during 1846, see *Baltimore Sun*, July 7, 28; August 9, 14, 19, 21, 29; September 5, 22; October 3; November 10; and see *Picayune*, quoted in *St. Louis Reveille*, November 4, 1846. The reference was to Kendall's imprisonment in Mexico City. *Picayune*, August 15, 1846.

8. Kendall in *Letters*, 111; Henry, *Spirit of the Times*, September 26, October 10, 1846; Haile in *Picayune*, September 12, 1846.

9. Haile in *Picayune*, August 25, 26, 1846.

10. Ibid., September 6, 1846.

11. Haile in ibid., October 6, 1846; Henry, *Spirit of the Times*, September 26, 1846. Another correspondent who met Kendall in the army camp reported that "Kendall is the best mounted man in the army, having two fine thoroughbreds at his command." *Spirit of the Times*, August 1, 1846; Copeland, *Kendall*, 168.

12. *Picayune*, October 6, 1846.

13. *Delta*, May 13, August 15, 1846. Also see Charles D. Spurlin, *Texas Veterans in the Mexican War* (St. Louis: Ingmire Publications, 1984), 30; and James Kimmins Greer, *Colonel Jack Hays* (1952; rev. ed., College Station: Texas A&M University Press, 1987).

14. *Delta*, September 6, 1846; Copeland, *Kendall of the* Picayune, 171.

15. *Picayune*, October 4, 1846.

16. Eisenhower, *So Far from God*, chap. 12.

17. *Picayune*, October 4, 1846.

18. Ibid., October 22, 1846.

19. Ibid., October 4, 1846.

20. Ibid., October 22, 1846; Allis was 6 feet, 1 inch—tall for the time. He was born in New Haven County, Connecticut, and was twenty-five years old. Letter from Thomas R. Kailbourn to the author regarding Allis's biography, July 13, 1992.

21. *Picayune*, October 4, 1846.

22. Copeland, *Kendall of the* Picayune, 172, Kendall, quoted on 173; *Picayune*, October 3, November 19, 1846.

23. Copeland, *Kendall of the* Picayune, 176–177; Lavender, *Climax at Buena Vista*, 118–120.

24. *Picayune*, October 21, 1846.

25. Ibid., October 4, 6, 1846. Haile later identified the courier as an employee of the army quartermaster named Myers. Ibid., February 2, 1847.

26. *Charleston Courier*, October 10, 1846; *Washington Union*, October 12, 1846; *Baltimore Sun*, October 12, 1846; *Philadelphia Public Ledger*, October 12, 1846; *New York Herald*, October 12, 1846; *Boston Daily Mail*, October 13, 1846; *St. Louis Republican*, October 15, 1846; *Cincinnati Enquirer*, October 16, 1846.

27. Smith, *War with Mexico*, 1:505–506.

28. *St. Louis Reveille*, November 13, 1846; *Baltimore Sun*, November 13, 1846.

29. *Charleston Courier*, November 22, 1847; *National Intelligencer*, quoted in *Philadelphia North American*, November 11, 1846.

30. *Picayune*, November 11, 1846.

31. Kendall quote in ibid., October 21, 1846; Haile's primary coverage of the battle appeared in the *Picayune* on October 4, 6, and 26 and November 3 and 4, 1846. Kendall letters appeared during this time primarily on October 21 but did not get into detailed accounts of the battle. Between October 4 and November 19 the *Picayune* printed thirty-four letters from Haile and eleven from Kendall. As army officers started arriving back at New Orleans from Monterrey, the *Picayune* interviewed them and reported, "We have no corrections to make in the first report which we gave of the battle. . . . [Those] who were in the battle bear witness to the fidelity of [Haile]." Ibid., October 21, 1846.

32. Ibid., November 3, 1846.

33. *Delta*, October 4, 6, November 3, 1846. "Soft soap" quote, November 6, 1847.

34. Ibid., June 16, 1846, November 6, 1847; also see Greer, *Colonel Jack Hays*, 141.

35. *Spirit of the Times*, November 7, 1846; "Ticket" quote, December 26, 1846.

36. Ibid., November 7, 28, 1846.

37. Ibid., October 31, November 7, 21, 1846. Henry eventually went public, but his wartime correspondence always carried his distinctive "G** de L**" signature.

38. *Picayune*, October 21, 1846. A good discussion of the controversial surrender terms is found in Chance, *Jefferson Davis's Mexican War Regiment*, 65–68.

39. Henry in *Spirit of the Times*, November 11, 28, 1846; Reid, *Scouting Expeditions*, 204. Reid wrote a straight summary of the battle for the *New Orleans Commercial Times*. It is reprinted in the Charleston *Mercury*, November 5, 1846.

40. Haile in *Picayune*, October 21, 1846; Robert Ryal Miller, *Shamrock and Sword: The Saint Patrick's Battalion in the U.S.-Mexican War* (Norman: University of Oklahoma Press, 1989), chap. 3; Henry and Kendall in *Picayune*, December 3, 1846; Henry about desertions in *Spirit of the Times*, May 16, 1846.

41. *Picayune*, November 3, 1846. A report long after the war estimated the Quartermaster Department had hired as many as 300 civilians to be express riders during the conflict. *Vedette* 2, no. 7, April 15, 1881, 7.

42. *Delta*, November 17, December 15, 1846.

43. *Picayune*, November 14, 1846.

44. Ibid., November 14, 29, 1846.

45. Ibid., October 6, 1846; *Charleston Courier*, October 10, 1846; *Baltimore Sun*, October 13, 1846; *New York Tribune*, October 13, 1846. Additional praise for Haile's reporting can be found in the *Picayune*, November 19, 1846; *Philadelphia North American*, December 8, 1846; *St. Louis Reveille*, October 15, 1846, April 20, 1847; *Matamoros American Flag*, April 28, 1847.

46. *Washington Union*, October 12, 13, 1846.

47. *Delta*, March 2, 1847. Twiggs's 1st Division was on the east front. Worth received so much newspaper praise for Monterrey that he wrote to his daughter,

"If not well poised my head would be turned." See William T. Worth, "Never before Published Letters of Famous General Worth, Written during the Mexican War." *New York Times Magazine Section*, July 16, 1916, 10–11. As the praise continued, however, Worth's head did turn and he started to see himself as a presidential prospect.

48. Kendall, undated note in Kendall Collection, Special Collections Division, University of Texas at Arlington Libraries; and George Wilkins Kendall, *The War between the United States and Mexico, Illustrated*, with illustrations by Carl Nebel (1851; reprint, Austin: Texas State Historical Association, 1994), 52.

49. *Spirit of the Times*, November 28, 1846. Months later the *Spirit* proudly observed that Taylor's reports "have sustained our correspondent" in every important detail. January 9, 1847; Reid, *Scouting Expeditions*, 168.

50. For biographical information on the three, see Bauer, *Zachary Taylor*; Wallace, *General William Jenkins Worth*; Thomas W. Cutrer, *Ben McCulloch and the Frontier Military Tradition* (Chapel Hill: University of North Carolina Press, 1993). Cutrer quote on 89–90. Taylor did not suffer, either; Reid and Henry warmly dedicated their popular 1847 books about Monterrey to the general.

Chapter 7. The "Americanization" of Tampico

1. *St. Louis Reveille*, January 9, 1847; *Albany Argus*, January 16, 1847; Justin H. Smith, *The War with Mexico*, 2 vols. (New York: Macmillan Co., 1919), vol. 1, chap. 18.

2. Peoples is identified as the correspondent for these papers in the *Bee* on May 1, 1847, in the *Delta* April 4, 1847, and in the *Crescent* August 7, 1848. He wrote fifty-eight letters to the *Bee* signed "The Corporal" between May 1846 and February 1847. He sent a fifty-ninth and final letter to the paper on May 1, 1847. Using "Chaparral," he wrote fifty-two letters to the *Delta* between November 1846 and May 1847. His "Chaparral" letters appeared in the *Crescent* fifty-six times between March 1848 and August 7, 1848, the date of his final war letter. The *New Orleans Tropic* also printed letters signed "The Corporal" early in the war, which may have been from Peoples, but the author is never clearly identified. See the *Tropic*, June 6, July 17, November 14, December 21, 1846. James Freaner used the signature "Corporal" briefly at the start of the war but switched to "Mustang" in early June 1846.

3. *Niles' National Register*, August 1, 1846, 341; *New Orleans Crescent*, March 31, 1848; also June 16, August 7, September 23, 1848; *Delta*, March 3, December 29, 1847, August 8, 1848. *Picayune*, September 1, 1848. *New Orleans Bee*, July 17, 1846, said, "Mr. Peoples is an able and ready writer," and the *Charleston Courier*, May 11, 1847, described his work as "able and intelligent."

4. Some biographical information on Peoples is available in Lota M. Spell, "The Anglo-Saxon Press in Mexico, 1846–1848," *American Historical Review* 38, no. 1 (October 1932): 20–31, esp. 25. Most of the research included in this chapter was obtained from reading Peoples's newspaper letters over the two-year period. The *San Francisco Daily Alta California*, April 17, 1850, reported Peoples was born in Raleigh, North Carolina, and moved to New Orleans in 1837. He served

briefly in the Army of the Republic of Texas in 1838 before returning to his printing career in New Orleans. One source, Oliver Goldsmith, met Peoples briefly in California in 1849 and noted, "Capt. Peoples . . . says he's from Lynchburg, Virginia." See Oliver Goldsmith, *Overland in Forty-Nine* (Detroit: Published by the author, 1896), 81. Praise of his character is in [U.S. Senate], *The History of the Raising of the American Flag on the Capital of Mexico* (Washington, D.C.: Printed by C. Wendell, 1856), 31–32; *Picayune*, April 8, 1849; *San Francisco Daily Alta California*, April 17, 1850.

5. Quoted in *Pensacola (Fla.) Gazette*, December 5, 1846.

6. *Delta*, November 22, December 27, 1846. In justice to Peoples, it should be noted his Tampico prediction did not appear in the *Delta* until after the army had departed for Victoria, thus not "leaking" its destination; march described in *Augusta (Ga.) Chronicle and Sentinel*, February 2, 1847.

7. *Delta*, January 27, 1847. This was a popular anecdote about Taylor and appeared in several newspapers with slight variations.

8. Ibid., February 4, 1847; *Picayune*, August 8, 1847. In this issue Kendall noted that the latest U.S. news had come to him from Mexico City newspapers, which were using the *New Orleans La Patria* as their source "about what is going on in our own country." He would not be able to safely send or receive newspapers "until we establish relations as friendly with the Mexican Government as those which the editors of *La Patria* have been able to form."

9. *Delta*, February 13, 1847. The army's procurement practice is described in John S. D. Eisenhower, *So Far from God: The U.S. War with Mexico, 1846–1848* (New York: Random House, 1989), 100.

10. *Delta*, February 14, 1847; "Truth" in *Spirit of the Times*, March 27, 1847; *Picayune*, March 18, 1847.

11. *Delta*, February 13, 17, 18, 25, 1847. *Aquadiente* was Mexican brandy and *muscal* a wine.

12. Ibid. A correspondent of the New York *Spirit of the Times* called the commercial exchange the "drinking house and billiard saloon of Tampico. . . . A prohibition exists against the sale of ardent spirits at the bar. Where was there an order of that nature that the ingenuity of man did not get around? You go quietly into the back room and visit what they call 'the Jackass,' a second edition of the 'striped pig.'" *Spirit of the Times*, March 27, 1847.

13. *Delta*, March 2, 1847. Attack on Peoples, April 16, 1847.

14. Spell, "The Anglo-Saxon Press," 25; Fayette Copeland, *Kendall of the* Picayune (Norman: University of Oklahoma Press, 1943), 187–188; Lumsden quotation in *Picayune*, February 18, 1847. Ownership of the *Sentinel* passed into the hands of John G. Gibson, a veteran newsman who had edited the *New Orleans True American*. Gibson, who also served as an American court official in Tampico, operated the *Sentinel* until his death in October 1847. It resumed publication in late October 1847 and was quoted in the New Orleans press as late as March 1848.

15. See Copeland, *Kendall of the* Picayune, chap. 3, for Lumsden's background. Lumsden and Kendall briefly served as court judges during the American

occupation. Ibid., 187. *Picayune*, January 2, 6, 1847; quote in *Pensacola (Fla.) Gazette*, March 6, 1847.

16. *Picayune*, February 3, March 16, 1847.

17. Ibid., January 7, 19, 1847.

18. Ibid., February 4, March 20, 1847.

19. Ibid., March 18, 1847; *Delta*, December 27, 1846, March 3, 16, 1847.

Chapter 8. Buena Vista—"Carpe Diem"

1. *Picayune*, February 23, 1847; *St. Louis Reveille*, March 28, 1847.

2. Justin H. Smith, *The War with Mexico*, 2 vols. (New York: Macmillan Co., 1919), 1:347–400.

3. See David Lavender, *Climax at Buena Vista* (Philadelphia and New York: J. B. Lippincott, 1966); James Henry Carleton, *Battle of Buena Vista* (New York: Harper & Bros., 1848); Joseph E. Chance, *Jefferson Davis's Mexican War Regiment* (Jackson: University Press of Mississippi, 1991), chaps. 7–8; John S. D. Eisenhower, *So Far from God: The U.S. War with Mexico, 1846–1848* (New York: Random House, 1989), chaps. 15–16.

4. For rumor examples, see *Washington Union*, March 5, 1847; *Baton Rouge Gazette*, March 20, 1847; *St. Louis Reveille*, March 23, 1847; *Baltimore Sun*, March 23, 1847; quote in *Charleston Courier*, February 24, 1847.

5. *St. Louis Reveille*, March 21, 1847; *Baltimore Sun*, March 23, 24, 1847; *New York Tribune*, March 25, 1847. Adding to the problems of the eastern editors was a heavy winter snowstorm that knocked down telegraph lines throughout the Northeast. Ibid., March 29, 1847.

6. *Picayune*, March 2, 1847. Kendall, quoted in ibid., March 19, 1847. Kendall was not present at Buena Vista, as is sometimes cited.

7. *New Orleans La Patria*, February 24, 1847, quoted in *Delta*, February 25, 1847; *Picayune*, March 9, 1847.

8. *Delta*, January 24, 1847. Tobin's unit (McCulloch's Texas Mounted Volunteers) was credited by Taylor with convincing him that Santa Anna's army had arrived from the south. Upon the advice of General John E. Wool, Taylor moved his army to the defensive position at Buena Vista. Walter Prescott Webb, H. Bailey Carroll, and Eldon Branda, eds., *The Handbook of Texas*, 3 vols. (1952; reprint, Austin: Texas State Historical Association, 1976), 113n; Eisenhower, *So Far from God*, 181. Tobin's quote is in *Matamoros American Flag*, December 26, 1846. Tobin was promoted to lieutenant in McCulloch's small detachment in March 1847. The unit was mustered out of service in July 1847. See Frederick Wilkins, *The Highly Irregular Irregulars: Texas Rangers in the Mexican War* (Austin, Tex.: Eakin Press, 1990), chap. 9. Tobin is referred to as "another Old 1st Texas man" on 133.

9. *Delta*, March 30, 1847. All quotes are from Tobin's main battle story.

10. Ibid., April 11, 1847. Other Tobin letters appear March 30, April 6, 1847. The Buena Vista casualty reports reached the public via Taylor's official report in the *Washington Union*.

11. See Josiah Gregg, *The Diary and Letters of Josiah Gregg*, ed. Maurice G. Fulton, 2 vols. (1941; reprint, Norman: University of Oklahoma Press, 1944). Among the newspapers Gregg wrote to were the *Louisville Daily Journal, Galveston Daily Advertiser, Van Buren Arkansas Intelligencer* and the *Shreveport Caddo Gazette* in Louisiana. *Niles' National Register*, August 1, 1846, quotes a letter from him in the *Boonslick (Mo.) Times*, n.d.

12. Josiah Gregg, *Commerce of the Prairies*, 2 vols. (New York: H. G. Langley, 1844). Also valuable for Gregg are Paul Horgan, *Josiah Gregg and His Vision of the Early West* (New York: Farrar Straus Giroux, 1979); and Edward Halsey Foster, *Josiah Gregg and Lewis H. Garrard* (Boise, Idaho: Boise State University, 1977). First quote is from Horgan, 78; second quote in Gregg, *Diary*, 1:259–260, 2:305, 79–84. An example of Gregg complaining about Wool can be seen in the *Louisville Daily Journal*, February 8, 1847. One historian noted: "As far as General Wool was concerned, Gregg was a nuisance and a malicious gossip whose stories for the press were far too critical. And to the men in the ranks, Gregg was anything but a comrade. His scientific and hypochondriac preoccupations became the butt of their jokes, and their pranks were merely encouraged by his indignation. Gregg thought enlisted men crude and the officers stupid." See Josiah Gregg, *Commerce of the Prairies*, ed. Max L. Moorhead (Norman: University of Oklahoma Press, 1954), xxiv.

13. Gregg, *Diary*, 1:347; Moorhead, in Gregg's *Commerce of the Prairies*, xxiii; Paul Horgan in Gregg, *Diary*, 2:5; also see Horgan, *Josiah Gregg and His Vision*, 79–91.

14. Gregg, *Diary*, 1:190. Bigelow apparently followed Gregg's admonition, for no clearly identified article by him appeared in the *Post* during the war. Gregg, Bigelow wrote, "was morbidly conscientious, and nothing would induce him to state anything that he did not positively know as if he did know it, or to overstate anything." Moorhead, in Gregg's *Commerce of the Prairies*, xxxvii.

15. *Louisville Journal*, March 8, 1847. In a letter in the *Journal* on February 8, 1847, Gregg said he was giving "sort of *carte blanche* license" to the paper to print his reports. The fact that Gregg's reports to newspapers were only incidental to other activities is clear from his method of handling his letters. They were sent as a personal letter to the editor. Whether the letters should be published or not was left to the editor. Gregg, *Diary*, 2:64n, 60–61.

16. *Louisville Journal*, April 7, 1847. Gregg also wrote a report of the battle for the *Caddo Gazette*. See *St. Louis Daily Reveille*, May 2, 1847.

17. Gregg, *Diary*, 2:52–56.

18. *Louisville Journal*, April 7, 1847. The *Journal* added a note of explanation, calling Gregg "our interesting correspondent" who "gives a graphic description of the great battle. We omit some of the first pages as they contain the same details already" published. Gregg remained at Buena Vista for five weeks after the battle, writing letters to newspapers, his family, and recording a detailed diary of the events.

19. Quotes in *Ottawa (Ill.) Free Trader*, April 16, 30, 1847. Hardin was an occasional correspondent for the *St. Louis Daily Missouri Republican*. Two other Illinois officers who wrote to newspapers—Lieutenants Edward F. Fletcher and Lauriston

Robbins—were killed with Hardin. Robbins was an occasional correspondent for the *Alton (Ill.) Telegraph* with Fletcher. Ibid., April 2, 9, 23, 1847. Robbins "was stabbed dead with his own sword" after he surrendered on the battlefield, an eyewitness wrote in the *New York Post*, April 28, 1847. Hardin used the pen name "Illinois." Examples of his letters can be seen in the *St. Louis Daily Missouri Republican*, March 9, 11, 12, 13, 16, 17, 23, and 24, 1847. The paper reports his death and identification on April 6, 30, 1847.

20. *Picayune*, March 27, 1847. Second quote in ibid., April 7, 1847.

21. *Jackson Mississippi Southron*, April 9, 1847.

22. Examples of Pike's pre–Buena Vista letters can be seen in the *Little Rock Arkansas State Gazette*, July 13, 1846, March 27, 1847. His career and bitter political feud with Yell are described in William W. Hughes, *Archibald Yell* (Fayetteville: University of Arkansas Press, 1988), chaps. 13–17; and Fred W. Allsopp, *Albert Pike: A Biography* (Little Rock, Ark.: Park-Harper, 1928). Pike also wrote letters to the *Spirit of the Times*. See also Albert Pike, *Prose Sketches and Poems*, ed. D. J. Weber with foreword by Tom L. Popejoy (Albuquerque, N.M.: Calvin Horn Publishers, 1967), xx–xxxii; and Walter Lee Brown, "The Mexican War Experiences of Albert Pike and the 'Mounted Devils' of Arkansas," *Arkansas Historical Quarterly* 12, no. 4 (Winter 1953): 301–315. Josiah Gregg considered Pike the best of the Arkansas officers but did not like him personally. Gregg, *Diary*, 1:219–220.

23. Pike's three-column account of the battle appeared in the *Little Rock Arkansas State Gazette* on April 24, 1847. A long, romantic poem by Pike titled "Buena Vista" appeared first in the New York magazine *Spirit of the Times*, May 1, 1847. It was widely reprinted. Pike also may be the author of an account of Buena Vista in the *Spirit of the Times*, May 1, 1847, under the signature "H. Von S." Hughes, *Archibald Yell*, 113, 135, notes Pike used this nom de plume; a source is not listed.

24. *Indianapolis State Journal*, January 26, 1847; Robert E. Morsberger and Katherine M. Morsberger, *Lew Wallace: Militant Romantic* (New York: McGraw-Hill, 1980), 31–35; Lew Wallace, *A Hoosier in the Mexican War* (Ft. Wayne, Ind.: Public Library of Ft. Wayne and Allen County, 1973); Oran Perry, *Indiana in the Mexican War* (Indianapolis: W. B. Burford, contractor for state printing, 1908).

25. The performance of the 2nd Indiana Regiment is described in Lavender, *Climax at Buena Vista*, chap.10, and 240n17; Eisenhower, *So Far from God*, 188; and Jeffrey L. Patrick, "A Question of Cowardice: The Second Indiana Regiment and the Mexican War," paper presented to Southwestern Historical Conference, Houston, March 1996.

26. Kingsbury's *Tropic* article appeared March 30, 1847; *Tropic*'s defense of his apology is repeated in Perry, *Indiana in the Mexican War*, 298–299, 320; *Washington Union*, April 2, 1847. Despite complaints, General Taylor did not change his critical report.

27. Arthur's quote is in Jackson *Mississippian*, April 9, 1847; Tobin in *Delta*, March 30, 1847; Osman in *Ottawa (Ill.) Free Trader*, April 16, 1847.

28. For a full discussion of "A little more grape, Captain Bragg," see Grady McWhiney, *Braxton Bragg and Confederate Defeat* (New York: Columbia University

Press, 1969), chap. 4. Also K. Jack Bauer, *Zachary Taylor* (Baton Rouge: Louisiana State University Press, 1985), chap. 10. Bragg is quoted in the *Mobile Register and Journal*, January 22, 1849, reprinted in *Picayune*, January 23, 1849. "Passport" quote is in *Picayune*, June 27, 1848.

29. *Picayune*, March, 13, 1847.

30. *Delta*, March 27, 1847; *Picayune*, March 24, 1847. The first American military couriers left Monterrey on March 4. Most of the correspondents' accounts were stuck at the U.S. Post Office in Monterrey.

31. *Picayune*, March 23, 1847. Army doctors were often utilized as messengers, causing Zachary Taylor to comment, "It seems that the medical dept. appears to be peculiarly fitted for carrying expresses." Zachary Taylor, *Letters of Zachary Taylor, from the Battle-fields of the Mexican War* (Rochester, N.Y.: Genesee Press, 1908), 91; see *Charleston Courier*, April 5, 15, 24, 1847; *Augusta (Ga.) Chronicle and Sentinel*, March 27, 29, 1847; *New York Tribune*, April 1847. From New Orleans, Pony Express riders carried the news to Augusta, Georgia. Then the news was placed on a train to Charleston, where a boat took the U.S. mail to Washington, D.C. At Washington, various newspaper agents telegraphed to other cities in the North. The news reached Charleston on March 28, Washington on March 30, and was in the papers of Baltimore, Philadelphia, New York, and Boston on March 31.

32. *Picayune* and *Delta*, March 14, 1847.

33. *Delta*, March 21, 1847.

34. The "good guess" quote is in *Delta*, March 25, 1847. For examples, see *Washington Union*, March 29, 1847; *Philadelphia North American*, March 30, 1847; *New York Tribune*, March 30, 1847. Critical of the *Delta*'s "guess" were the *Mobile Advertiser* and the *Savannah (Ga.) Republican*, quoted in *Delta*, March 27, 1847.

35. *Charleston Courier*, March 29, 1847

36. *Delta* and *Picayune*, March 23, 1847. Quote in *Picayune*, March 24, 1847. Also, Corydon Donnavan, *Adventures in Mexico* (Boston: George R. Holbrook & Co., 1848), 140–141.

37. Arthur quote is in *Jackson Mississippian*, April 9, 1847; Pike in *Little Rock Arkansas State Gazette*, April 24, 1847; Osman in *Ottawa Free Trader*, April 16, 1847; and Tobin in *Delta*, March 30, 1847.

Chapter 9. Siege at Veracruz

1. See *New York Herald*, May 8, 1846. The *Herald* had agitated for a Veracruz invasion even before the war broke out. On May 8, 1846, the paper ran a three-column woodcut showing the fortress of "San Juan D'Ulloa" with the underline, "The American fleet in the offing." In another example, on October 15, 1846, the *Savannah (Ga.) Republican* reported, "We learn from a gentleman who conversed with Lt. Berryman [a Navy messenger] on the [railroad] cars that it has been determined to attack Veracruz." For other examples, see *New York Tribune*, October 21, 24, 1846; *New York Sun*, January 30, 1847; and *Niles' National Register*, October 24, 1846, which commented, "We have strong reasons to believe, also, that Vera Cruz is

no longer to be spared; but that a co-operate attack by land and sea will follow close after the storming of Tampico."

2. Justin H. Smith, *The War with Mexico*, 2 vols. (New York: Macmillan Co., 1919), vol. 1, chap. 18; vol. 2, chap. 22; K. Jack Bauer, *Zachary Taylor* (Baton Rouge: Louisiana State University Press, 1985), chap. 13, and 142–144 for the naval landing; John S. D. Eisenhower, *So Far from God: The U.S. War with Mexico, 1846–1848* (New York: Random House, 1989), chap. 22.

3. For evidence the Mexicans learned of events from American newspapers, see José Fernando Ramírez, *Mexico during the War with the United States* (Columbia: University of Missouri Press, 1970), 91, 120. On February 19, 1847, the *New York Sun* quoted from the Veracruz *Locomotor and Indicator* that Veracruz was not as prepared as it should be for the pending attack by "25,000 Americans." "The Mexicans are well advised of our movements," the *Sun* observed.

4. Smith, *War with Mexico*, vol. 2, chap. 22. The battle ended on March 27, formal articles of capitulation were signed March 28, and the Americans occupied the city on March 29.

5. *Picayune*, March 26, 1847; see Fayette Copeland, *Kendall of the* Picayune (Norman: University of Oklahoma Press, 1943), chap. 16, for background.

6. Quoted in *Charleston Courier*, April 5, 1847.

7. *Picayune*, April 4, 1847.

8. *Spirit of the Times*, April 17, 1847.

9. *Philadelphia Pennsylvanian*, April 16, 1847. Diller added, "They, however, never forget their friends, as I can testify."

10. *Picayune*, April 4, 1847. In a separate note to his friend William Trotter Porter, editor of the *Spirit of the Times*, Kendall said of the American bombardment, "I hope they have an old room left untouched at the *Casa de Diligencias* I occupied four year ago." He added, "I would not have missed the show for anything." *Spirit of the Times*, April 17, 1847.

11. *Picayune*, February 5, 1847. For army life, see Richard Bruce Winders, *Mr. Polk's Army* (College Station: Texas A&M University Press, 1997); James M. McCaffrey, *Army of Manifest Destiny: The American Soldier in the Mexican War, 1846–1848* (New York: New York University Press, 1992).

12. *Picayune*, March 26, 1847.

13. Ibid.

14. Quoted in *St. Louis Republican*, April 15, 1847.

15. *Picayune*, March 25, 1847.

16. Ibid., March 26, 1847.

17. Ibid., February 20, 1847.

18. Ibid., March 26, 1847.

19. *St. Louis Reveille*, April 6, 1847.

20. *Picayune*, March 30, 1847.

21. Ibid., June 11, July 11, 30, 1847.

22. *Delta*, April 1, 4, 1847.

23. Ibid., March 19, 1847.

24. Ibid., April 1, 1847.

25. Ibid., April 11, 1847.

26. Ibid., March 12, 1847.

27. Ibid., March 30, 1847.

28. *Spirit of the Times*, April 10, 1847. Kendall appears to have referred to "Truth" when he wrote to the *Spirit*. "Tom B. is here and hearty as a horse. We have been sleeping under the same sand hill." "Truth" also referred to sleeping under a sand hill. Ibid., April 10, 17, 1847.

29. *Delta*, March 19, April 4, 1847.

30. Ibid., April 3, 4, 1847. Drinking also was widespread among the troops. A navy officer who commanded one of the land-based 8-inch guns during the Veracruz bombardment wrote to the *Spirit of the Times* (April 17, 1847), "Many of [the men] got tipsy the moment the firing ceased. . . . You may depend upon it the task of taking care of 42 drunken sailors was no sinecure."

31. *Picayune*, April 4, 1847.

32. Undated *Picayune* clipping in Kendall Collection, Special Collections Division, University of Texas at Arlington Libraries. Kendall from Boerne, Texas, September 12, 1867.

33. *Delta*, April 14, 1847.

34. *Picayune*, April 9, 1847.

35. *Delta*, April 14, 1847.

36. All Peoples's quotes from ibid., April 11, 1847. The special pass from Scott was to allow Peoples to find a printing press for a new camp newspaper, the *American Eagle*.

37. *Picayune*, April 9, 1847.

38. *Alton (Ill.) Telegraph*, April 23, 1847.

39. *Picayune*, April 4, 9, 1847.

40. "Piquant" in *Picayune*, May 6, 1847; "able and patriotic" in *St. Louis Reveille*, November 17, 1847; "of great versatility and power" in *Delta*, January 2, 1848.

41. *Ottawa (Ill.) Free Trader*, February 5, 1848. Tobey was born October 6, 1818, at Tonawanda, N.Y.

42. Francis B. Heitman, *Historical Register and Dictionary of the United States Army, from Its Organization, September 29, 1789 to March 2, 1903*, 2 vols. (Washington, D.C.: Government Printing Office, 1903), 1:193; *New York Tribune*, December 21, 1846; *New York Spirit of the Times*, November 20, 1847. Tobey enlisted on January 16, 1847, when the unit was at New Orleans, and was honorably discharged at Jalapa, Mexico, in May 1847 "upon a surgeon's certificate." He fought at Mexico City on a volunteer basis. Also see Randy W. Hackenburg, *Pennsylvania in the War with Mexico* (Shippensburg, Pa.: White Mane Publishing Co., 1992), 178.

43. *Philadelphia Pennsylvanian*, February 2, 1847.

44. *Philadelphia North American*, March 19, 1847. Seven dollars per month was a private's pay at the time.

45. Ibid., April 9, 1847. Also see April 15, 1847, for comments about the New Orleans reporters.

46. Ibid., April 15, 1847.

47. Ibid., April 9, 1847.

48. Ibid., April 15, 1847.

49. Ibid., April 16, 1847.

50. Ibid., April 17, 1847.

51. Ibid. Tobey had uneven luck with the delivery of his letters. At the close of the siege, Tobey was appointed to work in the Veracruz post office; that may account for his Veracruz letters reaching the *North American* so quickly. The last batch, dated March 28, arrived in Philadelphia on April 14, his fastest delivery of the war. The *North American* printed thirty-eight of Tobey's letters, usually a column in length, on twenty different dates between December 25, 1846, and June 19, 1847. His letters suddenly stopped at the end of June. In December 1847, the paper printed more letters from Tobey dated the previous June. Other batches of Tobey's letters appeared in April and June 1848, dated from Mexico City. After arriving in the Mexican capital in September 1847, Tobey started a new paper there, also called the *North American* (see Chapter 19 of this book). His correspondence to the Philadelphia paper dropped sharply after taking that assignment. *Philadelphia North American*, November 15, December 6, 1847.

52. For Haile's military record, see Old Military and Civil Records (NWCTB-Military), Textual Services Division, National Archives, Washington, DC; also *Picayune*, April 9, 1847, September 16, 1849.

53. *Veracruz American Eagle*, April 10, 1847. John Peoples started the new paper, and is probably the author of this item.

Chapter 10. Jane McManus Storms

1. Marcy quote in Frederick Merk, *Manifest Destiny and Mission in American History* (New York: Knopf, 1963), 200–201n. Also Bancroft to Storms, Washington, D.C., August 2, 1846, in George Bancroft Collection, Massachusetts Historical Society.

2. For background on Storms, see Tom Reilly, "Jane McManus Storms: Letters from the Mexican War, 1846–1848," *Southwestern Historical Quarterly* 81, no. 1 (July 1981): 21–44; Anna Kasten Nelson, "Jane Storms Cazneau: Disciple of Manifest Destiny," *Prologue* 18, no. 1 (Spring 1986): 24–40; Nelson, *Secret Agents: President Polk and the Search for Peace with Mexico* (New York and London: Garland Publishing, 1988), and "Mission to Mexico—Moses Y. Beach, Secret Agent," *New York State Historical Society Quarterly* 59, no. 3 (July 1975): 227–245; Robert E. May, "'Plenipotentiary in Petticoats': Jane M. Cazneau and American Foreign Policy in the Mid-Nineteenth Century," in *Women and American Foreign Policy: Lobbyists, Critics, and Insiders*, ed. Edward Crapol, 2nd ed. (Wilmington, Del.: SR Books, 1992); A. Brooke Caruso, *The Mexican Spy Company: United States Covert Operations in Mexico, 1845–1848* (Jefferson, N.C.: McFarland & Co., 1991), 138–146. Also see Robert Crawford Cotner's introduction to Cora Montgomery's *Eagle Pass, or Life on the Border* (1852; reprint, Austin, Tex.: Pemberton Press, 1966); Patricia

Kinkade, "Jane McManus Storms Cazneau: Journalist and Expansionist," in *Essays in History: The E.C. Barksdale Student Lectures, 1987–1988* (Arlington: University of Texas at Arlington Campus Printing Service, 1988), 7–30; Peggy Cashion, "Women and the Mexican War, 1846–1848" (M.A. thesis, University of Texas at Arlington, 1990), chap. 3; Edward T. James, ed., *Notable American Women, 1607–1950,* 3 vols. (Cambridge, Mass.: Belknap Press of Harvard University Press, 1971), 1:315–317; Walter Webb, H. Bailey Carroll, and Eldon Stephen Branda, eds., *The Handbook of Texas,* 3 vols. (1952; reprint, Austin: Texas State Historical Association, 1976), 2:122; obituaries in *New York Tribune,* December 31, 1878, *New York Sun,* January 2, 1879. For quotes, see *Baltimore Sun,* June 7, 1847; Henry Watterson, "Marse Henry": *An Autobiography,* 2 vols. (New York: George H. Doran, 1919), 1:57; James, ed., *Notable American Women,* 1:316. Benton may have been cooled by occasional critical remarks about him in her articles. See *New York Sun,* April 19, 1847.

3. James, ed., *Notable American Women,* 1:316–317; Nelson, "Mission to Mexico," 230–231; Webb et al., *The Handbook of Texas,* 1:122.

4. Edwin Emery and Michael Emery, *The Press and America,* 7th ed. (Englewood Cliffs, N.J.: Prentice Hall, 1992), 120–122. The growth of the *Sun* and the paper's role in the Mexican War are discussed in Frank M. O'Brien, *The Story of the* Sun: *New York, 1833–1928* (New York: D. Appleton, 1928), 89–120. The 45,000 figure is given in the *Sun* on April 18, 1846, and the 55,000 figure on January 1, 1848. It was a time, however, of inflated newspaper circulation figures. Representative editorials supporting the war may be read in the *Sun,* May 16, 29, 1846; May 19, 22, 1847. Editorials supporting annexation of Mexico are in the paper May 27, 1847, and January 13, 1848.

5. See Julius W. Pratt, "John L. O'Sullivan and Manifest Destiny," *New York History* 14 (July 1933): 213–234. Her views on Cuba and Mexico also can be found in two pamphlets, Cora Montgomery, *The King of Rivers* (New York, 1850), and *Queen of Islands* (New York, 1850), and a novel, *Eagle Pass.* Although she wrote for the *Sun* throughout the 1840s, there is no evidence Storms was a full-time staff member. Most of her writing for the *Sun* was in the form of editorials and political letters. Some editors occasionally mistook "Montgomery" for a man. References to her as a man are in the *New York Tribune,* January 14, 1847, and *Washington Union,* April 20, 27, 1847. She was blunt in her criticism of Polk in private letters. She wrote to Mirabeau B. Lamar that Senator John C. Calhoun of South Carolina was "worth at least two hundred and fifty thousand Polks." Storms to Lamar, October (?) 1845 (?), in Charles Adams Gulick Jr. and Katherine Elliott, eds., *The Papers of Mirabeau Buonaparte Lamar,* 6 vols. (Austin: Texas State Library, 1924), 4, pt. 1:108–110. In another letter to Lamar she commented, "Polk is a base, narrow souled man and would sell his mother's grave to buy up a Senator." Storms to Lamar, March 27, 1846, ibid., 130–131.

6. M. S. Beach, "A Secret Mission to Mexico," *Scribner's Monthly* 18 (May 1879) 136–140; Merk, *Manifest Destiny,* 132–33; quote from John Bassett Moore, ed., *The Works of James Buchanan,* 11 vols. (New York: New York Antiquarian Press, 1960), 7:119; Nelson, "Mission to Mexico," 230–234.

7. Merk, *Manifest Destiny*, 132; Moore, ed., *The Works of James Buchanan*, 7:119–120. Buchanan added that the government would pay Beach $6 per day for his services, plus travel expenses.

8. Beach, "Secret Mission," 137–139. Watterson, "Marse Henry" 1:57, said of Storms: "She possessed infinite knowledge of Spanish-American affairs, looked like a Spanish woman, and wrote and spoke the Spanish language fluently." The Havana meeting is discussed in Tom Chaffin, *Fatal Glory: Narcisco Lopez and the First Clandestine U.S. War against Cuba* (Charlottesville: University Press of Virginia, 1996), 11–15.

9. Storms wrote thirty-one letters to the *Sun* during the five-month trip, including eleven from Cuba and sixteen from Mexico. Most of her early letters concerned conditions in Cuba and appeared in the *Sun* on January 12, 13, 14, 15, 16, 25, 30, February 8, and March 17, 25, 26, 1847. Her Mexico letters appeared February 12, April 15, 16, 19, 24, 28, 30, May 3, 6, 7, 14, 21, 22, 24, 1847. She also wrote letters to the *New York Tribune* and *Philadelphia Public Ledger* during the trip. See the *Tribune*, January 14, 18, April 20, 30, 1847; *Public Ledger*, April 22, 1847. Some of her *Sun* letters were reprinted in the *Washington Union*, *New Orleans Delta*, and *St. Louis Union*, all proadministration papers. Her quotes about the navy are in the *Sun*, January 16, February 12, 1847. Other Storms letters criticizing the navy were in the *Sun*, April 4, June 13, 1846.

10. For the Mexican political situation, see Pedro Santoni, *Mexicans at Arms: Puro Federalists and the Politics of War, 1845–1848* (Fort Worth: Texas Christian University Press, 1996), chap. 6; Michael Costeloe, "The Mexican Church and the Rebellion of the Polkos," *Hispanic American Historical Review* 46 (May 1966): 170–178.

11. Justin H. Smith, *The War with Mexico*, 2 vols. (New York: Macmillan Co., 1919), 2:12–13, 331. In a report to the state department, Beach explained he supported the rebellion in order to detain the troops at the capital and keep them from marching to the support of Veracruz. The expense and action were "justified," he told Secretary of State Buchanan, because more than 5,000 Mexican troops were tied down by the civil war for 23 days. Ibid., 2:331. In a letter to the *Sun*, Beach said the civil war "checked business, killed an indefinite number of women and children, had a nautical air and above all else gave five thousand men an excuse to keep from the more serious business of going to the defense of Vera Cruz." *New York Sun*, May 27, 1847.

12. *New York Sun*, April 15, 1847.

13. Costeloe, "The Mexican Church," 173; Smith, *War with Mexico*, 2:14, 332; Beach, "Secret Mission," 140; Beach reported their trip to Tampico in a series of letters in the *Sun*, May 27, 28, 31, June 1, 5, 7, 8, 10, 11, 14, 15, 1847. Most only describe scenery.

14. Beach, "Secret Mission," 139–140; Storms quote in *New York Sun*, April 30, 1847; Smith, *War with Mexico*, 2:39; Edward S. Wallace, in *Destiny and Glory* (New York: Coward-McCann, 1957), 246–248, gives a more positive version of the meeting, although he provides no documentation.

15. *Sun*, May 6, 1847. The reference was to Taylor's heavy losses at Monterrey. In another letter to the *Sun*, January 25, 1847, she observed, "General Taylor is only a soldier and may be excused for his professional preference of the sword to the pen."

16. Ibid., April 19, 1847. She later told the *Baltimore Sun*'s Washington correspondent that she had interviewed several of Mexico's Catholic bishops and that they told her they were "perfectly willing to submit to any government which [would] rid them of their military tyrants . . . and protect their rights and property," meaning the American government. *Baltimore Sun*, June 7, 1847.

17. *New York Sun*, April 16, 18, 19, 28, May 3, 1847.

18. Ibid., April 30, May 3, 1847. The hanging incident Storms refers to is discussed in K. Jack Bauer, *The Mexican War, 1846–1848* (New York: Macmillan, 1974), 114–115. After Veracruz was captured, American military authorities did take steps to stop further disorders by the invading army. Smith, *War with Mexico*, 2:220–221.

19. *New York Sun*, May 3, 6, 7, 1847.

20. Polk quote in Milo M. Quaife, ed., *The Diary of James K. Polk, 1845–1849*, 4 vols. (Chicago: A. C. McLurg & Co., 1910), 3:25.

21. *New York Sun*, May 24, 1847.

Chapter 11. "I Am Requested by the President . . ."

1. *Pensacola (Fla.) Gazette*, April 3, 1847. Copies of McKinley's paper, carried by express riders, spread the story up the Eastern Seaboard. If the editor was aware of the article's impact, he made no mention of it in subsequent issues of the *Gazette*. Examples of the use of the Pensacola report can be seen in *Charleston Courier*, April 7, 8, 1847; *Baltimore Sun*, April 10, 1847; *Washington Union*, April 10, 1847; *Philadelphia Public Ledger*, April 10, 12, 1847; *New York Herald*, April 10, 11, 1847; *New York Sun*, April 10, 1847; *Boston Post*, April 12, 1847.

2. Reported in *Charleston Courier*, April 10, 1847. The *Evening Mercury* also obtained its story by interviewing officers on the *Princeton*.

3. *Picayune*, April 4, 1847.

4. *Delta*, April 4, 1847.

5. *Charleston Courier*, April 8, 1847; *Baltimore Sun*, April 10, 1847; *Washington Union*, April 12, 1847. The *New York Herald*, *Sun*, and *Tribune* also cooperated on the cost of an express to deliver copies of the *Baltimore Sun* with the fuller account, allowing the New York papers to issue a second extra edition the same afternoon (April 10). Winter storms had cut telegraph lines throughout the Northeast, making the express essential. *New York Herald*, April 10, 11, 1847.

6. *Baltimore Sun*, April 10, 1847.

7. Milo M. Quaife, ed., *The Diary of James K. Polk, 1845–1849*, 4 vols. (Chicago: A. C. McLurg & Co., 1910), 2:465. That same night the army's courier carrying Scott's official account reached Polk, and he released the reports immediately to the *Washington Union*.

8. *Baltimore Sun*, April 12, 1847.

9. See Tom Reilly, "A Spanish-Language Voice of Dissent in Antebellum New Orleans," *Louisiana History* 23 (Fall 1982): 325–339. Also see John S. D. Eisenhower, "Polk and His Generals," in *Essays on the Mexican War*, ed. Douglas W. Richmond (College Station: Texas A&M University Press, 1986), 34–65.

10. *La Patria*, December 31, 1846, reprinted in *Delta*, January 26, 1847.

11. *Washington National Intelligencer*, February 15, 1847.

12. *Charleston Courier*, December 30, 1846.

13. *Washington National Intelligencer*, February 16, 1847.

14. Benton's verification of *La Patria*'s story was widely criticized. See *New Orleans Commercial Bulletin*, January 23, 1847, and *Delta*, January 26, 1847.

15. Dix to Azariah C. Flagg, January 21, 1847, in Flagg Papers, New York Public Library.

16. *New Orleans Commercial Bulletin*, January 20, 1847.

17. *Washington Union*, February 12, 1847. In the same issue, however, the *Union* published a letter from an officer at Scott's headquarters, denying the general gave the editor the plan. Scott saw Gomez for less than five minutes, the officer wrote, adding, "If Gomez knew any war secrets he must have guessed them."

18. Quaife, ed., *Polk Diary*, 2:327–328.

19. A letter with Gomez's denial that Scott was the source is in the *Delta*, January 27, 1847. Scott's explanation is reported in the *Washington Union*, February 12, 1847, and the *Washington National Intelligencer*, February 16, 1847. Scott may have been distracted by Washington politics during his stay in New Orleans. He had just heard that Polk was attempting to supersede him by appointing Benton as a lieutenant general. Winfield Scott, *Memoirs of Lieut.-General Scott, LL.D.*, 2 vols. (New York: Sheldon, 1864), 2:399–400; and Charles Winslow Elliott, *Winfield Scott, The Soldier and the Man* (New York: Macmillan, 1937), 445–446.

20. A number of American newspapers had predicted an attack on Veracruz, the *New York Herald* as early as May 1846. Also see Alfred Hoyt Bill, *Rehearsal for Conflict: The War with Mexico, 1846–1848* (New York: History Book Club, 1947), 184; "Prying eyes" quote from Robert Johannsen, *To the Halls of the Montezumas* (New York: Oxford University Press, 1985), 19–20; *Mobile Register and Journal*, February 10, 1847. The Mobile paper added, "In the Mexican papers . . . we find no reports and scarcely a speculation about the movements of their armies and generals. Whatever the cause . . . this gives Mexico a great advantage in the war over the United States."

21. *La Patria*, January 24, 1847, quoted in *Delta*, January 27, 1847.

22. See Jones to Taylor, January 5, 1846, and Taylor to Jones, February 3, 1846, cited in Justin H. Smith Collection, Benson Latin American Collection, General Libraries, University of Texas at Austin, 11:1–4. Scott's note is added at the end of Taylor's letter. Scott contended that paragraph 203, page 38, of the *Army's General Regulations* prohibited officers writing such letters.

23. Justin H. Smith, *The War with Mexico*, 2 vols. (New York: Macmillan Co., 1919), 1:507; the letter is in the New York *Evening Express*, January 22, 1847. The

Express (February 12, 1847) explained that Dr. D. Francis Bacon of New York City received the letter from Gaines and gave it to the paper. The order does not appear to have slowed letters from officers in volunteer units.

24. Quotes are from *New York Express*, February 1, 1847; *New York Tribune*, February 3, 1847; *New York Sun*, February 2, 1847.

25. The *Picayune*, June 8, 1846, called Henry "the capital Army correspondent . . . whose graphic letters are universally read"; the *Philadelphia Pennsylvanian*, December 29, 1846, referred to him as "the elegant contributor to the New York *Spirit*"; the *Memphis Enquirer* called his battle descriptions "the best written and most satisfactory accounts"; his writing was "spirited" and he was "a shrewd observer," the magazine *Democratic Review* (December 1847 issue) stated; and the *Spirit of the Times* noted on several occasions (June 20, August 8, 1846) how widely his work was reprinted. When Henry returned to the States from Veracruz in summer 1847, the *Picayune* put a summary cap on his performance: "He writes with spirit and ease, is a clear-headed and right-hearted man who [did] justice to those who have distinguished themselves in war." *Picayune*, July 18, 1847.

26. *Spirit of the Times*, March 27, 1847. Henry still provided the magazine occasional non-battle-related sketches about army personalities and incidents. He spent most of 1847 on recruitment duty in the New England states and returned to Mexico in spring 1848 during the army's occupation of Mexico City. He resumed reporting occasionally at that time. *Spirit of the Times*, June 10, July 1, 1848. Historian Robert W. Johannsen, *To the Halls of the Montezumas*, 153, believes Henry may have been transferred from Scott's command to recruiting service because of official displeasure with his articles for the *Spirit of the Times*.

27. *Spirit of the Times*, March 27, 1847. "Truth" wrote only briefly for the *Spirit*—starting January 7, 1847, at Victoria, and concluding April 7, 1847, after the Veracruz campaign.

28. *Washington Union*, April 1, 9, 16, 1847.

29. Quaife, ed., *Polk Diary*, 2:236. When a *Picayune* article reported that Taylor did not want to be president, the administration's *Washington Union* (April 16, 1847) observed, "There is perhaps no paper in the Union which has a better claim than the *Picayune* to speak authoritatively . . . as to the wishes and feelings of General Taylor himself."

30. Zachary Taylor, *Letters of Zachary Taylor, from the Battle-fields of the Mexican War* (Rochester, N.Y.: Genesee Press, 1908), 105; Fayette Copeland, *Kendall of the* Picayune (Norman: University of Oklahoma Press, 1943), 211.

31. Quaife, ed., *Polk Diary*, 2:492–493, 3:17, 25. The messages came on April 30 and May 7, 1847, and appear related to the *Baltimore Sun*'s express deliveries. Polk reports on a success for the government express in September 1847, in *Diary*, 3:170–171. For his anxiety, see 3:159, 171–172, 180, 195, 220–221; New York *Express*, October 27, 1847. The president did not get the full reports he was waiting for until November 13, 1847.

Chapter 12. Battle of Cerro Gordo

1. The Americans' fear of yellow fever and its impact are discussed in Roger C. Miller, "Yellow Jack at Veracruz," *Prologue* 10 (Spring 1978) 1:42–53. For Cerro Gordo, see Justin H. Smith, *The War with Mexico*, 2 vols. (New York: Macmillan Co., 1919), 2:37–59; John S. D. Eisenhower, *So Far from God: The U.S. War with Mexico, 1846–1848* (New York: Random House, 1989), 266–283.

2. *Mexico City American Star*, May 30, 1848; J. Jacob Oswandel, *Notes of the Mexican War, 1846–47–48* (Philadelphia: Published by the author, 1885), 103; Lota M. Spell, "The Anglo-Saxon Press in Mexico, 1846–1848," *American Historical Review* 38, no. 1 (October 1932): 20–31.

3. Winfield Scott, *Memoirs of Lieut.-General Scott, LL.D.*, 2 vols. (New York: Sheldon, 1864), 2:393–396; William Seton Henry, *Campaign Sketches of the War with Mexico* (New York: Harper & Brothers, 1847), 202.

4. *Delta*, April 13, 1847; *Washington Union*, May 5, 1847; *Eagle*, quoted in *Delta* and *Picayune*, April 13, 15, 1847; also see *Mexico City American Star*, May 30, 1848.

5. *Picayune*, April 14, 1847; *Charleston Courier*, April 24, 1847; *Delta*, April 13, 1847. Storms's quote is in the *New York Sun*, April 28, 1847. Two weeks after the *Eagle* started, Peoples and Barnard left the paper to rejoin Scott. In June, with the onset of the summer heat and yellow fever season, Jewell announced the *Eagle* was suspending publication until September, however, it never resumed. *Picayune*, July 8, 1847.

6. *Picayune*, April 10, 23, 1847.

7. *Baltimore Sun*, December 2, 1847; *Boston Daily Mail*, January 11, 1848; *Picayune*, August 6, 1847; May 8, 1849.

8. *Picayune*, April 23, 1847.

9. Ibid., May 1, 1847.

10. Ibid., May 5, 6, 1847. *Charleston Courier*, May 8, 1847. See *Picayune*, May 2, 1847, for an example of the supplements. Kendall also jotted off a postbattle note to his friend William Trotter Porter at the *Spirit of the Times:* "The sheet of paper on which this is written was sure enough found in Santa Anna's magnificent carriage at the rout of Cerro Gordo, as was the gold leaf cigar which accompanies it. . . . When you smoke it call a General Council of the boys and take a whiff a piece all around, Indian fashion. The things is [*sic*] scarce!" Kendall also sent Porter a Mexican uniform and sword. He expressed the hope the war would end quickly so that he could start "for New Orleans and New York at a tolerably rapid rate." *Spirit of the Times*, June 12, 1847.

11. *Delta*, May 19, 1847.

12. Quotes in ibid., April 23, 1847; *New Orleans Bee*, May 1, 1847; *Augusta (Ga.) Chronicle and Sentinel*, May 7, 1847.

13. *Delta*, May 6, 1847.

14. *Picayune*, May 9, 1847; *New York Spirit of the Times*, May 29, 1847, also praised Peoples's account as "the most connected history of the events"; Oswandel, *Notes of the Mexican War*, 145, called it "a good little reading paper . . . you can see that those enterprising Yankees Messrs. Jewell, Peoples and Barnard are determined

to follow up the army, and publish the news, as we go along, in English." Peoples, quoted in *Delta*, May 18, 1847. Peoples continued to supply the *Delta* with regular correspondence from Puebla until May 8. Freaner returned to Mexico May 7 and resumed the main *Delta* reporting assignment.

15. *New York Tribune*, May 18, 1847; the *Jalapa Star* continued publication until May 13, when the owners announced they were going forward with the troops to Puebla and "ultimately to the city of Mexico." Jewell, Barnard, and Peoples had decided to dissolve their association "by mutual consent," Jewell continuing the *American Eagle* at Veracruz, while Peoples and Barnard continued the *Star* at another press in Puebla. *Picayune*, May 25, 1847.

16. *Alton (Ill.) Telegraph*, May 21, 1847.

17. *Philadelphia North American*, May 4, 1847.

18. Ibid., May 20, 1847.

19. *New York Sun*, May 24, 1847.

20. *Picayune*, May 1, August 8, 1847.

21. *Charleston Courier*, May 5, 1847; *Augusta (Ga.) Chronicle and Sentinel*, May 6, 1847.

22. See *Washington Union, Baltimore Sun, Philadelphia North American, New York Herald*, May 7, 1847, for examples. The problem of gaining access to the telegraph apparently hurt some newspapers, a *New York Tribune* (May 8, 1847) correspondent complaining, "The interruption and preoccupation of the telegraph prevents the receipt of full intelligence. We will send the details early in the morning."

23. *Washington Union*, May 7, 1847; *St. Louis Reveille*, May 7, 1847; *New York Sun*, May 11, 1847.

Chapter 13. "Mustang" of the *Delta*

1. See Robert W. Drexler, *Guilty of Making Peace: A Biography of Nicholas Trist* (Lanham, Md.: University Press of America, 1991), chaps. 7–11; John S. D. Eisenhower, *So Far from God: The U.S. War with Mexico, 1846–1848* (New York: Random House, 1989), chap. 25; Wallace Ohrt, *Defiant Peacemaker: Nicholas Trist in the Mexican War* (College Station: Texas A&M University Press, 1997).

2. *Delta*, October 15, 1847.

3. Ibid., May 18, 25, 28, 1847; Ohrt, *Defiant Peacemaker*, 108.

4. Trist Memorandum. Trist Papers, Library of Congress.

5. Ethan Allen Hitchcock, *Fifty Years in Camp and Field: Diary of Major General Ethan Allen Hitchcock, U.S.A*, ed. W. A. Croffut (New York: G. Putnam's Sons, 1909); J. F. H. Claiborne, *Life and Correspondence of John A. Quitman*, 2 vols. (New York: Harper & Bros., 1860), 1:399.

6. Barnard in *Corpus Christi (Tex.) Star*, September 8, 1849; Warland in *Boston Atlas*, April 3, September 11, 1848; *Picayune*, February 20, 1849.

7. See the *Picayune*, August 20, 1847, for examples.

8. *Delta*, July 8, 1847; *Picayune*, July 8, 1847. After publishing their seventeenth issue on August 7, 1847, the *Star's* publishers noted: "As we said in Jalapa, ours is

not a 'fixed' *Star*. We raise it where and whenever the gallant band, whose deeds we chronicle, shall repose." On the same day, the printers packed up their belongings and joined Scott's troops as they started the march to the Mexican capital. *Delta*, August 22, 1847.

9. *Delta*, July 8, 11, 1847.

10. Ibid., September 11, 1847; 30th Congress, 1st Session (Senate) Executive No. 65 (August 3, 1848), *Message from the President of the United States, Communicating, in Compliance with the Resolution of the Senate, the Proceedings of the Two Courts of Inquiry in the Case of Major General Pillow*, 14, 18–19. Scott refers to using these expresses in 30th Congress, 1st Session, Exec. Doc. 60, *Messages of the President*, 1014, 1039, 1082. Communications were greatly disrupted between Washington and Scott's army during this period. At one point, the War Department went five months without receiving an official communiqué from the general. It assured him, however, "we are not without authentic information of your" victories. See *Messages of the President*, 1005–1006, 1010. Also see Trist to "heddy parker," Puebla, August 6, 1847, in Trist Papers, vol. 24, Library of Congress.

11. *Delta*, May 27, 1847.

12. Ibid., July 30, August 22, September 11, 1847.

13. Relationship in ibid., November 17, 1847. May 14, 1848. Freaner wrote at least 126 letters to the *Delta* between May 20, 1846, and June 22, 1848. Of those, eighty-seven were written after he returned to Mexico in May 1847 to follow Scott's army to Mexico; sixty-eight were written from the capital.

14. *Picayune*, May 18, June 8, 22, August 7, 1847. See Fayette Copeland, *Kendall of the* Picayune (Norman: University of Oklahoma Press, 1943), 198–200, regarding Kendall's express riders.

15. *Picayune*, May 11, 23, 28, 1847.

16. Ibid., June 15, 1847. These comments were written from Jalapa the week Trist arrived at Scott's headquarters.

17. Ibid., June 15, August 8, 10, 11, 1847. At the *Picayune*, the editors decided to follow "this example until such time as the whole affair may be laid before the country."

18. George Wilkins Kendall, handwritten untitled manuscript on the Mexican War, Eugene C. Barker Texas History Collection, Briscoe Center for American History, University of Texas, Austin. Scott feared he was being undercut.

19. Trist memorandum, February 14, 1848, in Trist Papers, Library of Congress; Justin H. Smith, *The War with Mexico*, 2 vols. (New York: Macmillan Co., 1919), 2:401–403n5, 411n18.

20. *Picayune*, August 20, 1847.

21. Ibid., August 7, 8, 1847.

22. Kendall's comments in ibid., May 11, 19, June 8, October 15, 1847; criticism of *Sun*, November 7, 14, 1847.

23. *Picayune*, August 8, November 7, 1847.

24. *Philadelphia North American*, May 6, 1847; *Boston Atlas*, July 4, August 4, 11, 1847.

25. *Picayune*, June 8, 1847; Scully quote, October 26, 1847.

26. Hayes's experiences are from the *Delta*, August 20, September 1, 3, November 6, 1847; *Picayune*, August 31, September 1, 3, 1847; *Veracruz Sol de Anahuac*, quoted in *Picayune*, September 3, 1847. Hayes joined the Louisiana Volunteer Regiment, as did many of the New Orleans journalists. The *Picayune*, August 31, 1847, reports the attack on Haile's unit.

27. Conditions in Veracruz are described in the *Delta*, July 23, 1847, January 29, June 24, 1848; *Picayune*, July 30, December 9, 1847.

28. Letter from Louis D. Wilson to ?, Veracruz, July 31, 1847, cited in Justin H. Smith Collection, vol. 12, Benson Latin American Collection, General Libraries, University of Texas at Austin; *Delta*, September 5, 1847; Davis ("Gomez") in *St. Louis Republican*, November 15, 1847; Beraza is named in George Wilkins Kendall, *The War between the United States and Mexico, Illustrated*, with illustrations by Carl Nebel (1851; reprint, Austin: Texas State Historical Association, 1994), 35.

29. For praise of these men, see *Delta*, August 8, November 6, 1847; January 14, February 8, 13, 1848; *New Orleans Crescent*, May 4, August 7, 1848; *Picayune*, April 12, 1848; the *Baltimore Sun* reported that Clifton on occasion sent letters with summaries of the news; Allis's military records indicate the early discharge.

30. U.S. Army, Headquarters of the Army, Mexico, December 12, 1847, General Orders No. 372. The protection included any "follower of the American army."

31. *Picayune*, March 18, 1848. The *Picayune* ran a summary article titled "The Perils of Express Riding in Mexico" on August 8, 1847. The paper promised to persevere in delivering the news. For examples of express rider losses, see *Picayune*, August 8, September 26, October 5, 1847, February 20, March 18, 1848. On occasion, the American correspondents also used the more reliable delivery service of the English courier, who stopped in the American-occupied cities on his regular trips between Mexico City and Veracruz. *New York Tribune*, August 16, 1849.

32. Quotes in *Picayune*, July 23, 1847; *Boston Atlas*, March 1, 1848.

33. Kendall in *Picayune*, May 11, 1847; Scully's proposal, October 15, 1847.

Chapter 14. The Northern Occupation

1. Justin H. Smith, *The War with Mexico*, 2 vols. (New York: Macmillan Co., 1919), 2:60–78; K. Jack Bauer, *Zachary Taylor* (Baton Rouge: Louisiana State University Press, 1985), chap. 11.

2. For information on Durivage's background, see *St. Louis Reveille*, March 27, 1847; *Picayune*, March 30, 1847; *Delta*, September 9, 1846; *New York Herald*, April 15, 1846. The *Boston Post* (October 14, 1847) said Durivage was the nephew of Harvard president Edward Everett. Durivage also wrote letters to the *New York Herald* from New Orleans during a portion of the war but did not report from the field for the New York paper. *New York Herald*, April 30, May 11, 20, 1846. Durivage apparently had planned to report from the front from the start of the war in May 1846, but for unexplained reasons did not join the *Picayune* until spring 1847. *New York Herald*, May 20, 1846.

3. *Picayune*, May 25, 28, 1847.

4. Ibid., June 1, 1847.

5. Ibid., May 3, 13, June 1, 8, 1847. Once established, Durivage became a prolific writer. The *Picayune* published sixty-eight letters and reports from May to November 1847, under his distinctive "J.E.D." signature.

6. Ibid., June 18, September 7, October 9, 1847. For more on the Paine Mutiny, see Richard Bruce Winders's "Will the Regiment Stand It?" in *Dueling Eagles: Reinterpreting the U.S. Mexican War, 1846–1848*, ed. Richard V. Francaviglia and Douglas W. Richmonds (Fort Worth: Texas Christian University Press, 2000).

7. *Ottawa (Ill.) Free Trader*, March 19, April 2, 1847.

8. See *Little Rock Arkansas State Gazette*, July 13, 1846, for "strict disciplinarian" quote. Also March 27, July 22, 1847, for Pike's criticisms.

9. Ibid., March 27, 1847. Pike was later challenged to a duel by one of the Arkansas officers involved in the incident. Pike also was critical of the unit's performance at Buena Vista and demanded General Wool appoint a court of inquiry to investigate the various charges. The court ended quickly when the feuding Arkansas officers signed a statement agreeing it had all been a misunderstanding. The dispute did not end, however, and they continued to write newspaper letters accusing each other of cowardice. Ibid., July 22, 1848. The historical record sustains Pike's account of the massacre and the unit's poor performance in the field. See Samuel E. Chamberlain, *My Confession* (New York: Harper & Bros., 1956), chap. 11; Josiah Gregg, *The Diary and Letters of Josiah Gregg*, ed. Maurice G. Fulton, 2 vols. (1941; reprint, Norman: University of Oklahoma Press, 1944), 2:40. The dispute with Yell is in William W. Hughes, *Archibald Yell* (Fayetteville: University of Arkansas Press, 1988), chaps. 13–17. A captain whose unit was blamed for the killings charged that Pike influenced Zachary Taylor's decision to send the Arkansas volunteers to the rear in disgrace. Pike strongly denied communicating with Taylor "directly or indirectly" about the incident. *Arkansas State Gazette*, July 22, 1848.

10. Tobin is in *Picayune*, March 30, 1847; Durivage in ibid., June 24, 1847.

11. *Louisville Journal*, March 8, 1847.

12. Gregg quotes from *Louisville Daily Journal*, December 24, 1846; March 8, 1847; also see Gregg, *Diary*, 80–84, 202.

13. Davis's quotes are in *Alton (Ill.) Telegraph*, December 11, 1846; May 21, July 23, 1847.

14. Ibid., September 4, October 2, 1846; June 18, 1847. For more on disease and mortality among the volunteers, see Winders, *Mr. Polk's Army*, 139–166.

15. *Picayune*, June 15, 1847.

16. Ibid., August 6, 14, September 8, 1847.

17. Ibid., October 30, November 2, 10, 1847.

18. Ibid., October 2, 9, 1847; Durivage's appointment is in Orderbook, 1846–1847, "Army of Chihuahua," Centre Division, Order No. 422, August 25, 1847, John Ellis Wool Papers, New York State Archives, Albany.

19. The letters to Wool were from Joseph W. Moulton, July 18, September 8, 1847; John Ellis Wool Papers, New York State Archives, Albany. Carleton wrote

correspondence to newspapers, including the *Washington Union* and the *Picayune*, regarding the march into Mexico by Wool's division. He published a detailed account of Buena Vista after the war: James Henry Carleton, *The Battle of Buena Vista, with the Operations of the Army of Occupation for One Month* (New York: Harper & Bros., 1848). For his exchange of letters with Wool, see 177–184. One officer who disputed Wool's claim, Captain George W. Hughes of the Topographical Engineers, made his case in a letter to the *National Intelligencer*. Another example can be seen in the October 20, 1847, letter of Colonel George W. Hughes in the *Picayune*, undated clipping in Kendall Collection, Special Collections Division, University of Texas at Arlington Libraries. See Durivage reference in *Picayune*, October 19, 1847, and Tobin in *Delta*, June 2, 1847.

20. *Picayune*, November 27, 30, 1847.

21. Ibid., June 15, 1847; *Delta*, September 29, 1847. Also see ibid., December 26, 1847, for an example of Tobin's wry sense of humor. Durivage and Tobin became friends during this period and spent some of their time hunting and drinking together. *Memphis Daily Appeal*, November 21, 1847.

22. *New York Tribune*, November 19, 1847.

23. As evidence of collusion by the firing squad, Tobin wrote in the *Illinois Journal* on April 13, 1848: "The case was so strange that I asked about it; and as nearly as I can learn, twenty of the party had agreed to fire over his head, and only two fired at him . . . neither wound was mortal." A review of the court-martial records, however, and reports of volunteers who witnessed the execution provide no evidence of collusion by the firing squad to intentionally miss the Arkansas private, Victor Galbraith (R. B. Winders, personal communication, March 23, 2009).

24. *St. Louis Reveille*, March 28, 1848.

25. *Delta*, July 13, 1848.

Chapter 15. Contreras and Churubusco

1. Edward S. Wallace, *General William Jenkins Worth: Monterey's Forgotten Hero* (Dallas: Southern Methodist University Press, 1953), chap. 13; Justin H. Smith, *The War with Mexico*, 2 vols. (New York: Macmillan Co., 1919), 2:92–93.

2. Smith, vol. 2, chaps. 25–27; Bauer, *The Mexican War*, chap. 15; Jack Northrup [*sic*], "The Trist Mission," *Journal of Mexican American History* 3 (1973): 13–31; Kendall's comment about Contreras is in his unpublished history of the war, 695, Western History Collection, University of Oklahoma.

3. Deaths averaged eighty-two per day. *Delta*, August 12, September 7, 1847; *Picayune*, September 6, 15, 25, October 3, 15, 1847. The *New Orleans National* reported nine of its staff had contracted the illness. *National Intelligencer*, September 14, 1847.

4. *Picayune*, September 22, 1847. Storms on the Gulf of Mexico also contributed to the disruption. The *Delta* is quoted in *Washington Union*, August 28, 1847.

5. Freaner in *Augusta (Ga.) Chronicle and Sentinel*, August 30, 1847, and *Delta*, September 10, 11, 1847.

6. *Delta*, September 9, 10, 1847, and *Augusta (Ga.) Chronicle and Sentinel*, September 14, 1847; also see *Washington Union*, September 17, 1847, and *Philadelphia Public Ledger*, quoted in *Delta*, September 29, 1847.

7. *Picayune*, August 20, 1847.

8. Kendall quotes in handwritten unpublished notes titled "Valley of Mexico, Scott's Operations," chaps. 1–2, Eugene C. Barker, Texas History Center, University of Texas at Austin.

9. Kendall quote in ibid.; *Mexico City American Star*, November 17, 24, 1847.

10. Robert Ryal Miller, *Shamrock and Sword: The Saint Patrick's Battalion in the U.S.-Mexican War* (Norman: University of Oklahoma Press, 1989), 87–89. Kendall quotes in *Picayune*, September 9, 1847.

11. *Picayune*, September 3, 1847.

12. *Washington Union*, September 4, 1847.

13. *Philadelphia North American*, September 9, 1847; *New York Herald*, September 10, 1847.

14. *Delta* and *Picayune*, September 8, 9, 1847.

15. Recounted in the *Picayune*, September 23, 1847.

16. Raphael Semmes, *Service Afloat and Ashore during the Mexican War* (Cincinnati, Ohio: William H. Moore, 1851), 412; Thomas Pitcher Diary, "Battle of Contreras," August 19, 1847, Pitcher Family Papers, U.S. Army Military History Institute, Carlisle Barracks, Pa.

17. Quoted in Wallace, *General William Jenkins Worth*, 157–158.

18. *Picayune*, September 9, October 17, 1847.

19. Ibid., August 11, September 15, 1847.

20. *Delta*, September 26, 1847.

21. A memorandum written by Warland detailing his Mexico City experiences is attached to a file of the *American Star*, which he presented to Harvard University in 1849. The notes are dated January 1, 1849, and August 10, 1861, and are at Houghton Library, Harvard. Following the battles of Contreras and Churubusco, Colonel Trueman B. Ransom of the New England Regiment proposed that Warland start a newspaper with a small press the regiment discovered where it was quartered. Warland met the New Orleans journalists when they came to inspect the press and remained associated with them throughout the occupation. They decided to approach Santa Anna for access to a press after it was determined the type fonts of the captured equipment were not useable. *Mexico City American Star*, May 30, 1848.

22. *Picayune*, September 26, 1847; *American Star*, September 20, 1847.

23. *Picayune*, November 28, 1847, for Kendall mention in battle report; *Boston Post*, October 4, 1847; *Nashville Union*, October 13, 1847.

24. *Picayune*, October 21, 1847.

25. *Washington Union*, quoted in *Picayune*, September 25, 1847. The statement is made more sanctimonious by the *Union*'s own attack on Scott about the armistice. See *Picayune*, September 24, 1847.

Chapter 16. Disaster at Molino del Rey

1. Reprinted in *Delta*, July 31, 1847.

2. Ibid.; *Picayune*, August 1, 1847.

3. The *Philadelphia Pennsylvanian* of August 11, 1847, is quoted in *Delta*, August 20, 1847; *New York Tribune*, August 11, 14, 1847; *St. Louis Missouri Republican* is quoted in *Picayune*, August 22, 1847. For other false reports, see *Delta*, September 3, 9, 1847; Kendall's letter in the *Picayune*, August 7, 1847, was written from Puebla July 30, the same day as the *National*'s false report.

4. *Washington Union*, September 1847; *Picayune*, October 15, 1847. The reference was to *The Adventures of Baron Munchausen*. The *National Intelligencer* and *Journal of Commerce* are quoted in the same article. *Delta*, October 14, 1847. Typical of the papers fooled by the *Sun*'s hoax was the *Newport (R.I.) Mercury*, October 9, 1847, which called the report "fearfully interesting, not only as a vivid description of the combat, but as evidence of the desperate tenacity with which the Mexicans adhere to the defence [*sic*] of their country."

5. *Charleston Courier*, September 29, 1847; *New York Herald*, October 14, 1847; *Philadelphia North American*, October 5, 1847.

6. Justin H. Smith, *The War with Mexico*, 2 vols. (New York: Macmillan Co., 1919), vol. 2, chap. 27; 2:140–148.

7. Entry dated "Tucubaya, September 10, 1847," in Duncan Letterbook, James Duncan Papers, U.S. Military Academy Library, West Point; also Raphael Semmes, *Service Afloat and Ashore during the Mexican War* (Cincinnati, Ohio: William H. Moore, 1851), 443.

8. First quote, *Picayune*, October 14, 1847; second quote, Kendall, from an 830-page unpublished history of the Mexican War, typescript, chap. 4, 23; third quote, Kendall undated notes on the history of the Mexican War, in Kendall Collection, Special Collections Division, University of Texas at Arlington Libraries.

9. *Picayune*, October 14, 1847.

10. Freaner quotes from *Augusta (Ga.) Chronicle and Sentinel*, October 20, 1847.

11. *Delta*, October 27, 1847. This part of Freaner's correspondence was intercepted and did not appear in print until long after Kendall's account.

12. *Delta*, October 15, 1847.

13. Undated *New York Courier and Enquirer* clipping with dateline of "Mexico, May 18, 1848," in Kendall Collection, Special Collections Division, University of Texas at Arlington Libraries.

Chapter 17. The Halls of Montezuma

1. *Picayune*, October 14, 1847.

2. Justin H. Smith, *The War with Mexico*, 2 vols. (New York: Macmillan Co., 1919), 2:149–164; John S. D. Eisenhower, *So Far from God: The U.S. War with Mexico, 1846–1848* (New York: Random House, 1989), chap. 28.

3. *Picayune*, August 11, 1867. Kendall recounted the incident twenty years later.

4. Ibid., October 14, 1847.

5. Ibid., August 11, 1867.

6. Kendall recounted these events twenty years later in the *Picayune*, September 15, 1867. Also see Scott criticism and the same anecdote in a Kendall letter to the *Picayune*, written November 2, 1861, in Kendall Collection, Special Collections Division, University of Texas at Arlington Libraries. Kendall kept his word about not reporting future wars, although he briefly covered street fighting in Paris in 1848. See Fayette Copeland, *Kendall of the* Picayune (Norman: University of Oklahoma Press, 1943), chap. 21. Kendall wrote some commentary but did not report combat for the *Picayune* during the Civil War. Kendall's critical feelings toward Scott continued in his postwar writing, including in his unpublished history of the war in the University of Oklahoma Western History Collection. See 526–527, 566–567, for examples. On November 14, 1852, Kendall wrote to his wife, "Frank Pierce's majority for President is enormous—Gen. Scott is badly defeated and I was never so much rejoiced at the result of any election in my life: the news is glorious." Ibid.

7. *Picayune*, October 14, 1847.

8. Kendall, *Illustrated*, 48–49.

9. Freaner's reports are in the *Delta*, October 15, 27, 1847; also in *Augusta (Ga.) Chronicle and Sentinel*, October 20, 1847.

10. *Delta*, October 15, 1847; *Picayune*, October 15, 1847.

11. *Picayune*, November 30, 1847.

12. The incident is reported in the *Baltimore Sun*, December 2, 1847. Another version of the incident quoted Bugbee as replying, "None, Sir! I'm one of the printer's craft, from *Bosting!*" J. M. Wynkoop, ed., *Anecdotes and Incidents . . . of the Mexican War* (Pittsburgh: n.p., 1848), 20–21. Another former reporter who contributed to the reports of the battles for Chapultepec and Mexico City was T. Mayne Reid, a *New York Herald* writer who was serving as a lieutenant in the New York Volunteer Regiment. Using the pseudonym "Ecolair," Reid provided detailed accounts to the *Spirit of the Times* of the fighting under the title "Sketches by a Skirmisher." Reid, a native of Ireland, had worked as a reporter and editor for several years prior to the start of the war. He later became a noted writer of children's literature. Reid erroneously was reported killed at Chapultepec, and the *Spirit of the Times* carried an obituary about him on December 4, 1847. It is not clear if Reid wrote accounts to the *Herald*, although he may be the author of unsigned letters about the battles at Mexico City that appeared in the *Herald*. The *Spirit* printed Reid's battle sketches on December 11, 18, 1847. A poem he wrote about the battle of Monterrey ran in the *Spirit*, December 25, 1847. He also wrote occasionally for the *Newport (R.I.) News*.

13. Kendall's quote is in *Augusta (Ga.) Chronicle and Sentinel*, October 20, 1847; Freaner in the *Delta*, October 15, 1847.

14. Freaner in the *Delta*, October 23, 1847. The *Delta* reprinted the Freaner item from the *Arco Iris* after having it translated back to English. See ibid., October 26, 1847. Durivage is in *Picayune*, October 19, 1847.

15. *Picayune* and *Delta*, September 26, 1847.

16. *Delta*, September 26, 1847; *Picayune*, September 26, 29, October 2, 1847.

17. *Charleston Courier*, September 29, October 2, 1847.

18. *Picayune* and *Delta*, September 26, 1847.

19. *Charleston Courier*, October 1, 1847; *Washington Union*, October 3, 5, 1847.

20. Scully in *Picayune*, October 5, 1847; *Picayune* and *Delta*, October 14, 15, 1847.

21. On this occasion the news reached New York City via Havana and New Orleans almost simultaneously. The *New York Express*'s Havana correspondent forwarded accounts from the British mail boat that left Veracruz October 1 with full reports from Mexico City to September 28. The English government courier carried the battle news to Veracruz in three days. Three days later an English ship en route to Europe stopped at Havana, where local newspapers published the story and then relayed the accounts to New York.

Chapter 18. Backlash

1. *National Eagle* editor J. S. Walker made this comment after using a generous portion of Kendall's Contreras and Churubusco letters. The editor continued, "Why do they not describe to us the scenes in the hospital of the wounded? Fancy the eight hundred maimed and wounded wretches—*on our side alone*—crowded together in close quarters, under a tropical sun, in the hands of the surgeons. . . . Ah! The *untold* incidents of war would give us a better understanding of its results . . . every moral sentiment turns away in unaffected loathing and disgust."

2. *Washington Union*, October 21, 1847.

3. The bribe proposal is described in John S. D. Eisenhower, *Agent of Destiny: The Life and Times of General Winfield Scott* (New York: Free Press, 1997), 266–268; Justin H. Smith, *The War with Mexico*, 2 vols. (New York: Macmillan Co., 1919), 2:390–391n11; George T. M. Davis, *Autobiography of Col. George T. M. Davis* (New York: Executors of the Estate, 1892), 177. The *Mexico City American Star* (February 10, 1848) said "Gomez" was "well known to this army as a writer of some merit and an officer of some consequence." E. J. Gomez, controversial editor of the New Orleans *La Patria*, made a prudent announcement that he was not the *Republican*'s "Gomez." *Delta*, December 21, 1847.

4. First printing was in the *St. Louis Republican*, November 22, 1847. It became a national issue when reprinted in the *Baltimore Sun*, December 6, 1847.

5. Shields's testimony to the *Pillow Court of Inquiry*, June 7, 1848, quoted in the Justin H. Smith Collection in the Benson Latin American Collection, General Libraries, University of Texas at Austin.

6. Trist quote is in memorandum, Nicholas Trist Papers, Library of Congress; Smith, *War with Mexico*, 2:390–391n11. No action was taken against Davis.

7. *Washington Union*, October 23, 1847.

8. Quotes in *New York Herald*, October 23, 1847; *Washington Union*, October 23, 1847; *Boston Daily Mail*, April 22, 1848. Ritchie's compliment of Freaner is in the *Union*, September 17, 1847.

9. Letter, Pillow to "My Dear Sir," January 13, 1848, in Reynolds Correspondence, New-York Historical Society.

10. *Boston Post*, October 4, 1847. Pillow's case is discussed in Chapter 20.

11. *Nashville Union*, November 1, 1847. See also October 13, 1847.

12. *Boston Post*, November 18, 1847; *Washington Union*, December 4, 1847.

13. *Picayune*, October 21, 1847.

14. Ibid., November 2, 25, December 5, 1847.

15. Quotes in *Cincinnati Enquirer*, June 9, 1847; *Albany Argus*, August 18, 1847; *Washington National Intelligencer*, August 17, 1847; *Boston Daily Mail*, October 26, 1847; *U.S. Gazette*, quoted in *Cincinnati Enquirer*, June 9, 1847.

16. *Delta*, November 27, 1847.

17. Quotes from *Public Ledger* in *Delta*, September 29, 1847; *Cincinnati Daily Commercial* in *Delta*, October 1, 1847; *Louisville Journal* in *Delta*, October 2, 1847; *Boston Daily Mail*, April 22, 1848; *Galveston News* in *Delta*, October 3, 1847; *Boston Atlas*, October 25, 1847.

18. Quotes in *Delta*, December 14, 30, 1847.

19. *Picayune*, November 7, 1847.

20. Ibid., October 16, 17, 1847.

21. First quote, ibid., November 20, 1847; second quote, November 7; departure and return home is in Fayette Copeland, *Kendall of the* Picayune (Norman: University of Oklahoma Press, 1943), 232.

Chapter 19. The Yankee Press in Mexico City

1. Secretary of the Navy John Y. Mason made this statement in a speech to the University of North Carolina alumni association attended by President Polk. Quoted in *New York Herald*, August 5, 1847, *Delta*, October 13, 1847, and *Mexico City American Star*, February 5, 1848.

2. Quote in *Charleston Courier*, October 27, 1847. For an excellent study of the occupation, see George Towne Baker III, "Mexico City and the War of the United States: A Study in the Politics of Military Occupation" (Ph.D. diss., Duke University, 1969). Also see Dennis E. Berge, "A Mexican Dilemma: The Mexico City Ayuntamiento and the Question of Loyalty, 1846–1848," *Hispanic American Historical Review* 50, no. 2 (May 1970): 229–256; Edward S. Wallace, "The United States Army in Mexico City," *Military Affairs* 13, no. 3 (Fall 1949): 158–166; Justin H. Smith, "American Rule in Mexico," *American Historical Review* 23, no. 2 (January 1918): 287–302. Mexican politics are examined in Pedro Santoni, *Mexicans at Arms: Puro Federalists and the Politics of War, 1845–1848* (Fort Worth: Texas Christian University Press, 1996), 213–230.

3. Quote in *American Star*, May 30, 1848; see Lota M. Spell, "The Anglo-Saxon Press in Mexico, 1846–1848," *American Historical Review* 38, no. 1 (October 1932): 26–27. During their association on the paper, Barnard and Peoples ran it jointly for a period, and each took turns running it separately. They ran it jointly until December 1847, then Barnard took it until February 1848. Peoples was the editor-publisher thereafter. Charles Bugbee ran an express line from Mexico City during the occupation and was associated with the *Star*. See *American Star*, October 10, 12,

28, 1847; *North American*, January 22, 1848. Among the printers "furloughed" to work on the *Star* were Alexander Kenaday, John W. Ross, James Sawyer, Frank Bitting, Frederick K. Krauth, and Henry R. Courtney. *Vedette*, 9, no. 4 (1888): 9.

4. Quote in *American Star*, May 30, 1848; see Spell, "The Anglo-Saxon Press"; also see Robert Louis Bodson, "A Description of the United States Occupation of Mexico as Reported by American Newspapers Published in Vera Cruz, Puebla, and Mexico City, September 14, 1847 to July 31, 1848" (Ph.D. diss., Ball State University, 1971), 27; John H. Warland, memorandum detailing his Mexico City experiences, notes dated January 1, 1849, and August 10, 1861, attached to a file of the *American Star*, Houghton Library, Harvard University.

5. For an excellent study of this unit, see Robert Ryal Miller, *Shamrock and Sword: The Saint Patrick's Battalion in the U.S.-Mexican War* (Norman: University of Oklahoma Press, 1989).

6. The *Star*'s account is in the *Picayune*, October 15, 1847. Warland wrote a separate story to the *Boston Atlas*, August 10, 1848.

7. Kendall's comments are from *Picayune*, October 14, 15, 1847.

8. Edward S. Wallace, *General William Jenkins Worth, Monterey's Forgotten Hero* (Dallas: Southern Methodist University Press, 1953), 180–222. Warland was noted for his pro-Whig editorials as the editor of the *Lowell Courier*. He was born in Cambridge, April 20, 1807, and died July 7, 1872, in Lowell, age sixty-five. *New York Times*, July 11, 1872. Warland wrote approximately forty letters from Mexico to the *Atlas* and occasionally sent items to the *New Orleans Crescent* and *Picayune*. John H. Warland, memorandum detailing his Mexico City experiences, notes dated January 1, 1849, and August 10, 1861, attached to a file of the *American Star*, Houghton Library, Harvard University. Examples in *Boston Atlas*, March 23, April 6, May 26, August 2, 1848. Some of his prewar writings are compiled in John H. Warland, *The Plume: A Tuft of Literary Feathers* (Boston: Benjamin B. Mussey, 1847). Warland's career as a political editor is recounted by his former associate William Schouler in "Personal and Political Recollections No. 5," undated *Boston Journal* clipping, William Schouler Collection, Massachusetts Historical Society.

9. Summarized from the *Atlas*, March 1, September 11, 29, 1848; John H. Warland, memorandum detailing his Mexico City experiences, notes dated January 1, 1849, and August 10, 1861, attached to a file of the *American Star*, Houghton Library, Harvard University. The poem appeared in the *Star*, February 12, 1848.

10. Praise for the quality of *El Monitor Republicano* can be seen in the *Star*, September 28, 1847, February 2, 1848; background in Spell, "The Anglo-Saxon Press"; Berge, "A Mexican Dilemma," 241ff. See also Richard Bruce Winders, *Mr. Polk's Army* (College Station: Texas A&M University Press, 1997), for a discussion of the *North American* and *American Star*.

11. *Picayune*, October 14, 15, December 29, 1847; *New York Herald*, December 6, 1847.

12. Quotes praising Tobey and his newspaper are in *Philadelphia North American*, November 15, 1847; *Philadelphia Bulletin*, quoted in *Pensacola Gazette*, December 25, 1847; *Philadelphia Pennsylvanian*, quoted in *Chicago Journal*, May 19,

1848; *St. Louis Reveille*, November 17, December 4, 1847; *New York Spirit of the Times*, December 11, 1847; *Albany Argus*, December 21, 1847. Also see *Delta*, November 6, 1847.

13. Quote in *Picayune*, March 8, 1848; examples of use in ibid., March 30, 1848.

14. Baker, "Mexico City and the War of the United States," 251–261; for examples in the *Mexico City North American*, see November 12, December 17, 21, 24, 1847; January 31, February 4, 1848. For *American Star*, see October 29, November 21, 1847; February 1, 4, 1848.

15. See *Delta*, November 12, 1847; February 16, 1848, for republication of Tobey's articles.

16. Wallace, *General William Jenkins Worth*, 180; Spell, "The Anglo-Saxon Press," 27; *Mexico City North American*, February 8, 14, 1848; *American Star*, February 8, 1848. Edwin Tobey died in Mexico City on February 7, 1848, from typhus fever.

17. *Philadelphia North American*, June 4, 1847. Interestingly, some stateside political newspapers attacked Tobey after this article was printed, calling him a "striped" and "bogus" Democrat. Ibid., December 22, 1847.

18. Ibid., April 3, 1848; *Mexico City North American*, February 8, 1848.

19. Quotes from *American Star*, September 25, 30, 1847; *Mexico City North American*, October 12, 1847. Trist, quoted in Baker, "Mexico City and the War of the United States," 281.

20. Reilly, "Newspaper Suppression during the Mexican War," *Journalism Quarterly* 54 (Summer 1977): 262–270.

Chapter 20. "First Impressions": Gideon Pillow and the American Press in Mexico

1. The Robert E. Lee statement was in a letter to John MacKay, dated City of Mexico, October 2, 1847. Archives, U.S. Army Military History Institute, Carlisle Barracks, Penn.

2. *New Orleans Delta*, April 7, May 10, 1848; Edward S. Wallace, *General William Jenkins Worth: Monterey's Forgotten Hero* (Dallas: Southern Methodist University Press, 1953), 172–174.

3. For background about Pillow and his career, see Nathaniel Cheairs Hughes Jr. and Roy Stonesifer Jr., *The Life and Wars of Gideon J. Pillow* (Chapel Hill and London: University of North Carolina Press, 1993); Philip M. Hamer, "Gideon Johnson Pillow," *Dictionary of American Biography* 14:603–604; Patricia Bell, "Gideon Pillow: A Personality Profile," *Civil War Times Illustrated* 6 (October 1967): 13–19; Benjamin Franklin Cooling, "Lew Wallace and Gideon Pillow: Enigmas and Variations on an American Theme," *Lincoln Herald* 84, no. 2 (Summer 1981): 651–658; Roy Stonesifer Jr., "Gideon J. Pillow: A Study in Egotism," *Tennessee Historical Quarterly* 25, no. 4 (Winter 1966): 340–350; Timothy D. Johnson, *A Gallant Little Army: The Mexico City Campaign* (Lawrence: University Press of Kansas, 2007),

260–265; Timothy D. Johnson, "A Most Anomalous Affair: Gideon Pillow and Winfield Scott in the Mexico City Campaign," *Tennessee Historical Quarterly* 66, no. 1 (Spring 2007): 2–19. For historians' comments on Pillow's military abilities and the dispute, see John S. D. Eisenhower, *So Far from God: The U.S. War with Mexico, 1846–1848* (New York: Random House, 1989), 110–111, 351–355, 363–364, 371–373, and *Agent of Destiny*, chap. 29; K. Jack Bauer, *The Mexican War, 1846–1848* (New York: Macmillan, 1974), 371–374; Justin H. Smith, *The War with Mexico*, 2 vols. (New York: Macmillan Co., 1919), 2:187–188, 376, 378, 435, 437.

4. *Delta*, September 10, 1847; Wallace, *General William Jenkins Worth*, 173.

5. *Delta*, September 24, 1847; May 10, 1848; also see April 7, 1848, and September 9, 10, 1847.

6. Quotes in *Picayune*, April 23, May 2, 29, 1847. The trenches would have provided more protection for attackers, rather than the American defender, the story claimed. Also see Hughes and Stonesifer, *The Life and Wars of Gideon J. Pillow*, 47–48. For Pillow's defense, see *Washington Union*, October 21, 1847; *Delta*, September 24, 1847; *Nashville Union*, June 12, 1847.

7. *Picayune*, September 11, 19, 1847; *Delta*, September 20, 24, 1847.

8. *Delta*, September 22, 24, 1847; *Picayune*, September 20, 24, 1847; *New Orleans Commercial Bulletin*, September 18, 1847, quoted in *Picayune*, September 19, 1847.

9. *New York Tribune*, May 25, 1848. For the effect on Pillow's career, see Hughes and Stonesifer, *The Life and Wars of Gideon J. Pillow*, chap. 6.

10. Fayette Copeland, *Kendall of the* Picayune (Norman: University of Oklahoma Press, 1943), chaps. 16–19. Zachary Taylor won for the Whigs in 1848; Democrat Franklin Pierce beat Whig Winfield Scott in 1852; John C. Frémont unsuccessfully carried the Republican Party banner in 1856.

11. Letter (?) to Mr. Levert (of Pennsylvania) from National Bridge, Mexico, November 26, 1847. In Mexican War Collection, Special Collections Division, University of Texas at Arlington Libraries.

12. R. B. Reynolds to Major D. Graham, Veracruz, October 7, 1847, James K. Polk Papers, Library of Congress. Davis comments in *Alton (Ill.) Telegraph*, June 18, 1847.

13. Quotes in Trist Memorandum, February 14, 1848, Nicholas Trist Papers, Library of Congress; James T. McIntosh et al., eds., *The Papers of Jefferson Davis*, 3:88–91; Bragg in Smith, *War with Mexico*, 2:436; Ulysses Simpson Grant, *The Papers of Ulysses S. Grant*, ed. John Y. Simon (Carbondale: Southern Illinois University Press, 1967), 1:115.

14. Emma Jerome Blackwood, ed., *To Mexico with Scott: Letters of Captain E. Kirby Smith to His Wife* (Cambridge, Mass.: Harvard University Press, 1917), 213–214; A. F. Caldwell to Jarvis Jackson, Mexico City, January 28, 1848, in *Mexican War Letters*, Center for American History, General Libraries, University of Texas at Austin; Robert Anderson, *An Artillery Officer in the Mexican War* (New York: G. Putnam's Sons, 1911), 77; "Indicator" is in *New Orleans Tropic*, March 25, 1847.

15. Frederic Hudson, *Journalism in the United States, from 1690 to 1872* (New York: Harper, 1873), 145. Hudson mentioned Jefferson Davis and Braxton Bragg

as two examples. Kendall's views are in an undated *Picayune* article, written from Paris, France, June 12, 1854, in Kendall Collection, Special Collections Division, University of Texas at Arlington Libraries. In 1849, after hearing of Worth's death, Kendall wrote: "Worth had his faults, as who has not; but men overlooked the failings, which owed their origins to an impetuous temper, in the dash and daring of a gallant soldier . . . [all who served with him] will remember his soldierly bearing, his gallant deportment, or the natural goodness of his heart." See Kendall letter to Picayune from Paris, June 25, 1849, in Kendall Collection, Special Collections Division, University of Texas at Arlington Libraries.

16. *Mexico City American Star*, October 22, 1847; Wallace, *General William Jenkins Worth*, 172; Charles Winslow Elliott, *Winfield Scott, The Soldier and the Man* (New York: Macmillan, 1937), chap. 41.

17. Smith, *War with Mexico*, 1:347, 507. Only a few antiadministration newspapers, such as the *New York Express* and the *New York Tribune*, complained of "the gag order," Horace Greeley noting prophetically, "We think the Administration has only hurt itself by this covert assault on the General and that the President will yet rue the day when the odious order was revived" (*New York Tribune*, February 3, 1847). Also see the exchange of letters between Marcy and Zachary Taylor in *Messages of the President of the United States, with the Correspondence, Therewith Communicated, between the Secretary of War and Other Officers of the Government, on the Subject of the Mexican War*, Exec. Doc. 60, 30th Congress, 1st Session (Washington: Wendell & Benthuysen Printers, 1848), 391–392, 809–810. *Augusta (Ga.) Chronicle and Sentinel*, February 10, 1847. The order had first appeared in the *General Regulations of the Army* in 1825 but had been excluded when the regulations were reprinted in 1841.

18. Originals of both orders are in the Garrett Collection, Special Collections Division, University of Texas at Arlington Libraries.

19. Duncan admitted in a letter to the *Mexico City North American*, November 16, 1847, that he wrote the letter. Also see Wallace, *General William Jenkins Worth*, 174–175.

20. John Sanders to Duncan, Philadelphia, January 1, 1848, James Louis Mason to Duncan, Newport, R.I., January 14, 1848, both in James Duncan Collection, U.S. Military Academy Library, West Point. In the midst of the Duncan dispute, Lieutenant Colonel Ethan Allen Hitchcock admitted to the court of inquiry that he was the author of a long letter defending Scott's Lake Chalco decision that appeared in the *New York Courier and Enquirer*, March 12, 1848. Hitchcock used the same "letter to a friend" defense. Ethan Allen Hitchcock, *Fifty Years in Camp and Field: Diary of Major General Ethan Allen Hitchcock, U.S.A*, ed. W. A. Croffut (New York: G. Putnam's Sons, 1909).

21. The Duncan-Peoples comments are in the *Mexico City American Star*, November 16, 17, 1847, and *Mexico City North American*, November 16, 1847. Also see Duncan to Kendall, Mexico City, November 22, 1847, in Kendall Collection, Special Collections Division, University of Texas at Arlington Libraries; Worth to Duncan, Washington, D.C., August 5, 1848, Duncan Collection, U.S. Military Academy Library, West Point.

22. *Delta*, April 7, 1848; Hughes and Stonesifer, *The Life and Wars of Gideon J. Pillow*, chap. 6. It was a complicated inquiry, lasting from November 1847 until July 1848. Soon after he brought the charges, Scott's temper cooled, and he offered to drop the whole affair. Worth and Duncan accepted, but Pillow demanded his own court proceedings continue. The court held hearings in Mexico City and the United States. President Polk changed Scott's order for a court-martial to a court of inquiry and appointed army officers who supported Pillow. In the end the court recommended no action be taken against Pillow. "Message from the President of the United States, Communicating, in Compliance with Resolution of the Senate, the Proceedings of the Two Courts of Inquiry in the Case of Major General Pillow," 1st Session (Senate), Executive No. 65 (August 3, 1848).

23. The dates on the letters, place of origin, and dates published in the *Pennsylvanian* are November 19, 1846, from Camargo, published December 24, 1846; January 22, 1847, from Brazos, published February 12, 1847; February 27, 1847, from Tampico, published March 25, 1847; April 30, 1847, from Veracruz, published May 21, 1847; May 30, 1847, from Jalapa, published June 29, 1847; and June 7, 1847, from Jalapa, published June 30, 1847. Quotes from *Pennsylvanian*, March 25, May 21, 1847. Examples of Pillow's defense can be seen in the *Pennsylvanian*, June 10, 26, September 23, 1847; April 3, 21, May 19, 1848.

24. The unpublished Leonidas, dated Mexico City, September 25, 1847, is in the Trist Papers, Library of Congress. Freaner, Trist, and Scott were aware of the unpublished version.

25. Pillow to Major Robert B. Reynolds, November 27 and December 27, 1847; Pillow to "My Dear Major," April 5, 1847; Pillow to "My Dear Sir," January 13, 1848, all in Reynolds Correspondence, New-York State Historical Society.

26. Executive Document No. 65, 116–118. In an earlier letter to Peoples, Pillow denied he wrote the Leonidas letter. *Mexico City American Star*, October 23, 1847. Quitman in George T. M. Davis, *Autobiography of Col. George T. M. Davis* (New York: Executors of the Estate, 1892), 283–285.

27. Pillow to Polk, November 26, Polk Papers, Library of Congress; Pillow to Major Robert B. Reynolds, November 27, 1847, Reynolds Papers, New-York State Historical Society. Request for Tobey, Pillow to Polk, November 26, Polk Papers.

28. *New Orleans Picayune*, October 27, 1847.

29. Ibid., February 10, 1848. Burns's letter was dated January 26, 1848, from Mexico City.

30. Executive Document No. 65, 13–15; *Delta*, May 10, 1848.

31. Trist Papers, vol. 24, Library of Congress. Trist believed he accidentally mailed the Leonidas Letter.

32. Quotes in Executive Document No. 65, 13–15; *Delta*, May 10, 1848.

33. *Mexico City American Star*, May 30, 1848.

34. *Delta*, April 7, May 23, 1848; for criticism of Freaner, see *Mobile Register and Journal*, April 4, 1848.

35. *Boston Daily Mail*, April 22, 1848.

36. Executive Document No. 65, 32–37; 43–46. A celebrated stateside case had preceded Scott's, when Lieutenant Colonel John C. Frémont was court-martialed

for failure to obey the orders of General Stephen Kearney while in California. The court met in Virginia. At first the *New York Herald* was excited at the prospect of the trial and thanked the court for "the facilities extended to the press gang, whose judgment goes largely to make up the judgment of the public." Initial coverage was heavy, but the trial quickly bogged down in charges and countercharges. The press and public expressed exasperation at the bickering. Two months later the *Herald* wrote, "We request our reporter at Washington to pick up his hat and leave the court martial upon Col. Fremont; it is not worthy of any further reporting. . . . [it] has degenerated into one of the smallest and silliest pieces of trifling we have ever seen." *New York Herald*, November 4, December 27, 1847.

37. *Boston Atlas*, September 11, 1848.

38. *New Orleans Crescent*, May 4, 14, 1848.

39. *Delta*, April 7, 1848; Elliott, *Winfield Scott*, 573; Smith, *War with Mexico*, 2:436–437.

40. *Delta*, April 11, 1848; *Crescent*, May 22, 1848; Alexander Walker to Trist, May 16, 1848, Trist Papers, Library of Congress.

41. Smith, *War with Mexico*, 2:437; Hughes and Stonesifer, *The Life and Wars of Gideon J. Pillow*, 120.

42. See J. Cutler Andrews, *The North Reports the Civil War* (Pittsburgh: University of Pittsburgh Press, 1955), for a discussion of this problem; Hughes and Stonesifer, *The Life and Wars of Gideon J. Pillow*.

Chapter 21. Stereotypes

1. Thorpe in *New Orleans Tropic*, July 1, 1846; Durivage in *Picayune*, September 7, 1847.

2. *Boston Atlas*, July 25, August 24, 1848.

3. *Picayune*, August 26, September 8, 1846.

4. Tobey, quoted in *Philadelphia North American*, June 4, 1847; "Indicator" in *Tropic*, June 20, 1846; Thorpe in *Our Army at Monterey*, 122–123.

5. Durivage's views are in *Picayune*, October 1, November 2, 1847.

6. *Alton (Ill.) Telegraph*, April 23, 1847.

7. Peoples is quoted in *New Orleans Crescent*, April 22, 1848; Freaner in *Augusta (Ga.) Chronicle and Sentinel*, November 12, 1847.

8. Tobey's views are from *Philadelphia North American*, May 4, June 5, 1847.

9. From *New Orleans Commercial Times*, n.d., reprinted in Charleston *Mercury*, November 5, 1846.

10. Kendall in *Picayune*, June 27, 1846; Reid, *Scouting Expeditions*, 89.

11. Callahan in *Picayune*, December 19, 1847; Peoples in *Mexico City American Star*, November 9, 1847. For other examples of correspondents using "greasers," see Kendall, *Picayune*, June 27, July 19, 1846; Freaner, *Delta*, November 14, 1846; Durivage, *Picayune*, October 1, 1847; Peoples, *Delta*, February 25, 1847, and *New Orleans Crescent*, April 22, 1848; Tobin, *Memphis Daily Appeal*, November 21, 1847, and *St. Louis Reveille*, March 28, 1848; S. D. Allis uses "yellow bellies" in *Picayune*, October 22, 1846; Tobey uses "yellow bellies" and "yellowskins" in *Philadelphia*

North American, March 19, April 9, 1847; George Davis refers to "yellow skins," *Alton (Ill.) Telegraph*, April 7, July 2, 1847.

12. *Picayune*, April 21, 1847.

13. Warland in *Boston Atlas*, April 14, 1848; *Mexico City American Star*, March 17, 1848.

14. See Raymund Paredes, "The Image of the Mexican in American Literature" (Ph.D. diss., University of Texas, Austin, 1973), 109; Henry in the New York *Spirit of the Times*, August 1, 1846.

Chapter 22. Mustang Delivers the Treaty

1. *Delta*, March 16, 1848. The *Nashville Union*, April 1, 1848, citing the *Delta*, related a similar story. After he left Buchanan, Freaner went to Secretary of War William Marcy's house to deliver Scott's official letters. Again, a servant would not let the correspondent in, so Freaner sat in a hallway chair. After a wait, a woman came and said Marcy was taking a nap and could not be disturbed. "Fine, I haven't slept for six days and I'll join him in this chair," Freaner responded. Shocked, the woman left and woke Marcy, who came quickly, "surprised and embarrassed." Polk and Buchanan thought Trist was coming with the treaty. Freaner apparently sent Buchanan a telegram from Charleston using Trist's secret code, but it was garbled in transmission. Milo M. Quaife, ed., *The Diary of James K. Polk, 1845–1849*, 4 vols. (Chicago: A. C. McLurg & Co., 1910), 3:344.

2. See John Edward Weems, *To Conquer a Peace* (Garden City, N.Y.: Doubleday & Co., 1974), 345–450.

3. Quote in Justin H. Smith, *The War with Mexico*, 2 vols. (New York: Macmillan Co., 1919), 2:233; excellent accounts of the events leading to the treaty are in Richard Griswold del Castillo, *The Treaty of Guadalupe Hidalgo: A Legacy of Conflict* (Norman: University of Oklahoma Press, 1990), particularly chaps. 1–4; Robert W. Drexler, *Guilty of Making Peace: A Biography of Nicholas Trist* (Lanham, Md.: University Press of America, 1991); and Pedro Santoni, *Mexicans at Arms: Puro Federalists and the Politics of War, 1845–1848* (Fort Worth: Texas Christian University Press, 1996), 213–230. Also see Norman A. Graebner, "Party Politics and the Trist Mission," *Journal of Southern History* 19 (1953): 135–156; Jack Northrup [*sic*], "The Trist Mission," *Journal of Mexican American History* 3 (1973): 13–31; and "Nicholas Trist's Mission to Mexico: A Reinterpretation," *Southwestern Historical Quarterly* 71 (January 1968): 321–346.

4. For background, see John Douglas Pitts Fuller, *The Movement for the Acquisition of All Mexico, 1846–1848* (Baltimore: Johns Hopkins University Press, 1936); Frederick Merk, *Manifest Destiny and Mission in American History* (New York: Knopf, 1963); and Paul F. Lambert, "The Movement for Acquisition of All Mexico," *Journal of the West* 11, no. 2 (April 1972): 317–327. Also see Griswold del Castillo, *The Treaty of Guadalupe Hidalgo*, chap. 3; Smith, *War with Mexico*, 2:239, 465; Thomas J. Farnham, "Nicholas Trist and James Freaner and the Mission to Mexico," *Arizona and the West* 11, no. 3 (Autumn 1969): 247–260.

5. Weems, *To Conquer a Peace*, 446; Drexler, *Guilty of Making Peace*, chaps. 8–11.

6. Smith, *War with Mexico*, 2:465; Farnham, "Nicholas Trist and James Freaner," 252–255.

7. Trist to his wife, Virginia, February 2, 1848. Trist Papers, Library of Congress; also Farnham, "Nicholas Trist and James Freaner," 254; Quaife, ed., *Polk Diary*, 3:285–287, for example.

8. For examples and praise of Freaner's reporting, see *Augusta (Ga.) Chronicle and Sentinel*, November 12, 1847; *Philadelphia North American*, January 4, 1848; *Charleston Courier*, January 20, 1848; *Franklin (La.) Planter's Banner*, May 25, 1848. For quotes, see *Delta*, November 12, December 22, 1847; February 16, 1848.

9. Quote in *Delta*, January 14, 1848. Also, ibid., January 29, 1848. The *Delta* said it received regular correspondence from Veracruz, Orizaba, Puebla, and Querétaro in addition to Freaner at Mexico City. Ibid., March 5, 7, 1848.

10. Trist Papers, Library of Congress, vol. 30.

11. Quoted in Drexler, *Guilty of Making Peace*, 113. Also see Trist Papers, "My Disobedience of Instructions"; George Towne Baker III, "Mexico City and the War of the United States: A Study in the Politics of Military Occupation" (Ph.D. diss., Duke University, 1969), 272–276; Robert Arthur Brent, "Nicholas Philip Trist, Biography of a Disobedient Diplomat" (Ph.D. diss., University of Virginia, 1950), 210–211. Brent notes Trist wrote to Secretary of State Buchanan "that Freaner should be considered in the employ of the government from December 9th, 1847, until his arrival in Washington. Freaner had insisted that he would be happy to serve his government without salary, but Trist would not entrust a non-government employee with the treaty."

12. *Delta*, December 23, 24, 1847.

13. Ibid., October 19, November 17, 1847. Freaner also shared Trist's view that large numbers of Mexicans, "a degenerate race" in Freaner's words, should not be incorporated into the U.S. population.

14. Ibid., January 15, 1848.

15. *Washington Union*, February 21, 1848; Seymour V. Connor and Odie B. Faulk, *North America Divided: The Mexican War, 1846–1848* (New York: Oxford University Press, 1971), 168–169. Copies of the treaty were enclosed in three tin boxes with leather cases, which Trist had asked Freaner to procure in Mexico City. A receipt from Freaner for $12 for the boxes is in the Trist Papers, Library of Congress. Also, Ethan Allen Hitchcock, *Fifty Years in Camp and Field: Diary of Major General Ethan Allen Hitchcock, U.S.A*, ed. W. A. Croffut (New York: G. Putnam's Sons, 1909), 315.

16. Memorandum from Freaner to Trist, January 18, 1848, in Trist Papers, Library of Congress.

17. Undated memorandum to Scott in Trist Papers, Library of Congress.

18. *Washington Union*, February 21, 1848. The British courier went directly from Querétaro to Veracruz, while Freaner departed from Mexico City.

19. *American Star*, February 5, 11, 13, 1848.

20. *Picayune*, March 10, 1848.

21. Ibid., March 23, 1848; Smith, *War with Mexico*, vol. 2, chap. 23; Drexler, *Guilty of Making Peace*, chaps. 10–11. There is no evidence Trist participated in such speculation.

22. Quote in *Picayune*, March 10, 1848; also, John J. Schroeder, *Mr. Polk's War: American Opposition and Dissent, 1846–1848* (Madison: University of Wisconsin Press, 1973), 157–159.

23. *Delta*, March 7, 1848.

24. Fayette Copeland, *Kendall of the* Picayune (Norman: University of Oklahoma Press, 1943), 234–236. See also *Charleston Courier*, March 6, 1848. The loss of the two days was related in a letter, Virginia Trist to Rosella (?), March 5, 1848, Trist Papers, Library of Congress.

25. There is a possibility, although there is no hard evidence, that the *Picayune*'s former correspondent Christopher Haile was the source that the paper had so much confidence in regarding the treaty. Haile, an army captain at the time, returned aboard *New Orleans*. Freaner and Haile were acquaintances, having met on several occasions at Mexico City prior to the conclusion of the treaty. A number of correspondents saw Freaner at Veracruz and knew he was on an important mission. Presumably, Haile heard these reports, too, while waiting for the ship to carry him to New Orleans. *Delta*, February 13, 15, 1848.

26. For examples, see the *Washington Union*, February 21, 1848; *Picayune*, February 16, 1848; *Charleston Courier*, February 17, 18, 1848; *New York Sun*, February 22, 1848. Also see quote in *American Star*, February 8, 27, 1848, and *North American*, February 7, 1848.

27. *Charleston Courier*, February 17, 1848; *Mobile Register and Journal*, February 14, 1847. Quotes in *Mobile Daily Advertiser*, February 14, 1848, and New Orleans *Bulletin*, February 14, 1848.

28. Quote in *Charleston Courier*, February 18, 1848; quote in *New York Tribune*, February 22, 1848.

29. *Philadelphia North American*, February 22, 1848; *Augusta (Ga.) Chronicle and Sentinel*, February 17, 1848, quoting *Charleston Chronicle* of February 16, 1848; *New York Sun* quote, February 22, 1848. Also, *New York Tribune*, February 22, 1848.

30. Copeland, *Kendall of the* Picayune, 237–238; see *Philadelphia North American*, February 22, 23, 1848, and *New York Sun*, February 22, 1848.

31. *Atlas*, quoted in *Delta*, March 16, 1848; other quotes in *Washington Union*, February 21, 1848; *American Star*, February 27, 1848.

32. Trist to his wife, Virginia, Mexico City, February 2, 1848. Trist Papers, vol. 30. Freaner did visit the Trist family while in Washington. Virginia Trist to her husband, February 23, 1848, Trist Papers, vol. 30.

33. William R. Manning, ed., *Diplomatic Correspondence of the United States: Inter-Latin American Affairs, 1831–1860*, 12 vols. (Washington, D.C.: Carnegie Endowment for International Peace, 1932–1939), 8:1059–1060.

34. *Philadelphia North American*, March 1, 1848; *Picayune*, March 10, 1848; *New York Tribune*, February 23, 1848; Quaife, ed., *Polk Diary*, 3:357.

35. Smith, *War with Mexico*, 2:264–267; the Washington press had another incident with the telegraph operators the night the treaty was approved. The vote came late—almost 10 P.M., the time the Washington telegraph office closed for the night. Correspondents for the *New York Tribune, Herald, Journal of Commerce*, and *Philadelphia North American* raced by carriage to the telegraph office, only to find the doors locked. W. E. Robinson of the *Tribune* railed at such "outrageous conduct" when "the country was all agape for the news in detail." He argued "the telegraph *must* be taught" to stay open when the news is important. The writers searched for the operators at their boardinghouses before one was located and a short summary transmitted. *New York Tribune*, March 11, 13, 15, 1848.

36. *Washington National Intelligencer*, quoted in Schroeder, *Mr. Polk's War*, 157–159; for the Nugent story, see Frederick B. Marbut, *News from the Capital: The Story of Washington Reporting* (Carbondale: Southern Illinois University Press, 1971), 85–93. Brent, "Nicholas Philip Trist," 220, examined seventeen papers and found thirteen supported the treaty; see *New York Tribune*, February 22, March 1, 13, 1848. Greeley wanted fast acceptance: "Sign anything, ratify anything, pay anything, to end the guilt, the bloodshed, the shame, the enormous waste of this horrible contest. . . . Even with the most unfit, unstable boundary of the Rio Grande, give us Peace; and then for the reckoning!" *New York Tribune*, January 27, 1848. Quote in *Picayune*, March 9, 1848.

Chapter 23. Withdrawal Pains

1. *New York Herald*, March 23, 1848; *Picayune*, April 21, 1848.

2. *Picayune*, March 24, 1848; October 23, 1856; Granada, Nicaragua, *El Nicaraguense*, July 5, 1856.

3. Quotes in *Picayune*, December 19, 23, 1847; January 20, March 24, July 28, 1848.

4. Scully's background has been obtained from his military records in the National Archives; Justin H. Smith, *The War with Mexico*, 2 vols. (New York: Macmillan Co., 1919), 1, chap. 11:427; *Picayune*, June 8, 1848; Fayette Copeland, *Kendall of the* Picayune (Norman: University of Oklahoma Press, 1943), 160, 163, 165, 189, 230. Scully spent most of the war in rear areas as an agent and correspondent for the *Picayune*.

5. Quotes in *Picayune*, January 30, February 13, 15, 18, March 10, 1848.

6. Tobey in *Philadelphia North American;* Henry reprinted in *Mexico City North American*, January 28, 1848.

7. *Picayune*, February 15, March 10, April 16, 1848; the reference to Scully is in Lane's report in *Message from the President of the United States . . .* , Executive Document No. 1, 30th Congress, 2nd Session (Washington, D.C.: Wendell & Van Benthuysen, 1848), 94.

8. The reports were published in the *Picayune*, February 15, 18, March 9, 1848. "Mr. Henderson," an occasional correspondent for the *Delta*, provided coverage of the Lane expedition for his paper. *Delta*, March 21, 1848.

9. Scully in *Picayune*, March 24, 1848; Warland in *Atlas*, April 20, 1848; Peoples in *Crescent*, April 22, 1848; Freaner in *Delta*, May 19, 1848.

10. Edward S. Wallace, "The United States Army in Mexico City," *Military Affairs* 13, no. 3 (Fall 1949): 163; Callahan in *Picayune*, January 30, 1848; Scully in ibid., April 23, 1848; Warland in *Atlas*, June 23, 1848.

11. *Crescent*, April 13, 14, May 19, 1848; *Delta*, May 19, 1848; Scully in *Picayune*, March 24, 1848.

12. Freaner quote in *Delta*, December 23, 1847. Recommendations in ibid., May 20, 1848.

13. Reprinted in *St. Louis Republican*, May 23, 1848.

14. Undated *New York Courier and Enquirer* clippings datelined "Mexico," May 12, 18, 1848, in Kendall Collections, Special Collections Division, University of Texas at Arlington Libraries.

15. Peoples in *Crescent*, April 22, 1848; John H. Warland, memorandum detailing his Mexico City experiences, notes dated January 1, 1849, and August 10, 1861, attached to a file of the *American Star*, Houghton Library, Harvard University.

16. *Crescent*, May 27, 1848.

Chapter 24. The Last Story

1. Justin H. Smith, *The War with Mexico*, 2 vols. (New York: Macmillan, 1919), 2:248–252.

2. For coverage examples, see *Crescent*, April 4, May 8, 1848; *Delta*, April 23, May 23, 1848; *Picayune*, March 24, April 23, May 23, 1848. Peoples is quoted from *Crescent*, May 8, 1848.

3. *Crescent*, March 30, 1848.

4. *Picayune*, April 23, 1848.

5. *Crescent*, May 8, 1848; *Picayune*, April 23, 1848.

6. *Picayune*, May 27, 1848.

7. *Delta*, April 23, 1848.

8. John H. Warland, memorandum detailing his Mexico City experiences, notes dated January 1, 1849, and August 10, 1861, attached to a file of the *American Star*, Houghton Library, Harvard University.

9. *Delta*, May 23, 1848.

10. *Picayune*, March 24, 1848.

11. Ibid., April 23, 1848. The letters from the Querétaro writer (the first dated April 13) started running in the *Picayune* on May 4 and continued until after the American troops departed Mexico City in June.

12. Smith, *War with Mexico*, 2:251; *Picayune*, June 15, 1848; *Crescent*, June 16, 1848.

13. *Picayune*, June 15, 1848.

14. *Delta*, May 21, 31, 1848; *Crescent*, May 31, 1848. These often were official Mexican government express riders.

15. See *Picayune* of those dates.

16. *Delta*, May 31, June 4, 6, 1848. The British courier made the fast trips to the coast in order to put the news aboard the regular bimonthly British government mail ship bound for Liverpool. Freaner's correspondent at Querétaro, who had shipped his letters to "Mustang" in the Mexican government's official express, concluded, "My friend, all has terminated happily."

17. *Picayune*, June 8, 1848. Also see *Delta* and *Crescent*, same date.

18. Smith, *War with Mexico*, 2:251; see examples in *Washington Union*, June 13, 17, 1848. Some of the New Orleans papers still objected to the treaty as too lenient. See *Crescent*, May 31, 1848.

19. *Crescent*, June 16, 1848; *Boston Atlas*, July 25, 1848. Warland complained in the same issue it was "a mistake" to release the San Patricio prisoners.

20. John H. Warland, memorandum detailing his Mexico City experiences, notes dated January 1, 1849, and August 10, 1861, attached to a file of the *American Star*, Houghton Library, Harvard University. *Boston Atlas*, July 25, 1848; *Crescent*, June 8, 16, 1848. Peoples quote is in *American Star*, May 30, 1848.

21. *Crescent*, May 27, 1848.

22. Ibid., June 12, 1848.

23. Ibid., June 8, 15, 16, 1848. The American government wanted to dampen the various filibustering projects. The War Department and not General Butler issued the orders on where and how the troops were to be mustered out of service. Executive Document No. 1, 170–173. The government required the troops go to U.S. military posts for discharge. Also see *Crescent*, June 21, 27, July 3, 9, 1848.

24. Ibid., July 28, 1848.

25. Ibid., October 18, 1848.

26. Ibid., July 28, 1848.

27. *Delta*, June 6, 1848.

28. Ibid., June 16, 22, 1848. Freaner was ill in bed his last two weeks in Mexico City.

29. *Crescent*, June 16, 21, 1848.

30. *Boston Atlas*, August 10, September 11, 1848.

Epilogue

1. "European news" quote, *Picayune*, July 23, 1848. Peoples in *Crescent*, August 7, 1848. Description of last day in Veracruz in *Picayune*, August 6, 1848.

2. Bugbee's death is in *Picayune*, May 8, 1849; Haile, ibid., September 15, 1849; Henry in George W. Cullum, *Biographical Register of the Officers and Graduates of the U.S. Military Academy at West Point . . .* , 3rd ed. (Boston and New York: Houghton, Mifflin, 1891), 618; and *Spirit of the Times*, March 29, 1851.

3. For Peoples, see *Corpus Christi (Tex.) Star*, February 24, August 11, 1849; Fred B. Rogers, *Soldiers of the Overland* (San Francisco: Grabhorn Press, 1938), 5–8, and "Bear Flag Lieutenant, Part IV," *California Historical Society Quarterly* 30, no. 1 (March 1951): 49–66; *Message from the President of the United States, Calling for Further Information in Relation to the Formation of a State Government in*

California . . . , Executive Document No. 52, U.S. 31st Congress (Senate), 1st Session, 1849–1850 (Washington, D.C.: U.S. Department of State, 1850); J. Goldsborough Bruff, *Gold Rush* (1944; reprint, New York: Columbia University Press, 1949), 654–656; obituaries in *San Francisco Alta California*, April 17, 1850; *Delta*, May 29, 1850. Gregg's death is in Max L. Moorhead's "Introduction" to Josiah Gregg, *Commerce of the Prairies*, ed. Max L. Moorhead (Norman: University of Oklahoma Press, 1954), xxvi–xxix; Freaner in Thomas J. C. Williams, *A History of Washington County, Maryland* (Hagerstown, Md.: John M. Runk & L. R. Titsworth, 1906), 241, 281–282; *San Francisco Alta California*, August 10, September 8, 1852.

4. For Durivage, see letters about his difficult trip to California in "Through Mexico to California, Letters and Journal of John Durivage" in *Southern Trails to California in 1849*, ed. Ralph B. Bieber (Glendale, Calif.: Arthur H. Clarke Co., 1937), 157–255. Durivage joined E. C. Kimble as coeditor of the *Alta California* on December 10, 1849, and continued until October 15, 1851. On his departure, the paper wrote he was "fitted in a remarkable degree by experience, education and talent for the arduous profession of a daily newspaper [and] he has largely contributed by the effusions of his ready, humorous and sensible pen." Tobin is discussed in Edward S. Wallace, *Destiny and Glory* (New York: Coward-McCann, 1957), 40–45; Callahan's death is in the *Picayune*, October 23, 1856; also see William Walker, *The War in Nicaragua* (Mobile, Ala.: S. H. Goetzel & Co., 1860), 286.

5. Warland's career and illness are described by his friend William Schouler in "Personal and Political Recollections No. 5," undated *Boston Journal* clipping, William Schouler Collection, Massachusetts Historical Society; Tobey's death is in *Harrisburg (Pa.) Herald*, August 3, 1854; Pike is in Fred W. Allsopp, *Albert Pike: A Biography* (Little Rock, Ark.: Park-Harper, 1928); Scully is mentioned in *Cohen's New Orleans Directory for 1855* (New Orleans: Printed at the office of the *Picayune*, 1855), 211; Thorpe is in Milton Rickels, *Thomas Bangs Thorpe, Humorist of the Old Southwest* (Baton Rouge: Louisiana State University Press, 1962); for Reid, see J. Cutler Andrews, *The South Reports the Civil War* (Princeton, N.J.: Princeton University Press, 1970), 48–49; Storms is in Edward T. James, ed., *Notable American Women, 1607–1950*, 3 vols. (Cambridge, Mass.: Belknap Press of Harvard University Press, 1971), 1:315–317.

6. For Lumsden quote, see *Picayune*, July 30, 1847; and Fayette Copeland, *Kendall of the* Picayune (Norman: University of Oklahoma Press, 1943), 289, for his death; for Kendall, ibid., chap. 27. Kendall's "complete justice" quote is in *Picayune*, November 7, 1847.

7. Kendall's views are in *Picayune* clippings from Paris, June 19, 1854, in Kendall Family Collection, Special Collections Division, University of Texas at Arlington Libraries.

Bibliography

Allsopp, Fred W. *Albert Pike: A Biography.* Little Rock, Ark.: Park-Harper, 1928.

Anderson, John Q. *With the Bark On.* Nashville: Vanderbilt University Press, 1967.

Anderson, Robert. *An Artillery Officer in the Mexican War.* New York: G. P. Putnam's Sons, 1911.

Andrews, J. Cutler. *The North Reports the Civil War.* Pittsburgh: University of Pittsburgh Press, 1955.

———. *The South Reports the Civil War.* Princeton, N.J.: Princeton University Press, 1970.

Baker, George Towne, III. "Mexico City and the War of the United States: A Study in the Politics of Military Occupation." Ph.D. diss., Duke University, 1969.

Barringer, Graham A., ed. "The Mexican War Journal of Henry S. Lane." *Indiana Magazine of History* 53 (December 1957): 422–434.

Bauer, K. Jack. *The Mexican War, 1846–1848.* New York: Macmillan, 1974.

———. *Zachary Taylor.* Baton Rouge: Louisiana State University Press, 1985.

Beach, M. S. "A Secret Mission to Mexico." *Scribner's Monthly* 18 (May 1879): 136–140.

Bell, Patricia. "Gideon Pillow: A Personality Profile." *Civil War Times Illustrated* 6 (October 1967): 13–19.

Berge, Dennis E. "A Mexican Dilemma: The Mexico City Ayuntamiento and the Question of Loyalty, 1846–1848." *Hispanic American Historical Review* 50, no. 2 (May 1970): 229–256.

Bieber, Ralph B., ed. *Southern Trails to California in 1849.* Glendale, Calif.: Arthur H. Clarke, 1937.

Bill, Alfred Hoyt. *Rehearsal for Conflict: The War with Mexico, 1846–1848.* New York: History Book Club, 1942.

Blackwood, Emma Jerome, ed. *To Mexico with Scott: Letters of Captain E. Kirby Smith to His Wife.* Cambridge, Mass.: Harvard University Press, 1917.

Blair, Walter. *Horse Sense in American Humor.* Chicago: University of Chicago Press, 1942.

Bloom, John Porter. "With the American Army into Mexico, 1846–1848." Ph.D. diss., Emery University, 1956.

Bodson, Robert Louis. "A Description of the United States Occupation of Mexico as Reported by American Newspapers Published in Vera Cruz, Puebla, and Mexico City, September 14, 1847 to July 31, 1848." Ph.D. diss., Ball State University, 1971.

Brasher, Thomas L. *Whitman as Editor of the Brooklyn Daily Eagle.* Detroit: Wayne State University Press, 1970.

Brent, Robert Arthur. "Nicholas Philip Trist, Biography of a Disobedient Diplomat." Ph.D. diss., University of Virginia, 1950.

Brinley, Francis. *The Life of William T. Porter.* New York: D. Appleton, 1860.

Brooks, William T. H. Papers. U.S. Army Military History Collection. Carlisle Barracks, Pa.

Brown, Walter Lee. "The Mexican War Experiences of Albert Pike and the 'Mounted Devils' of Arkansas." *Arkansas Historical Quarterly* 12, no. 4 (Winter 1953): 301–315.

Bruff, J. Goldsborough. *Gold Rush.* 1944; reprint, New York: Columbia University Press, 1949.

Bryan, Jimmy L. Jr., comp. "Correspondents of the U.S.-Mexican War (1846–1848) from the *New Orleans Delta.*" Center for Southwestern Studies and the History of Cartography, University of Texas at Arlington, 1998.

Bullard, F. Lauriston. *Famous War Correspondents.* Boston: Little, Brown, 1914.

Carleton, James Henry. *Battle of Buena Vista.* New York: Harper & Bros., 1848.

Carr, Albert Z. *The World and William Walker.* New York: Harper & Row, 1963.

Caruso, A. Brooke. *The Mexican Spy Company: United States Covert Operations in Mexico, 1845–1848.* Jefferson, N.C.: McFarland & Co., 1991.

Cashion, Peggy. "Women and the Mexican War, 1846–1848." M.A. thesis, University of Texas at Arlington, 1990.

Chaffin, Tom. *Fatal Glory: Narciso Lopez and the First Clandestine U.S. War against Cuba.* Charlottesville: University Press of Virginia, 1996.

Chamberlain, Samuel E. *My Confession.* New York: Harper & Bros., 1956.

Chance, Joseph E. *Jefferson Davis's Mexican War Regiment.* Jackson: University Press of Mississippi, 1991.

Claiborne, J. F. H. *Life and Correspondence of John A. Quitman.* 2 vols. New York: Harper & Bros., 1860.

Connor, Seymour V., and Odie B. Faulk. *North America Divided: The Mexican War, 1846–1848.* New York: Oxford University Press, 1971.

Cooling, Benjamin Franklin. "Lew Wallace and Gideon Pillow: Enigmas and Variations on an American Theme." *Lincoln Herald* 84, no. 2 (Summer 1981): 651–658.

Copeland, Fayette. *Kendall of the* Picayune. Norman: University of Oklahoma Press, 1943.

Corcoran, Denis. *Pickings from the* Picayune. Philadelphia: Carey & Hart, 1846.

Costeloe, Michael P. "The Mexican Church and the Rebellion of the Polkos." *Hispanic American Historical Review* 46 (May 1966): 170–178.

Cullum, George W. *Biographical Register of the Officers and Graduates of the U.S. Military Academy at West Point . . . ,* 3rd ed. Boston and New York: Houghton, Mifflin, 1891.

Current-Garcia, Eugene. "Thomas Bangs Thorpe and the Literature of the Antebellum Southwest Frontier." *Louisiana Historical Quarterly* 34, no. 2 (April 1956): 199–222.

Cutrer, Thomas W. *Ben McCulloch and the Frontier Military Tradition*. Chapel Hill: University of North Carolina Press, 1993.

Dabney, Thomas Ewing. *One Hundred Great Years: The Story of the* Times-Picayune *from Its Founding to 1940*. Baton Rouge: Louisiana State University Press, 1944.

DePalo, William A., Jr. "James L. Freaner." In *The United States and Mexico at War*, ed. Donald S. Frazier. New York: Simon & Schuster Macmillan, 1998.

Donnavan, Corydon. *Adventures in Mexico*. Boston: George R. Holbrook & Co., 1848.

Drexler, Robert W. *Guilty of Making Peace: A Biography of Nicholas P. Trist*. Lanham, Md.: University Press of America, 1991.

Eisenhower, John S. D. "Polk and His Generals." In *Essays on the Mexican War*, ed. Douglas W. Richmond, 34–65. College Station: Texas A&M University Press, 1986.

———. *So Far from God: The U.S. War with Mexico, 1846–1848*. New York: Random House, 1989.

———. *Agent of Destiny: The Life and Times of General Winfield Scott*. New York: Free Press, 1997.

Elliott, Charles Winslow. *Winfield Scott, The Soldier and the Man*. New York: Macmillan, 1937.

Emery, Edwin, and Michael Emery. *The Press and America*. 7th ed. Englewood Cliffs, N.J.: Prentice Hall, 1992.

Estes, David C., ed. *A New Collection of Thomas Bangs Thorpe's Sketches of the Old Southwest*. Baton Rouge: Louisiana State University Press, 1989.

Farnham, Thomas J. "Nicholas Trist & James Freaner and the Mission to Mexico." *Arizona and the West* 11, no. 3 (Autumn 1969): 247–260.

Foster, Edward Halsey. *Josiah Gregg and Lewis H. Garrard*. Boise, Idaho: Boise State University, 1977.

Fuller, John Douglas Pitts. *The Movement for the Acquisition of All Mexico, 1846–1848*. Baltimore: Johns Hopkins University Press, 1936.

Furneaux, Rupert. *The First War Correspondent, William Howard Russell of* The Times. London: Cassell & Co., 1944.

Garrett Collection, Special Collections Division, University of Texas at Arlington Libraries.

Gilley, B. H. "'Polk's War' and the Louisiana Press." *Louisiana History* 20 (1979): 5–23.

Goldsmith, Oliver. *Overland in Forty-Nine*. Detroit: Published by the author, 1896.

Graebner, Norman A. "Party Politics and the Trist Mission." *Journal of Southern History* 19 (1953): 135–156.

Grant, Ulysses Simpson. *The Papers of Ulysses S. Grant*, ed. John Y. Simon. Carbondale: Southern Illinois University Press, 1967.

Greer, Jack Kimmins. *Colonel Jack Hays*. 1952. Rev. ed., College Station: Texas A&M University Press, 1987.

———. *Colonel Jack Hays*. New York: E. P. Dutton & Co., 1952.

Gregg, Josiah. *Commerce of the Prairies*. 2 vols. New York: H. G. Langley, 1844.

———. *Commerce of the Prairies.* Edited by Max L. Moorhead. Norman: University of Oklahoma Press, 1954.

———. *The Diary and Letters of Josiah Gregg.* Edited by Maurice G. Fulton. 2 vols. 1941; reprint, Norman: University of Oklahoma Press, 1944.

Griswold del Castillo, Richard. *The Treaty of Guadalupe Hidalgo: A Legacy of Conflict.* Norman: University of Oklahoma Press, 1990.

Gulick, Charles Adams, Jr., and Katherine Elliott, eds. *The Papers of Mirabeau Buonaparte Lamar.* 6 vols. Austin: Texas State Library, 1924.

Gutierrez, Felix. "Spanish-Language Media in America: Background, Resources, History." *Journalism History* 4, no. 2 (Summer 1977): 34–41, 65–67.

Hackenburg, Randy W. *Pennsylvania in the War with Mexico.* Shippensburg, Pa.: White Mane Publishing, 1992.

Hall, Oakey. *The Manhattener in New Orleans.* New York: J. S. Redfield, Clinton Hall, 1851.

Heitman, Francis B. *Historical Register and Dictionary of the United States Army, from Its Organization September 29, 1789, to March 2, 1903.* 2 vols. Washington, D.C.: Government Printing Office, 1903.

Henry, Robert Selph. *The Story of the Mexican War.* New York: Frederick Ungar Publishing, 1950.

Henry, William Seton. *Campaign Sketches of the War with Mexico.* New York: Harper & Bros., 1847.

Hitchcock, Ethan Allen. *Fifty Years in Camp and Field: Diary of Major General Ethan Allen Hitchcock, U.S.A.*, ed. W. A. Croffut. New York: G. P. Putnam's Sons, 1909.

Horgan, Paul. *Josiah Gregg and His Vision of the Early West.* New York: Farrar Straus Giroux, 1979.

Hudson, Frederic. *Journalism in the United States, from 1690 to 1872.* New York: Harper, 1873.

Hughes, Nathaniel Cheairs, Jr., and Roy P. Stonesifer Jr. *The Life and Wars of Gideon J. Pillow.* Chapel Hill and London: University of North Carolina Press, 1993.

Hughes, William W. *Archibald Yell.* Fayetteville: University of Arkansas Press, 1988.

James, Edward T., ed. *Notable American Women, 1607–1950.* 3 vols. Cambridge, Mass.: Belknap Press of Harvard University Press, 1971.

Johannsen, Robert. *To the Halls of the Montezumas.* New York: Oxford University Press, 1985.

Johnson, Timothy D. *A Gallant Little Army: The Mexico City Campaign.* Lawrence: University Press of Kansas, 2007.

———. "A Most Anomalous Affair: Gideon Pillow and Winfield Scott in the Mexico City Campaign." *Tennessee Historical Quarterly* 66, no. 1 (Spring 2007): 2–19.

Kendall Family Collection, Special Collections Division, University of Texas at Arlington Libraries.

Kendall, George Wilkins. *Narrative of the Texan Santa Fe Expedition.* 2 vols. New York: Harper & Bros., 1844.

———. *Narrative of the Texan Santa Fe Expedition*. Chicago: Lakeside Press, 1929.

———. Handwritten untitled manuscript. Eugene C. Barker Texas History Collection, Briscoe Center for American History, University of Texas, Austin. N.d.

———. *Letters from a Texas Sheep Ranch*, ed. James Harry Brown. Urbana: University of Illinois Press, 1959.

———. *The War between the United States and Mexico, Illustrated*. Illustrations by Carl Nebel. 1851; reprint, Austin: Texas State Historical Association, 1994.

———. *Dispatches from the Mexican War*, ed. and with an introduction by Lawrence Delbert Cress. Norman: University of Oklahoma Press, 1999.

Kendall, John S. "Early New Orleans Newspapers." *Louisiana Historical Quarterly* 10 (1927): 383–402.

———. "The Foreign Language Press of New Orleans." *Louisiana Historical Quarterly* 12 (1929): 363–380.

Kieffer, Chester L. *Maligned General: The Biography of Thomas Sidney Jesup*. San Rafael, Calif.: Presidio Press, 1979.

Kinkade, Patricia. "Jane McManus Storms Cazneau: Journalist and Expansionist." In *Essays in History: The E. C. Barksdale Student Lectures, 1987–1988*. Arlington: University of Texas at Arlington Campus Printing Service, 1988.

Knightley, Phillip. *The First Casualty*. New York: Harcourt Brace Jovanovich, 1975.

Lambert, Paul F. "The Movement for Acquisition of All Mexico." *Journal of the West* 11, no. 2 (April 1972): 317–327.

Lavender, David. *Climax at Buena Vista*. Philadelphia & New York: J. B. Lippincott Co., 1966.

———. "How to Make It to the White House without Really Trying." *American Heritage* 18, no. 4 (June 1967): 78–86.

Lecompte, Janet. "Manuel Armijo, George Wilkins Kendall and the Baca-Caballero Conspiracy." *New Mexico Historical Review* 59, no. 1 (January 1984): 49–65.

Lee, James Melvin. *A History of American Journalism*. 1917; reprint, Garden City, N.Y.: Garden City Publishing Co., 1923.

MacCurdy, Raymond R. *A History and Bibliography of Spanish-Language Newspapers and Magazines in Louisiana, 1808–1949*. Albuquerque: University of New Mexico Press, 1951.

Manning, William R., ed. *Diplomatic Correspondence of the United States: Inter-Latin American Affairs, 1831–1860*. 12 vols. Washington, D.C.: Carnegie Endowment for International Peace, 1932–1939.

Marbut, Frederick B. *News from the Capital: The Story of Washington Reporting*. Carbondale: Southern Illinois University Press, 1971.

Mathews, Joseph J. *Reporting the wars*. Minneapolis: University of Minnesota Press, 1957.

May, Robert E. "'Plenipotentiary in Petticoats': Jane M. Cazneau and American Foreign Policy in the Mid-nineteenth Century." In *Women and American Foreign Policy: Lobbyists, Critics, and Insiders*, ed. Edward P. Crapol. 2nd ed. Wilmington, Del.: SR Books, 1992.

McCaffrey, James W. *The Army of Manifest Destiny: The American Soldier in the Mexican War, 1846–1848.* New York: New York University Press, 1992.

McElderry Bruce R., Jr., ed. *The Realistic Movement in American Writing.* New York: Odyssey Press, 1965.

McIntosh, James T., Lynda L. Crist, and Mary S. Dix, eds. Vol. 3 of *The Papers of Jefferson Davis.* 12 vols. Baton Rouge: Louisiana State University Press, 1981.

McWhiney, Grady. *Braxton Bragg and Confederate Defeat.* New York: Columbia University Press, 1969.

McWilliams, Carey. *North from Mexico.* Reprint, New York: Greenwood Press, 1968.

Meade, George. *The Life and Letters of George Gordon Meade.* 2 vols. New York: Scribners, 1913.

Merk, Frederick. *Manifest Destiny and Mission in American History.* New York: Knopf, 1963.

Mexican War Letters. Center for American History, General Libraries, University of Texas at Austin.

Miller, Roger C. "Yellow Jack at Veracruz." *Prologue* 10, no. 1 (Spring 1978): 42–53.

Miller, Robert Ryal. *Shamrock and Sword: The Saint Patrick's Battalion in the U.S.-Mexican War.* Norman: University of Oklahoma Press, 1989.

Montgomery, Cora. *The King of Rivers.* New York: Charles Wood, 1850.

———. *Queen of Islands.* New York: Charles Wood, 1850.

———. *Eagle Pass, or Life on the Border.* New York: George P. Putnam & Co., 1852.

Morsberger, Robert E., and Katherine M. Morsberger. *Lew Wallace: Militant Romantic.* New York: McGraw-Hill Co., 1980.

Mott, Frank Luther. *American Journalism.* 3rd ed. New York: Macmillan, 1962.

Myers, William Starr, ed. *The Mexican War Diary of George B. McClellan.* Princeton, N.J.: Princeton University Press, 1917.

Nelson, Anna Kasten. "Mission to Mexico — Moses Y. Beach, Secret Agent." *New York State Historical Society Quarterly* 59, no. 3 (July 1975): 227–245.

———. "Jane Storms Cazneau: Disciple of Manifest Destiny." *Prologue* 18, no. 1 (Spring 1986): 24–40.

———. *Secret Agents: President Polk and the Search for Peace with Mexico.* New York and London: Garland Publishing, 1988.

Northrup [*sic*], Jack. "The Trist Mission." *Journal of Mexican American History* 3 (1973): 13–31.

Nortrup, Jack. "Nicholas Trist's Mission to Mexico: A Reinterpretation." *Southwestern Historical Quarterly* 71 (January 1968): 321–346.

O'Brien, Frank M. *The Story of the Sun: New York, 1833–1928.* New York: D. Appleton, 1928.

Official Register of the Officers and Cadets of the U.S. Military Academy (1832–1835).

Ohrt, Wallace. *Defiant Peacemaker: Nicholas Trist in the Mexican War.* College Station: Texas A&M University Press, 1997.

Osthaus, Carl R. *Partisans of the Southern Press: Editorial Spokesmen of the Nineteenth Century.* Lexington: University Press of Kentucky, 1994.

Oswandel, J. Jacob. *Notes of the Mexican War 1846–47–48.* Philadelphia: Published by the author, 1885.

Paredes, Raymund. "The Image of the Mexican in American Literature." Ph.D. diss., University of Texas at Austin, 1973.

———. "The Mexican Image in American Travel Literature, 1831–1869." *New Mexico Historical Review* 52, no. 1 (January 1977): 5–29.

Patrick, Jeffrey L. "A Question of Cowardice: The Second Indiana Regiment and the Mexican War." Paper presented to Southwestern Historical Conference, Houston, March 1996.

Perry, Oran. *Indiana in the Mexican War.* Indianapolis: W. B. Burford, contractor for state printing, 1908.

Pike, Albert. *Prose Sketches and Poems.* Edited by D. J. Weber with foreword by Tom L. Popejoy. Albuquerque, N.M.: Calvin Horn Publishers, 1967.

Pitcher, Thomas. Diary. "Battle of Contreras," August 19, 1847. Pitcher Family Papers. U.S. Army Military History Institute. Carlisle Barracks, Pa.

Pratt, Julius W. "John L. O'Sullivan and Manifest Destiny." *New York History* 14 (July 1933): 213–234.

Quaife, Milo M., ed. *The Diary of James K. Polk, 1845–1849.* 4 vols. Chicago: A. C. McClurg, 1910.

Ramírez, José Fernando. *Mexico during the War with the United States.* Columbia: University of Missouri Press, 1970.

Reid, Samuel Chester Jr. *Scouting Expeditions of McCulloch's Texas Rangers.* Philadelphia: G. B. Sieber & Co., 1847.

Reilly, Tom. "American Reporters and the Mexican War." Ph.D. diss., University of Minnesota, 1975.

———. "Jane McManus Storms: Letters from the Mexican War, 1846–1848." *Southwestern Historical Quarterly* 81 (July 1981) 1:21–44.

———. "A Spanish-Language Voice of Dissent in Antebellum New Orleans." *Louisiana History* 23 (Fall 1982): 325–339.

Reinders, Robert Clemens. *End of an Era.* New Orleans: Pelican Publishing, 1969.

Rickels, Milton. *Thomas Bangs Thorpe, Humorist of the Old Southwest.* Baton Rouge: Louisiana State University Press, 1962.

Robinson, Cecil. *With the Ears of Strangers: The Mexican in American Literature.* Tucson: University of Arizona Press, 1963.

Rogers, Fred B. *Soldiers of the Overland.* San Francisco: Grabhorn Press, 1938.

———. "Bear Flag Lieutenant, Part IV." *California Historical Society Quarterly* 30, no. 1 (March 1951): 49–66.

Rutland, Robert. *The Newsmongers: Journalism in the Life of the Nation, 1690–1972.* New York: Dial Press, 1973.

Santoni, Pedro. *Mexicans at Arms: Puro Federalists and the Politics of War, 1845–1848.* Fort Worth: Texas Christian University Press, 1996.

Schroeder, John J. *Mr. Polk's War: American Opposition and Dissent, 1846–1848.* Madison: University of Wisconsin Press, 1973.

Semmes, Raphael. *Service Afloat and Ashore during the Mexican War.* Cincinnati, Ohio: William H. Moore, 1851.

Sibley, Marilyn McAdams. *Travelers in Texas, 1761–1860.* Austin and London: University of Texas Press, 1967.

Sinclair, Harold, *The Port of New Orleans.* Garden City, N.Y.: Doubleday, Doran & Co., 1942.

Smith, Justin H. "American Rule in Mexico." *American Historical Review* 23, no. 2 (January 1918): 287–302.

———. *The War with Mexico.* 2 vols. New York: Macmillan, 1919.

Spell, Lota M. "The Anglo-Saxon Press in Mexico, 1846–1848." *American Historical Review* 38, no. 1 (October 1932): 20–31.

Spurlin, Charles D. *Texas Veterans in the Mexican War.* St. Louis: Ingmire Publications, 1984.

Stonesifer, Roy P., Jr. "Gideon J. Pillow: A Study in Egotism." *Tennessee Historical Quarterly* 25, no. 4 (Winter 1966): 340–350.

Taylor, Zachary. *Letters of Zachary Taylor, from the Battle-fields of the Mexican War.* Rochester, N.Y.: Genesee Press, 1908.

Thayer Memorial Edition, *Register of Graduates and Former Cadets of the United States Military Academy, 1964.* West Point, N.Y.: West Point Alumni Foundation, 1964.

Thonhoff, Robert H. "Taylor's Trail in Texas." *Southwestern Historical Quarterly* 70, no. 1 (July 1966): 7–22.

Thorpe, Thomas Bangs. *Our Army on the Rio Grande.* Philadelphia: Carey & Hart, 1846.

———. *Our Army at Monterey.* Philadelphia: Carey & Hart, 1847.

Tinker, Edward Larocque. *Bibliography of the French Newspapers and Periodicals of Louisiana.* Worcester, Mass.: American Antiquarian Society, 1933.

Trist Papers. Library of Congress.

U.S. Congress. *Messages of the President of the United States, with the Correspondence, therewith Communicated, between the Secretary of War and Other Officers of the Government, on the Subject of the Mexican War.* Executive Document No. 60, 30th Congress, 1st Session. Washington, D.C.: Wendell & Benthuysen Printers, 1848.

U.S. Congress. Senate. *Message from the President of the United States, Communicating, in Compliance with the Resolution of the Senate, the Proceedings of the Two Courts of Inquiry in the Case of Major General Pillow.* Executive Document No. 65, 30th Congress, 1st Session (August 3, 1848). Washington, D.C.

———. Senate. *Message from the President of the United States, Calling for Further Information in Relation to the Formation of a State Government in California . . . .* Executive Document No. 52. Washington, D.C.: U.S. Department of State, 1850.

———. Senate. *The History of the Raising of the American Flag on the Capital of Mexico.* Washington, D.C.: Printed by C. Wendell, 1856.

U.S. Military Academy Cadet Application Papers, 1805–1866. National Archives Microfilm Publication 688.

Walker, William. *The War in Nicaragua*. Mobile, Ala.: S. H. Goetzel & Co., 1860.

Wallace, Edward S. "The United States Army in Mexico City." *Military Affairs* 13, no. 3 (Fall 1949): 158–166.

———. *General William Jenkins Worth: Monterey's Forgotten Hero*. Dallas: Southern Methodist University Press, 1953.

———. *Destiny and Glory*. New York: Coward-McCann, 1957.

Wallace, Lew. *A Hoosier in the Mexican War*. Ft. Wayne, Ind.: Public Library of Ft. Wayne and Allen County, 1973.

Watterson, Henry. *"Marse Henry": An Autobiography*. 2 vols. New York: George H. Doran, 1919.

Webb, Walter Prescott, H. Bailey Carroll, and Eldon Branda, eds. *The Handbook of Texas*. 3 vols. 1952; reprint, Austin: Texas State Historical Association, 1976.

Weems, John Edward. *To Conquer a Peace*. Garden City, N.Y.: Doubleday & Co., 1974.

Wilkins, Frederick. *The Highly Irregular Irregulars: Texas Rangers in the Mexican War*. Austin, Tex.: Eakin Press, 1990.

Williams, Thomas J. C. *A History of Washington County, Maryland*. Hagerstown, Md.: John M. Runk & L. R. Titsworth, 1906.

Winders, Richard Bruce. *Mr. Polk's Army: The American Military Experience in the Mexican War*. College Station: Texas A&M University Press, 1997.

———. "Will the Regiment Stand It?" In *Dueling Eagles: Reinterpreting the U.S. Mexican War, 1846–1848*, ed. Richard V. Francaviglia and Douglas W. Richmonds. Fort Worth: Texas Christian University Press, 2000.

———. *Crisis in the Southwest: The United States, Mexico, and the Struggle over Texas*. Wilmington, Del.: SR Books, 2002.

Winwar, Frances. *American Giant*. New York: Tudor Publishing, 1941.

Wool, John Ellis. *The Battle of Buena Vista, with the Operations of the Army of Occupation for One Month*. New York: Harper & Bros., 1848.

Wynkoop, J. M., ed. *Anecdotes and Incidents . . . of the Mexican War*. Pittsburgh: n.p., 1848.

Yates, Norris W. *William T. Porter and the Spirit of the Times*. Baton Rouge: Louisiana State University Press, 1957.

Index

Page numbers in italics refer to illustrations.